Injury & Trauma Sourcebook

Learning Disabilities Sourcebook, 4th Edition

Leukemia Sourcebook

Liver Disorders Sourcebook

Medical Tests Sourcebook, 4th Edition

Men's Health Concerns Sourcebook, 4th Edition

Mental Health Disorders Sourcebook, 5th Edition

Mental Retardation Sourcebook

Movement Disorders Sourcebook, 2nd Edition

Multiple Sclerosis Sourcebook

Muscular Dystrophy Sourcebook

Obesity Sourcebook

Osteoporosis Sourcebook

Pain Sourcebook, 4th Edition

Pediatric Cancer Sourcebook

Physical & Mental Issues in Aging Sourcebook

Podiatry Sourcebook, 2nd Edition

Pregnancy & Birth Sourcebook, 3rd Edition

Prostate & Urological Disorders Sourcebook

Prostate Cancer Sourcebook

Rehabilitation Sourcebook

Respiratory Disorders Sourcebook, 3rd Edition

Sexually Transmitted Diseases Sourcebook, 5th Edition

Sleep Disorders Sourcebook, 3rd Edition

Smoking Concerns Sourcebook

Sports Injuries Sourcebook, 4th Edition

Stress-Related Disorders Sourcebook, 3rd Edition

Stroke Sourcebook, 3rd Edition

Surgery Sourcebook, 3rd Edition

Thyroid Disorders Sourcebook

Transplantation Sourcebook

Traveler's Health Sourcebook

Urinary Tract & Kidney Diseases & Disorders Sourcebook, 2nd Edition

Vegetarian Sourcebook

Women's Health Concerns Sourcebook, 4th Edition

Workplace Health & Safety Sourcebook

Worldwide Health Sourcebook

Abuse & Violence ...

Accident & Safety Information for Teens

Alcohol Information for Teens, 3rd Edition

Allergy Information for Teens, 2nd Edition

Asthma Information for Teens, 2nd Edition

Body Information for Teens

Cancer Information for Teens, 3rd Edition

Complementary & Alternative Medicine Information for Teens, 2nd Edition

Diabetes Information for Teens, 2nd Edition

Diet Information for Teens, 3rd Edition

Drug Information for Teens, 3rd Edition

Eating Disorders Information for Teens, 3rd Edition

Fitness Information for Teens, 3rd Edition

Learning Disabilities Information for Teens

Mental Health Information for Teens, 4th Edition

Pregnancy Information for Teens, 2nd Edition

Sexual Health Information for Teens, 3rd Edition

Skin Health Information for Teens, 3rd Edition

Sleep Information for Teens

Sports Injuries Information for Teens, 3rd Edition

Stress Information for Teens, 2nd Edition

Suicide Information for Teens, 2nd Edition

Tobacco Information for Teens, 2nd Edition

Congenital Disorders

Disorders

SOURCEBOOK

Third Edition

Health Reference Series

Third Edition

Congenital Disorders

SOURCEBOOK

Basic Consumer Information about Nonhereditary Birth Defects and Disorders Related to Prematurity, Gestational Injuries, Prenatal and Perinatal Infections, Maternal Health Conditions during Pregnancy, and Birth Complications, Including Cerebral Palsy, Cleft Lip and Palate, Heart Defects, Hydrocephalus, Spina Bifida, and More

Along with Facts about Risk Factors and Birth Defect Prevention, Prenatal Care, Fetal Surgery Techniques, and Other Treatment Options, a Glossary of Related Terms, and a Directory of Resources for Additional Help and Information

Edited by
Sandra J. Judd

Omnigraphics

155 W. Congress, Suite 200, Detroit, MI 48226

Bibliographic Note

Because this page cannot legibly accommodate all the copyright notices, the Bibliographic Note portion of the Preface constitutes an extension of the copyright notice.

Edited by Sandra J. Judd

Health Reference Series
Karen Bellenir, *Managing Editor*
David A. Cooke, MD, FACP, *Medical Consultant*
Elizabeth Collins, *Research and Permissions Coordinator*
EdIndex, Services for Publishers, *Indexers*

* * *

Omnigraphics, Inc.
Matthew P. Barbour, *Senior Vice President*
Kevin M. Hayes, *Operations Manager*

* * *

Peter E. Ruffner, *Publisher*
Copyright © 2013 Omnigraphics, Inc.
ISBN 978-0-7808-1295-6
E-ISBN 978-0-7808-1296-3

Library of Congress Cataloging-in-Publication Data

Congenital disorders sourcebook : basic consumer information about nonhereditary birth defects and disorders related to prematurity, gestational injuries, prenatal and perinatal infections, maternal health conditions during pregnancy, and birth complications, including cerebral palsy, cleft lip and palate, heart defects, hydrocephalus, spina bifida, and more, along with facts about risk factors and birth defect prevention, prenatal care, fetal surgery techniques, and other treatment options, a glossary of related terms, and a directory of resources for additional help and information / edited by Sandra J. Judd. -- Third edition.
  pages cm
Includes bibliographical references and index.
  Summary: "Provides basic consumer health information about nonhereditary birth defects and disorders, including facts about prevention and treatment options. Includes index, glossary of related terms, and other resources"-- Provided by publisher.
  ISBN 978-0-7808-1295-6 (hardcover : alk. paper) 1. Abnormalities, Human--Popular works. 2. Developmental disabilities--Popular works. I. Judd, Sandra J., editor.
  [DNLM: 1. Congenital, Hereditary, and Neonatal Diseases and Abnormalities--Popular Works.]
  RG626.C597 2013
  618.92'8588--dc23
                                                          2013005206

The information in this publication was compiled from the sources cited and from other sources considered reliable. While every possible effort has been made to ensure reliability, the publisher will not assume liability for damages caused by inaccuracies in the data, and makes no warranty, express or implied, on the accuracy of the information contained herein.

∞

This book is printed on acid-free paper meeting the ANSI Z39.48 Standard. The infinity symbol that appears above indicates that the paper in this book meets that standard.

Printed in the United States

Table of Contents

Visit www.healthreferenceseries.com to view *A Contents Guide to the Health Reference Series*, a listing of more than 16,000 topics and the volumes in which they are covered.

Part III: Structural Abnormalities and Functional Impairments

Preface

About This Book

According to the March of Dimes, 120,000 babies—one in thirty-three—are born each year with a birth defect. In fact, birth defects are the leading cause of death in the first year of life. Yet the future is brightening. Recent medical advances have enabled doctors to diagnose and treat some birth defects before birth, affording affected children a much greater chance at survival. Additionally, advances in our understanding of the causes of birth defects allow prospective parents to take steps to minimize the chance that an infant will be born with these types of disorders.

Congenital Disorders Sourcebook, Third Edition describes the most common types of nonhereditary birth defects and disorders related to prematurity, gestational injuries, prenatal and perinatal infections, maternal health conditions during pregnancy, and birth complications, including cerebral palsy, cleft lip and palate, fetal alcohol syndrome, spina bifida, and disorders of the heart, brain, gastrointestinal tract, musculoskeletal system, urinary tract, and reproductive organs. Causes, prevention strategies, and diagnostic tests are explained, and innovative treatment strategies, including fetal surgery, are described. The book concludes with a glossary of related terms and a directory of resources for further help and information.

How to Use This Book

This book is divided into parts and chapters. Parts focus on broad areas of interest. Chapters are devoted to single topics within a part.

Part I: Prenatal Concerns and Preventing Birth Defects describes what is known about the causes of birth defects and what can be done to prevent them. It details the most common risk factors for congenital disorders, including medications, environmental elements, and infectious diseases and other maternal health conditions with known adverse fetal effects. Disorders of the amniotic fluid, placenta, and umbilical cord are also discussed. Additionally, the part offers facts about other pregnancy complications that can affect fetal health, and it describes the steps that can be taken to help ensure a healthy pregnancy. This portion of the book concludes with a description of fetal surgery and other fetal treatment techniques that can correct or lessen defects before birth and improve the chances of survival for infants with congenital disorders.

Part II: Prematurity and Other Birth Complications provides basic information about the types of complications that can affect premature infants, including apnea of prematurity, persistent pulmonary distress syndrome, retinopathy of prematurity, and persistent pulmonary hypertension. It addresses the most common health concerns with twins and other multiple births, including twin reversed arterial perfusion sequence, unequal placental sharing, and twin-twin transfusion syndrome. It also describes the types of infections that can be passed from mother to infant at birth, explains the screening tests that are given to newborns, and details what parents can expect in labor and delivery and in the first days after birth when a baby has a health problem.

Part III: Structural Abnormalities and Functional Impairments offers detailed information about the most common types of physical defects, including spina bifida, cerebral palsy, craniofacial and musculoskeletal defects, and defects of the brain, heart, kidney, liver, pancreas, reproductive organs, gastrointestinal tract, and urinary tract. It describes the causes and symptoms of each disorder, the diagnostic tests and treatment techniques used with each, and the research advances that are improving prevention efforts and treatment outcomes.

Part IV: Additional Help and Information includes a glossary of terms related to congenital disorders and a directory of resources offering additional help and support.

Bibliographic Note

This volume contains documents and excerpts from publications issued by the following U.S. government agencies: AIDSinfo.gov; Centers for Disease Control and Prevention (CDC); National Dissemination Center for Children with Disabilities; National Eye Institute; National

Heart Lung and Blood Institute; National Institute of Child Health and Human Development; National Institute of Diabetes and Digestive and Kidney Diseases; National Institute of Neurological Disorders and Stroke; National Institute on Deafness and Other Communication Disorders; National Institutes of Health; U.S. Department of Health and Human Services, Office on Women's Health; and the U.S. Food and Drug Association.

In addition, this volume contains copyrighted documents from the following organizations: A.D.A.M., Inc.; American Academy of Orthopaedic Surgeons; American Heart Association; American Pregnancy Association; American Society of Clinical Oncology; Avenues; Boston Children's Hospital; California Department of Public Health-California Birth Defects Monitoring Program; Children's Craniofacial Association; Children's Hospital at Vanderbilt; Children's Hospital Colorado; Children's Hospitals and Clinics of Minnesota; Cleveland Clinic; Dartmouth-Hitchcock; FACES: National Craniofacial Association; Fetal Hope Foundation; Fetal Treatment Program of New England; Georgia Urology; Hennepin County Human Services and Public Health Department; Hospital for Sick Children; Indiana State Department of Health; March of Dimes; Nemours Foundation; Organization of Teratology Information Specialists; St. Louis Fetal Care Institute; Spina Bifida Association; University of California San Francisco Benioff Children's Hospital; University of Iowa Hospitals and Clinics; University of Maryland Medical Center; University of Missouri Children's Hospital; Urology Care Foundation; and the Utah Department of Health.

Full citation information is provided on the first page of each chapter or section. Every effort has been made to secure all necessary rights to reprint the copyrighted material. If any omissions have been made, please contact Omnigraphics to make corrections for future editions.

Acknowledgements

Thanks go to the many organizations, agencies, and individuals who have contributed materials for this *Sourcebook* and to medical consultant Dr. David Cooke and prepress services provider WhimsyInk. Special thanks go to managing editor Karen Bellenir and permissions coordinator Liz Collins for their help and support.

About the Health Reference Series

The *Health Reference Series* is designed to provide basic medical information for patients, families, caregivers, and the general public.

Each volume takes a particular topic and provides comprehensive coverage. This is especially important for people who may be dealing with a newly diagnosed disease or a chronic disorder in themselves or in a family member. People looking for preventive guidance, information about disease warning signs, medical statistics, and risk factors for health problems will also find answers to their questions in the *Health Reference Series*. The *Series*, however, is not intended to serve as a tool for diagnosing illness, in prescribing treatments, or as a substitute for the physician/patient relationship. All people concerned about medical symptoms or the possibility of disease are encouraged to seek professional care from an appropriate healthcare provider.

A Note about Spelling and Style

Health Reference Series editors use *Stedman's Medical Dictionary* as an authority for questions related to the spelling of medical terms and the *Chicago Manual of Style* for questions related to grammatical structures, punctuation, and other editorial concerns. Consistent adherence is not always possible, however, because the individual volumes within the *Series* include many documents from a wide variety of different producers and copyright holders, and the editor's primary goal is to present material from each source as accurately as is possible following the terms specified by each document's producer. This sometimes means that information in different chapters or sections may follow other guidelines and alternate spelling authorities. For example, occasionally a copyright holder may require that eponymous terms be shown in possessive forms (Crohn's disease *vs.* Crohn disease) or that British spelling norms be retained (leukaemia *vs.* leukemia).

Locating Information within the Health Reference Series

The *Health Reference Series* contains a wealth of information about a wide variety of medical topics. Ensuring easy access to all the fact sheets, research reports, in-depth discussions, and other material contained within the individual books of the series remains one of our highest priorities. As the *Series* continues to grow in size and scope, however, locating the precise information needed by a reader may become more challenging.

A *Contents Guide to the Health Reference Series* was developed to direct readers to the specific volumes that address their concerns. It presents an extensive list of diseases, treatments, and other topics of general interest compiled from the Tables of Contents and major index headings. To access *A Contents Guide to the Health Reference Series*, visit www.healthreferenceseries.com.

Medical Consultant

Medical consultation services are provided to the *Health Reference Series* editors by David A. Cooke, MD, FACP. Dr. Cooke is a graduate of Brandeis University, and he received his M.D. degree from the University of Michigan. He completed residency training at the University of Wisconsin Hospital and Clinics. He is board-certified in Internal Medicine. Dr. Cooke currently works as part of the University of Michigan Health System and practices in Ann Arbor, MI. In his free time, he enjoys writing, science fiction, and spending time with his family.

Our Advisory Board

We would like to thank the following board members for providing guidance to the development of this series:

Dr. Lynda Baker, Associate Professor of Library and Information Science, Wayne State University, Detroit, MI

Nancy Bulgarelli, William Beaumont Hospital Library, Royal Oak, MI

Karen Imarisio, Bloomfield Township Public Library, Bloomfield Township, MI

Karen Morgan, Mardigian Library, University of Michigan-Dearborn, Dearborn, MI

Rosemary Orlando, St. Clair Shores Public Library, St. Clair Shores, MI

Health Reference Series *Update Policy*

The inaugural book in the *Health Reference Series* was the first edition of *Cancer Sourcebook* published in 1989. Since then, the *Series* has been enthusiastically received by librarians and in the medical community. In order to maintain the standard of providing high-quality health information for the layperson the editorial staff at Omnigraphics felt it was necessary to implement a policy of updating volumes when warranted.

Medical researchers have been making tremendous strides, and it is the purpose of the *Health Reference Series* to stay current with the most recent advances. Each decision to update a volume is made on an individual basis. Some of the considerations include how much new information is available and the feedback we receive from people who use the books. If there is a topic you would like to see added to the update list, or an area of medical concern you feel has not been adequately addressed, please write to:

Editor
Health Reference Series
Omnigraphics, Inc.
155 W. Congress, Suite 200
Detroit, MI 48226
E-mail: editorial@omnigraphics.com

Part One

Prenatal Concerns and Preventing Birth Defects

Chapter 1

What Are Birth Defects: An Overview

About 120,000 babies (1 in 33) in the United States are born each year with birth defects.[1] A birth defect is an abnormality of structure, function, or metabolism (body chemistry) present at birth that results in physical or mental disabilities or death. Thousands of different birth defects have been identified.[2] Birth defects are the leading cause of death in the first year of life.[3]

What causes birth defects?

Genetic and environmental factors, or a combination of these factors, can cause birth defects. However, the causes of about 70 percent of birth defects are unknown.[1]

How are genetic disorders passed on to the child?

There are three main categories of genetic birth defects.

Single-gene defects: A mutation (change) in a single gene can cause birth defects. Every human being has about twenty thousand to twenty-five thousand genes that determine traits like eye and hair color.[4] Genes also direct the growth, development, and functioning of every system in the body. Genes are packaged into each of the forty-six chromosomes inside our cells.

A child gets half its genes from each parent. A person can inherit a genetic disease when one parent (who may or may not have the disease) passes along a single faulty gene. This is called dominant inheritance. Each child of a parent with the gene has a 50-percent chance of inheriting the disorder. Examples include:

- achondroplasia (a form of dwarfism);
- Marfan syndrome (a connective-tissue disease).

Other genetic diseases are inherited when both parents (who do not have the disease) carry an abnormality in the same gene and pass it on to a child. This is called recessive inheritance. Each child of two parents who have the abnormal gene has a 25-percent chance of inheriting the disorder. Examples include:

- Tay-Sachs disease (a fatal nervous system disorder);
- cystic fibrosis (a serious disorder of lungs and other organs, affecting mainly Caucasians).

X-linked is another form of inheritance in which sons can inherit a genetic disease from a mother who carries an abnormal gene (usually with no effect on her own health). Each son of a mother who carries an abnormal gene has a 50 percent chance of inheriting the disorder. Daughters usually do not inherit the disorder, but they may be carriers like their mother. Examples include:

- hemophilia (a blood-clotting disorder);
- Duchenne muscular dystrophy (progressive muscle weakness).

Chromosomal birth defects: Abnormalities in the number or structure of chromosomes can cause many birth defects. Chromosomal abnormalities usually are caused by an error that occurred when an egg or sperm cell was developing. Because of the error, a baby can be born with too many or too few chromosomes, or with one or more chromosomes that are broken or rearranged. Examples include:

- *Down syndrome (an extra copy of chromosome 21 or other rearrangements resulting in extra genetic material from this chromosome)*: Affected children have varying degrees of intellectual disabilities, characteristic facial features and, often, heart defects and other problems.

- *Trisomies 18 and 13 (an extra copy of chromosome 18 or 13)*: Affected babies have multiple birth defects and often die in the first months of life.

4

- *Sex chromosome abnormalities (missing or extra copies of the sex chromosomes, X and Y):* These disorders affect sexual development and may cause infertility, growth abnormalities, and behavioral and learning problems. However, most affected individuals live fairly normal lives. Examples include Turner syndrome (in which a girl is missing all or part of an X chromosome) and Klinefelter syndrome (in which a boy has one or more extra X chromosomes).

Multifactorial birth defects: Some birth defects appear to be caused by a combination of genes and environmental exposures. This is called multifactorial inheritance. In some cases, an individual may inherit one or more genes that make him more likely to have a birth defect if he is exposed to certain environmental substances, such as cigarette smoke. These individuals have a genetic predisposition to a birth defect. But if the individual is not exposed to the environmental substance before birth, he probably won't have the birth defect. Examples of multifactorial birth defects include:

- cleft lip/palate (opening in the lip and/or roof of the mouth);

- neural tube defects (NTDs; serious birth defects of the brain and spinal cord, including spina bifida and anencephaly);

- heart defects

What environmental factors contribute to birth defects?

Environmental substances that can cause birth defects are called teratogens. These include alcohol, certain drugs/medications, infections, and certain chemicals.

Alcohol: Each year between one thousand and six thousand babies in the United States are born with fetal alcohol syndrome (FAS).[5] FAS is a pattern of mental and physical birth defects that is common in babies of mothers who drink heavily during pregnancy. Women who are pregnant or planning pregnancy should not drink any alcohol. Even moderate or light drinking during pregnancy may harm the baby.

Drugs: Illegal drugs, including cocaine, marijuana, and Ecstasy, may cause birth defects. Pregnant women should not take illegal drugs and should tell their providers if they need help to quit. Some prescription drugs also can cause birth defects. A woman taking any of the following prescription drugs should talk to her provider before getting pregnant. She may need to switch to a safer drug for pregnancy:

- Angiotensin-converting enzyme (ACE) inhibitors (enalapril or captopril)
- Androgens and testosterone by-products
- Anticancer drugs
- Antifolic acid drugs, like methotrexate or aminopterin
- Carbamazepine
- Levothyroxine
- Lithium
- Phenytoin
- Streptomycin and kanamycin
- Tetracycline
- Trimethadione and paramethadione
- Valproic acid
- Warfarin and other coumarin by-products

If a woman is pregnant and taking any of the following drugs, she should stop taking the medicine immediately and call her health care provider:

- Accutane, Amnesteem, Claravis, Sotret (isotretinoin) and other retinoids
- Soriatane (acitretin)
- Thalomid (thalidomide)
- Revlimid (lenalidomide)

A woman who is pregnant or thinking about getting pregnant should tell her provider about any drugs she takes to make sure they are safe for pregnancy.

Infections: Certain infections can cause birth defects when a woman gets them during pregnancy. About thirty thousand babies a year (about 1 in 150 newborns) in this country are born with a viral infection called cytomegalovirus (CMV).[6] About eight thousand infected babies each year develop permanent disabilities, including mental retardation and loss of vision and hearing.[6] Pregnant women often get CMV from young children who have few or no symptoms.

Sexually transmitted infections (STIs): STIs in the mother can endanger the fetus and newborn. For example, untreated syphilis can cause stillbirth, newborn death, or bone defects. About 350 babies were affected by congenital syphilis in the United States in 2006.[7]

Chemicals: Little information is known about the effects of most chemicals during pregnancy. However, a small number of chemicals are known to be harmful to an unborn baby. Most of these are found in the workplace. For example, workplace exposure to organic solvents (chemicals that dissolve other substances), such as alcohols, degreasers, paint thinners, and varnish removers, are suspected of increasing the risk of birth defects. High levels of exposure to pesticides, on the job or at home, also may contribute to birth defects and other pregnancy complications. Pregnant women should avoid pesticides whenever possible, and those who work with chemicals should follow all preventive measures to reduce their exposure. A woman who is pregnant or planning pregnancy should also discuss all workplace chemical exposures with her health care provider to see if additional on-the-job protections are advisable.

What are the most common birth defects?

Some of the most common birth defects include:

- **Heart defects:** As many as 1 in 100 babies in the United States are born with heart defects each year.[1] While advances in surgery have dramatically improved the outlook for affected babies, heart defects remain the leading cause of birth defect-related infant deaths.[8]

- **Cleft lip/palate:** About 1 in 700 babies is born with cleft lip/palate each year.[1] Affected babies can have problems with eating, speech, and language. Some have a small cleft that can be corrected with one surgical procedure, while others have severe clefts and need multiple surgeries.

- **Down syndrome:** This chromosomal abnormality affects about 1 in 800 babies in the United States.[1] Early intervention programs and treatment of associated health problems have greatly improved the outlook for affected individuals.

- **Spina bifida (open spine):** This disorder affects about 1 in 2,500 babies in the United States each year.[1] Affected babies have varying degrees of paralysis and bladder and bowel problems.

Other common birth defects include musculoskeletal defects (including arm and leg defects), gastrointestinal defects (including defects of the esophagus, stomach, and intestines), and eye defects. These birth defects usually are multifactorial.

What are birth defects of body chemistry?

In 2004, about four thousand babies in the United States were born with disorders affecting body chemistry.[9] These are called metabolic disorders. Most metabolic disorders are recessive genetic diseases. These disorders are not visible, but they can be harmful or even fatal. Many metabolic disorders can be routinely detected with newborn screening tests, allowing early treatment and healthy development. The March of Dimes recommends that all newborns be screened for thirty disorders (including hearing loss) for which effective treatment is available. Examples of the thirty disorders include:

- **Phenylketonuria (PKU):** Affected babies cannot process a part of protein, which builds up and damages the brain. Affected babies are placed on a special diet that prevents mental retardation. Affected individuals generally should follow a special diet throughout life.

- **Galactosemia:** Affected babies cannot process galactose (a sugar in milk), which builds up and can lead to mental retardation, blindness, and death. Affected individuals are treated with a special diet free of dairy products.

Some metabolic disorders cannot yet be treated. An example is Tay-Sachs disease. Affected babies lack an enzyme needed to break down certain fatty substances in brain cells. These substances build up and destroy brain cells, resulting in blindness, paralysis, and death by age five.

Can birth defects be prevented?

There are a number of steps a woman can take before and during pregnancy to reduce her risk of having a baby with a birth defect:

- Get a preconception checkup with a health care provider. This is a medical checkup a woman gets before getting pregnant. During this visit, the provider can identify and often treat health conditions that can pose a risk in pregnancy. A preconception visit is especially crucial for women with chronic health conditions, like diabetes, high blood pressure, and epilepsy, that can affect pregnancy. For example, women with diabetes who have poor blood-sugar control are several times more likely than women without diabetes to have a baby with a serious birth defect. However, if their blood sugar levels are well controlled before pregnancy, they are almost as likely to have a healthy baby as women without diabetes.[10]

- Make sure her vaccinations are up-to-date. All women should be tested for immunity to rubella (German measles) and chickenpox before getting pregnant and consider being vaccinated if they are not immune. After being vaccinated, a woman should wait one month before becoming pregnant. Rubella poses a high risk of birth defects if a woman gets infected during pregnancy. Chickenpox also can cause birth defects, though the risk is low.

- Take a multivitamin containing 400 micrograms of folic acid daily starting before pregnancy and in early pregnancy to help prevent NTDs. If a woman already has had a pregnancy affected by an NTD, she should consult her provider before pregnancy about how much folic acid to take. Generally a higher dose, 4 milligrams, is recommended.[11] Women with diabetes or epilepsy or who are obese are at increased risk of having a baby with these birth defects. They should ask their providers before pregnancy about whether they should take the larger dose of folic acid.

- Eat healthy foods, including foods containing folic acid and folate, the form of folic acid that occurs naturally in foods. Foods high in folic acid include fortified breakfast cereals, enriched grain products, beans, leafy green vegetables, and orange juice.

- Get early and regular prenatal care.

- Don't eat undercooked meat or change a cat's litter box. Both are possible sources of toxoplasmosis, an infection that can cause birth defects.

- Avoid contact with all rodents, including hamsters, mice, and guinea pigs. These animals can carry a virus that can harm a baby.

- Don't eat fish that contain high amounts of mercury. These fish include shark, swordfish, king mackerel, or tilefish. It's all right for a pregnant woman to eat up to twelve ounces a week of fish that have small amounts of mercury, such as shrimp, salmon, pollock, catfish, and canned light tuna. But she should not eat more than six ounces of albacore (white) tuna per week. Women also should check local advisories about the safety of fish caught in local waters.

- Begin pregnancy at a healthy weight (not too heavy or too thin).

- Don't smoke and avoid secondhand smoke.

- Don't drink alcohol.

- Don't use any drug, even over-the-counter medications or herbal preparations, unless recommended by a health care provider who knows the woman is pregnant.

Can some birth defects be diagnosed before birth?

Providers can diagnose some birth defects before birth using one or more prenatal tests, including ultrasound, amniocentesis, and chorionic villus sampling (CVS). Ultrasound can help diagnose structural birth defects, such as spina bifida, heart defects, and some urinary tract defects. Amniocentesis and CVS are used to diagnose or rule out chromosomal abnormalities, such as Down syndrome and many genetic birth defects. Most women have screening tests (blood tests) to see if they are at increased risk of certain birth defects, including Down syndrome and spina bifida. These screening tests cannot diagnose a condition, but they can suggest that further diagnostic testing is needed.

Can birth defects be treated before birth?

A small percentage of couples learn through prenatal diagnosis that their baby has a birth defect. While this news can be devastating, prenatal diagnosis sometimes can improve the outlook for the baby. It is now possible to treat some birth defects before birth. For example, biotin dependence and methylmalonic academia, two life-threatening inherited metabolic disorders, have been diagnosed by amniocentesis and treated in the womb, resulting in the births of healthy babies.

Prenatal surgery has saved babies with urinary tract blockages and rare lung tumors. However, prenatal surgery poses a number of serious risks for mother and baby, including preterm birth. The National Institutes of Health is conducting a study to compare the safety and effectiveness of surgery before and after birth for babies with spina bifida. Doctors also have saved babies with serious heart-rhythm disturbances by treating the pregnant woman with medications.

Even when a fetus has a condition for which prenatal treatment is not yet possible, prenatal diagnosis permits parents to prepare themselves emotionally and to plan with their provider the safest timing, hospital facility, and method of delivery.

Couples who have had a baby with a birth defect or who have a family history of birth defects should consider consulting a genetic counselor. These health professionals help families understand what is known about the causes of a birth defect and the chances of the birth defect recurring in another pregnancy. Genetic counselors can provide referrals to medical experts as well as to appropriate support groups in the community. Genetic counseling is available at most large medical centers and teaching hospitals. To find a genetic counselor in their area, individuals can ask their health care provider or visit the National Society of Genetic Counselors.

References

1. Centers for Disease Control and Prevention (CDC). Birth Defects. Retrieved March 11, 2009.

2. National Institutes of Health (NIH). Birth Defects. Retrieved May 11, 2009.

3. Mathews, T.J. and MacDorman, M.F. Infant Mortality Statistics from the 2005 Period Linked Birth/Infant Death Data Set. *National Vital Statistics Reports*, volume 57, number 2, July 30, 2008.

4. National Human Genome Research Institute. A Brief Guide to Genomics. Retrieved December 23, 2008.

5. Centers for Disease Control and Prevention (CDC). Erratum: Volume 54, No. RR-11. *Morbidity and Mortality Weekly Report*, volume 55, number 20, May 26, 2006, page 568.

6. Centers for Disease Control and Prevention (CDC). Cytomegalovirus. Retrieved November 3, 2008.

7. Centers for Disease Control and Prevention (CDC). Syphilis—CDC Fact Sheet. Updated 1/4/08.

8. Kung, H., et al. Deaths: Final Data for 2005. *National Vital Statistics Report*, volume 56, number 10, April 24, 2008.

9. *Overview of NBS Programs: States of the States.* Briefing Presented at the First Meeting of the Advisory Committee on Heritable Disorders and Genetic Diseases in Newborns and Children, June 7–8, 2004, Washington, DC.

10. American College of Obstetricians and Gynecologists (ACOG). Pregestational Diabetes Mellitus. *ACOG Practice Bulletin*, number 60, March 2005 (reaffirmed 2007).

11. Centers for Disease Control and Prevention (CDC). Folic Acid: Questions and Answers. Updated March 31, 2009.

Chapter 2

Steps to a Healthy Pregnancy

Chapter Contents

Section 2.1

Prenatal Care

Excerpted from "Prenatal Care Fact Sheet," U.S. Department
of Health and Human Services Office on Women's Health, March 6, 2009.

What is prenatal care?

Prenatal care is the health care you get while you are pregnant. Take care of yourself and your baby by doing the following things:

- Get early prenatal care. If you know you're pregnant, or think you might be, call your doctor to schedule a visit.

- Get regular prenatal care. Your doctor will schedule you for many checkups over the course of your pregnancy. Don't miss any—they are all important.

- Follow your doctor's advice.

Why do I need prenatal care?

Prenatal care can help keep you and your baby healthy. Babies of mothers who do not get prenatal care are three times more likely to have a low birth weight and five times more likely to die than those born to mothers who do get care.

Doctors can spot health problems early when they see mothers regularly. This allows doctors to treat them early. Early treatment can cure many problems and prevent others. Doctors also can talk to pregnant women about things they can do to give their unborn babies a healthy start to life.

I am thinking about getting pregnant. How can I take care of myself?

You should start taking care of yourself before you start trying to get pregnant. This is called preconception health. It means knowing how health conditions and risk factors could affect you or your unborn baby if you become pregnant. For example, some foods, habits, and medicines can harm your baby—even before he or she is conceived. Some health problems also can affect pregnancy.

Talk to your doctor before pregnancy to learn what you can do to prepare your body. Women should prepare for pregnancy before becoming sexually active. Ideally, women should give themselves at least three months to prepare before getting pregnant.

The five most important things you can do before becoming pregnant are as follows:

1. Take 400 to 800 micrograms (400 to 800 mcg or 0.4 to 0.8 mg) of folic acid every day for at least three months before getting pregnant to lower your risk of some birth defects of the brain and spine. You can get folic acid from some foods. But it's hard to get all the folic acid you need from foods alone. Taking a vitamin with folic acid is the best and easiest way to be sure you're getting enough.

2. Stop smoking and drinking alcohol. Ask your doctor for help.

3. If you have a medical condition, be sure it is under control. Some conditions include asthma, diabetes, depression, high blood pressure, obesity, thyroid disease, or epilepsy. Be sure your vaccinations are up to date.

4. Talk to your doctor about any over-the-counter and prescription medicines you are using. These include dietary or herbal supplements. Some medicines are not safe during pregnancy. At the same time, stopping medicines you need also can be harmful.

5. Avoid contact with toxic substances or materials at work and at home that could be harmful. Stay away from chemicals and cat or rodent feces.

I'm pregnant. What should I do—or not do—to take care of myself and my unborn baby?

Follow these do's and don'ts to take care of yourself and the precious life growing inside you.

Health care do's and don'ts:

*   Get early and regular prenatal care. Whether this is your first pregnancy or third, health care is extremely important. Your doctor will check to make sure you and the baby are healthy at each visit. If there are any problems, early action will help you and the baby.

- Take a multivitamin or prenatal vitamin with 400 to 800 micrograms (400 to 800 mcg or 0.4 to 0.8 mg) of folic acid every day. Folic acid is most important in the early stages of pregnancy, but you should continue taking folic acid throughout pregnancy.

- Ask your doctor before stopping any medicines or starting any new medicines. Some medicines are not safe during pregnancy. Keep in mind that even over-the-counter medicines and herbal products may cause side effects or other problems. But not using medicines you need could also be harmful.

- Avoid x-rays. If you must have dental work or diagnostic tests, tell your dentist or doctor that you are pregnant so that extra care can be taken.

- Get a flu shot. Pregnant women can get very sick from the flu and may need hospital care.

Food do's and don'ts:

- Eat a variety of healthy foods. Choose fruits, vegetables, whole grains, calcium-rich foods, and foods low in saturated fat. Also, make sure to drink plenty of fluids, especially water.

- Get all the nutrients you need each day, including iron. Getting enough iron prevents you from getting anemia, which is linked to preterm birth and low birth weight. Eating a variety of healthy foods will help you get the nutrients your baby needs. But ask your doctor if you need to take a daily prenatal vitamin or iron supplement to be sure you are getting enough.

- Protect yourself and your baby from food-borne illnesses, including toxoplasmosis and listeria. Wash fruits and vegetables before eating. Don't eat uncooked or undercooked meats or fish. Always handle, clean, cook, eat, and store foods properly.

- Don't eat fish with lots of mercury, including swordfish, king mackerel, shark, and tilefish.

Lifestyle do's and don'ts:

- Gain a healthy amount of weight. Your doctor can tell you how much weight gain you should aim for during pregnancy.

- Don't smoke, drink alcohol, or use drugs. These can cause long-term harm or death to your baby. Ask your doctor for help quitting.

- Unless your doctor tells you not to, try to get at least two hours and thirty minutes of moderate-intensity aerobic activity a week. It's best to spread out your workouts throughout the week. If you worked out regularly before pregnancy, you can keep up your activity level as long as your health doesn't change and you talk to your doctor about your activity level throughout your pregnancy.

- Don't take very hot baths or use hot tubs or saunas.

- Get plenty of sleep and find ways to control stress.

- Get informed. Read books, watch videos, go to a childbirth class, and talk with moms you know.

- Ask your doctor about childbirth education classes for you and your partner. Classes can help you prepare for the birth of your baby.

Environmental do's and don'ts:

- Stay away from chemicals like insecticides, solvents (like some cleaners or paint thinners), lead, mercury, and paint (including paint fumes). Not all products have pregnancy warnings on their labels. If you're unsure if a product is safe, ask your doctor before using it. Talk to your doctor if you are worried that chemicals used in your workplace might be harmful.

- If you have a cat, ask your doctor about toxoplasmosis. This infection is caused by a parasite sometimes found in cat feces. If not treated, toxoplasmosis can cause birth defects. You can lower your risk of by avoiding cat litter and wearing gloves when gardening.

- Avoid contact with rodents, including pet rodents, and with their urine, droppings, or nesting material. Rodents can carry a virus that can be harmful or even deadly to your unborn baby.

- Take steps to avoid illness, such as washing hands frequently.

- Stay away from secondhand smoke.

I don't want to get pregnant right now. But should I still take folic acid every day?

Yes. Birth defects of the brain and spine happen in the very early stages of pregnancy, often before a woman knows she is pregnant. By the time she finds out she is pregnant, it might be too late to prevent those birth defects. Also, half of all pregnancies in the United States are not planned. For these reasons, all women who are able to get pregnant need 400 to 800 mcg of folic acid every day.

How often should I see my doctor during pregnancy?

Your doctor will give you a schedule of all the doctor's visits you should have while pregnant. Most experts suggest you see your doctor on the following schedule:

- About once each month for weeks four through twenty-eight
- Twice a month for weeks twenty-eight through thirty-six
- Weekly for weeks thirty-six to birth

If you are older than thirty-five or your pregnancy is high risk, you'll probably see your doctor more often.

What happens during prenatal visits?

During the first prenatal visit, you can expect your doctor to do the following things:

- Ask about your health history, including diseases, operations, or prior pregnancies
- Ask about your family's health history
- Do a complete physical exam, including a pelvic exam and Pap test
- Take your blood and urine for lab work
- Check your blood pressure, height, and weight
- Calculate your due date
- Answer your questions

At the first visit, you should ask questions and discuss any issues related to your pregnancy. Find out all you can about how to stay healthy.

Later prenatal visits will probably be shorter. Your doctor will check on your health and make sure the baby is growing as expected. Most prenatal visits will include the following:

- Checking your blood pressure
- Measuring your weight gain

- Measuring your abdomen to check your baby's growth (once you begin to show)

- Checking the baby's heart rate

While you're pregnant, you also will have some routine tests. Some tests are suggested for all women, such as blood work to check for anemia, your blood type, human immunodeficiency virus (HIV), and other factors. Other tests might be offered based on your age, your personal or family health history, your ethnic background, or the results of routine tests you have had.

Section 2.2

Healthy Eating during Pregnancy

Do you wonder how it's reasonable to gain 25 to 35 pounds (on average) during your pregnancy when a newborn baby weighs only a fraction of that? Although it varies from woman to woman, this is how those pounds may add up:

- 7.5 pounds: average baby's weight

- 7 pounds: extra stored protein, fat, and other nutrients

- 4 pounds: extra blood

- 4 pounds: other extra body fluids

- 2 pounds: breast enlargement

- 2 pounds: enlargement of your uterus

- 2 pounds: amniotic fluid surrounding your baby

- 1.5 pounds: the placenta

Of course, patterns of weight gain during pregnancy vary. It's normal to gain less if you start out heavier and more if you're having twins or triplets—or if you were underweight before becoming pregnant. More important than how much weight you gain is what makes up those extra pounds.

When you're pregnant, what you eat and drink is the main source of nourishment for your baby. In fact, the link between what you consume and the health of your baby is much stronger than once thought. That's why doctors now say, for example, that no amount of alcohol consumption should be considered safe during pregnancy.

The extra food you eat shouldn't just be empty calories—it should provide the nutrients your growing baby needs. For example, calcium helps make and keep bones and teeth strong. While you're pregnant, you still need calcium for your body, plus extra calcium for your developing baby. Similarly, you require more of all the essential nutrients than you did before you became pregnant.

A Nutrition Primer for Expectant Mothers

Whether or not you're pregnant, a healthy diet includes proteins, carbohydrates, fats, vitamins, minerals, and plenty of water. The U.S. government publishes dietary guidelines that can help you determine how many servings of each kind of food to eat every day. Eating a variety of foods in the proportions indicated is a good step toward staying healthy.

Here are some of the most common nutrients you need and the foods that contain them.

Important Nutrients

Scientists know that your diet can affect your baby's health—even before you become pregnant. For example, recent research shows that folic acid helps prevent neural tube defects (including spina bifida) from occurring during the earliest stages of fetal development—so it's important to consume plenty of it before you become pregnant and during the early weeks of your pregnancy.

Even though many foods, particularly breakfast cereals, are fortified with folic acid, doctors now encourage women to take folic acid supplements before and throughout pregnancy (especially for the first twenty-eight days). Be sure to ask your doctor about folic acid if you're considering becoming pregnant.

Calcium is another important nutrient. Because your growing baby's calcium demands are high, you should increase your calcium

Table 2.1. Common Nutrients and Their Sources

Nutrient	Needed for	Best sources
Protein	Cell growth and blood production	Lean meat, fish, poultry, egg whites, beans, peanut butter, tofu
Carbohydrates	Daily energy production	Breads, cereals, rice, potatoes, pasta, fruits, vegetables
Calcium	Strong bones and teeth, muscle contraction, nerve function	Milk, cheese, yogurt, sardines or salmon with bones, spinach
Iron	Red blood cell production (to prevent anemia)	Lean red meat, spinach, iron-fortified whole-grain breads and cereals
Vitamin A	Healthy skin, good eyesight, growing bones	Carrots, dark leafy greens, sweet potatoes
Vitamin C	Healthy gums, teeth, and bones; assistance with iron absorption	Citrus fruit, broccoli, tomatoes, fortified fruit juices
Vitamin B6	Red blood cell formation; effective use of protein, fat, and carbohydrates	Pork, ham, whole-grain cereals, bananas
Vitamin B12	Formation of red blood cells, maintaining nervous system health	Meat, fish, poultry, milk (Note: vegetarians who don't eat dairy products need supplemental B12)
Vitamin D	Healthy bones and teeth; aids absorption of calcium	Fortified milk, dairy products, cereals, and breads
Folic acid	Blood and protein production, effective enzyme function	Green leafy vegetables, dark yellow fruits and vegetables, beans, peas, nuts
Fat	Body energy stores	Meat, whole-milk dairy products, nuts, peanut butter, margarine, vegetable oils (Note: limit fat intake to 30 percent or less of your total daily calorie intake)

consumption to prevent a loss of calcium from your own bones. Your doctor will also likely prescribe prenatal vitamins for you, which contain some extra calcium.

Your best food sources of calcium are milk and other dairy products. However, if you have lactose intolerance or dislike milk and milk products, ask your doctor about a calcium supplement. (Signs of lactose intolerance include diarrhea, bloating, or gas after eating milk or milk products. Taking a lactase capsule or pill, or using lactose-free milk products may help.) Other calcium-rich foods include sardines or salmon with bones, tofu, broccoli, spinach, and calcium-fortified juices and foods.

Doctors don't usually recommend starting a strict vegan diet when you become pregnant. However, if you already follow a vegetarian diet, you can continue to do so during your pregnancy—but do it carefully. Be sure your doctor knows about your diet. It's challenging to get the nutrition you need if you don't eat fish and chicken, or milk, cheese, or eggs. You'll likely need supplemental protein and may also need to take vitamin B12 and D supplements.

To ensure that you and your baby receive adequate nutrition, consult a registered dietitian for help with planning meals.

Food Cravings during Pregnancy

You've probably known women who craved specific foods during pregnancy, or perhaps you've had such cravings yourself. Some theories held that a hunger for a particular type of food indicated that a woman's body lacked the nutrients that food contains. Although this turned out not to be so, it's still unclear why these urges occur.

Some pregnant women crave chocolate, spicy foods, fruits, and comfort foods, such as mashed potatoes, cereals, and toasted white bread. Other women crave nonfood items, such as clay and cornstarch. The craving and eating of nonfood items is known as pica. Consuming things that aren't food can be dangerous to both you and your baby. If you have urges to eat nonfood items, notify your doctor.

But following your cravings is fine as long as you crave foods that contribute to a healthy diet. Often, these cravings let up about three months into the pregnancy.

Food and Drinks to Avoid during Pregnancy

No level of alcohol consumption is considered safe during pregnancy. Also, check with your doctor before you take any vitamins or herbal products. Some of these can be harmful to the developing fetus.

And although many doctors feel that one or two six- to eight-ounce cups per day of coffee, tea, or soda with caffeine won't harm your baby, it's probably wise to avoid caffeine altogether if you can. High caffeine consumption has been linked to an increased risk of miscarriage, so limit your intake or switch to decaffeinated products.

When you're pregnant, it's also important to avoid food-borne illnesses, such as listeriosis and toxoplasmosis, which can be life-threatening to an unborn baby and may cause birth defects or miscarriage. Foods to steer clear of include:

- soft, unpasteurized cheeses (often advertised as "fresh") such as feta, goat, Brie, Camembert, and blue cheese;

- unpasteurized milk, juices, and apple cider;

- raw eggs or foods containing raw eggs, including mousse and tiramisu;

- raw or undercooked meats, fish, or shellfish;

- processed meats such as hot dogs and deli meats (these should be well cooked);

- fish that are high in mercury, including shark, swordfish, king mackerel, or tilefish.

If you've eaten these foods at some point during your pregnancy, try not to worry too much about it now; just avoid them for the remainder of the pregnancy. If you're really concerned, talk to your doctor.

More about Fish

Fish and shellfish can be an extremely healthy part of your pregnancy diet—they contain beneficial omega-3 fatty acids and are high in protein and low in saturated fat. But limit the types of fish you eat while pregnant because some contain high levels of mercury, which can cause damage to the developing nervous system of a fetus.

Mercury, which occurs naturally in the environment, is also released into the air through industrial pollution and can accumulate in streams and oceans, where it turns into methylmercury. The methylmercury builds up in fish, especially those that eat other fish.

Because canned albacore (or white) tuna and tuna steaks are generally considered to be higher in mercury than canned light tuna, the U.S. Food and Drug Administration (FDA) recommends that you eat no more than six ounces a week. A 2006 review by Consumer Reports, though, showed that some canned light tuna can contain levels of mercury even higher than that of white tuna. But the FDA maintains that the levels are safe if consumption of the fish is limited, and that the current recommendations should stand.

It can be confusing when recommendations from trusted sources differ. But since this analysis indicates that amounts of mercury in tuna may be higher than previously reported, some women may want to eliminate tuna from their diet while pregnant or when trying to become pregnant.

Almost all fish and shellfish contain small amounts of mercury, but you can safely eat up to twelve ounces (two average meals) a week of a variety of fish and shellfish that are lower in mercury, such as salmon, shrimp, clams, pollock, catfish, and tilapia.

Talk with your doctor if you have any questions about how much—and which fish—you can eat.

Managing Some Common Problems

Because the iron in prenatal vitamins and other factors may cause constipation during pregnancy, try to consume more fiber than you did before you became pregnant. Try to eat about twenty to thirty grams of fiber a day. Your best sources are fresh fruits and vegetables and whole-grain breads, cereals, or muffins.

Some people also use fiber tablets or drinks or other high-fiber products available at pharmacies and grocery stores, but check with your doctor before trying them. (Don't use laxatives while you're pregnant unless your doctor advises you to do so. And avoid the old wives' remedy—castor oil—because it can actually interfere with your body's ability to absorb nutrients.)

If constipation is a problem for you, your doctor may prescribe a stool softener. Be sure to drink plenty of fluids, especially water, when increasing fiber intake, or you can make your constipation worse. One of the best ways to avoid constipation is to get more exercise. You should also drink plenty of water between meals each day to help soften your stools and move food through your digestive system. Sometimes hot tea, soups, or broth can help. Also, keep dried fruits handy for snacking.

Some pregnant women find that broccoli, spinach, cauliflower, and fried foods give them heartburn or gas. You can plan a balanced diet to avoid these foods. Carbonated drinks also cause gas or heartburn for some women, although others find they calm the digestive system.

If you're frequently nauseated, eat small amounts of bland foods, like toast or crackers, throughout the day. If nothing else sounds good, try cereal with milk or a sweet piece of fruit. To help combat nausea, you can also:

- Take your prenatal vitamin before going to bed after you've eaten a snack—not on an empty stomach.

- Eat a small snack when you get up to go to the bathroom early in the morning.

- Suck on hard candy.

Section 2.3

Folic Acid: An Important Part of a Healthy Pregnancy

"Folic Acid and Pregnancy," November 2011, reprinted with permission from www.kidshealth.org. This information was provided by KidsHealth®, one of the largest resources online for medically reviewed health information written for parents, kids, and teens. For more articles like this, visit www.KidsHealth.org, or www.TeensHealth.org. Copyright © 1995–2012 The Nemours Foundation. All rights reserved.

Having a healthy baby means making sure you're healthy, too. One of the most important things you can do to help prevent serious birth defects in your baby is to get enough folic acid every day—especially before conception and during early pregnancy.

About Folic Acid

Folic acid, sometimes called folate, is a B vitamin (B9) found mostly in leafy green vegetables like kale and spinach, orange juice, and enriched grains.

Many studies have shown that women who get 400 micrograms (0.4 milligrams) daily prior to conception and during early pregnancy reduce the risk that their baby will be born with a serious neural tube defect (a birth defect involving incomplete development of the brain and spinal cord) by up to 70 percent.

The most common neural tube defects are:

- spina bifida, an incomplete closure of the spinal cord and spinal column;

- anencephaly, severe underdevelopment of the brain;

- encephalocele, when brain tissue protrudes out to the skin from an abnormal opening in the skull.

All of these defects occur during the first twenty-eight days of pregnancy—usually before a woman even knows she's pregnant.

That's why it's so important for all women of childbearing age to get enough folic acid—not just those who are planning to become pregnant.

Only 50 percent of pregnancies are planned, so any woman who could become pregnant should make sure she's getting enough folic acid.

Doctors and scientists still aren't completely sure why folic acid has such a profound effect on the prevention of neural tube defects, but they do know that this vitamin is crucial in the development of deoxyribonucleic acid (DNA). As a result, folic acid plays a large role in cell growth and development, as well as tissue formation.

Getting Enough Folic Acid

The Centers for Disease Control and Prevention (CDC) recommends that all women of childbearing age—and especially those who are planning a pregnancy—consume about 400 micrograms (0.4 milligrams) of folic acid every day. Adequate folic acid intake is very important before conception and at least three months afterward to potentially reduce the risk of having a fetus with a neural tube defect.

So, how can you make sure you're getting enough folic acid? In 1998, the U.S. Food and Drug Administration mandated that folic acid be added to enriched grain products—so you can boost your intake by looking for breakfast cereals, breads, pastas, and rice containing 100 percent of the recommended daily folic acid allowance.

But for most women, eating fortified foods isn't enough. To reach the recommended daily level, you'll probably need a vitamin supplement. During pregnancy, you require more of all of the essential nutrients than you did before you became pregnant.

Although prenatal vitamins shouldn't replace a well-balanced diet, taking them can give your body—and, therefore, your baby—an added boost of vitamins and minerals. Some health care providers even recommend taking a folic acid supplement in addition to your regular prenatal vitamin. Talk to your doctor about your daily folic acid intake and ask whether he or she recommends a prescription supplement, an over-the-counter brand, or both.

Also talk to your doctor if you've already had a pregnancy that was affected by a neural tube defect. He or she may recommend that you increase your daily intake of folic acid (even before getting pregnant) to lower your risk of having another occurrence.

Section 2.4

Vaccinations for a Healthy Pregnancy

Excerpted from "Immunizations for Pregnant Women," Centers for Disease Control and Prevention, June 15, 2012. Table 2.2 is reprinted from "Immunization and Pregnancy," Centers for Disease Control and Prevention, October 2011.

Vaccines can help keep you and your growing family healthy. It is important to make sure that your immunizations are up to date before becoming pregnant according to the recommended immunization schedule. Some vaccine-preventable diseases, such as rubella, can pose a serious risk to your health and that of your unborn baby. If you are pregnant or planning a pregnancy, the specific vaccinations you need are determined by factors such as your age, lifestyle, high-risk conditions, type and locations of travel, and previous vaccinations.

Vaccine Safety Before, During, and After Pregnancy

The Centers for Disease Control and Prevention (CDC) has guidelines for the vaccines you need before, during, and after pregnancy. Live vaccines, such as the measles, mumps rubella vaccine, should be given a month or more before pregnancy. Inactivated vaccines, such as hepatitis B and some flu vaccines, can be given before or during pregnancy. It is safe for a woman to receive vaccines right after giving birth, even while she is breastfeeding. Be sure to discuss each vaccine with your health care professional prior to getting vaccinated. See Table 2.2, which shows the vaccines you may need before, during, and after pregnancy.

Important Vaccines for Pregnant Women to Consider

- **Rubella (German measles):** Rubella infection in pregnant women can cause unborn babies to have serious birth defects with devastating, lifelong consequences, or even die before birth. Make sure you have a pre-pregnancy blood test to see if you are immune to the disease. Most women were vaccinated as children

27

with the combination measles, mumps, rubella vaccine (MMR) but you should confirm this with your doctor. If you need to get vaccinated for rubella, you should avoid becoming pregnant until one month after receiving the MMR vaccine and, ideally, not until your immunity is confirmed by a blood test.

- **Hepatitis B:** Hepatitis B is a serious liver disease that can lead to an incurable chronic (long-term) infection that may result in liver damage and liver cancer. A baby whose mother has hepatitis B is at highest risk for becoming infected with hepatitis B during delivery. The Hepatitis B virus is spread through exposure to blood or body fluids. If you live with someone infected with hepatitis B, talk to your health care professional about getting testing for hepatitis B and whether or not you should be vaccinated.

- **Whooping Cough (Pertussis):** Whooping cough (pertussis) is one of the most common vaccine-preventable diseases in the United States. It is caused by bacteria that spread easily from person to person through personal contact, coughing, and sneezing. It can be very serious for babies and can cause them to stop breathing. Hundreds of babies are hospitalized each year for whooping cough, and some die from it. Many infants who get pertussis catch it from their older brothers and sisters, or from their parents—who might not even know they have the disease. Pregnant women who have not been previously vaccinated with the tetanus, diphtheria, and acellular pertussis vaccine (Tdap) should receive one dose of Tdap during the second or third trimester or postpartum before leaving the hospital or birthing center. In addition, all family members and caregivers of new infants should also get vaccinated with Tdap.

- **Flu:** It is safe, and very important, for a woman who is pregnant during flu season to receive the inactivated flu vaccine. A pregnant woman who gets the flu is at risk for serious complications, and pregnant woman with flu also have a greater chance for serious problems for their unborn baby, including premature labor and delivery. Pregnant women can receive the flu shot at any time, during any trimester. In addition, because babies younger than six months are too young to receive flu vaccine, it is important that everyone who cares for your baby also get a flu vaccine. You should continue to get a yearly flu vaccine as the first and most important step in protecting you and your family against flu viruses.

Table 2.2. Vaccines Needed Before, During, and After Pregnancy

Vaccine	Before pregnancy	During pregnancy	After pregnancy	Type of Vaccine	Route
Hepatitis A	Yes, if at risk	Yes, if at risk	Yes, if at risk	Inactivated	IM
Hepatitis B	Yes, if at risk	Yes, if at risk	Yes, if at risk	Inactivated	IM
Human Papillomavirus (HPV)	Yes, if 9 through 26 years of age	No, under study	Yes, if 9 through 26 years of age	Inactivated	IM
Influenza TIV	Yes	Yes	Yes	Inactivated	IM, ID (18–64 years)
Influenza LAIV	Yes, if less than 50 years of age and healthy; avoid conception for four weeks	No	Yes, if less than 50 years of age and healthy; avoid conception for four weeks	Live	Nasal spray
MMR	Yes, avoid conception for four weeks	No	Yes, give immediately postpartum if susceptible to rubella	Live	SC
Meningococcal Polysaccharide	If indicated	If indicated	If indicated	Inactivated	SC
Meningococcal Conjugate	If indicated	If indicated	If indicated	Inactivated	IM
Pneumococcal Polysaccharide	If indicated	If indicated	If indicated	Inactivated	IM or SC
Tetanus/ Diphtheria Td	Yes, Tdap preferred	Yes, Tdap preferred if twenty weeks gestational age or more	Yes, Tdap preferred	Toxoid	IM
Tdap, one dose only	Yes, preferred	Yes, preferred	Yes, preferred	Toxoid/ inactivated	IM
Varicella	Yes, avoid conception for four weeks	No	Yes, give immediately postpartum if susceptible	Live	SC

- **Vaccines for travel:** If you are pregnant and planning international travel, you should talk to your doctor at least four to six weeks before your trip to discuss any special precautions or vaccines that you may need. Many vaccine-preventable diseases that are rare in the United States are still common in other parts of the world. Depending on where you plan to travel, you may need

29

additional vaccinations. However, there are some vaccines that should be avoided during pregnancy, so it's best to weigh the risks and benefits of vaccination based on your destination.

Chapter 3

Prenatal Tests

Every parent-to-be hopes for a healthy baby, but it can be hard not to worry: What if the baby has a serious or untreatable health problem? What would I do? Is there anything I can do to prevent problems?

Concerns like these are completely natural. Fortunately, though, a wide array of tests for pregnant women can help to reassure them and keep them informed throughout their pregnancies.

Prenatal tests can help identify health problems that could endanger both you and your unborn child, some of which are treatable. However, these tests do have limitations. As an expectant parent, it's important to educate yourself about them and to think about what you would do if a health problem is detected in either you or your baby.

Why Are Prenatal Tests Performed?

Prenatal tests can identify several different things:

- Treatable health problems in the mother that can affect the baby's health

- Characteristics of the baby, including size, sex, age, and placement in the uterus

- The chance that a baby has certain congenital, genetic, or chromosomal problems

- Certain types of fetal abnormalities, including some heart problems

The last two items on this list may seem the same, but there's a key difference. Some prenatal tests are screening tests and only reveal the possibility of a problem. Other prenatal tests are diagnostic, which means they can determine—with a fair degree of certainty—whether a fetus has a specific problem. In the interest of making the more specific determination, the screening test may be followed by a diagnostic test.

Prenatal testing is further complicated by the fact that more abnormalities can be diagnosed in a fetus than can be treated or cured.

What Do Prenatal Tests Find?

Among other things, routine prenatal tests can determine key things about the mother's health, including:

- her blood type;

- whether she has gestational diabetes;

- her immunity to certain diseases;

- whether she has a sexually transmitted disease (STD) or cervical cancer.

All of these conditions can affect the health of the fetus.

Prenatal tests also can determine things about the fetus's health, including whether it's one of the 2 to 3 percent of babies in the United States that the American College of Obstetricians and Gynecologists (ACOG) says have major congenital birth defects.

Categories of defects that can be picked up by prenatal tests include the following disorders.

Dominant Gene Disorders

When one parent is affected by a dominant gene disorder, there's a 50 percent chance a child will inherit the gene from the affected parent and have the disorder.

Dominant gene disorders include:

- Achondroplasia, a rare abnormality of the skeleton that causes a form of dwarfism. It can be inherited from a parent who has it, but most cases occur without a family history.

- Huntington disease, a disease of the nervous system that causes a combination of mental, cognitive, and movement disorders.

Recessive Gene Disorders

Because there are so many genes in each cell, everyone carries some abnormal genes, but most people don't have a defect because the normal gene overrules the abnormal recessive one. But if a fetus has a pair of abnormal recessive genes (one from each parent), the child will have the disorder. It can be more likely for this to happen in children born to certain ethnic groups.

Recessive gene disorders include:

- Cystic fibrosis, most common among people of northern European descent, is life threatening and causes severe lung damage and nutritional deficiencies.

- Sickle cell disease, most common among people of African descent, is a disease in which red blood cells form a "sickle" shape (rather than the typical doughnut shape) that can get caught in blood vessels and damage organs and tissues.

- Tay-Sachs disease, most common among people of eastern European (Ashkenazi) Jewish descent, can cause mental retardation, blindness, seizures, and death.

- Beta thalassemia, most common among people of Mediterranean descent, this disorder can cause anemia.

X-Linked Disorders

These disorders are determined by genes on the X chromosome. The X and Y chromosomes are the chromosomes that determine sex. These disorders are much more common in boys because the pair of sex chromosomes in males contains only one X chromosome (the other is a Y chromosome).

If the disease gene is present on the one X chromosome, the X-linked disease shows up because there's no other paired gene to "overrule" the disease gene. One such X-linked disorder is hemophilia, which prevents the blood from clotting properly.

Chromosomal Disorders

Chromosomal disorders occur when there is an abnormality in the number or structure of chromosomes, which contain the genetic material. Some chromosomal disorders are inherited but most are caused by a random error in the genetics of the egg or sperm.

The chance of a child having these disorders increases with the age of the mother. For example, according to ACOG, 1 in 1,477 live babies born to twenty-year-olds have Down syndrome, which causes mental retardation and physical defects. That number changes to 1 in 353 for thirty-five-year-olds and 1 in 85 for forty-year-olds.

Multifactorial Disorders

This category includes disorders that are caused by a mix of genetic and environmental factors. Their frequency varies from location to location, and some can be detected during pregnancy.

Multifactorial disorders include neural tube defects, which occur when the tube enclosing the spinal cord doesn't form properly. Neural tube defects, which often can be prevented by taking folic acid (which is in prenatal vitamins) around the time of conception and during pregnancy, include:

- **Spina bifida:** Also called "open spine," this defect happens when the lower part of the neural tube doesn't close during embryo development. The spinal cord and nerves may be covered only by skin or might be open to the environment, leaving them unprotected.

- **Anencephaly:** This defect occurs when the brain and head don't develop properly, and parts of the brain are completely absent or malformed.

Other multifactorial disorders include:

- congenital heart defects;

- obesity;

- diabetes;

- cancer.

Who Has Prenatal Tests?

Certain prenatal tests are considered routine—that is, almost all pregnant women receiving prenatal care get them. Other nonroutine tests are recommended only for certain women, especially those with high-risk pregnancies. These may include women who:

- are age thirty-five or older;

- are adolescents;

- have had a premature baby;

- have had a baby with a birth defect—especially heart or genetic problems;

- are carrying more than one baby;

- have high blood pressure, diabetes, lupus, heart disease, kidney problems, cancer, a sexually transmitted disease, asthma, or a seizure disorder;

- have an ethnic background in which genetic disorders are common (or a partner who does);

- have a family history of mental retardation (or a partner who does).

Although your health care provider (who may be your obstetrician-gynecologist [OB-GYN], family doctor, or a certified nurse-midwife) may recommend these tests, it's ultimately up to you to decide whether to have them.

Also, if you or your partner have a family history of genetic problems, you may want to consult with a genetic counselor to help you look at the history of problems in your family, and to determine the risk to your children.

To decide which tests are right for you, it's important to carefully discuss with your health care provider:

- what these tests are supposed to measure;

- how reliable they are;

- the potential risks;

- your options and plans if the results indicate a disorder or defect

Prenatal Tests During the First Visit

During your first visit to your health care provider for prenatal care, you can expect to have a full physical, which may include a pelvic and rectal examination, and you'll undergo certain tests regardless of your age or genetic background.

You may have a urine test to check for protein, sugar, or signs of infection.

Blood tests check for:

L.W. Nixon Library
Butler Community College
901 South Haverhill Road
El Dorado, Kansas 67042-3280

35

- Your blood type and Rh factor. If your blood is Rh negative and your partner's is Rh positive, you may develop antibodies that prove dangerous to your fetus. This can be prevented through a course of injections given to you.

- Anemia (a low red blood cell count).

- Hepatitis B, syphilis, and human immunodeficiency virus (HIV).

- Immunity to German measles (rubella) and chickenpox (varicella).

- Cystic fibrosis. Health care providers now routinely offer this screening even when there's no family history of the disorder.

Cervical tests (also called Pap smears) check for:

- STDs such as chlamydia and gonorrhea;

- changes that could lead to cervical cancer.

To do a Pap smear, your health care provider uses what looks like a very long mascara wand or cotton swab to gently scrape the inside of your cervix (the opening to the uterus that's located at the very top of the vagina). This may be a little uncomfortable, but it is over quickly.

Prenatal Tests Throughout or Later in Pregnancy

After the initial visit, your health care provider will order other tests based on, among other things, your personal medical history and risk factors, as well as the current recommendations. These tests may include:

- Urine tests for sugar, protein, and signs of infection. The sugar in urine may indicate gestational diabetes—diabetes that occurs during pregnancy; the protein can indicate preeclampsia—a condition that develops in late pregnancy and is characterized by a rise in blood pressure, with fluid retention and protein in the urine.

- Group B streptococcus (GBS) infection. GBS bacteria are found naturally in the vaginas of many women but can cause serious infections in newborns. This test involves swabbing the vagina and rectum, usually between the thirty-fifth and thirty-seventh weeks of pregnancy. If the test comes back positive, it is important to go to the hospital as soon as your labor begins so that intravenous antibiotics can be started in order to reduce the chance of the baby being infected.

- Sickle cell trait tests for women of African or Mediterranean descent, who are at higher risk for having sickle cell anemia—a chronic blood disease—or carrying the trait, which can be passed on to their children.

Other Tests

Here are some other tests that might be performed during pregnancy.

Ultrasound

Why is this test performed? In this test, sound waves are bounced off the baby's bones and tissues to construct an image showing the baby's shape and position in the uterus. Ultrasounds were once used only in high-risk pregnancies but have become so common that they're often part of routine prenatal care.

Also called a sonogram, sonograph, echogram, or ultrasonogram, an ultrasound is used:

- to determine whether the fetus is growing at a normal rate;
- to verify the expected date of delivery;
- to record fetal heartbeat or breathing movements;
- to see whether there might be more than one fetus;
- to identify a variety of abnormalities that might affect the remainder of the pregnancy or delivery;
- to make sure the amount of amniotic fluid in the uterus is adequate;
- to indicate the position of the placenta in late pregnancy (which may be blocking the baby's way out of the uterus);
- to detect pregnancies outside the uterus;
- as a guide during other tests such as amniocentesis.

Ultrasounds also are used to detect:

- structural defects such as spina bifida and anencephaly;
- congenital heart defects;

- gastrointestinal and kidney malformations;

- cleft lip or palate.

Should I have this test? Most women have at least one ultrasound. The test is considered to be safe. Some women will have multiple ultrasounds during the pregnancy; others do not have any. Ask your health care provider if he or she thinks you will have ultrasounds during your pregnancy.

When should I have this test? An ultrasound is usually performed at eighteen to twenty weeks to look at your baby's anatomy. If you want to know your baby's gender, you may be able to find out during this time—that is, if the genitals are in a visible position.

Ultrasounds also can be done sooner or later and sometimes more than once, depending on the health care provider and the pregnancy. For example, some providers will order an ultrasound to date the pregnancy, usually during the first three months. And others may want to order one during late pregnancy to make sure the baby's turned the right way before delivery.

Women with high-risk pregnancies may need to have multiple ultrasounds using more sophisticated equipment. Results can be confirmed when needed using special three-dimensional (3-D) equipment that allows the technician to get a more detailed look at the baby.

How is this test performed? Women need to have a full bladder for a transabdominal ultrasound (an ultrasound of the belly) to be performed in the early months—you may be asked to drink a lot of water and not urinate. You'll lie on an examining table and your abdomen will be coated with a special ultrasound gel. A technician will pass a wand-like instrument called a transducer back and forth over your abdomen. You may feel some pressure as the technician presses on the bladder. High-frequency sound waves "echo" off your body (and the fetus) and create a picture of the fetus inside on a computer screen.

You may want to ask to have the picture interpreted for you, even in late pregnancy—it often doesn't look like a baby to the untrained eye.

Sometimes, if the technician isn't able to see a good enough image from the ultrasound, he or she will determine that a transvaginal ultrasound is necessary. This is especially common in early pregnancy. For this procedure, your bladder should be empty. Instead of a transducer being moved over your abdomen, a slender probe called an endovaginal transducer is placed inside your vagina. This technique often provides improved images of the uterus and ovaries.

Some health care providers may have the equipment and trained personnel necessary to provide in-office ultrasounds, whereas others may have you go to a local hospital or radiology center. Depending on where you have the ultrasound done, you may be able to get a printed picture (or multiple pictures) of your baby and/or a disc of images you can view on your computer and even send to friends and family.

When are the results available? Although the technician can see the images immediately, a full evaluation by a physician may take up to one week.

Depending on where you have the ultrasound done, the technician may be able to tell you that day whether everything looks OK. However, most radiology centers or health care providers prefer that technicians not comment until a specialist has taken a look—even when everything is OK.

Glucose Screening

Why is this test performed? Glucose screening checks for gestational diabetes, a short-term form of diabetes that develops in some women during pregnancy. Gestational diabetes is increasing in frequency in the United States, and may occur in 3 to 8 percent of pregnancies. Gestational diabetes can cause health problems for the baby, especially if it is not diagnoses or treated.

Should I have this test? Most women have this test in order to diagnose and treat gestational diabetes, reducing the risk to the baby.

When should I have this test? Screening for gestational diabetes usually takes place at twenty-four to twenty-eight weeks. Testing may be done earlier for women who are at higher risk of having gestation diabetes, such as those who:

- have previously had a baby that weighs more than nine pounds (4.1 kilograms);

- have a family history of diabetes;

- are obese;

- are older than age twenty-five;

- have sugar in the urine on routine testing;

- have high blood pressure;

- have polycystic ovary syndrome.

How is the test performed? This test involves drinking a sugary liquid and then having your blood drawn after an hour. If the sugar level in the blood is high, you'll have a glucose-tolerance test, which means you'll drink a glucose solution on an empty stomach and have your blood drawn once every hour for three hours.

When are the results available? The results are usually available within one to two days. Ask if your health care provider will call you with the results if they are normal or only if the reading is high and you need to come in for another test.

Chorionic Villus Sampling (CVS)

Why is this test performed? Chorionic villi are tiny finger-like units that make up the placenta (a disk-like structure that sticks to the inner lining of the uterus and provides nutrients from the mother to the fetus through the umbilical cord). They have the same chromosomes and genetic makeup as the fetus.

This alternative to an amniocentesis removes some of the chorionic villi and tests them for chromosomal abnormalities, such as Down syndrome. Its advantage over an amniocentesis is that it can be performed earlier, allowing more time for expectant parents to receive counseling and make decisions.

The risks of CVS are higher than with amniocentesis so the risks and benefits of the test must be weighed.

Should I have this test? Your health care provider may recommend this test if you:

- are older than age thirty-five;

- have a family history of genetic disorders (or a partner who does);

- have a previous child with a genetic disorder or had a previous pregnancy with a chromosomal abnormality;

- have had an earlier screening test that indicates that there may be a concern.

Possible risks of this test include:

- approximately one percent risk of miscarriage (the risk is higher with the transcervical method than with the transabdominal method);

- infection;

- spotting or bleeding (this is more common with the transcervical method—see below)

- birth defects when the test is done too early in pregnancy.

When should I have this test? At ten to twelve weeks.

How is this test performed? This test is done in one of two ways:

- *Transcervical:* Using ultrasound as a guide, a thin tube is passed from the vagina into the cervix. Gentle suction removes a sample of tissue from the chorionic villi. Some women experience cramping with the removal.

- *Transabdominal:* A needle is inserted through the abdominal wall with ultrasound guidance, and a sample of the chorionic villi is removed. Cramping may be felt with this approach as well.

After the sample is taken, the doctor may check the fetus' heart rate. You should rest for several hours afterward.

When are the results available? Usually one to two weeks depending on what the test is being used to look for.

Maternal Blood Screening/Triple Screen/Quadruple Screen

Why is this test performed? Doctors use this to test to screen for Down syndrome and neural tube defects. Alpha-fetoprotein (AFP) is a protein produced by the fetus, and it appears in varying amounts in the mother's blood and the amniotic fluid at different times during pregnancy. A certain level in the mother's blood is considered normal, but higher or lower levels may indicate a problem.

This test also looks at the levels of two pregnancy hormones—estriol and human chorionic gonadotropin (HCG)—which is why it's sometimes called a "triple screen" or "triple marker." The test is called a "quadruple screen" ("quad screen") or "quadruple marker" ("quad marker") when the level of an additional substance—inhibin A—is also measured. The greater number of markers increases the accuracy of the screening and better identifies the possibility of a problem.

This test, which also is called a multiple-marker screening or maternal serum screening, calculates a woman's individual risk based on the levels of the three (or more) substances plus:

- her age;

- her weight;
- her race;
- whether she has diabetes requiring insulin treatment;
- whether she is carrying one fetus or multiple ones.

Sometimes this test is done along with an ultrasound and blood work during the first trimester, which makes it even more accurate than the second trimester blood work alone.

It's important to note, though, that each of these screening tests determine risk only—they don't diagnose a condition.

Should I have this test? All women are offered some form of this test. Some practitioners include more parts of it than others. Remember that this is a screening, not a definitive test—it indicates whether a woman is likely to be carrying an affected fetus. It's also not foolproof—Down syndrome, another chromosomal abnormality, or a neural tube defect may go undetected, and some women with abnormal levels have been found to be carrying a healthy baby. Further testing is recommended to confirm a positive result.

When should I have this test? The blood tests are typically done between fifteen and twenty weeks. When first-trimester screening is added, the initial tests are done at about eleven to thirteen weeks.

How is the test performed? Blood is drawn from the mother. When first-trimester screening is added, an ultrasound can be included.

When are the results available? Usually within a week, although it may take up to two weeks.

Amniocentesis

Why is this test performed? This test is most often used to detect:

- Down syndrome and other chromosome abnormalities;
- structural defects such as spina bifida and anencephaly;
- inherited metabolic disorders.

Late in the pregnancy, this test can reveal if a baby's lungs are strong enough to allow the baby to breathe normally after birth. This can help the health care provider make decisions about inducing labor or trying to prevent labor, depending on the situation. For instance, if a mother's water breaks early, the health care provider may want to try to hold off on delivering the baby as long as possible to allow the baby's lungs to mature.

Other common birth defects, such as heart disorders and cleft lip and palate, can't be determined using this test.

Should I have this test? Your health care provider may recommend this test if you:

- are older than age thirty-five;

- have a family history of genetic disorders (or a partner who does);

- have a previous child with a birth defect, or had a previous pregnancy with a chromosomal abnormality or neural tube defect;

- had an abnormal screening test.

This test can be very accurate—close to 100 percent—but only certain disorders can be detected. The rate of miscarriage with this procedure is between one in three hundred and one in five hundred. It also carries a low risk of uterine infection, which can also cause miscarriage, leakage of amniotic fluid, and injury to the fetus.

When should I have this test? Amniocentesis is usually performed between fifteen and twenty weeks.

How is the test performed? While watching with an ultrasound, the doctor inserts a needle through the abdominal wall into the uterus to remove some (about one ounce) of the amniotic fluid. Some women report that they experience cramping when the needle enters the uterus or pressure while the doctor retrieves the sample.

The doctor may check the fetus' heartbeat after the procedure to make sure it's normal. Most doctors recommend rest for several hours afterward.

The cells in the withdrawn fluid are grown in a special culture and then analyzed (the specific tests conducted on the fluid depend on personal and family medical history).

When are the results available? Timing varies; depending on what is being tested for, the results are usually available within one to two weeks. Tests of lung maturity are often available within a few hours.

Nonstress Test

Why is this test performed? A nonstress test (NST) can determine if the baby is responding normally to a stimulus. Used mostly in high-risk pregnancies or when a health care provider is uncertain of fetal movement, an NST can be performed at any point in the pregnancy after the twenty-sixth to twenty-eighth week when fetal heart rate can appropriately respond by accelerating and decelerating.

This test may also be done if you've gone beyond your due date. The NST can help a doctor make sure that the baby is receiving enough oxygen and is responding to stimulation. However, an unresponsive baby isn't necessarily in danger, though further testing might be needed.

Sometimes, a biophysical profile is done, which is when an NST and ultrasound are performed, looking at the breathing, movement, amount of amniotic fluid, and tone of the fetus, in addition to the heart rate response.

Should I have this test? Your health care provider may recommend this if you have a high-risk pregnancy, if there are concerns during your pregnancy, or if you have a low-risk pregnancy but are past your due date.

When should I have this test?

An NST may be recommended any time after twenty-six to twenty-eight weeks, depending on why it is needed.

How is the test performed?

The health care provider will measure the response of the fetus' heart rate to each movement the fetus makes as reported by the mother or observed by the doctor on an ultrasound screen. If the fetus doesn't move during the test, he or she may be asleep and the health care provider may use a buzzer to wake the baby. You also may be asked to drink or eat to try to stimulate the baby more.

When are the results available? Immediately.

Contraction Stress Test

Why is this test performed? This test stimulates the uterus with Pitocin, a synthetic form of oxytocin (a hormone secreted during childbirth), to determine the effect of contractions on fetal heart rate. It may be recommended when a nonstress test or biophysical profile indicates a problem and can determine whether the baby's heart rate remains stable during contractions.

Should I have this test? This test may be ordered if the nonstress test or biophysical profile indicates a problem. However, it can induce labor.

When should I have this test? Your doctor may schedule it if he or she is concerned about how the baby will respond to contractions or feels that it is the appropriate test to determine the fetal heart rate response to a stimulus.

How is the test performed? Mild contractions are brought on either by injections of pitocin or by squeezing the mother's nipples (which causes oxytocin to be secreted). The fetus' heart rate is then monitored.

When are the results available? Immediately.

Percutaneous Umbilical Blood Sampling (PUBS)

Why is this test performed? This test obtains fetal blood by guiding a needle into the umbilical cord. It's primarily used in addition to an ultrasound and amniocentesis if your health care provider needs to quickly check your baby's chromosomes for defects or disorders or is concerned that your baby may have another problem, such as a low platelet count or a thyroid condition.

The advantage to this test is its speed. There are situations (such as when a fetus shows signs of distress) in which it's helpful to know whether the fetus has a fatal chromosomal defect. If the fetus is suspected to be anemic or to have a platelet disorder, this test is the only way to confirm this because it provides a blood sample rather than amniotic fluid. It also allows transfusion of blood or needed fluids into the baby while the needle is in place.

Should I have this test? This test may be used:

- after an abnormality has been noted on an ultrasound;

- when results from other tests, such as amniocentesis, aren't conclusive;

- if the fetus may have Rh disease;

- if you've been exposed to an infectious disease that could potentially affect fetal development.

Risks are associated with this procedure, such as miscarriage or infection, so the risks and benefits should be discussed with your health care provider.

When should I have this test? After eighteen weeks.

How is the test performed? A fine needle is passed through your abdomen and uterus into the umbilical cord and blood is withdrawn for testing.

When are the results available? Usually within three days.

Talking to Your Health Care Provider

Some prenatal tests can be stressful, and because many aren't definitive, even a negative result may not completely relieve any anxiety you might be experiencing. Because many women who have abnormal tests end up having healthy babies and because some of the problems that are detected can't be treated, some women decide not to have some of the tests.

One important thing to consider is what you'll do in the event that a birth defect or chromosomal abnormality is discovered. Your health care provider or a genetic counselor can help you establish priorities, give you the facts, and discuss your options.

It's also important to remember that tests are offered to women— they are not mandatory. You should feel free to ask your health care provider why he or she is ordering a certain test, what the risks and benefits are, and, most important, what the results will—and won't— tell you.

If you think that your health care provider isn't answering your questions adequately, you should say so. Things you might want to ask include:

- How accurate is this test?
- What are you looking to get from these test results?/What do you hope to learn?
- How long before I get the results?
- Is the procedure painful?
- Is the procedure dangerous to me or the fetus?
- Do the potential benefits outweigh the risks?
- What could happen if I don't undergo this test?
- How much will the test cost?
- Will the test be covered by insurance?
- What do I need to do to prepare?

You also can ask your health care provider for literature about each type of test.

Preventing Birth Defects

The best thing that mothers-to-be can do to avoid birth defects and problems with the pregnancy is to take care of their bodies by:

- not smoking (and avoiding secondhand smoke);

- avoiding alcohol and other drugs;

- checking with the doctor about the safety of prescription and over-the-counter medications;

- avoiding fumes, chemicals, radiation, and excessive heat;

- eating a healthy diet;

- taking prenatal vitamins—if possible, even before becoming pregnant;

- getting exercise (after discussing it with the doctor);

- getting plenty of rest;

- getting prenatal care—if possible, beginning with a preconception visit to the doctor to see if anything needs to change before you get pregnant.

Chapter 4

Substance Use and Pregnancy

Chapter Contents

Section 4.1

Alcohol Use and Pregnancy

"Alcohol and Pregnancy," © 2010 Organization of Teratology Information Specialists (OTIS). Reprinted with permission. The OTIS website features fact sheets answering frequently asked questions about a wide variety of exposures during pregnancy and lactation. For the most current information, visit www .otispregnancy.org. Member programs of OTIS are located throughout the U.S. and Canada. To find the Teratogen Information Service in your area, call OTIS toll-free at 866-626-OTIS (866-626-6847), or visit www.otispregnancy.org.

This section talks about the risks that exposure to alcohol can have during pregnancy. With each pregnancy, all women have a 3 to 5 percent chance of having a baby with a birth defect. This information should not take the place of medical care and advice from your health care provider.

What is alcohol?

Alcohol is the ingredient that gives beer, wine, or hard liquor its intoxicating ("high") effect. This section will focus on the effects of recreational alcohol exposure during pregnancy. The same amount of alcohol is found in a standard serving of beer, wine, or hard liquor. A standard serving is considered to be 12 ounces of beer, 4 to 5 ounces of wine, or 1.5 ounces of hard liquor.

Is there a safe amount of alcohol I can drink during pregnancy?

No, there is no safe level of alcohol established during pregnancy.

Alcohol crosses the placenta easily, but differences in genetics and metabolism of alcohol by both the mother and the developing baby may result in a wide range of risk. The risk may be different even in the same mother in different pregnancies.

Can drinking alcohol make it harder for me to get pregnant?

Some studies have shown an increase in fertility problems among women with heavy alcohol exposure. It is best to avoid alcohol while trying to get pregnant.

Can drinking alcohol cause a miscarriage?

Some studies have found higher rates of miscarriage and stillbirth with alcohol use during pregnancy.

Can drinking alcohol during my pregnancy cause a birth defect?

Yes. Drinking alcohol during pregnancy is a leading cause of mental retardation. When a mother uses alcohol in large amounts and/or regularly during pregnancy, her baby is at risk for fetal alcohol syndrome (FAS). The features of FAS include a pattern of certain birth defects that include small head and body size, specific facial features, and learning and behavioral problems. FAS is the most severe outcome of alcohol use during pregnancy. When a child has some but not all of the findings of FAS, doctors may use another term, such as fetal alcohol spectrum disorder (FASD).

The risks from heavy alcohol use and daily alcohol use have been well established. The risks from infrequent binge drinking (five or more standard drinks at one sitting) are less clear. The risks for occasional use of lower amounts of alcohol are also not clear.

Are there long-term issues with FASD?

Yes. FASD is associated with lifelong challenges, such as difficulties with learning and memory. Individuals with FASD are more likely to have difficulty understanding the consequences of their actions, have poor judgment, and have difficulty with social relationships. Higher rates of dropping out of school, mental health problems, and alcohol or drug abuse have also been reported in individuals with FASD.

I just found out I am six weeks pregnant and last weekend I had one beer. Will my baby have FASD?

While there is no known safe amount of alcohol, a single drink is unlikely to cause a problem. The best thing you can do for your baby is to avoid further use of alcohol during your pregnancy.

Is binge drinking on only some days of the week as risky as drinking alcohol every day but at lower amounts?

Possibly but it is not clear. Binge drinking provides the highest alcohol dose to the developing baby at one time. However, studies on alcohol use during pregnancy often calculate weekly averages, so the effects of certain patterns of drinking alcohol are not well studied.

Is it ok to drink after the first trimester?

No. Alcohol has a direct effect on brain development. The brain develops throughout the whole pregnancy. This means drinking any time in pregnancy increases the risk for having alcohol-related brain damage. Therefore, there is no safe period to drink during pregnancy.

Can a baby go through withdrawal after birth?

Yes, if the mother has been drinking close to delivery. There are reports of withdrawal symptoms in infants whose mothers consumed alcohol near delivery. Symptoms included tremors, increased muscle tone, restlessness, and excessive crying.

How will I know if alcohol has hurt my baby?

If you or others are concerned about your alcohol intake, it is important to discuss this with your doctor. A detailed ultrasound may be offered to you to look for birth defects. Usually, an ultrasound cannot see whether alcohol has affected the baby's brain. However, one of the signs of FASD is decreased growth, which can be evaluated on an ultrasound.

Once your baby is born, it is also recommended you tell your pediatrician about your alcohol use during pregnancy. Your baby can be evaluated for effects of alcohol exposure. Services and support are available for children with alcohol-related problems.

Is there any hope for a baby who has been exposed to alcohol throughout pregnancy?

Yes. It is always recommended for a pregnant woman to stop her alcohol use, regardless of how far along in her pregnancy she is. The baby will benefit by no longer being exposed to alcohol. Though FASD cannot be cured, children with FASD benefit from early diagnosis. The best outcomes occur when these children are diagnosed early and receive appropriate support and assistance. Being raised in a stable and nurturing home where basic living and social skills can be taught leads to better outcomes for children with FASD.

Can I drink alcohol while breastfeeding?

Alcohol passes into the breast milk. The concentration of alcohol in the breast milk is close to the concentration of alcohol in the woman's bloodstream. Alcohol can pass back and forth from the bloodstream into the breast milk. Only time can reduce the amount of alcohol in the breast milk. It takes about 2 to 2.5 hours for each standard drink to clear from breast milk. For each additional drink, a woman must wait another 2 to 2.5 hours. Alcohol may reduce the amount of milk you produce.

Effects on the infant from alcohol in the breast milk are not well studied but there have been reports of reduced infant feeding and changes in infant sleep patterns. Impaired motor development following exposure to alcohol in the breast milk was seen in one study but not another.

Since breastfeeding has documented benefits for the baby, speak with your pediatrician about your specific alcohol intake before avoiding breastfeeding.

What if the father of the baby drinks alcohol?

There is no evidence to suggest that a father's exposure to alcohol causes birth defects. In general, exposures that the father has do not increase risk to a pregnancy because the father does not share a blood connection with the developing baby. Studies have shown that hormone levels, sexual desire, and sperm quality are reduced among men who are dependent on alcohol.

Selected References

Adams et al. 2002. Statement of the Public Affairs Committee of the Teratology Society on the fetal alcohol syndrome. *Teratology* 66(6):344–47.

Anderson K et al. 2010 Lifestyle factors in people seeking infertility treatment—A review. *Aust N Z J Obstet Gynaecol* 50(1):8–20.

Coles CD, et al. 1984. Neonatal ethanol withdrawal: characteristics in clinically normal, nondysmorphic neonates. *J Pediatr* 105(3):445–51.

Ho et al. 2001. Alcohol and breast feeding: calculation of time to zero level in milk. *Biol Neonate* 80(3):219–22.

Jones KL et al. 1973. Pattern of malformation in offspring of chronic alcoholic mothers. *Lancet* 1(7815):1267–71, 1973.

Little RE, et al. 1989. Maternal alcohol use during breast-feeding and infant mental and motor development at one year. *N Engl J Med* 321:425–30.

Little RE, et al. 2002. Alcohol, breastfeeding, and development at 18 months. *Pediatrics* 109:e72–77.

Matteson et al. 2010. Toward a Neurobehavioral Profile of Fetal Alcohol Spectrum Disorders. *Alcohol Clin Exp Res* 1;34(9):1640–50.

Muthusami KR and Chinnaswamy P. 2005. Effect of chronic alcoholism on male fertility hormones and semen quality. *Fertil Steril* 84(4):919–24.

OLeary CM. 2004. Fetal alcohol syndrome: diagnosis, epidemiology, and developmental outcomes. *J Paediatr Child Health* 40(1–2):2–7.

Rasmussen C. 2005. Executive functioning and working memory in fetal alcohol spectrum disorder. *Alcohol Clin Exp Res* 29(8):1359–67.

Spohr H-L, et al. 2007. Fetal alcohol spectrum disorders in young adulthood. *J Pediatr* 150(2):175–79.

Strandberg-Larsen K, et al. 2008. Binge drinking in pregnancy and risk of fetal death. *Obstet Gynecol* 111(3):602–9.

Warren KR and Li T-K. 2005. Genetic polymorphisms: impact on the risk of fetal alcohol spectrum disorders. Birth Defects *Res A Clin Mol Teratol* 73(4):195–203.

Section 4.2

Tobacco Use and Pregnancy

Excerpted from the Centers for Disease Control
and Prevention, March 23, 2012.

What are the effects of smoking during pregnancy on the health of mothers and their babies?

Most people know that smoking causes cancer, heart disease, and other major health problems. But women who smoke during pregnancy put themselves and their unborn babies at risk for other health problems. The dangers of smoking during pregnancy include premature birth (being born too early), certain birth defects, and infant death.

- Smoking makes it harder for a woman to get pregnant.

- Women who smoke during pregnancy are more likely than other women to have a miscarriage.

- Smoking can cause problems with the placenta—the source of the baby's food and oxygen during pregnancy. For example, the placenta can separate from the womb too early, causing bleeding, which is dangerous to the mother and baby.

- Smoking during pregnancy can cause a baby to be born too early or to have low birth weight—making it more likely the baby will be sick and have to stay in the hospital longer. A few babies may even die.

- Smoking during and after pregnancy is a risk factor of sudden infant death syndrome (SIDS), deaths among babies of no immediately obvious cause.

- Babies born to women who smoke are more likely to have certain birth defects, like a cleft lip or cleft palate.

How many women smoke during pregnancy?

According to the 2008 Pregnancy Risk Assessment and Monitoring System (PRAMS) data from 29 states:

- Approximately 13 percent of women reported smoking during the last three months of pregnancy.

- Of women who smoked three months before pregnancy, 45 percent quit during pregnancy. Among women who quit smoking during pregnancy, 50 percent relapsed within six months after delivery.

What are the benefits of quitting?

Quitting smoking will help you feel better and provide a healthier environment for your baby.

When you stop smoking:

- Your baby will get more oxygen, even after just one day of not smoking.

- There is less risk that your baby will be born too early.

- There is a better chance that your baby will come home from the hospital with you.

- You will be less likely to develop heart disease, stroke, lung cancer, chronic lung disease, and other smoke-related diseases.

- You will be more likely to live to know your grandchildren.

- You will have more energy and breathe more easily.

- You will have more money that you can spend on other things.

- Your clothes, hair, and home will smell better.

- Your food will taste better.

- You will feel good about what you have done for yourself and your baby.

What are the effects of other people's smoke (secondhand smoke) on my health and my child's health?

Breathing other people's smoke can make children and adults who do not smoke sick:

- Pregnant women who breathe other people's cigarette smoke are more likely to have a baby who weighs less than if they did not breathe other people's cigarette smoke.

- Babies who are around cigarette smoke are more likely to have ear infections and more frequent asthma attacks than babies who are not around other people's smoke.

- Babies who breathe in other people's cigarette smoke are more likely to die from sudden infant death syndrome (SIDS) than are infants who are not exposed to cigarette smoke.

Section 4.3

Illicit Drug
Use and Pregnancy

When you are pregnant, it is important that you watch what you put into your body. Consumption of illegal drugs is not safe for the unborn baby or for the mother. Studies have shown that consumption of illegal drugs during pregnancy can result in miscarriage, low birth weight, premature labor, placental abruption, fetal death, and even maternal death. The following information can help you understand these drugs and their effects.

Marijuana

Common slang names: Pot, weed, grass and reefer.

What happens when a pregnant woman smokes marijuana? Marijuana crosses the placenta to your baby. Marijuana, like cigarette smoke, contains toxins that keep your baby from getting the proper supply of oxygen that he or she needs to grow.

How can marijuana affect the baby? Studies of marijuana in pregnancy are inconclusive because many women who smoke marijuana also use tobacco and alcohol. Smoking marijuana increases the levels of carbon monoxide and carbon dioxide in the blood, which reduces the oxygen supply to the baby. Smoking marijuana during pregnancy can increase the chance of miscarriage, low birth weight, premature births, developmental delays, and behavioral and learning problems.

What if I smoked marijuana before I knew I was pregnant?
According to Dr. Richard S. Abram, author of *Will it Hurt the Baby,* "occasional use of marijuana during the first trimester is unlikely to cause birth defects." Once you are aware you are pregnant, you should stop smoking. Doing this will decrease the chance of harming your baby.

Cocaine

Common slang names: Bump, toot, C, coke, crack, flake, snow, and candy.

What happens when a pregnant woman consumes cocaine?
Cocaine crosses the placenta and enters your baby's circulation. The elimination of cocaine is slower in a fetus than in an adult. This means that cocaine remains in the baby's body much longer than it does in your body.

How can cocaine affect my baby? According to the Organization of Teratology Information Services (OTIS), during the early months of pregnancy cocaine exposure may increase the risk of miscarriage. Later in pregnancy, cocaine use can cause placental abruption. Placental abruption can lead to severe bleeding, preterm birth, and fetal death. OTIS also states that the risk of birth defects appears to be greater when the mother has used cocaine frequently during pregnancy. According to the American Congress of Obstetricians and Gynecology (ACOG), women who use cocaine during their pregnancy have a 25 percent increased chance of premature labor. Babies born to mothers who use cocaine throughout their pregnancy may also have a smaller head and be growth restricted. Babies who are exposed to cocaine later in pregnancy may be born dependent and suffer from withdrawal symptoms such as tremors, sleeplessness, muscle spasms, and feeding difficulties. Some experts believe that learning difficulties may result as the child gets older. Defects of the genitals, kidneys, and brain are also possible.

What if I consumed cocaine before I knew I was pregnant?
There have not been any conclusive studies done on single doses of cocaine during pregnancy. Birth defects and other side effects are usually a result of prolonged use, but because studies are inconclusive, it is best to avoid cocaine altogether. Cocaine is a very addictive drug and experimentation often leads to abuse of the drug.

Heroin

Common slang names: Horse, smack, junk, and H-stuff.

What happens when a pregnant woman uses heroin? Heroin is a very addictive drug that crosses the placenta to the baby. Because this drug is so addictive, the unborn baby can become dependent on the drug.

How can heroin affect my baby? Using heroin during pregnancy increases the chance of premature birth, low birth weight, breathing difficulties, low blood sugar (hypoglycemia), bleeding within the brain (intracranial hemorrhage), and infant death. Babies can also be born addicted to heroin and can suffer from withdrawal symptoms. Withdrawal symptoms include irritability, convulsions, diarrhea, fever, sleep abnormalities, and joint stiffness. Mothers who inject narcotics are more susceptible to human immunodeficiency virus (HIV), which can be passed to their unborn children.

What if I am addicted to heroin and I am pregnant? Treating an addiction to heroin can be complicated, especially when you are pregnant. Your health care provider may prescribe methadone as a form of treatment. It is best that you communicate with your health care provider, so he or she can provide the best treatment for you and your baby.

Phenylcyclohexylpiperidine (PCP) and Lysergic Acid Diethylamide (LSD)

What happens when a pregnant woman takes PCP and LSD? PCP and LSD are hallucinogens. Both PCP and LSD users can behave violently, which may harm the baby if the mother hurts herself.

How can PCP and LSD affect my baby? PCP use during pregnancy can lead to low birth weight, poor muscle control, brain damage, and withdrawal syndrome if used frequently. Withdrawal symptoms include lethargy, alternating with tremors. LSD can lead to birth defects if used frequently.

What if I experimented with LSD or PCP before I knew I was pregnant? No conclusive studies have been done on one time use effects of these drugs on the fetus. It is best not to experiment if you are trying to get pregnant or think you might be pregnant.

Methamphetamine

Common slang names: Meth, speed, crystal, glass, and crank.

What happens when a pregnant woman takes methamphetamine? Methamphetamine is chemically related to amphetamine, which causes the heart rate of the mother and baby to increase.

How can methamphetamine affect my baby? Taking methamphetamine during pregnancy can result in problems similar to those seen with the use of cocaine in pregnancy. The use of speed can cause the baby to get less oxygen, which can lead to low birth weight. Methamphetamine can also increase the likelihood of premature labor, miscarriage, and placental abruption. Babies can be born addicted to methamphetamine and suffer withdrawal symptoms that include tremors, sleeplessness, muscle spasms, and feeding difficulties. Some experts believe that learning difficulties may result as the child gets older.

What if I experimented with methamphetamine before I knew I was pregnant? There have not been any significant studies done on the effect of one time use of methamphetamine during pregnancy. It is best not to experiment if you are trying to get pregnant or think you might be pregnant.

What Does the Law Say?

Currently there are no states that hold prenatal substance abuse as a criminal act of child abuse and neglect. But many have expanded their civil child-welfare requirements to include substance abuse during pregnancy as grounds for terminating parental rights in relation to child abuse and neglect. The laws that address prenatal substance abuse are as follows:

- Iowa, Minnesota, and North Dakota's health care providers are required to test for and report prenatal drug exposure. Kentucky health care providers are only required to test.

- Alaska, Arizona, Illinois, Louisiana, Massachusetts, Michigan, Montana, Oklahoma, Utah, Rhode Island, and Virginia's, health care providers are required to report prenatal drug exposure. Reporting and testing can be evidence used in child welfare proceedings.

- Some states consider prenatal substance abuse as part of their child welfare laws. Therefore prenatal drug exposure can provide grounds for terminating parental rights because of child abuse or neglect. These states include: Arkansas, Colorado, Florida, Illinois, Indiana, Iowa, Louisiana, Minnesota, Nevada, Rhode Island, South Carolina, South Dakota, Texas, Virginia, and Wisconsin.

- Some states have policies that enforce admission to an inpatient treatment program for pregnant women who use drugs. These states include: Minnesota, South Dakota, and Wisconsin.

- In 2004, Texas made it a felony to smoke marijuana while pregnant, resulting in a prison sentence of two to twenty years.

How Can I Get Help?

You can get help from counseling, support groups, and treatment programs. Popular groups include the twelve-step program.

Chapter 5

Environmental Risks and Pregnancy

Having a healthy pregnancy is more than just eating healthy and getting good prenatal care. It's also important to keep your environment (where you live and work) safe from things that can harm you and your baby, like radiation, chemicals, and some metals.

Harmful substances can get into your body through your skin or when you breathe, eat, or drink. Some can be immediately dangerous to you and your baby. With other substances, you have to come in contact with large amounts for a long time for them to cause harm.

Some jobs, like farming and working in dry cleaning stores or factories, may force you to be around or in contact with harmful substances. If you work in these kinds of jobs, talk to your health care provider and your employer about how you can protect yourself before and during pregnancy. You may need extra protection at work or a change in your job duties to stay safe.

You also can take steps to protect yourself and your baby from harmful substances at home.

Can radiation harm your pregnancy?

Radiation is a kind of energy. It travels as rays or particles in the air. Radiation can attach itself to materials like dust, powder, or liquid. These materials can become radioactive, which means that they give off radiation.

You come in contact with small amounts of radiation nearly every day. This radiation comes from natural sources (such as sun rays) and man-made sources (such as microwaves and medical x-rays) that don't cause harm. However, a nuclear power plant accident or similar emergency could put you in contact with larger, more dangerous amounts of radiation.

2011 nuclear power plant crisis in Japan: Since the Fukushima Daiichi nuclear power plant accident in Japan in 2011, very small amounts of radiation have been found in the United States. The Centers for Disease Control and Prevention (CDC) says that it's not enough radiation to cause health problems. So you don't need to take any drugs to treat radiation sickness. These drugs are only given to people who come in close contact with large amounts of radiation. In fact, these drugs can cause health problems in people who don't need them.

Radiation during pregnancy: During pregnancy, your body works hard to protect your baby from radiation that you come in contact with every day. Most babies born to moms who come in contact with low amounts of radiation during pregnancy aren't at increased risk for birth defects.

However, some radiation may cause health problems in you and your baby. It depends on the amount of radiation that your body takes in, the kind of radiation, and the length of time that you're in contact with it.

If you're in contact with large amounts of radioactive material, and this material gets inside your body (you swallow it or breathe it), it may cause harm to your baby during pregnancy.

When radioactive material gets into your bloodstream, it can pass through the umbilical cord to your baby. It also can be dangerous if radioactive material builds up in areas of your body that are close to your uterus (womb), such as your bladder.

If you come in contact with large amounts of radiation early in your pregnancy, your baby may be at risk for birth defects. Exposure to large amounts of radiation, equal to having more than five hundred chest x-rays at one time, is not common. But some pregnant women in Japan came in contact with this much radiation after the atomic bombs dropped on Hiroshima and Nagasaki in 1945. If you do come in contact with large amounts of radiation, you may not feel sick, but the radiation may be enough to cause serious problems in your baby. Radiation can slow his growth, cause birth defects, affect brain development, or lead to cancer.

Extremely large amounts of radiation later in pregnancy can cause severe health risks for your baby. Exposure to extremely large amounts of radiation, equal to having more than five thousand chest x-rays at one time, is not common. But some women came in contact with this much radiation from the 1986 Chernobyl nuclear power plant accident in the Ukraine. If you come in contact with extremely large amounts of radiation, you may show signs of radiation sickness. Early symptoms include vomiting, diarrhea, and fever. Later signs of radiation sickness range from fatigue to hair loss or bloody stools.

If you're pregnant, contact your health care provider immediately if you think you've been exposed to large amounts of radiation. CDC offers tips to prepare for radiation emergencies and steps you can take to stay safe after being exposed to radiation.

Can lead harm your pregnancy?

Lead is a metal. It was once used in gasoline and house paint but is no longer used in any products. With most lead used in products, you can't see, smell, or taste it. Today the most common sources of lead are house paint (used before 1978) and water that comes from wells or through lead pipes.

Lead can be harmful to everyone, but it's especially harmful to young children and pregnant women. Contact with lead during pregnancy can put you at risk for miscarriage, and your baby may be at risk for preterm birth, low birth weight, and developmental delays. Most women in this country don't come in contact with high levels of lead. But if you think you have, your health care provider can check your lead levels with a blood test.

Lead paint: If you live in a home built before 1978, you could be in contact with lead. Older homes were once painted with house paint that had lead.

If you live in an older home and the paint isn't crumbling or peeling, there's little risk to your health. However, crumbling paint can lead to dust with lead substances, which can be harmful to your health.

If you need to remove lead paint from your home, hire experts to do it. Stay out of your home until the job is done. You can learn more about lead paint and removing lead at the U.S. Environmental Protection Agency (EPA) website.

Lead in water: If you have lead plumbing in your house or if you have well water, lead could get into your drinking water. Boiling your water does not get rid of lead.

If you think you have lead plumbing:

- Use only cold water for drinking and cooking. Water from the cold water pipe has less lead than water from the hot pipe.

- Run water for fifteen to thirty seconds before drinking it, using it for cooking, or making baby formula, especially if you haven't used water for a few hours. If you use a water filter, get one that is certified by NSF International to remove lead.

- Contact your local health department or water supplier to find out how to get pipes tested for lead.

If you use well water, contact the EPA Safe Drinking Water Hotline at 800-426-4791 for information on testing your well water for lead and other substances that can harm your health.

Other sources of lead in the home: Lead can be found in other parts of the home, including:

- Lead crystal glassware and some ceramic dishes. Don't use these items. Ceramics you buy in a store are generally safer than those made by craftspeople because stores have to follow certain safety guidelines.

- Some arts and crafts supplies, including oil paints, ceramic glazes, and stained glass materials. Use lead-free art supplies during pregnancy and breastfeeding.

- Vinyl mini blinds that come from other countries.

- Old painted toys and some new toys and jewelry. The U.S. Consumer Product Safety Commission website has information on recalls.

- Make-up, such as lipstick, that has surma or kohl. Check the label on your make-up for a list of ingredients.

- Canned food from other countries.

- Candy from Mexico called Chaca Chaca. Lead in this candy may come from ingredients like chili powder and tamarind, or from ink on plastic or paper wrappers.

Lead on the job: If you work in a job that puts you in contact with large amounts of lead, your health could be at risk. These jobs include painting, plumbing, auto repair, battery manufacturing, and certain kinds of construction.

To help you stay safe:

- Change your clothes (including shoes) before coming home.
- Shower at work to avoid bringing lead into your home.
- Wash your work clothes at work or wash them at home separately from the rest of the laundry.

Can mercury harm your pregnancy?

Mercury is a metal. There are two kinds of mercury that can be harmful during pregnancy: elemental (pure) mercury and methylmercury.

Elemental mercury: Elemental mercury is used in some dental fillings (used to fill in cavities in teeth), older thermometers, and fluorescent light bulbs.

A dental filling that is silver-colored is called an amalgam. Amalgam contains elemental mercury, silver, and other metals. Small amounts of mercury from amalgam fillings can get into the air you breathe.

While amalgams are safe in adults and children over age six, there's not enough information to know if they're safe during pregnancy. If you're concerned about having an amalgam filling, talk with your dentist.

Mercury in older thermometers and fluorescent bulbs is surrounded by glass and doesn't pose any health risk unless the glass breaks. If the glass breaks, small amounts of mercury can get into the air you breathe.

If you break a thermometer, don't vacuum the spilled mercury. Instead, use a piece of paper to roll the beads of mercury onto another piece of paper. Seal the paper in a plastic bag. Contact your local health department to ask how to throw the mercury away.

Fluorescent bulbs have much less mercury in them than old thermometers. But you still have to be careful to clean up the mercury if you break an old bulb. The EPA has guidelines for cleaning up fluorescent bulbs.

Methylmercury: Methylmercury is made when mercury in the air gets into the water supply. The mercury comes from natural sources (such as volcanoes) and man-made sources (such as burning coal and other pollution).

You can get methylmercury in your body by eating fish that swim in waters with methylmercury. Methylmercury is mostly found in certain large fish, like swordfish, shark, king mackerel, and tilefish. During pregnancy, don't eat these kinds of fish because the mercury in them can cause harm to your baby.

It's ok for pregnant women to eat a limited amount of fish that have small amounts of mercury. You can eat up to twelve ounces of these fish a week. The twelve ounces can include shrimp, salmon, pollock, catfish, and canned light tuna. If you eat albacore (white) tuna, don't eat more than six ounces a week.

Mercury on the job: If you're pregnant and work in a dental office or at a job (like electrical, chemical, and mining jobs) that uses mercury to make products, talk with your health care provider about how to stay safe.

Can arsenic harm your pregnancy?

Arsenic is a metal. It gets into the environment through natural sources (crumbling rocks and forest fires) and man-made sources (mining and making electronic products).

Small amounts of arsenic normally found in the environment are unlikely to harm your baby during pregnancy. But if you come in contact with higher levels of arsenic, it may be harmful to your pregnancy and cause problems like miscarriage and birth defects.

Arsenic also can be harmful to children. If children are in contact with arsenic for a long period of time, it may lead to lowered intelligence quotient (IQ).

You may be in contact with harmful levels of arsenic if you:

- Work or live near metal smelters (where metal is made).

- Live near harmful waste sites or incinerators (used to burn garbage).

- Drink well water that has high levels of arsenic. This may be well water found near metal smelters, waste sites or incinerators. Or it may be well water in areas of the country, like parts of New England and the Midwest, that have naturally high levels of arsenic in rock.

If you live in areas that may have high arsenic levels, follow these steps to protect yourself:

- Limit your contact with soil.

- Get your well water tested for arsenic to make sure it's safe to drink.

- Seal decks and outdoor play sets made before 2003. Arsenic was once used in these products. You can use a special stain or sealant to reduce your chances of coming in contact with arsenic.

- Change out of work clothes and shoes that were in contact with arsenic before you go home.

Can pesticides harm your pregnancy?

Pesticides are chemicals used to kill or keep away insects and rodents. You can use some pesticides in your home. Others are for use only outside or on crops.

Being in contact with large amounts of pesticides may be harmful during pregnancy. It may lead to miscarriage, preterm birth, low birth weight, birth defects, and learning problems. If you live or work in an area with crops, you may be exposed to large amounts of pesticides. During pregnancy, stay away from pesticides whenever you can.

If you need pest or rodent control in your home:

- Try to use traps, like mousetraps or sticky traps, instead of pesticides. Be careful not to set traps in places where children can get to them.

- Have someone else put the pesticide in your home. Ask them to follow the directions on the product label.

- Put food, dishes, and utensils away before using the pesticide.

- Have someone open the windows to air out your home and wash off all surfaces where food is made after using the pesticide.

If you use pesticides outside your home:

- Close all the windows and turn off the air conditioning. This helps keep pesticides in the air from coming into the home.

- Wear rubber gloves when gardening to avoid touching pesticides.

Insect repellants: Insect repellants are products you put on your skin or clothes to help keep insects, like mosquitoes and ticks, away. This helps prevent insect bites. You don't want any insect bites during pregnancy because some insects carry infections that may be harmful to you and your baby.

Insect repellants are safe to use during pregnancy. Follow directions on the product label. You also can prevent bites by staying indoors in the early morning or late afternoon when mosquitoes are most likely to bite. Wearing long pants and long sleeves when going outdoors helps, too.

Can solvents harm your pregnancy?

Solvents are chemicals that get rid of other substances. Solvents include alcohols, degreasers, paint thinners, and stain and varnish removers. Lacquers, silk-screening inks, and paints also contain solvents.

If you inhale (breathe in) solvents at any time, you risk liver, kidney, and brain damage and even death. During pregnancy, being in contact with solvents, especially if you work with them, can be harmful. It may lead to miscarriage, slow your baby's growth, or cause premature birth and birth defects.

If you work with solvents or if you do arts and crafts using solvents, here's how you can stay safe:

• Air out your work area. Open a window or use a fan.

• Wear safety clothes, like gloves and a face mask.

• Don't eat or drink in your work area.

Can air pollution harm your pregnancy?

Air pollution is a mixture of small substances and gases that are in the air. Most women who live in areas with high levels of air pollution (such as large cities) have healthy babies.

However, research shows that if you come into contact with high levels of certain air pollutants (like car exhaust), you may be slightly more likely than other women to have a premature or small baby. Some research shows that these air pollutants may lower a child's IQ.

If you live in a large city with high levels of air pollution, limit your outdoor activities, especially exercise, on days when the air in your area is unhealthy.

Can household cleaning products harm your pregnancy?

Household cleaning products are products (like soaps and cleansers) you use to clean your home. When using household cleaning products, read labels carefully. Don't use products that may be toxic (harmful). Products that are toxic (like some oven cleaners and carpet cleaners) say so on the label. If the label doesn't have any safety information, don't use the product. Or contact the product maker to make sure the product is safe to use during pregnancy.

Products that have ammonia or chlorine (bleach) in them probably don't harm your baby during pregnancy. But their smell may cause nausea. When using these products:

- Open windows and doors.

- Wear rubber gloves.

- Don't mix products. Mixing ammonia and chlorine can cause dangerous fumes.

Instead of cleaning products, use safer, more natural products. For example, use baking soda to scrub greasy areas, pots and pans, sinks, tubs, and ovens. And mix vinegar and water to clean floors and countertops.

Can chemicals in plastics harm your pregnancy?

Plastics are made from certain chemicals. Two of these chemicals are phthalates and bisphenol A (BPA). Phthalates make plastic soft and flexible. They are found in toys, medical equipment (such as tubing), shampoos, cosmetics, and food packaging. BPA makes plastics clear and strong. It's sometimes used in baby bottles, metal cans, and water bottles.

Some research shows that being in contact with phthalates and BPA may be harmful during pregnancy. Since 2009, phthalates are no longer used in toys or other children's products. While there isn't a ban on BPA, many products are BPA-free.

More research needs to be done to know for certain if chemicals in plastics can harm your pregnancy or baby.

Here's how to limit your contact with harmful plastics:

- Don't use plastic containers with the number 7 or the letters PC (stands for polycarbonate, a kind of chemical) in the triangle found on the bottom.

- Limit use of canned food.

- Don't microwave food in plastic containers or put plastics in the dishwasher.

Here's how to limit your baby's contact with harmful plastics:

- Breastfeed your baby so you don't have to use baby bottles.

- Use baby bottles made of glass, polypropylene, or polyethylene.

- Give your baby only plastic toys that are made after February 2009 or that are labeled phthalate-free or BPA-free.

- Don't use baby lotions or powders that contain phthalates. Check the product label to make sure.

Chapter 6

X-Rays During Pregnancy: Are They Safe?

Pregnancy is a time to take good care of yourself and your unborn child. Many things are especially important during pregnancy, such as eating right, cutting out cigarettes and alcohol, and being careful about the prescription and over-the-counter drugs you take. Diagnostic x-rays and other medical radiation procedures of the abdominal area also deserve extra attention during pregnancy. This chapter will help you understand the issues concerning x-ray exposure during pregnancy.

Diagnostic x-rays can give the doctor important and even life-saving information about a person's medical condition. But like many things, diagnostic x-rays have risks as well as benefits. They should be used only when they will give the doctor information needed to treat you.

You'll probably never need an abdominal x-ray during pregnancy. But sometimes, because of a particular medical condition, your physician may feel that a diagnostic x-ray of your abdomen or lower torso is needed. If this should happen, don't be upset. The risk to you and your unborn child is very small, and the benefit of finding out about your medical condition is far greater. In fact, the risk of not having a needed x-ray could be much greater than the risk from the radiation. But even small risks should not be taken if they're unnecessary.

You can reduce those risks by telling your doctor if you are, or think you might be, pregnant whenever an abdominal x-ray is prescribed.

"X-Rays, Pregnancy and You," U.S. Food and Drug Administration, March 4, 2010.

If you are pregnant, the doctor may decide that it would be best to cancel the x-ray examination, to postpone it, or to modify it to reduce the amount of radiation. Or, depending on your medical needs, and realizing that the risk is very small, the doctor may feel that it is best to proceed with the x-ray as planned. In any case, you should feel free to discuss the decision with your doctor.

What kind of x-rays can affect the unborn child?

During most x-ray examinations—like those of the arms, legs, head, teeth, or chest—your reproductive organs are not exposed to the direct x-ray beam. So these kinds of procedures, when properly done, do not involve any risk to the unborn child. However, x-rays of the mother's lower torso—abdomen, stomach, pelvis, lower back, or kidneys—may expose the unborn child to the direct x-ray beam. They are of more concern.

What are the possible effects of x-rays?

There is scientific disagreement about whether the small amounts of radiation used in diagnostic radiology can actually harm the unborn child, but it is known that the unborn child is very sensitive to the effects of things like radiation, certain drugs, excess alcohol, and infection. This is true, in part, because the cells are rapidly dividing and growing into specialized cells and tissues. If radiation or other agents were to cause changes in these cells, there could be a slightly increased chance of birth defects or certain illnesses, such as leukemia, later in life.

It should be pointed out, however, that the majority of birth defects and childhood diseases occur even if the mother is not exposed to any known harmful agent during pregnancy. Scientists believe that heredity and random errors in the developmental process are responsible for most of these problems.

What if I'm x-rayed before I know I'm pregnant?

Don't be alarmed. Remember that the possibility of any harm to you and your unborn child from an x-ray is very small. There are, however, rare situations in which a woman who is unaware of her pregnancy may receive a very large number of abdominal x-rays over a short period. Or she may receive radiation treatment of the lower torso. Under these circumstances, the woman should discuss the possible risks with her doctor.

How can I help minimize the risks?

Most important, tell your physician if you are pregnant or think you might be. This is important for many medical decisions, such as drug prescriptions and nuclear medicine procedures, as well as x-rays. And remember, this is true even in the very early weeks of pregnancy.

Occasionally, a woman may mistake the symptoms of pregnancy for the symptoms of a disease. If you have any of the symptoms of pregnancy—nausea, vomiting, breast tenderness, fatigue—consider whether you might be pregnant and tell your doctor or x-ray technologist (the person doing the examination) before having an x-ray of the lower torso. A pregnancy test may be called for.

If you are pregnant, or think you might be, do not hold a child who is being x-rayed. If you are not pregnant and you are asked to hold a child during an x-ray, be sure to ask for a lead apron to protect your reproductive organs. This is to prevent damage to your genes that could be passed on and cause harmful effects in your future descendants.

Whenever an x-ray is requested, tell your doctor about any similar x-rays you have had recently. It may not be necessary to do another. It is a good idea to keep a record of the x-ray examinations you and your family have had taken so you can provide this kind of information accurately.

Feel free to talk with your doctor about the need for an x-ray examination. You should understand the reason x-rays are requested in your particular case.

Chapter 7

Medications with Adverse Fetal Effects

Chapter Contents

Section 7.1

Pregnancy and Medicines: Basic Facts

"Pregnancy and Medicines Fact Sheet," U.S. Department of Health and Human Services Office on Women's Health, April 14, 2010.

Is it safe to use medicine while I am pregnant?

There is no clear-cut answer to this question. Before you start or stop any medicine, it is always best to speak with the doctor who is caring for you while you are pregnant. Read on to learn about deciding to use medicine while pregnant.

How should I decide whether to use a medicine while I am pregnant?

When deciding whether or not to use a medicine in pregnancy, you and your doctor need to talk about the medicine's benefits and risks:

- **Benefits:** what are the good things the medicine can do for me and my growing baby (fetus)?

- **Risks:** what are the ways the medicine might harm me or my growing baby (fetus)?

There may be times during pregnancy when using medicine is a choice. Some of the medicine choices you and your doctor make while you are pregnant may differ from the choices you make when you are not pregnant. For example, if you get a cold, you may decide to "live with" your stuffy nose instead of using the "stuffy nose" medicine you use when you are not pregnant.

Other times, using medicine is not a choice—it is needed. Some women need to use medicines while they are pregnant. Sometimes, women need medicine for a few days or a couple of weeks to treat a problem like a bladder infection or strep throat. Other women need to use medicine every day to control long-term health problems like asthma, diabetes, depression, or seizures. Also, some women have a pregnancy problem that needs treatment with medicine. These problems might include severe nausea and vomiting, earlier pregnancy losses, or preterm labor.

Where do doctors and nurses find out about using medicines during pregnancy?

Doctors and nurses get information from medicine labels and packages, textbooks, and research journals. They also share knowledge with other doctors and nurses and talk to the people who make and sell medicines.

The Food and Drug Administration (FDA) is the part of our country's government that controls the medicines that can and can't be sold in the United States. The FDA lets a company sell a medicine in the United States if it is safe to use and works for a certain health problem. Companies that make medicines usually have to show FDA doctors and scientists whether birth defects or other problems occur in baby animals when the medicine is given to pregnant animals. Most of the time, drugs are not studied in pregnant women.

The FDA works with the drug companies to make clear and complete medicine labels. But in most cases, there is not much information about how a medicine affects pregnant women and their growing babies. Many prescription medicine labels include the results of studies done in pregnant animals. But a medicine does not always affect growing humans and animals in the same way. Here is an example: A medicine is given to pregnant rats. If the medicine causes problems in some of the rat babies, it may or may not cause problems in human babies. If there are no problems in the rat babies, it does not prove that the medicine will not cause problems in human babies.

The FDA asks for studies in two different kinds of animals. This improves the chance that the studies can predict what may happen in pregnant women and their babies.

There is a lot that FDA doctors and scientists do not know about using medicine during pregnancy. In a perfect world, every medicine label would include helpful information about the medicine's effects on pregnant women and their growing babies. Unfortunately, this is not the case.

How do prescription and over-the-counter (OTC) medicine labels help my doctor choose the right medicine for me when I am pregnant?

Doctors use information from many sources when they choose medicine for a patient, including medicine labels. To help doctors, the FDA created pregnancy letter categories to help explain what is known about using medicine during pregnancy. This system assigns letter categories to all prescription medicines. The letter category is listed in the label of a prescription medicine. The label states whether studies were done in pregnant women or pregnant animals and if so, what happened. Over-the-counter (OTC) medicines do not have a pregnancy letter category. Some OTC medicines were prescription medicines first and used to have a letter category. Talk to your doctor and follow the instructions on the label before taking OTC medicines.

Prescription medicines: The FDA chooses a medicine's letter category based on what is known about the medicine when used in pregnant women and animals.

The FDA is working hard to gather more knowledge about using medicine during pregnancy. The FDA is also trying to make medicine labels more helpful to doctors. Medicine label information for prescription medicines is now changing, and the pregnancy part of the label will change over the next few years. As this prescription information is updated, it is added to an online information clearinghouse called DailyMed that gives up-to-date, free information to consumers and health care providers.

OTC medicines: All OTC medicines have a drug facts label. The drug facts label is arranged the same way on all OTC medicines. This makes information about using the medicine easier to find. One section of the drug facts label is for pregnant women. With OTC medicines, the label usually tells a pregnant woman to speak with her doctor before using the medicine. Some OTC medicines are known to cause certain problems in pregnancy. The labels for these medicines give pregnant women facts about why and when they should not use the medicine. Here are some examples:

- Nonsteroidal anti-inflammatory drugs (NSAIDs) like ibuprofen (Advil, Motrin), naproxen (Aleve), and aspirin (acetylsalicylate), can cause serious blood flow problems in the baby if used during the last three months of pregnancy (after twenty-eight weeks). Also, aspirin may increase the chance for bleeding problems in the mother and the baby during pregnancy or at delivery.

- The labels for nicotine therapy drugs, like the nicotine patch and lozenge, remind women that smoking can harm an unborn child. While the medicine is thought to be safer than smoking, the risks of the medicine are not fully known. Pregnant smokers are told to try quitting without the medicine first.

What if I'm thinking about getting pregnant?

If you are not pregnant yet, you can help your chances for having a healthy baby by planning ahead. Schedule a pre-pregnancy checkup.

Table 7.1. Definition of medicine categories

Pregnancy category	Definition	Examples of drugs
A	In human studies, pregnant women used the medicine and their babies did not have any problems related to using the medicine.	• Folic acid • Levothyroxine (thyroid hormone medicine)
B	In humans, there are no good studies. But in animal studies, pregnant animals received the medicine, and the babies did not show any problems related to the medicine; or, in animal studies, pregnant animals received the medicine, and some babies had problems. But in human studies, pregnant women used the medicine and their babies did not have any problems related to using the medicine.	• Some antibiotics like amoxicillin. • Zofran (ondansetron) for nausea • Glucophage (metformin) for diabetes • Some insulins used to treat diabetes such as regular and NPH insulin.
C	In humans, there are no good studies. In animals, pregnant animals treated with the medicine had some babies with problems. However, sometimes the medicine may still help the human mothers and babies more than it might harm; or, no animal studies have been done, and there are no good studies in pregnant women.	• Diflucan (fluconazole) for yeast infections • Ventolin (albuterol) for asthma • Zoloft (sertraline) and Prozac (fluoxetine) for depression
D	Studies in humans and other reports show that when pregnant women use the medicine, some babies are born with problems related to the medicine. However, in some serious situations, the medicine may still help the mother and the baby more than it might harm.	• Paxil (paroxetine) for depression • Lithium for bipolar disorder • Dilantin (phenytoin) for epileptic seizures • Some cancer chemotherapy
X	Studies or reports in humans or animals show that mothers using the medicine during pregnancy may have babies with problems related to the medicine. There are no situations where the medicine can help the mother or baby enough to make the risk of problems worth it. These medicines should never be used by pregnant women.	• Accutane (isotretinoin) for cystic acne • Thalomid (thalidomide) for a type of skin disease

At this visit, you can talk to your doctor about the medicines, vitamins, and herbs you use. It is very important that you keep treating your health problems while you are pregnant. Your doctor can tell you if you need to switch your medicine. Ask about vitamins for women who are trying to get pregnant. All women who can get pregnant should take a daily vitamin with folic acid (a B vitamin) to prevent birth defects of the brain and spinal cord. You should begin taking these vitamins before you become pregnant or if you could become pregnant. It is also a good idea to discuss caffeine, alcohol, and smoking with your doctor at this time.

Is it safe to use medicine while I am trying to become pregnant?

It is hard to know exactly when you will get pregnant. Once you do get pregnant, you may not know you are pregnant for ten to fourteen days or longer. Before you start trying to get pregnant, it is wise to schedule a meeting with your doctor to discuss medicines that you use daily or every now and then. Sometimes, medicines should be changed, and sometimes they can be stopped before a woman gets pregnant. Each woman is different. So you should discuss your medicines with your doctor rather than making medicine changes on your own.

What if I get sick and need to use medicine while I am pregnant?

Whether or not you should use medicine during pregnancy is a serious question to discuss with your doctor. Some health problems need treatment. Not using a medicine that you need could harm you and your baby. For example, a urinary tract infection (UTI) that is not treated may become a kidney infection. Kidney infections can cause preterm labor and low birth weight. You need an antibiotic to cure a UTI. Ask your doctor whether the benefits of taking a certain medicine outweigh the risks for you and your baby.

I have a health problem. Should I stop using my medicine while I am pregnant?

If you are pregnant or thinking about becoming pregnant, you should talk to your doctor about your medicines. Do not stop or change them on your own. This includes medicines for depression, asthma, diabetes, seizures (epilepsy), and other health problems. Not using medicine that you need may be more harmful to you and your baby than using the medicine.

For women living with human immunodeficiency virus (HIV), the Centers for Disease Control and Prevention (CDC) recommends using zidovudine (AZT) during pregnancy. Studies show that HIV-positive women who use AZT during pregnancy greatly lower the risk of passing HIV to their babies. If a diabetic woman does not use her medicine during pregnancy, she raises her risk for miscarriage, stillbirth, and some birth defects. If asthma and high blood pressure are not controlled during pregnancy, problems with the fetus may result.

Are vitamins safe for me while I am pregnant?

Women who are pregnant should not take regular vitamins. They can contain doses that are too high. Ask about special vitamins for pregnant women that can help keep you and your baby healthy. These prenatal vitamins should contain at least 400 to 800 micrograms (µg) of folic acid. It is best to start taking these vitamins before you become pregnant or if you could become pregnant. Folic acid reduces the chance of a baby having a neural tube defect, like spina bifida, where the spine or brain does not form the right way. Iron can help prevent a low red blood cell count (anemia). It's important to take the vitamin dose prescribed by your doctor. Too many vitamins can harm your baby. For example, very high levels of vitamin A have been linked with severe birth defects.

Are herbs, minerals, or amino acids safe for me while I am pregnant?

No one is sure if these are safe for pregnant women, so it's best not to use them. Even some "natural" products may not be good for women who are pregnant or breastfeeding. Except for some vitamins, little is known about using dietary supplements while pregnant. Some herbal remedy labels claim that they will help with pregnancy. But, most often there are no good studies to show if these claims are true or if the herb can cause harm to you or your baby. Talk with your doctor before using any herbal product or dietary supplement. These products may contain things that could harm you or your growing baby during your pregnancy.

In the United States, there are different laws for medicines and for dietary supplements. The part of the FDA that controls dietary supplements is the same part that controls foods sold in the United States. Only dietary supplements containing new dietary ingredients that were not marketed before October 15, 1994 submit safety information for review by the FDA. However, unlike medicines, the FDA does not approve herbal remedies and "natural products" for safety or for what they say they will do. Most have not even been evaluated for their potential to cause harm to you or the growing fetus, let alone shown to be safe for use in pregnancy. Before a company can sell a medicine, the company must complete many studies and send the results to the FDA. Many scientists and doctors at the FDA check the study results. The FDA allows the medicine to be sold only if the studies show that the medicine works and is safe to use.

In the future, will there be better ways to know if medicines are safe to use during pregnancy?

At this time, drugs are rarely tested for safety in pregnant women for fear of harming the unborn baby. Until this changes, pregnancy exposure registries help doctors and researchers learn how medicines affect pregnant mothers and their growing babies. A pregnancy exposure registry is a study that enrolls pregnant women who are using a certain medicine. The women sign up for the study while pregnant and are followed for a certain length of time after the baby is born. Researchers compare babies of mothers who used the medicine while pregnant to babies of mothers who did not use the medicine. This type of study compares large groups of pregnant mothers and babies to look for medicine effects. A woman and her doctor can use registry results to make more informed choices about using medicine while pregnant.

If you are pregnant and are using a medicine or were using one when you got pregnant, check to see if there is a pregnancy exposure registry for that medicine. The Food and Drug Administration has a list of pregnancy exposure registries that pregnant women can join.

Section 7.2

Accutane and Other Retinoids

Isotretinoin is a prescription medication used to treat a severe form of acne (nodular or cystic acne) that has not been helped by other treatments, including oral antibiotics. Accutane, the original brand of isotretinoin, has been discontinued. Other brands (Amnesteem, Claravis, Sotret) are still available.

Isotretinoin is a member of a family of drugs called retinoids, which are related to vitamin A. When taken during pregnancy, isotretinoin and other retinoids can cause miscarriage or very serious birth defects.

Who should not take isotretinoin?

Women who are pregnant, planning pregnancy, having sex without birth control, or breastfeeding should not take isotretinoin.

What birth defects are caused by use of isotretinoin during pregnancy?

There is an extremely high risk of birth defects if a woman takes isotretinoin during pregnancy, even if she takes a small amount of the drug for a short period. Birth defects caused by isotretinoin include:[1]

- hydrocephaly (enlargement of the fluid-filled spaces in the brain);

- microcephaly (small head and brain);

- mental retardation;

- ear and eye abnormalities;

- cleft palate and other facial abnormalities;

- heart defects.

Isotretinoin can cause birth defects in the early weeks after conception when a woman may not know she is pregnant. Even babies born without obvious birth defects may have mental retardation or learning disabilities.[1] The drug also increases the risk of premature birth and infant death.

What is nodular acne?

Nodular acne causes many red, swollen lumps in the skin and can leave permanent scars. This form of acne sometimes does not respond to treatments other than isotretinoin. The drug clears the skin of most affected individuals for prolonged periods.

What is iPLEDGE?

All patients, including men, who take isotretinoin, must participate in a risk-management program called iPLEDGE. This program was started in 2005 by the Food and Drug Administration (FDA) with two goals:[2]

- to ensure that no pregnant woman starts taking isotretinoin;
- to ensure that no woman taking isotretinoin becomes pregnant.

The FDA approved the first form of the drug, Accutane, in 1982. Before it was approved, testing had shown that the drug could cause birth defects in animals. The manufacturer of Accutane, Roche Pharmaceuticals (a division of Hoffmann-La Roche, Inc.), warned against its use by pregnant women, but pregnancies resulting in birth defects still occurred. Subsequently, the FDA and the manufacturers of all brands of isotretinoin implemented voluntary risk-management plans to prevent pregnant women from using the drug. These programs were not successful in preventing drug exposure during pregnancy. As a result, the FDA started iPLEDGE, a stronger, mandatory risk-management program.

What should a woman of childbearing age do before taking isotretinoin?

A woman should discuss with a health care provider who is experienced in isotretinoin treatment whether the drug is right for her. Besides causing birth defects, isotretinoin can cause serious side effects for the woman, possibly including mental health problems.[3] In many cases, safer treatments may work to clear up acne.

If a woman decides to take isotretinoin, she must follow the steps required by iPLEDGE.

What does iPLEDGE require for women who can become pregnant?

iPLEDGE requires that a woman follow these steps before, during and after isotretinoin treatment.

Before treatment:[3]

- have two negative pregnancy tests, including one right before starting the drug;

- sign a patient information/consent form containing warnings about the risk of birth defects if the fetus is exposed to isotretinoin;

- agree to use two effective forms of birth control, which must be used at the same time (unless abstinence is the chosen method), for at least one month before treatment with the drug, during treatment with the drug, and for one month after she stops taking the drug;

- register with iPLEDGE by phone (866-495-0654) or on the internet, and agree to follow all instructions in the iPLEDGE program.

During treatment:

- Each month a woman receives a thirty-day supply of isotretinoin. To refill her prescription, she must:

  - have a negative pregnancy test;

  - enter her two types of birth control into the iPLEDGE system (by phone or internet);

  - answer questions about the iPLEDGE program and preventing pregnancy (by phone or internet).

After treatment:

- have a pregnancy test after her last dose;

- continue to use two forms of birth control for one month;

- have another pregnancy test one month after her last dose.

If a woman taking isotretinoin does become pregnant, she should stop taking the drug and call her health care provider. She or her provider must report the pregnancy to the FDA at (800) FDA-1088 and to iPLEDGE.[3] Reporting allows the FDA and the drug companies who make isotretinoin to monitor the success of the iPLEDGE program and to make any necessary changes to prevent pregnancy exposures.

A woman should never attempt to get isotretinoin over the internet because she will miss out on important safeguards to protect her health. The FDA provides more information about the dangers of buying isotretinoin on its website.

Is it safe to breastfeed while taking isotretinoin?

Women should not breastfeed while using isotretinoin and for one month after stopping the drug because it is not known whether it could harm the baby.[3]

What other precautions should a woman take during treatment with isotretinoin?

Most women are treated with isotretinoin for about four to five months.[3] During this time a woman should check with her provider before taking any other medications. A woman should avoid certain drugs and supplements while she is taking isotretinoin:[3]

- **St. John's wort:** This herbal preparation may cause birth control pills to work less effectively and put a woman at increased risk of pregnancy.

- **Tetracycline:** This antibiotic can increase the risk of serious side effects, including increased pressure in the brain, when taken with isotretinoin.

- **Dilantin (phenytoin):** This anti-seizure medication, when taken with isotretinoin, can weaken bones.

- **Corticosteroids:** These medicines are used to treat arthritis, severe asthma, and a number of other conditions. When taken with isotretinoin, they can weaken bones.

- **Progestin-only birth control pills:** When taken with isotretinoin, this form of birth control may not be effective.

- **Vitamin A supplements:** These vitamins are related to isotretinoin and can increase the risk of serious side effects.

Women and men who use isotretinoin should not give blood while taking the drug and for one month afterward, because the drug might cause birth defects if a pregnant woman receives the blood.[3] Individuals should never share their prescription for isotretinoin with anyone else.

What are other iPLEDGE requirements?

All providers who prescribe the drug and pharmacists who sell it must register with iPLEDGE.[1] Each must agree to certain responsibilities for preventing pregnant women from taking the drug. For example, providers are responsible for counseling women about birth control and the risks of isotretinoin, explaining the iPLEDGE program, and documenting in iPLEDGE a negative pregnancy test for women taking the drug each month. Pharmacists can fill a prescription only after receiving authorization from iPLEDGE. These requirements should help ensure that each woman has had an appropriately timed negative pregnancy test before starting the drug and each month before she refills her prescription. The requirements also should help ensure that all women of childbearing age receive continuing counseling about the safety precautions necessary to prevent fetal exposure to the drug.

Are there safer acne medications for women of childbearing age?

Most women with acne do not have severe nodular acne, and their skin problems often respond to safe topical (applied to the skin) or oral medications. Topical preparations of the antibiotics erythromycin or clindamycin are safe choices during pregnancy, as is benzoyl peroxide, an antibacterial agent that also dries the skin.[4]

If topical preparations do not clear the skin, a woman's provider may recommend oral treatment with antibiotics, such as erythromycin, that have not been associated with birth defects. If she is not planning pregnancy, treatment with oral contraceptives (which should not be used during pregnancy) also may be effective.[4]

Are topical retinoids safe in pregnancy?

Topical retinoids are used to treat acne and sun-damaged skin. These include topical tretinoin (Retin A, Renova), adapalene (Differin), and tazarotene (Tazorac). Small amounts of these drugs may be absorbed through the skin into the bloodstream.

Studies suggest that topical retinoids do not cause birth defects.[5,6,7] However, some questions about their safety remain due to a few reports of birth defects in babies of women who used these preparations during pregnancy.[5,6,7] Until more is known about the safety of topical retinoids during pregnancy, it's best for women who are pregnant or planning pregnancy to avoid them.

Are there other retinoids that are unsafe during pregnancy?

All oral retinoids pose a risk of birth defects similar to those caused by isotretinoin and should be avoided during pregnancy. As with isotretinoin, women should have a pregnancy test before starting these drugs and another each month. Women also should use two reliable forms of birth control during treatment and for varying periods of time after discontinuing use of these drugs:

- **Soriatane (acitretin):** This retinoid is used to treat severe psoriasis, a chronic disfiguring skin disease. Soriatane can remain in the body for an extended period. It should not be used by any woman who plans to become pregnant within three years after stopping the drug.[8] Women should continue to use two reliable forms of contraception for at least three years after they stop taking the drug.[8] Women should not drink alcohol while taking the drug or for two months afterward.[8] This combination causes the body to turn Soriatane into etretinate (the active ingredient in Tegison), which may remain in the body for many years after treatment ends.

- **Tegison (etretinate):** This psoriasis medicine has been replaced by Soriatane and is no longer sold in the United States. Tegison stays in the body for a prolonged period. Any woman who has used Tegison should discuss with her provider if and when it may be safe for her to attempt pregnancy.

- **Vesanoid (tretinoin):** This drug is used to treat a blood cancer called acute promyelocytic leukemia. Women should continue to use two forms of contraception for one month after stopping treatment.[9]

- **Targretin (bexarotene):** This retinoid is used to treat a form of blood cancer called T-cell lymphoma. A woman should continue using two reliable forms of contraception for one month after she stops taking the drug.[10]

A number of new retinoids are being tested for their effectiveness in treating and, in some cases, preventing various forms of cancer, including breast, ovarian, and lung cancer. These drugs appear to cause cancer cells to behave like normal cells, possibly leading to remission of some cancers. If these drugs prove successful, women and their providers should pay careful attention to the risks for birth defects associated with use of these drugs.

Can high doses of vitamin A cause birth defects?

Vitamin A is crucial for normal fetal growth and development. However, too much of it may cause birth defects. A 1995 study found that women who took more than 10,000 IU (international units) of vitamin A daily in the first two months of pregnancy doubled their risk of having a baby with birth defects.[11] The birth defects were similar to those seen in isotretinoin-exposed babies.

The FDA's current daily value (DV) for vitamin A is 5,000 IU.[12] Other studies have suggested that doses less than 25,000 IU probably do not cause birth defects, but the lowest dose that can cause birth defects is unknown.[13]

The body makes its own vitamin A, when needed, from vitamin A precursors, such as beta carotene. Beta carotene is found in yellow and green vegetables and some multivitamins. This form of the vitamin is believed to be completely safe during pregnancy.

However, much of the vitamin A we consume is the preformed vitamin which, in excessive amounts, can cause birth defects. Preformed vitamin A is found in many vitamin supplements and some foods, including meats (especially liver), eggs, dairy products, and fortified breakfast cereals.

A pregnant woman should be sure that her multivitamin or prenatal supplement contains no more than 5,000 IU of preformed vitamin A, and she should not take any vitamin A supplements beyond that amount. She also should limit the amount of liver she eats.

What is the role of the March of Dimes in the study of retinoids?

The March of Dimes has supported research on isotretinoin and was instrumental in bringing to public attention the need for more stringent guidelines concerning its use. The March of Dimes continues to support research on the role of retinoids in both normal and abnormal fetal development, in order to better understand how these drugs may cause birth defects, with the ultimate goal of learning how to prevent them.

References

1. iPLEDGE. (2005). About Isotretinoin: Contraindications and Warnings. Retrieved September 24, 2009.

2. iPLEDGE. (2005). About iPLEDGE. Retrieved September 24, 2009.

3. iPLEDGE. (2007). The iPLEDGE Program Patient Introductory Brochure. Retrieved September 24, 2009.

4. Deitch, H. & Hillard, P. (2002). A Gynecologist's Guide to Acne. *Contemporary Ob/Gyn*, 47(1), 88–93.

5. Reproductive Toxicology Center. (2008). Tretinoin. Retrieved September 22, 2009.

6. Reproductive Toxicology Center. (2008). Adapalene. Retrieved September 22, 2009.

7. Reproductive Toxicology Center. (2008). Tazarotene. Retrieved September 22, 2009.

8. Stiefel Laboratories. Do Your P.A.R.T. (2007). Retrieved September 24, 2009.

9. Roche U.S. Pharmaceuticals. (2008). Complete Product Information: Vesanoid (Tretinoin) Capsules. Retrieved September 24, 2009.

10. Eisai, Inc. (2007). Targretin (Bexarotene) Capsules: Patient's Instructions for Use. Retrieved September 22, 2009.

11. Rothman, K., Moore, L., Singer, M., Uyen-Sa, D.T.N., Mannino, S., et al. (1995). Teratogenicity of High Vitamin A Intake. *The New England Journal of Medicine*, 333(21), 1369–73.

12. National Institutes of Health (NIH) Office of Dietary Supplements. (2006). Dietary Supplement Fact Sheet: Vitamin A and Carotenoids. Retrieved September 24, 2009.

13. Reproductive Toxicology Center. (2008). Vitamin A. Retrieved September 21, 2009.

Section 7.3

Antiretroviral Drugs

Pregnant women with human immunodeficiency virus (HIV) can prevent passing the acquired immune deficiency syndrome (AIDS)–causing virus to their babies by taking antiretroviral drugs, but there remains a possibility that some of these medications might cause birth defects, such as cleft lip and palate, according to a new study.

Antiretroviral drugs have been found to reduce the risk of mothers passing HIV on to their children from between 15 and 25 percent to less than 1 percent. These drugs, however, are still under investigation and not considered safe during pregnancy, the study authors noted.

To analyze the possible association between antiretroviral drugs and birth defects, Vassiliki Cartsos, an associate professor and director of graduate orthodontics at Tufts University School of Dental Medicine in Boston, and colleagues examined five years of adverse events compiled by the U.S. Food and Drug Administration.

Their findings are published in the January 2012 issue of *Cleft Palate—Craniofacial Journal*.

The investigators found seven antiretroviral drugs were associated with twenty-six incidents of cleft lip and palate. However, the authors noted, uncovering an association does not prove a cause-and-effect relationship.

In other words, although the study findings should serve as a red flag, the researchers pointed out that the findings do not confirm that the antiretroviral drugs caused the birth defects.

Those drugs included lamivudine (Epivir); efavirenz (known as EFV); nelfinavir (Viracept); and the combination of abacavir sulfate (Ziagen), lamivudine, and zidovudine (Retrovir).

The study authors concluded in a journal news release that more research is needed to determine if there is a link between antiretroviral drugs and cleft lip and palate, a congenital malformation believed to have several causes, including genetic and environmental factors.

Section 7.4

Paroxetine (Paxil)

This section talks about the risks that exposure to paroxetine can have during pregnancy. With each pregnancy, all women have a 3 to 5 percent chance of having a baby with a birth defect. This information should not take the place of medical care and advice from your health care provider.

What is paroxetine?

Paroxetine is a medication used to treat depression, social anxiety disorder, obsessive compulsive disorder, and panic disorder. Paroxetine belongs to the class of antidepressants known as selective serotonin reuptake inhibitors or SSRIs. Some brand names for paroxetine are Paxil, Aropax, and Seroxat.

I am taking paroxetine, but I would like to stop taking it before becoming pregnant. How long does paroxetine stay in my body?

While everyone breaks down medication at a different rate, on average it takes four to five days for most of the paroxetine to be gone from the body after taking the last dose. If you choose to stop taking paroxetine, the dosage should be gradually lowered before quitting completely to prevent withdrawal symptoms. Please discuss the benefits and risks of stopping your medication with your health care provider.

94

Can taking paroxetine make it more difficult for me to become pregnant?

Some animal studies have suggested reduced fertility with exposure to paroxetine. Animal studies do not always predict what will happen in humans. There are no reports in humans suggesting that taking paroxetine would make it harder to become pregnant.

Can taking paroxetine cause a miscarriage?

There have been some studies suggesting exposure to antidepressant medications may slightly increase the risk for miscarriage. Other studies have not supported this association. If there is an increase risk for miscarriage with antidepressants it is probably small.

Can taking paroxetine during my pregnancy cause birth defects?

Several studies have suggested that exposure to paroxetine may be associated with an increased risk for heart defects. In the general population, the background risk for heart defects is 1 percent. These studies showed that paroxetine use during the first trimester of pregnancy may increase this risk to 2 percent. One of the heart defects seen most often involves the wall dividing the right and left sides of the heart. This type of defect can range from very mild (no treatment needed) to more significant, which may require surgery. It has been suggested that because infants exposed to paroxetine are followed more closely at birth, mild heart defects that might otherwise not be discovered are found. There have also been recent studies that have not supported the association between paroxetine and heart defects. Currently the information is uncertain, but if the risk exists it is likely to be small. Women who take paroxetine during the first trimester can consider asking their doctor for a fetal echocardiogram (ultrasound of the baby's heart) at twenty weeks of pregnancy.

Most studies have not found paroxetine to be associated with birth defects other than heart defects.

I need to take paroxetine throughout my entire pregnancy. Will it cause withdrawal symptoms in my baby?

Possibly. If you are taking paroxetine at the time of delivery, your baby may have some difficulties for the first few days of life. Your baby may have jitteriness, increased muscle tone, irritability, altered sleep patterns, tremors, difficulty eating, and some problems with breathing. While in most cases these effects are mild and go away on their own, some babies may need to stay in a special care nursery for several days until the effects from paroxetine and withdrawal go away. Not all babies exposed to paroxetine will have these symptoms.

Are there any other problems paroxetine can cause when used in the third trimester?

Two studies have suggested that babies whose mothers take SSRIs like paroxetine during the second half of the pregnancy may be at an increased risk for pulmonary hypertension, a serious lung problem at birth. Other studies have not supported this association. Further study is needed but if any increased risk does exist, it is felt to be small. You should inform your obstetrician and your baby's pediatrician that you are taking paroxetine so that any extra care can be readily provided.

Should I wean off paroxetine before the third trimester?

It is important to discuss with your doctor the risks associated with taking paroxetine during pregnancy as compared to the risks of stopping it. Studies have shown that when depression is left untreated during pregnancy, there may be increased risks for miscarriage, pre-eclampsia, preterm delivery, low birth weight, and a number of other harmful effects on the mother and the baby. Only you and your doctor know your medical history and can best determine whether or not you should stop taking paroxetine during pregnancy. Some women can gradually wean off of paroxetine before delivery. For other women, the effects from stopping paroxetine may be more harmful than the possible risks to the baby if they continue to take it. The benefits of taking paroxetine for your specific situation and the potential risks to the baby should be considered before a decision is made.

Will taking paroxetine have any long-term effect on my baby's behavior and development?

There have been some small studies on the long-term development of infants exposed to selective serotonin reuptake inhibitors during pregnancy. Some of the infants involved in those studies were exposed to paroxetine. These studies suggest that SSRI exposure does not appear to have any significant long-term effects on brain development in babies exposed during pregnancy. While reassuring, further long-term studies on infants exposed to paroxetine are needed before we will know if there are any effects on the fetal brain and on the baby's behavior and development.

Can I take paroxetine while breastfeeding?

Paroxetine crosses into the breast milk in very low amounts. No adverse effects in breastfed infants have been seen in several reports. Some authors consider paroxetine one of the safer SSRIs to take while breastfeeding. Long-term studies on infants exposed to paroxetine in breast milk have not been conducted. You should discuss the risks and benefits of breastfeeding while taking paroxetine with your health care provider.

What if the father of the baby takes paroxetine?

There are no studies looking at possible risks to a pregnancy when the father takes paroxetine. In general, medications the father takes do not increase the risk to a pregnancy because the father does not share a blood connection with the developing baby.

Selected References

Alwan S, et al. 2007. Use of selective serotonin-reuptake inhibitors in pregnancy and the risk of birth defects. *N Engl J Med* 356(26):2684–92.

Andrade S, et al. 2009. Antidepressant use and risk of persistent pulmonary hypertension of the newborn. *Pharmacoepidemiol Drug Saf* 18(3):246–52.

Bonari L, et al. 2004. Perinatal risks of untreated depression during pregnancy. *Can J Psychiatry* 49(11):726–35.

Chambers C, et al. 2006. Selective serotonin-reuptake inhibitors and risk of persistent pulmonary hypertension of the newborn. *N Engl J Med* 354(6)579–87.

Costei A, et. al. 2002. Perinatal outcome following third trimester exposure to paroxetine. *Arch Pediatr Adolesc Med* 156:1129–32.

Diav-Citrin O, et al. 2008. Paroxetine and fluoxetine in pregnancy: a prospective, multicentre, controlled observational study. *Br J Clin Pharmacol* 66(5): 695–705.

Einarson A, et al. 2008. Evaluation of the risk of congenital cardiovascular defects associated with use of paroxetine during pregnancy. *Am J Psychiatry* AiA:1–5.

Einarson A, et al. 2009. Rates of spontaneous and therapeutic abortions following use of antidepressants in pregnancy: results from a large prospective database. *J Obstet Gynaecol Can* 31:452–56.

Hendrick V, et al. 2001. Use of sertraline, paroxetine and fluvoxamine by nursing women. *Br J Psychiatry* 179:163–66.

Hernandez-Diaz S. 2007. Risk factors for persistent pulmonary hypertension of the newborn. *Pediatrics* 120 (2):e272–82.

Kallen B, et al. 2008. Maternal use of selective serotonin re-uptake inhibitors and persistent pulmonary hypertension of the newborn. *Pharmacoepidemiol Drug Saf* 17(8):801–6.

Levinson-Castiel R, et al. 2006. Neonatal abstinence syndrome after in utero exposure to selective serotonin reuptake inhibitors in term infants. *Arch Pediatr Adolesc Med* 160:173–76.

Louik C, et al. 2007. First-trimester use of selective serotonin-reuptake inhibitors and the risk of birth defects. *N Engl J Med* 356(26):2675–83.

Misri S, et al. 2000. Paroxetine levels in postpartum depressed women, breastmik, and infant serum. *J Clin Psychiatry* 61(11):828–32.

Nakhai-Pour HR, et al. 2010. Use of antidepressants during pregnancy and the risk of spontaneous abortion. *CMAJ* 182(10):1031–37.

Nulman I, et al. 1997. Neurodevelopment of children exposed in utero to antidepressant drugs. *NEJM* 336(4):258–62.

Sanz E, et al. 2005. Selective serotonin reuptake inhibitors in pregnant women and neonatal withdrawal syndrome: a database analysis. *Lancet* 365:482–87.

Stowe Z, et al. 2000. Paroxetine in human breastmilk and nursing infants. *Am J Psychiatry* 157(2):185–89.

Weissman AM, et al. 2004. Pooled analysis of antidepressant levels in lactating mothers, breast milk, and nursing infants. *Am J Psychiatry* June; 161(6): 1066–78.

Wichman CL, et al. 2009. Congenital heart disease associated with selective serotonin reuptake inhibitor use during pregnancy. *Mayo Clin Proc* 84(1):23–27.

Wurst K, et al. 2010. First trimester paroxetine use and the prevalence of congenital, specifically cardiac, defects: a meta-analysis of epidemiological studies. *Birth Defects Res A Clin Mol Teratol* 88(3):159–70.

Section 7.5

Selective Serotonin Reuptake Inhibitors (SSRIs)

"FDA Drug Safety Communication: Selective Serotonin Reuptake Inhibitor (SSRI) Antidepressant Use During Pregnancy and Reports of a Rare Heart and Lung Condition in Newborn Babies," U.S. Food and Drug Administration, January 9, 2012.

The U.S. Food and Drug Administration (FDA) is updating the public on the use of selective serotonin reuptake inhibitor (SSRI) antidepressants by women during pregnancy and the potential risk of a rare heart and lung condition known as persistent pulmonary hypertension of the newborn (PPHN). The initial Public Health Advisory in July 2006[1] on this potential risk was based on a single published study. Since then, there have been conflicting findings from new studies evaluating this potential risk, making it unclear whether use of SSRIs during pregnancy can cause PPHN.

Facts about selective serotonin reuptake inhibitors (SSRIs):

- Marketed under various brand and generic drug names (see Table 7.2).

- Used to treat depression and other psychiatric disorders.

- Are commonly used drugs to treat depression during pregnancy in the United States.[1,2]

- There are no adequate and well-controlled studies of SSRIs in pregnant women.

At this time, FDA advises health care professionals not to alter their current clinical practice of treating depression during pregnancy. Healthcare professionals should report any adverse events involving SSRIs to the FDA MedWatch Program.[2]

FDA has reviewed the additional new study results and has concluded that, given the conflicting results from different studies, it is premature to reach any conclusion about a possible link between SSRI use in pregnancy and PPHN. FDA will update the SSRI drug labels to reflect the new data and the conflicting results.

PPHN occurs when a newborn baby does not adapt to breathing outside the womb. Newborns with PPHN may require intensive care support including a mechanical ventilator to increase their oxygen level. If severe, PPHN can result in multiple organ damage, including brain damage, and even death.

Additional Information for Patients

If you are pregnant or plan to become pregnant, talk with your health care professional if you are depressed or undergoing treatment for depression to determine your best treatment option during pregnancy.

Talk to your health care professional about the potential benefits and risks of taking an SSRI during pregnancy.

Do not stop taking an SSRI antidepressant without first talking to your health care professional. Stopping an SSRI antidepressant suddenly may cause unwanted side effects or a relapse of depression.

Report any suspected side effects of SSRI use in pregnancy to your health care professional and to the FDA MedWatch program.

Additional Information for Health Care Professionals

It is unclear whether SSRI use during pregnancy can cause PPHN, because the available data are conflicting.

Health care professionals and their patients must weigh the small potential risk of PPHN that may be associated with SSRI use in pregnancy against the substantial risks associated with undertreatment or no treatment of depression during pregnancy.

Untreated depression during pregnancy may lead to poor birth outcomes, including low birth weight, preterm delivery, lower Apgar scores, poor prenatal care, failure to recognize or report signs of labor; and an increased risk of fetal abuse, neonaticide, or maternal suicide.[3,4]

The published joint 2009 American Psychiatric Association (APA) and American College of Obstetrics and Gynecology (ACOG) guidelines for the management of depression during pregnancy includes treatment paradigms for the appropriate management of depression in pregnancy.[2]

Report adverse events involving SSRIs to the FDA MedWatch program.

Data Summary

It is well documented in the medical literature that SSRIs are used during pregnancy.[1,2] In general, most epidemiology studies show that adverse events in pregnant patients are similar to those in nonpregnant patients, and many studies find no major fetal abnormalities in excess of the 1 to 3 percent found in the general population.[5] Two studies suggest an increased risk for PPHN with SSRI use in pregnancy.[3,6] Three other studies do not support this association, and the potential risk with SSRI use during pregnancy remains unknown.[5,7,8]

PPHN affects between one and two infants per thousand live births in the general population, a relatively uncommon event, but one associated with significant infant morbidity and mortality as well as long term sequelae.[7,8,9] A neonate with primary PPHN is typically a term or late-preterm infant who presents within hours after birth with severe respiratory failure and who often requires mechanical ventilation. These neonates have no radiographic lung abnormalities and no evidence of parenchymal lung disease. Secondary PPHN may be associated with other problems with the fetus, such as meconium aspiration, neonatal infection, or congenital heart malformations.[8,9,10]

The 2006 study by Chambers et al. found a sixfold increase in PPHN among neonates whose mothers were exposed to an SSRI after twenty weeks of gestation, and provided the rationale for the current SSRI product label warning under Usage in Pregnancy: Nonteratogenic Effects stating, "Infants exposed to SSRIs in late pregnancy may have an increased risk for persistent pulmonary hypertension of the newborn (PPHN)."[3] A more recent study by Källén, et al. also found a statistically significant association between SSRI use and PPHN, although the majority of exposures occur during the first trimester of pregnancy.[6] The results of these two studies reporting an increase in risk are interpreted by some to show a strong association between SSRI use in pregnancy and the development of PPHN.

A review of the published literature also identified three studies reporting no increase in risk of PPHN.[5,7,8] The 2006 study by Wichman et al. is a retrospective cohort study of obstetric deliveries within a defined geographic area conducted by the Mayo Clinic. The study identified sixteen neonates with PPHN and no exposures to an SSRI in utero.[5] The 2009 study by Andrade et al. is a well-designed retrospective cohort study from four health plans in an ongoing health maintenance organization (HMO) research network study of birth outcomes. The authors found no association between SSRI exposure during the third trimester of pregnancy and PPHN.[7] Lastly, the smaller 2011 retrospective case-control study by Wilson et al. identified fifty-eight neonates with PPHN and no SSRI exposure in utero.[8]

Design features in each of the above five published studies preclude the demonstration, either individually or collectively, of a definitive association between SSRI use and PPHN. Each study incorporates a different study design, uses a different method of collecting exposure information during gestation, and gives incomplete attention to potentially important factors including Cesarean delivery. FDA recommends caution be used when interpreting results of studies with statistical associations, as statistical significance in an epidemiologic study does not always correlate with clinical significance and good clinical decision making.[11,12]

At present, FDA does not find sufficient evidence to conclude that SSRI use in pregnancy causes PPHN, and therefore recommends that health care providers treat depression during pregnancy as clinically appropriate. FDA will update the SSRI labels as any new data regarding SSRI use and PPHN become available.

Table 7.2. Selective Serotonin Reuptake Inhibitor (SSRI) Drugs

Generic name	Found in Brand name(s)
Citalopram	Celexa
Escitalopram	Lexapro
Fluoxetine	Prozac, Sarafem, Symbyax
Fluvoxamine	Luvox, Luvox CR
Paroxetine	Paxil, Paxil CR, Pexeva
Sertraline	Zoloft
Vilazodone	Viibryd

References

1.   Cooper WO, Willey ME, Pont SJ, Ray WA. Increasing use of antidepressants in pregnancy. *Am L Obstet Gynecol* 2007;196:544 e1–544.e5.

2.   Yonkers KA, Wisner KL, Stewart DE, Oberlander TF, Dell DL, Stotland N, Ramin S, Chaudron L, Lockwood C. The management of depression during pregnancy: a report from the American Psychiatric Association and the American College of Obstetricians and Gynecologists. *General Hospital Psychiatry* 2009;31:403–13.

3.   Chambers CD, Hernandez-Diaz S, Van Marter LJ, Werler MM, Louik C, Jones KL, Mitchell AA. Selective Serotonin-Reuptake Inhibitors and Risk of Persistent Pulmonary Hypertension of the Newborn. *NEJM* 2006;354(6):579–87.

4. O'Keane V, Marsh SM. Depression during pregnancy. *BMJ* 2007;334:1003–5.

5. Wichman CL, Morre KM, Lang TR, St. Sauver JL, Heise RH, Watson WJ. Congenital heart disease associated with selective serotonin reuptake inhibitor use during pregnancy. *Mayo Clin Proc* 2009;84(1):23–27.

6. Källén B and Olausson PO. Maternal use of selective serotonin re-uptake inhibitors and persistent pulmonary hypertension of the newborn. *Pharmacoepidemiol Drug Safety* 2008;17:801–6.

7. Andrade SE, McPhillips H, Loren D, Raebel MA, lane K, Livingston J, Boudreau DM, Smith DH, Davis RI, Willy ME, Platt R. Antidepressant medication use and risk of persistent pulmonary hypertension of the newborn. *Pharmacoepidemiol Drug Safety* 2009;18:246–52.

8. Wilson KL, Zelig CM, Harvey JP, Cunningham BS, Dolinsky BM, Napolitano PG. Persistent pulmonary hypertension of the newborn is associated with mode of delivery and not with maternal use of selective serotonin reuptake inhibitors. *Am J Perinatol* 2011;28(1):19–24.

9. Hernandez-Diaz S, VanMarter LJ, Werler MM, Louik C, Mitchell AA. Risk Factors for Persistent Pulmonary Hypertension of the Newborn. *Pediatrics* 2007;120:e272–e282.

10. Levine, EM, Ghai V, Barton JJ, Storm CM. Mode of delivery and risk of respiratory disease in newborns. *Obstetrics and Gynecology* 2001;97:3:439–42.

11. Chambers C. Selective serotonin reuptake inhibitors and congenital malformations. *BMJ* 2009;339:b3525.

12. Nonacs, R. SSRIs and PPHN: a review of the data. Boston (MA): Massachusetts General Hospital, Center for Women's Mental Health; posted 2009, Nov 10. Available from: http://www.womensmentalhealth.org/posts/ssris-and-pphn-a-review-of-the-data/4.

Section 7.6

Thalidomide

This section talks about the risks that exposure to thalidomide can have during pregnancy. With each pregnancy, all women have a 3 to 5 percent chance of having a baby with a birth defect. This information should not take the place of medical care and advice from your health care provider.

What is thalidomide?

Thalidomide is a sedative agent that also changes the body's immune response and reduces the ability of the body to grow new blood vessels. Thalidomide was one of the first drugs recognized to cause birth defects in humans. Although thalidomide was not released in the United States until 1998, it is now being used for treatment of several medical conditions including leprosy, cancer, and complications from human immunodeficiency virus (HIV) infection.

After I stop taking thalidomide, how long should I wait to become pregnant?

The half-life of thalidomide is 8.7 hours, which is the time it takes for 50 percent of the drug to be cleared from your body. Therefore, after a few days to a week, any remaining drug level would be fairly low.

To be safe, it is recommended that women stop use of thalidomide one month before conception to reduce the risk of thalidomide-related birth defects.

There are no studies on pregnancy outcome in women who only used thalidomide prior to conception. All infants known to have thalidomide-related birth defects were exposed during the first trimester of pregnancy.

Can thalidomide make it more difficult for me to become pregnant?

No. To date, there are no reports linking thalidomide use and infertility. However, because thalidomide can damage the developing fetus early in pregnancy, often before a woman recognizes she is pregnant, it is important that very effective methods of birth control be used. Therefore, it is recommended that two different and reliable methods of birth control be used if a woman is taking thalidomide. The manufacturer developed the STEPS (System for Thalidomide Education and Prescribing Safety) program to help prevent exposure to pregnant women.

Can taking thalidomide during pregnancy cause birth defects in my baby?

Yes. When a pregnant woman takes thalidomide thirty-four to fifty days (4.5 to 7 weeks) after the beginning of her last menstrual period, there is a risk of approximately 20 percent or greater to have a baby with birth defects such as extremely short or missing arms and legs, missing ears (both outside and inside), and deafness. There is also a risk of other problems such as heart defects, missing or small eyes, paralysis of the face, kidney abnormalities, gastrointestinal abnormalities, poor growth, and mental retardation. The risk for fetal harm if the drug is taken after the first trimester is unknown.

Will taking thalidomide have an effect on my baby's behavior and development?

The only long-term studies of thalidomide exposure during pregnancy have been done on children born with birth defects. Some of these children were mentally retarded or had behavioral conditions such as autism. The possible long-term effects on children exposed to thalidomide but who were not born with birth defects are unknown.

Does thalidomide cause an increased risk for miscarriage or infant death?

Yes. The fetal and infant death rate with maternal thalidomide use is estimated to be as high as 40 percent or greater. The cause of death has been attributed to the severe birth defects caused by the thalidomide exposure.

If I get pregnant while taking thalidomide, what should I do?

Contact your health care provider right away. Your health care provider will discuss whether you should discontinue your medication, as well as the possibilities for prenatal testing. Prenatal testing involves a detailed ultrasound to look at the baby's body and organs. Ultrasound can visualize many birth defects, but is not able to detect all potential fetal problems caused by a thalidomide exposure.

If a man uses thalidomide, will it cause birth defects in his children?

There are no reports in the literature that suggest the use of thalidomide in men is associated with an increased risk of birth defects. However, thalidomide is excreted in semen, often at levels higher than found in blood. It is recommended that men taking thalidomide use condoms during intercourse as a precautionary measure.

Can I take thalidomide while breastfeeding?

Thalidomide has not been studied during breastfeeding. Based on its chemical properties, it is expected to pass into breast milk. The drug may cause drowsiness in a breastfed infant, but the exact effects of thalidomide on the breastfed infant are unknown. Until more is known, it is not recommended that women breastfeed while taking thalidomide.

Selected References

Brooks C, et al. 1977. Linear growth of children with limb deformities following exposure to thalidomide in utero. *Acta Paediatr Scan* 66:673–75.

Castilla E, et al. 1996. Thalidomide, a current teratogen in South America. *Teratology* 54:273–77.

Gollop T, et al. 1987. Prenatal diagnosis of thalidomide syndrome. *Prenat Diagn* 7:295–98.

Miller et al 2009. Thalidomide and misoprostol: ophthalmologic manifestations and associations both expected and unexpected. *Birth Defects Res A Clin Mol Teratol* 85(8):667–76.

Smithells R. 1992. Recognition of thalidomide defects. *J Med Genet* 29:716–23.

Sterling D, et al. 1997. Thalidomide: a surprising recovery. *J Am Pharm Assn* 3:306–13.

Stromland K, et al. 1993. Thalidomide embryopathy: revisited 27 years later. *Acta Ophthalmol (Copen)* 71:238–45.

Tseng S, et al. 1996. Rediscovering thalidomide: a review of its mechanism of action, side effects and potential uses. *J Am Acad Dermatol* 35:969–79.

Teo S, et al. 2001. Thalidomide is distributed into human semen after oral dosing. *Drug Metab Dispos* 29:1355–57.

Section 7.7

New Research in Medications Affecting Fetal Health

"Research," Centers for Disease Control and Prevention, November 17, 2011.

Like many families affected by birth defects, the U.S. Centers for Disease Control and Prevention (CDC) wants to find out what causes them. Understanding risk factors, such as certain medications, that might increase the chance of having a baby with a birth defect will help us learn more about the causes. Better information on the safety or risk of specific medications will allow women and their doctors to make informed decisions about treatment during pregnancy.

To learn about birth defects, CDC coordinates and collaborates with many other researchers on one of the largest U.S. studies to understand the causes and risk factors for birth defects, the National Birth Defects Prevention Study. This study of major birth defects helps identify a number of specific medications associated with an increased risk of birth defects.

Gaps in Current Knowledge

A 2011 study of all medications approved by FDA from 1980 through 2010 found that 91 percent of the medications approved for use by adults in general had insufficient data to determine the risk of using the medication during pregnancy.[1] CDC and its collaborators are working to fill this gap and continue to study medication use during pregnancy in order to understand how specific medications might affect the unborn baby. Although the studies mentioned below are just one step toward determining the risk of different medications during pregnancy, they contribute to the information available to help women and their doctors make treatment decisions during pregnancy.

Some recent findings on possible associations between certain medications and birth defects are described below.

Over-the-Counter Medications

Taking acetaminophen (used for pain relief) during the first trimester of pregnancy did not appear to increase the risk of major birth defects in the baby. In addition, it might decrease the risk of some birth defects in the baby when the woman uses it because she has a fever, because untreated fever can increase the risk of some birth defects.

Antidepressants

Depression is a serious illness. Women should not change medications or stop taking medications without first talking with their doctor about the available options.

- One recent study found that taking bupropion (used for depression and to stop smoking) during pregnancy might increase the risk of having a baby with certain heart defects.

- A number of studies have identified risks to the fetus and newborn associated with use of antidepressant medications. Several studies have shown an increased risk for heart defects associated with taking selective serotonin-reuptake inhibitors (SSRIs) during early pregnancy. SSRIs are a common group of antidepressant medications. Data from the National Birth Defects Prevention Study (NBDPS) showed that taking SSRIs during pregnancy might increase the risk of anencephaly, craniosynostosis, or omphalocele.

Medications to Treat Diseases

Maternal diseases are serious conditions. Women should not change medications or stop taking medications without first talking with their doctor about the available options.

- Pregnant women with asthma who use certain medications might have an increased risk of having a baby with a heart defect. One type of asthma medication, bronchodilators, showed an increased risk in one study. Another type of medication used to treat asthma, corticosteroids, might increase the risk of having a baby born with cleft lip and/or cleft palate. However, it is important that asthma be well controlled in pregnancy. Women should discuss the best treatment options with their doctor before pregnancy.

- Recent studies suggest that pregnant women who have a thyroid disorder might have an increased risk of having a baby with craniosynostosis, hydrocephaly, or hypospadias.

- One study found that pregnant women who have high blood pressure (hypertension) or took certain hypertension medication appeared to have an increased risk of having a baby with left or right obstructive heart defects or septal heart defects. Hypertension is a serious disorder, particularly in pregnancy. Women should talk to their doctor about the best medication options to treat their condition during pregnancy.

- Some recent case reports suggested that pregnant women taking mycophenolate mofetil (MMF; CellCept), which is used to help prevent transplant organ rejection or to treat lupus nephritis, might have an increased risk of having a baby with birth defects. However, these are serious disorders and pregnant women should not stop or start taking any type of medication that they need without first talking with a doctor.

Medications to Help with Infertility

- Taking clomiphene citrate (commonly used to help women who have difficulty getting pregnant) just before or during early pregnancy might increase the risk of having a baby with certain birth defects. It is difficult to determine whether these findings are due to the use of the clomiphene citrate or because these women had difficulty getting pregnant due to some underlying conditions that affected fertility.

- Taking progestins (used to help with infertility and found in birth control pills) during early pregnancy might increase the risk of having a baby with hypospadias.

Medications to Treat Infections

- In one study, taking penicillins, erythromycins, or cephalosporins (antibiotics used to treat infections) did not appear to increase the risk of birth defects in the baby. However, sulfonamide, which is often in used in combination with trimethoprim (which is thought to increase the risk for birth defects) or nitrofurantoin use was associated with several birth defects.

References

1. Adam MP, Polifka JE, & Friedman JM. Evolving Knowledge of the Teratogenicity of Medications in Human Pregnancy. *Am J Med Genet Part C*. 2011;157:175–82.

Chapter 8

Maternal Health Conditions Affecting Pregnancy

Chapter Contents

Section 8.1

Asthma and Pregnancy

"Asthma and Pregnancy," © 2010 Organization of Teratology Information Specialists (OTIS). Reprinted with permission. The OTIS website features fact sheets answering frequently asked questions about a wide variety of exposures during pregnancy and lactation. For the most current information, visit www.otispregnancy.org. Member programs of OTIS are located throughout the U.S. and Canada. To find the Teratogen Information Service in your area, call OTIS toll-free at 866-626-OTIS (866-626-6847), or visit www.otispregnancy.org.

This section talks about asthma during pregnancy. With each pregnancy, all women have a 3 to 5 percent chance of having a baby with a birth defect. This information should not take the place of medical care and advice from your health care provider.

What is asthma?

Asthma refers to inflammation (swelling and tightening) in the airways of the lungs. When an asthma attack occurs, it is more difficult for air to pass through the lungs, which leads to wheezing, coughing, and trouble breathing. Asthma is often treated with a combination of short-acting inhalers for immediate symptom relief and daily medicines to reduce inflammation.

Triggers that can cause an asthma attack vary from person to person. Common triggers include breathing in cold air, cold/flu viruses, strenuous exercise, chemicals, cigarette smoke, and allergies to dust, animals, pollen, or mold. Avoiding these triggers can reduce the number of asthma attacks.

I have asthma and am planning on getting pregnant. Is there anything I need to know?

Asthma management during pregnancy should continue to include the medicines that best control an individual's asthma symptoms.

It is not possible to predict how a woman's asthma will act during pregnancy. For about one-third of women, symptoms will improve during pregnancy, another one-third will have no change in asthma symptoms, and a final one-third of women will have worsening of symptoms. It appears that the more severe the asthma is when you conceive, the more likely it is that the symptoms will get worse during pregnancy. Therefore, it is very important that a woman's asthma be in good control with carefully chosen medications prior to getting pregnant.

Can asthma cause birth defects?

Some studies have suggested an increased risk for birth defects while others have not. In these studies, it is difficult to determine whether the adverse effects seen were due to the mother's asthma, medicines needed to control the asthma, or other factors. If a pregnant woman has trouble breathing she will take in less oxygen. This could lead to a reduced amount of oxygen getting to the baby. Reduced oxygen for the developing baby could cause problems in organ development.

If there is a risk from asthma itself, it is expected to be very low. The vast majority of women with asthma have babies without birth defects.

Can asthma lead to any other pregnancy problems?

Yes. Maternal asthma, especially poorly controlled asthma, is associated with higher rates of pregnancy complications, such as placental problems, high blood pressure, premature delivery, higher rates of cesarean section, and low birth weight. It is important for women who are pregnant to speak with their health care provider about the best way to treat their asthma during pregnancy. The benefits of treating asthma during pregnancy generally outweigh the potential risks of the medication.

Can taking medicine for asthma during pregnancy cause birth defects?

Most asthma medicines have not been shown to have harmful effects on the developing baby. Speak with your health care provider with questions about your specific medicines.

Fast-acting inhalers (like albuterol) and inhaled corticosteroids are considered preferred treatments for asthma during pregnancy. Inhaled medications are absorbed into the body in lower amounts compared to oral (taken by mouth) medicines, so less of the medication should reach the developing baby. For many women, fast-acting inhalers and inhaled corticosteroids are very effective for treating asthma during pregnancy.

Some studies have suggested an increased risk for cleft lip with or without cleft palate (split in the lip or roof of the mouth) when corticosteroid pills are taken during the first trimester. Based on the available information, if there is a real risk for cleft lip and/or palate, the absolute risk would be small (less than 1 percent).

Can taking medicine for asthma during pregnancy cause other pregnancy problems?

Lower birth weights have been associated with corticosteroid pills but it isn't clear whether that is due to the medicine alone, to the maternal disease being treated, or a combination of both.

If I have asthma, can I breastfeed my baby?

Most asthma medicines are compatible with breastfeeding. For example, the amount of medicine in breast milk from fast-acting inhalers and inhaled corticosteroids is expected to be too small to be harmful for an infant.

What if the father of the baby has asthma?

A father's asthma or a father's use of asthma medicines does not increase the chance for birth defects or pregnancy complications because the father is not physically connected to the developing baby.

Selected References

Blais L, et al. 2010. Effect of maternal asthma on the risk of specific congenital malformations: A population-based cohort study. *Birth Defects Res A* 88(4):216–22.

Kallen B 2007. The safety of asthma medications during pregnancy. *Expert Opin Drug Saf* 6(1):15–26.

Kwon HL, et al. 2006. The epidemiology of asthma during pregnancy: prevalence, diagnosis, and symptoms. *Immunol Allergy Clin North Am* 26(1):29–62.

Murphy VE, et al. 2005. Asthma during pregnancy: mechanisms and treatment implications. *Eur Respir* 25:731–50.

National Asthma Education and Prevention Program. Working Group. 2004. Report on managing asthma during pregnancy: Recommendations for pharmacologic treatment. Update 2004. NIH publication No. 05-

5236. Bethesda, MD: U.S. Department of Health and Human Services; National Institutes of Health; National Heart, Lung and Blood Institute.

Schatz M and Dombrowski MP 2009. Clinical practice: Asthma in pregnancy. *N Engl J Med* 360(18):1862–69.

Section 8.2

Cancer and Pregnancy

Cancer during pregnancy is rare, occurring in approximately one out of every one thousand pregnancies, and little research is available to guide women and doctors. However, a pregnant woman with cancer is capable of giving birth to a healthy baby, and some cancer treatments are safe during pregnancy. Cancer rarely affects the fetus directly. Although some cancers may spread to the placenta (a temporary organ that connects the mother and fetus), most cancers cannot spread to the fetus itself.

The cancers that tend to occur during pregnancy are those that are more common in younger people, such as cervical cancer, breast cancer, thyroid cancer, Hodgkin lymphoma, and melanoma. In addition, a gestational trophoblastic tumor is a rare cancer that occurs in a woman's reproductive system. It is most commonly the result of an abnormal combination of a sperm and an egg; in other cases, it begins from a normal placenta.

Because age is the most significant risk factor for cancer, the rate of cancer during pregnancy may be increasing as more women are waiting until they are older to have children.

Diagnosis

Being pregnant often delays a cancer diagnosis because some cancer symptoms such as abdominal bloating, frequent headaches, or rectal bleeding are common during pregnancy and are not considered suspicious.

Breast cancer is the most common cancer in pregnant women, affecting approximately one in three thousand pregnancies. Pregnancy-related breast enlargement may make it difficult to detect small breast tumors, and mammograms are not regularly done during pregnancy.

If cancer is suspected during pregnancy, women and their doctors may be concerned about diagnostic tests such as x-rays. However, research has shown that the level of radiation in diagnostic x-rays is too low to harm the fetus. When possible, women may use a lead shield that covers the abdomen for extra protection. Other diagnostic tests—such as magnetic resonance imaging (MRI), ultrasound, and biopsy—are also considered safe during pregnancy because they don't use ionizing radiation.

Sometimes, pregnancy can uncover cancer that had previously gone undetected. For example, a Pap test performed as part of standard prenatal care can detect cervical cancer. Similarly, an ultrasound performed during pregnancy can find ovarian cancer that might otherwise go undiagnosed.

Treatment

When making treatment decisions for cancer during pregnancy, the doctor considers the best treatment options for the mother and the possible risks to the fetus. The type of treatment given depends on many factors, including gestational age of the fetus (stage of the pregnancy); the type, location, size, and stage of the cancer; and the wishes of the expectant mother and family. Because some cancer treatments can harm the fetus, especially during the first trimester (the first three months of pregnancy), treatment may be delayed until the second or third trimesters. When cancer is diagnosed later in pregnancy, doctors may wait to start treatment until after the baby is born, or they may consider inducing labor early. In some cases, such as early-stage (stage 0 or IA) cervical cancer, doctors may wait to treat the cancer until after delivery.

Some cancer treatments may be used during pregnancy but only after careful consideration and treatment planning to optimize the safety of the mother and the unborn baby. These include surgery, chemotherapy, and rarely, radiation therapy.

Surgery: Surgery is the removal of the tumor and surrounding tissue during an operation. It poses little risk to the fetus and is considered the safest cancer treatment option during pregnancy. In some instances, more extensive surgery can be done to avoid having to use chemotherapy or radiation therapy.

Chemotherapy: Chemotherapy is the use of drugs to kill cancer cells, usually by stopping the cancer cells' ability to grow and divide. Chemotherapy can harm the fetus, particularly if it is given during the first trimester of pregnancy when the fetus's organs are still developing. Chemotherapy during the first trimester may cause birth defects or even the loss of the unborn baby. During the second and third trimesters, some types of chemotherapy may be given without necessarily harming the fetus. The placenta acts as a barrier between the mother and the fetus, and some drugs cannot pass through the barrier, or they pass through only minimally. If the planned chemotherapy includes a drug that is not safe during any stage of pregnancy, the doctor can sometimes substitute another drug. Although chemotherapy in the later stages of pregnancy may not directly harm the fetus, it may cause side effects—such as malnutrition and anemia, meaning a low red blood cell count—for the mother that may indirectly harm the fetus. In addition, chemotherapy given during the second and third trimesters often causes early labor and low birth weight, both of which may lead to further health concerns for the mother and the baby. The baby may struggle to gain weight and fight infections, and the mother may have trouble breastfeeding.

Radiation therapy: Radiation therapy is the use of high-energy x-rays or other particles to kill cancer cells. Because radiation therapy can harm the fetus, particularly during the first trimester, doctors generally avoid using this treatment. Even in the second and third trimesters, the use of radiation therapy is rare, and it depends on the dose of radiation and the area of the body being treated.

Breastfeeding

Although cancer cells cannot pass to the infant through breast milk, doctors advise women who are being treated for cancer not to breastfeed. Chemotherapy can be especially dangerous because the drugs may be transferred to the infant through the breast milk, causing harm. Similarly, radioactive components that are taken internally, such as radioactive iodine used in treating thyroid cancer, also cross into breast milk and can harm the infant.

How Pregnancy Affects Chance of Recovery from Cancer

The prognosis (chance of recovery) for a pregnant woman with cancer is often the same, compared with other women of the same age with the same type and stage of cancer. However, if a woman's diagnosis is delayed during pregnancy, the extent of the cancer at the time of diagnosis may be greater, resulting in a worse overall prognosis. In addition, pregnancy sometimes affects the behavior of some cancers. For example, there is some evidence to suggest that the hormonal changes of pregnancy may stimulate the growth of malignant melanoma.

Pregnancy after Cancer Treatment

As more young people are surviving cancer, more women are considering whether they should have a baby after having cancer. In general, pregnancy after cancer treatment is considered safe for both the mother and the baby, and pregnancy does not appear to increase the chances of cancer recurring (coming back). However, because some cancers do recur, women are usually advised to wait a number of years after completing cancer treatment until the risk of recurrence has decreased. The amount of time a patient may be advised to wait before trying to become pregnant depends on the type and stage of cancer, the type of treatment the patient received, and the patient's preferences.

Sometimes, cancer treatments can damage specific areas of the body, such as the heart or lungs. Before becoming pregnant, your doctor may need to evaluate these organs to be sure that the pregnancy will be safe.

Unfortunately, some cancer treatments also cause infertility, making it difficult or impossible for some women to have children. All women of childbearing age who are interested in having children in the future should talk with their doctor about treatment-related infertility risks and fertility preservation strategies before beginning treatment.

Section 8.3

Diabetes and Pregnancy

"Type 1 or Type 2 Diabetes and Pregnancy,"
Centers for Disease Control and Prevention, June 16, 2010.

Problems of Diabetes in Pregnancy

Blood sugar that is not well controlled in a pregnant woman with type 1 or type 2 diabetes could lead to problems for the woman and the baby.

Birth Defects

The organs of the baby form during the first two months of pregnancy, often before a woman knows that she is pregnant. Blood sugar that is not in control can affect those organs while they are being formed and cause serious birth defects in the developing baby, such as those of the brain, spine, and heart.

An Extra Large Baby

Diabetes that is not well controlled causes the baby's blood sugar to be high. The baby is "overfed" and grows extra large. Besides causing discomfort to the woman during the last few months of pregnancy, an extra large baby can lead to problems during delivery for both the mother and the baby. The mother might need a Cesarean section to deliver the baby. The baby can be born with nerve damage due to pressure on the shoulder during delivery.

Cesarean Section (C-Section)

A C-section is a surgery to deliver the baby through the mother's belly. A woman who has diabetes that is not well controlled has a higher chance of needing a C-section to deliver the baby. When the baby is delivered by a C-section, it takes longer for the woman to recover from childbirth.

119

High Blood Pressure (Preeclampsia)

When a pregnant woman has high blood pressure, protein in her urine, and often swelling in fingers and toes that doesn't go away, she might have preeclampsia. It is a serious problem that needs to be watched closely and managed by her doctor. High blood pressure can cause harm to both the woman and her unborn baby. It might lead to the baby being born early and also could cause seizures or a stroke (a blood clot or a bleed in the brain that can lead to brain damage) in the woman during labor and delivery. Women with type 1 or type 2 diabetes have high blood pressure more often than women without diabetes.

Early (Preterm) Birth

Being born too early can result in problems for the baby, such as breathing problems, heart problems, bleeding into the brain, intestinal problems, and vision problems. Women with type 1 or type 2 diabetes are more likely to deliver early than women without diabetes.

Low Blood Sugar (Hypoglycemia)

People with diabetes who take insulin or other diabetes medications can develop blood sugar that is too low. Low blood sugar can be very serious, and even fatal, if not treated quickly. Seriously low blood sugar can be avoided if women watch their blood sugar closely and treat low blood sugar early.

If a woman's diabetes was not well controlled during pregnancy, her baby can very quickly develop low blood sugar after birth. The baby's blood sugar must be watched for several hours after delivery.

Miscarriage or Stillbirth

A miscarriage is a loss of the pregnancy before twenty weeks. Stillbirth means that after twenty weeks, the baby dies in the womb. Miscarriages and stillbirths can happen for many reasons. A woman who has diabetes that is not well controlled has a higher chance of having a miscarriage or stillbirth.

Seven Tips for Women with Diabetes

If a woman with diabetes keeps her blood sugar well controlled before and during pregnancy, she can reduce the chance of having a baby with birth defects. Controlling blood sugar also reduces the chance that a woman will develop common problems of diabetes, or that the problems will get worse during pregnancy.

Steps women can take before and during pregnancy to help prevent problems:

Plan for pregnancy: Before getting pregnant, see your doctor. The doctor needs to look at the effects that diabetes has had on your body already, talk with you about getting and keeping control of your blood sugar, change medications if needed, and plan for frequent follow-up. If you are overweight, the doctor might recommend that you try to lose weight before getting pregnant as part of the plan to get your blood sugar in control.

See your doctor early and often: During pregnancy, a woman with diabetes needs to see the doctor more often than a pregnant woman without diabetes. Together, you and your doctor can work to prevent or catch problems early.

Eat healthy foods: Eat healthy foods from a meal plan made for a person with diabetes. A dietitian can help you create a healthy meal plan. A dietitian can also help you learn how to control your blood sugar while you are pregnant.

Exercise regularly: Exercise is another way to keep blood sugar under control. It helps to balance food intake. After checking with your doctor, you can exercise regularly before, during, and after pregnancy. Get at least thirty minutes of moderate-intensity physical activity at least five days a week. This could be brisk walking, swimming, or actively playing with children.

Take pills and insulin as directed: If diabetes pills or insulin are ordered by your doctor, take it as directed in order to help keep your blood sugar under control.

Control and treat low blood sugar quickly: Keeping blood sugar well controlled can lead to a chance of low blood sugar at times. If you are taking diabetes pills or insulin, it's helpful to have a source of quick sugar, such as hard candy, glucose tablets, or gel on hand at all times. It's also good to teach family members and close co-workers or friends how to help in case of a severe low blood sugar reaction.

Monitor blood sugar often: Because pregnancy causes the body's need for energy to change, blood sugar levels can change very quickly. You need to check your blood sugar often, as directed by your doctor. It is important to learn how to adjust food intake, exercise, and insulin, depending on the results of your blood sugar tests.

Section 8.4

Epilepsy and Pregnancy

Women with epilepsy who want to get pregnant can do so safely, as long as they are cautious to avoid one particular drug that may cause higher rates of birth defects. That is the main finding of new epilepsy guidelines for women developed by the American Academy of Neurology and the American Epilepsy Society. The guidelines were published in the April 27, 2009, online issue of *Neurology*, the medical journal of the American Academy of Neurology.

"Women who have epilepsy should feel assured that they can have a safe pregnancy without increased risk of Caesarean section, premature delivery, or other complications," explains Jennifer Hopp, M.D., an assistant professor of neurology at the University of Maryland School of Medicine who is one of the authors of the new treatment guidelines.

"What's exciting about the findings is that they focus specifically on how epilepsy medications affect women, who have some different health concerns from men. We examined how these drugs could specifically affect a range of women's health issues from bone density to birth defects, and we found some areas of concern," adds Dr. Hopp, who is a neurologist and epilepsy specialist at the University of Maryland Medical Center.

The guidelines recommend that pregnant women with epilepsy should avoid taking the commonly used drug valproate due to an increased risk for fetal deformities and decreased cognitive skills in children. This higher risk was seen whether the drug was used by itself or in combination with other medications. The neurologists also found that these women should work with their doctors to limit the number of medications taken during pregnancy since taking more than one seizure medication also showed an increased risk for birth defects.

"Our extensive review of the best scientific studies indicates that women with epilepsy can have a safe pregnancy. However, we advise that they still consider having their blood tested regularly. Levels of antiseizure medicine in the blood tend to fall during pregnancy. To ensure these women remain seizure-free, the medication doses may need to be adjusted throughout the pregnancy," says guideline author Allan Krumholz, M.D., director of the University of Maryland Epilepsy Center and professor of neurology at the University of Maryland School of Medicine.

The guideline also cautions physicians about prescribing the drugs phenytoin and phenobarbital to women who are pregnant, because of the potential risk of decreased cognitive skills in children. Additionally, pregnant women with epilepsy should not smoke because it may increase the risk of premature contractions and premature delivery.

"Because of their seizures and worries about medications, many women with epilepsy have been fearful of becoming pregnant. These new guidelines, rooted in strong scientific research, should help allay these concerns," adds guideline author Tricia Ting, M.D., assistant professor of neurology at the University of Maryland School of Medicine and a neurologist at the University of Maryland Medical Center.

Epilepsy is a neurological condition that causes recurrent seizures, affecting about forty million Americans, including an estimated five hundred thousand women of childbearing age. The new epilepsy guidelines were presented April 27, 2009, at the American Academy of Neurology's annual meeting in Seattle.

"Involvement in important projects such as this reflects the University of Maryland School of Medicine's commitment to advancing the practice of medicine. These guidelines will help women have the best information for a healthy pregnancy," says E. Albert Reece, M.D., Ph.D., M.B.A, vice president for medical affairs, University of Maryland, and dean, University of Maryland School of Medicine.

Section 8.5

High Blood Pressure and Pregnancy

Excerpted from "High Blood Pressure in Pregnancy," National Heart Lung and Blood Institute, National Institutes of Health. This document is available online at http://www.nhlbi.nih.gov/health/putlic/heart/hbp/hbp_preg.htm; accessed April 4, 2012.

What is high blood pressure?

Blood pressure is the amount of force exerted by the blood against the walls of the arteries. A person's blood pressure is considered high when the readings are greater than 140 mm Hg systolic (the top number in the blood pressure reading) or 90 mm Hg diastolic (the bottom number). In general, high blood pressure, or hypertension, contributes to the development of coronary heart disease, stroke, heart failure, and kidney disease.

What are the effects of high blood pressure in pregnancy?

Although many pregnant women with high blood pressure have healthy babies without serious problems, high blood pressure can be dangerous for both the mother and the fetus. Women with pre-existing, or chronic, high blood pressure are more likely to have certain complications during pregnancy than those with normal blood pressure. However, some women develop high blood pressure while they are pregnant (often called gestational hypertension).

The effects of high blood pressure range from mild to severe. High blood pressure can harm the mother's kidneys and other organs, and it can cause low birth weight and early delivery. In the most serious cases, the mother develops preeclampsia—or "toxemia of pregnancy"—which can threaten the lives of both the mother and the fetus.

What is preeclampsia?

Preeclampsia is a condition that typically starts after the twentieth week of pregnancy and is related to increased blood pressure and protein in the mother's urine (as a result of kidney problems). Preeclampsia affects the placenta, and it can affect the mother's kidneys, liver, and brain. When preeclampsia causes seizures, the condition is known as eclampsia—the second-leading cause of maternal death in the United States. Preeclampsia is also a leading cause of fetal complications, which include low birth weight, premature birth, and stillbirth.

There is no proven way to prevent preeclampsia. Most women who develop signs of preeclampsia, however, are closely monitored to lessen or avoid related problems. The only way to "cure" preeclampsia is to deliver the baby.

Who is more likely to develop preeclampsia?

- Women with chronic hypertension (high blood pressure before becoming pregnant).

- Women who developed high blood pressure or preeclampsia during a previous pregnancy, especially if these conditions occurred early in the pregnancy.

- Women who are obese prior to pregnancy.

- Pregnant women under the age of twenty or over the age of forty.

- Women who are pregnant with more than one baby.

- Women with diabetes, kidney disease, rheumatoid arthritis, lupus, or scleroderma.

How is preeclampsia detected?

Unfortunately, there is no single test to predict or diagnose pre-eclampsia. Key signs are increased blood pressure and protein in the urine (proteinuria). Other symptoms that seem to occur with pre-eclampsia include persistent headaches, blurred vision or sensitivity to light, and abdominal pain.

All of these sensations can be caused by other disorders; they can also occur in healthy pregnancies. Regular visits with your doctor help him or her to track your blood pressure and level of protein in your urine, to order and analyze blood tests that detect signs of preeclamp-sia, and to monitor fetal development more closely.

How can women with high blood pressure prevent problems during pregnancy?

If you are thinking about having a baby and you have high blood pressure, talk first to your doctor or nurse. Taking steps to control your blood pressure before and during pregnancy—and getting regular prenatal care—go a long way toward ensuring your well-being and your baby's health.

Before becoming pregnant:

- Be sure your blood pressure is under control. Lifestyle changes such as limiting your salt intake, participating in regular physical activity, and losing weight if you are overweight can be helpful.

- Discuss with your doctor how hypertension might affect you and your baby during pregnancy, and what you can do to prevent or lessen problems.

- If you take medicines for your blood pressure, ask your doctor whether you should change the amount you take or stop taking them during pregnancy. Experts currently recommend avoiding angiotensin-converting enzyme (ACE) inhibitors and angiotensin II (AII) receptor antagonists during pregnancy; other blood pressure medications may be okay for you to use. Do not, however, stop or change your medicines unless your doctor tells you to do so.

While you are pregnant:

- Obtain regular prenatal medical care.

- Avoid alcohol and tobacco.

- Talk to your doctor about any over-the-counter medications you are taking or are thinking about taking.

Does hypertension or preeclampsia during pregnancy cause long-term heart and blood vessel problems?

The effects of high blood pressure during pregnancy vary depending on the disorder and other factors. According to the National High Blood Pressure Education Program (NHBPEP), preeclampsia does not in general increase a woman's risk for developing chronic hypertension or other heart-related problems. The NHBPEP also reports that in women with normal blood pressure who develop preeclampsia after the twentieth week of their first pregnancy, short-term complications—including increased blood pressure—usually go away within about six weeks after delivery.

Some women, however, may be more likely to develop high blood pressure or other heart disease later in life. More research is needed to determine the long-term health effects of hypertensive disorders in pregnancy and to develop better methods for identifying, diagnosing, and treating women at risk for these conditions.

Even though high blood pressure and related disorders during pregnancy can be serious, most women with high blood pressure and those who develop preeclampsia have successful pregnancies. Obtaining early and regular prenatal care is the most important thing you can do for you and your baby.

Section 8.6

Obesity and Pregnancy

Being overweight or obese during pregnancy can cause complications for you and your baby. The more overweight you are, the greater the chances for pregnancy complications. But there are things you can do before and during pregnancy to help you have a healthy baby.

To know if you're overweight or obese, find out your body mass index (BMI) before you get pregnant. BMI is a calculation based on your weight and height:

- If you're overweight, your BMI is 25.0 to 29.9 before pregnancy. Two in three women (66 percent) of reproductive age (fifteen to forty-four years) in the United States are overweight.

- If you're obese, your BMI is 30.0 or higher before pregnancy. About one in four women (25 percent) is obese.

What kinds of pregnancy complications can overweight and obesity cause?

If you're overweight or obese, you're more likely than pregnant women at a healthy weight to have certain medical problems during pregnancy. The more overweight you are, the higher your risk for problems. These problems include:

- Infertility, not being able to get pregnant.

- Miscarriage, when a baby dies in the womb before twenty weeks of pregnancy.

- Stillbirth, when a baby dies in the womb before birth but after twenty weeks of pregnancy.

- High blood pressure and preeclampsia, a form of high blood pressure that only pregnant women get. It can cause serious problems for mom and baby.

- Gestational diabetes, diabetes that some women get during pregnancy.

- Complications during labor and birth, including having a really big baby (called large-for-gestational-age) or needing a cesarean section (c-section).

Some of these problems, like preeclampsia, can increase your chances of preterm birth. Preterm birth is birth before thirty-seven completed weeks of pregnancy. This is too soon and can cause serious health problems for your baby.

Can overweight and obesity during pregnancy cause problems for your baby?

Most babies of overweight and obese women are born healthy. But overweight and obesity during pregnancy can cause health problems for your baby. These include:

- Birth defects, including neural tube defects (NTDs). NTDs are birth defects of the brain and spine.

- Preterm birth.

- Injury, like shoulder dystocia, during birth because the baby is large.

- Death after birth.

- Being obese during childhood.

What can you do before pregnancy to improve your chances of having a healthy pregnancy and a healthy baby?

Get a preconception checkup. This is a medical checkup you get before pregnancy. Your health care provider can help you with ways to eat healthy and exercise. This can help you lose weight before you get pregnant.

What can you do during pregnancy to improve your chances of having a healthy pregnancy and a healthy baby?

Here's what you can do:

- Get early and regular prenatal care. Go to every checkup, even if you're feeling fine.

- Talk to your provider about how much weight to gain during pregnancy. Overweight women should gain about fifteen to twenty-five pounds during pregnancy. Obese women should gain about eleven to twenty pounds during pregnancy. Don't try to lose weight during pregnancy.

- Don't diet during pregnancy. Some diets can reduce the nutrients your baby needs for growth and health. Visit the special section of choosemyplate.gov that's just for pregnant women and breastfeeding moms. Or see a nutritionist to help you plan your meals.

- Exercise on most days. But talk to your provider before you start any exercise program. Walking, swimming, riding a stationary bike, or taking pregnancy aerobic or yoga classes are safe forms of exercise for pregnant women.

Does weight-loss surgery reduce your chances of pregnancy complications?

Yes. More than fifty thousand women each year in the United States have weight-loss surgery. Women who lose weight after weight-loss surgery are less likely than obese women who haven't had surgery to have fertility problems. They're also less likely to have pregnancy complications, like gestational diabetes and high blood pressure. And their babies are less likely to be born too early or with birth defects.

If you have weight-loss surgery, your provider may recommend that you wait at least one year after surgery before you try to get pregnant. You may lose a lot of weight really quickly during that year after surgery. If you're pregnant, this rapid weight loss could cause problems for your baby.

It's not common, but weight-loss surgery can cause pregnancy complications for some women. If you've had weight-loss surgery, tell your surgeon right away if you have pain in your belly during pregnancy. You may need to be checked for blocked intestines or similar problems.

Remember that you don't have to have weight-loss surgery to lose weight. Healthy eating, exercise, and other lifestyle changes can help you lose weight without surgery. Talk to your provider about your pregnancy plans and how weight-loss surgery may affect them.

Section 8.7

Phenylketonuria and Pregnancy

"Maternal PKU and Pregnancy," © 2010 Organization of Teratology Information Specialists (OTIS). Reprinted with permission. The OTIS website features fact sheets answering frequently asked questions about a wide variety of exposures during pregnancy and lactation. For the most current information, visit www.otispregnancy.org. Member programs of OTIS are located throughout the U.S. and Canada. To find the Teratogen Information Service in your area, call OTIS toll-free at 866-626-OTIS (866-626-6847), or visit www.otispregnancy.org.

This section talks about the risks that having phenylketonuria (PKU) can have during pregnancy. With each pregnancy, all women have a 3 to 5 percent chance of having a baby with a birth defect. This information should not take the place of medical care and advice from your health care provider.

What is PKU?

PKU stands for phenylketonuria, an inherited condition where the body is missing an enzyme that is needed to break down an amino acid called phenylalanine, or Phe for short. Since people with PKU cannot properly digest Phe, Phe and similar compounds build up in the body. This can lead to problems with brain development and mental retardation. However, treatment with a special diet can decrease the levels of Phe in the body so that this damage does not occur. Newborns in North American are checked for PKU at birth.

Is there any reason to continue the diet in adulthood?

Currently, medical professionals recommend staying on the diet life-long to ensure the healthiest development. It is particularly important for females with PKU to stay on the diet, since increased Phe levels during a pregnancy can cause problems for an unborn baby. This is referred to as maternal PKU effects. Since half of all pregnancies are not planned, it is especially important for women with PKU to maintain the diet even if they are not actively trying to get pregnant.

What effects do high levels of Phe have on a developing baby?

Babies born to mothers with untreated PKU (women who are not on the special diet) are commonly born smaller, have microcephaly (an abnormally small head), mental retardation, behavior problems, characteristic facial features similar to those of the fetal alcohol syndrome, and have higher risks of heart defects.

Is there anything I can do to prevent these effects?

The same diet you were on as a child can reduce your Phe levels, which in turn reduces the chance for your baby to have any of the problems related to maternal PKU. The goal is to get your Phe levels below 6 mg/dl (or 360 mol/l). Dietary control should start before conception, because it may take some women longer than others to get their Phe levels down. The diet should be continued throughout pregnancy.

One large study looked at over 550 pregnancies in women with PKU, some of which were on a restricted diet before conception and others who began the diet once the pregnancy was recognized. Babies born to mothers on the special diet before conception or before eight to ten weeks of pregnancy had similar brain development as babies born to women without PKU. Women who did not start the diet until after the first trimester (after twelve weeks of pregnancy) had babies who did poorer on developmental tests. Therefore, the special diet should be started as soon as possible in order to increase your chances of having a healthy baby.

It is important to talk to a dietician and a geneticist before getting pregnant; they will provide you with more specific information on the diet and will follow you throughout your pregnancy. Getting enough protein (other than Phe) and vitamins, especially vitamins from the B group like folic acid and vitamin B12, is also important for your baby's development.

I am eleven weeks pregnant. Will it help if I go on the diet now?

Yes. Your baby continues to grow and the brain develops throughout the pregnancy. Untreated PKU has a direct effect on growth and brain development. So, it is still a good idea to go on the diet and maintain low levels of Phe. However, the first twelve weeks of pregnancy are the critical period for the organs, including the heart, to form. Therefore, starting the diet after the first trimester does not lower the risk for birth defects. Consult a dietician and a geneticist as soon as possible when you find out you're pregnant.

What does the diet consist of?

The diet replaces foods containing high amounts of Phe, such as meats, dairy products, and nuts, with low-protein foods such as certain grain products, fruits, and some vegetables. There is also a special low-Phe formula to make sure that you will get the essential nutrients. A dietician or other health care professional familiar with PKU can provide you with more specific information on the diet.

Is there any treatment other than the diet that could help me to maintain low Phe levels during pregnancy?

In recent years, drugs and nutritional supplements, like sapropterin (Kuvan) and BH4 (tetrahydrobiopterin), have been used to help reduce blood Phe levels with or without a restricted diet. Not all people who have PKU will respond to these drugs.

Individual reports on seven pregnancies with restricted diet and sapropterin therapy have been promising. More studies are needed on the safety and efficacy of these treatments.

Is there any way to know if my baby will have problems related to maternal PKU?

A detailed ultrasound around eighteen to twenty weeks of pregnancy can look for a heart defect or a growth problem, including microcephaly. However, changes in learning and behavior cannot be seen before a baby is born.

Will my baby need to be on the diet?

Your baby will only need to be on the special low phenylalanine diet if he or she also has PKU. In all states and provinces in North America, newborns are tested for PKU before they leave the hospital.

Can I breastfeed my baby if I have PKU?

If the baby does not have PKU, breastfeeding is not a problem. If you stay on the diet after you deliver, the baby should not be exposed to high levels of Phe. Your doctor can also measure the Phe levels in the baby to make sure they are not elevated after breastfeeding.

Babies with PKU can be breastfed, but they need to be followed strictly by a dietician and a geneticist and their Phe blood level checked to make sure they receive the correct amount of phenylalanine. Alternating breastfeeding with a special PKU formula (with low Phe levels) is usually done. Different approaches are possible, depending on the experience of the medical team taking care of you and your baby.

What if the father of the baby has PKU?

There have been two small studies that suggest that there is no increased risk for birth defects when the father has PKU. In some men, PKU may reduce their fertility.

What is the chance that my baby will have PKU as I do?

A baby can only have PKU if both the mother and the father carry a specific genetic change for PKU. Since you have PKU, you have two nonworking genes for PKU, one from your mother and one from your father. You will always pass on one nonworking gene for PKU to your children. A person who has only one nonworking gene for PKU is called a carrier for PKU. Carriers of PKU are healthy.

If the father of the baby does not have PKU and is not a carrier, none of your children will have PKU, but they will all be carriers. However, if you have children with someone who is a carrier of PKU, then there is a 50 percent chance for each child to have PKU. Finally, if you have children with someone who also has PKU, all of your children will have PKU. Testing to find out if a partner is a carrier of PKU is possible in some families, and if the specific genetic change is found, prenatal testing may also be available. A genetic counselor or other health care professional can provide more information.

Selected References

American College of Obstetricians and Gynecologists Committee on Genetics. 2009. ACOG Committee Opinion no. 449: Maternal phenylketonuria. *Obstet Gynecol* 114(6):1432–33.

Burgard P, et al. 1997. Neuropsychologic functions of early treated patients with phenylketonuria, on and off Diet: Results of a cross-national and cross-sectional study. *Pediatr Res* 41(3):368–74.

Fisch RO, et al. 1991. Children of fathers with phenylketonuria: An international survey. *J Pediatr* 118(5): 739–41.

Fox-Bacon C, et al. 1997. Maternal PKU and breastfeeding: case report of identical twin mothers. *Clin Pediatr* 36(9):539–42.

Koch R, et al. 2003. The Maternal Phenylketonuria International Study: 1984–2002. *Pediatrics* 112(suppl): 1523–29.

Koch R, el al. 2005. Tetrahydrobiopterin and maternal PKU. *Mol Gen Met* 86: S139–41.

Koch R, et al. 2010. Psychosocial issues and outcomes in maternal PKU. *Mol Genet Metab.* 99 Suppl 1:S68–74.

Lenke RR and Levy HL. 1980. Maternal phenylketonuria and hyperphenylalaninemia: An international survey of the outcome of untreated and treated pregnancies. *NEJM* 303(21):1202–8.

Levy HL, et al. 1991. Paternal phenylketonuria. *J Pediatr* 118(5):741–43.

Levy HL, et al. 1996. Fetal ultrasonagraphy in maternal PKU. *Prenat Diagn* 16:599–604.

Michals-Matalon K et al. 2003. Role of nutrition in pregnancy with phenylketonuria and birth defects. *Pediatrics* 112(suppl): 1534–36.

Trefz FK, et al. 2003. Potential role of tetrahydrobiopterin in the treatment of maternal phenylketonuria. *Pediatrics* 112(suppl): 1566–69.

Rouse B, et al. 1997. Maternal phenylketonuria Collaborative Study (MPUCS) offspring: Facial anomalies, malformations, and early neurological sequelae. *Am J Med Genet* 69:89–95.

Schmidt E, et al. 1994. Sustained attention in adult phenylketonuria: the influence of the concurrent phenylalanine-bloodlevel. *J Clin Exp Neuropsych* 16(5):681–88.

Van Rijn M, et al. 2003. A different approach to breast-feeding of the infant with phenylketonuria. *Eur J Pediatr* 162:323–26.

Section 8.8

Thyroid Disease and Pregnancy

"Pregnancy and Thyroid Disease," National Institute of Diabetes and Digestive and Kidney Diseases, National Institutes of Health, April 2012.

What Is Thyroid Disease?

Thyroid disease is a disorder that affects the thyroid gland. Sometimes the body produces too much or too little thyroid hormone. Thyroid hormones regulate metabolism—the way the body uses energy—and affect nearly every organ in the body. Too much thyroid hormone is called hyperthyroidism and can cause many of the body's functions to speed up. Too little thyroid hormone is called hypothyroidism and can cause many of the body's functions to slow down.

Thyroid hormone plays a critical role during pregnancy both in the development of a healthy baby and in maintaining the health of the mother.

Women with thyroid problems can have a healthy pregnancy and protect their fetuses' health by learning about pregnancy's effect on the thyroid, keeping current on their thyroid function testing, and taking the required medications.

What Is the Thyroid?

The thyroid is a two-inch-long, butterfly-shaped gland weighing less than one ounce. Located in the front of the neck below the larynx, or voice box, it has two lobes, one on either side of the windpipe. The thyroid is one of the glands that make up the endocrine system. The glands of the endocrine system produce, store, and release hormones into the bloodstream. The hormones then travel through the body and direct the activity of the body's cells.

The thyroid gland makes two thyroid hormones, triiodothyronine (T3) and thyroxine (T4). T3 is the active hormone and is made from T4. Thyroid hormones affect metabolism, brain development, breathing, heart and nervous system functions, body temperature, muscle strength, skin dryness, menstrual cycles, weight, and cholesterol levels.

Thyroid hormone production is regulated by thyroid-stimulating hormone (TSH), which is made by the pituitary gland in the brain. When thyroid hormone levels in the blood are low, the pituitary releases more TSH. When thyroid hormone levels are high, the pituitary responds by decreasing TSH production.

How Does Pregnancy Normally Affect Thyroid Function?

Two pregnancy-related hormones—human chorionic gonadotropin (hCG) and estrogen—cause increased thyroid hormone levels in the blood. Made by the placenta, hCG is similar to TSH and mildly stimulates the thyroid to produce more thyroid hormone. Increased estrogen produces higher levels of thyroid-binding globulin, also known as thyroxine-binding globulin, a protein that transports thyroid hormone in the blood.

These normal hormonal changes can sometimes make thyroid function tests during pregnancy difficult to interpret.

Thyroid hormone is critical to normal development of the baby's brain and nervous system. During the first trimester, the fetus depends on the mother's supply of thyroid hormone, which comes through the placenta. At around twelve weeks, the baby's thyroid begins to function on its own.

The thyroid enlarges slightly in healthy women during pregnancy, but not enough to be detected by a physical exam. A noticeably enlarged thyroid can be a sign of thyroid disease and should be evaluated. Thyroid problems can be difficult to diagnose in pregnancy due to higher levels of thyroid hormone in the blood, increased thyroid size, fatigue, and other symptoms common to both pregnancy and thyroid disorders.

Hyperthyroidism

What Causes Hyperthyroidism in Pregnancy?

Hyperthyroidism in pregnancy is usually caused by Graves disease and occurs in about one of every five hundred pregnancies.[1] Graves disease is an autoimmune disorder. Normally, the immune system protects people from infection by identifying and destroying bacteria, viruses, and other potentially harmful foreign substances. But in autoimmune diseases, the immune system attacks the body's own cells and organs.

With Graves disease, the immune system makes an antibody called thyroid-stimulating immunoglobulin (TSI), sometimes called TSH receptor antibody, which mimics TSH and causes the thyroid to make too much thyroid hormone. In some people with Graves disease, this antibody is also associated with eye problems such as irritation, bulging, and puffiness.

Although Graves disease may first appear during pregnancy, a woman with preexisting Graves disease could actually see an improvement in her symptoms in her second and third trimesters. Remission—a disappearance of signs and symptoms—of Graves disease in later pregnancy may result from the general suppression of the immune system that occurs during pregnancy. The disease usually worsens again in the first few months after delivery. Pregnant women with Graves disease should be monitored monthly.[2]

Rarely, hyperthyroidism in pregnancy is caused by hyperemesis gravidarum—severe nausea and vomiting that can lead to weight loss and dehydration. This extreme nausea and vomiting is believed to be triggered by high levels of hCG, which can also lead to temporary hyperthyroidism that goes away during the second half of pregnancy.

How Does Hyperthyroidism Affect the Mother and Baby?

Uncontrolled hyperthyroidism during pregnancy can lead to any of the following:

- Congestive heart failure
- Preeclampsia—a dangerous rise in blood pressure in late pregnancy
- Thyroid storm—a sudden, severe worsening of symptoms
- Miscarriage
- Premature birth
- Low birth weight

If a woman has Graves disease or was treated for Graves disease in the past with surgery or radioactive iodine, the TSI antibodies can still be present in the blood, even when thyroid levels are normal. The TSI antibodies she produces may travel across the placenta to the baby's bloodstream and stimulate the fetal thyroid. If the mother is being treated with antithyroid medications, hyperthyroidism in the baby is less likely because these medications also cross the placenta.

Women who have had surgery or radioactive iodine treatment for Graves disease should inform their health care provider, so the baby can be monitored for thyroid-related problems later in the pregnancy.

Hyperthyroidism in a newborn can result in rapid heart rate, which can lead to heart failure; early closure of the soft spot in the skull; poor weight gain; irritability; and sometimes an enlarged thyroid that can press against the windpipe and interfere with breathing. Women with Graves disease and their newborns should be closely monitored by their health care team.

How Is Hyperthyroidism in Pregnancy Diagnosed?

Health care providers diagnose hyperthyroidism in pregnant women by reviewing symptoms and doing blood tests to measure TSH, T3, and T4 levels.

Some symptoms of hyperthyroidism are common features in normal pregnancies, including increased heart rate, heat intolerance, and fatigue.

Other symptoms are more closely associated with hyperthyroidism: rapid and irregular heartbeat, a slight tremor, unexplained weight loss or failure to have normal pregnancy weight gain, and the severe nausea and vomiting associated with hyperemesis gravidarum.

A blood test involves drawing blood at a health care provider's office or commercial facility and sending the sample to a lab for analysis. Diagnostic blood tests may include the following:

- **TSH test:** If a pregnant woman's symptoms suggest hyperthyroidism, her doctor will probably first perform the ultrasensitive TSH test. This test detects even tiny amounts of TSH in the blood and is the most accurate measure of thyroid activity available. Generally, below-normal levels of TSH indicate hyperthyroidism. However, low TSH levels may also occur in a normal pregnancy, especially in the first trimester, due to the small increase in thyroid hormones from HCG.

- **T3 and T4 test:** If TSH levels are low, another blood test is performed to measure T3 and T4. Elevated levels of free T4—the portion of thyroid hormone not attached to thyroid-binding protein—confirm the diagnosis. Rarely, in a woman with hyperthyroidism, free T4 levels can be normal but T3 levels are high. Because of normal pregnancy-related changes in thyroid function, test results must be interpreted with caution.

- **TSI test:** If a woman has Graves disease or has had surgery or radioactive iodine treatment for the disease, her doctor may also test her blood for the presence of TSI antibodies.

How Is Hyperthyroidism Treated During Pregnancy?

During pregnancy, mild hyperthyroidism, in which TSH is low but free T4 is normal, does not require treatment. More severe hyperthyroidism is treated with antithyroid medications, which act by interfering with thyroid hormone production.

Radioactive iodine treatment is not an option for pregnant women because it can damage the fetal thyroid gland. Rarely, surgery to remove all or part of the thyroid gland is considered for women who cannot tolerate antithyroid medications.

Antithyroid medications cross the placenta in small amounts and can decrease fetal thyroid hormone production, so the lowest possible dose should be used to avoid hypothyroidism in the baby.

Antithyroid medications can cause side effects in some people, including the following:

- Allergic reactions such as rashes and itching

- A decrease in the number of white blood cells in the body, which can lower a person's resistance to infection

- Liver failure, in rare cases

Stop your antithyroid medication and call your health care provider right away if you develop any of the following signs and symptoms while taking antithyroid medications:

- Fatigue

- Weakness

- Vague abdominal pain

- Loss of appetite

- A skin rash or itching

- Easy bruising

- Yellowing of the skin or whites of the eyes, called jaundice

- Persistent sore throat

- Fever

In the United States, health care providers prescribe the antithyroid medication methimazole (Tapazole, Northyx) for most types of hyperthyroidism.

Experts agree that women in their first trimester of pregnancy should probably not take methimazole due to the rare occurrence of damage to the fetus. Another antithyroid medication, propylthiouracil (PTU), is available for women in this stage of pregnancy or for women who are allergic to or intolerant of methimazole and have no other treatment options.

Health care providers may prescribe PTU for the first trimester of pregnancy and switch to methimazole for the second and third trimesters.

Some women are able to stop antithyroid medication therapy in the last four to eight weeks of pregnancy due to the remission of hyperthyroidism that occurs during pregnancy. However, these women should continue to be monitored for recurrence of thyroid problems following delivery.

Studies have shown that mothers taking antithyroid medications may safely breastfeed. However, they should take only moderate doses, less than ten to twenty milligrams daily, of the antithyroid medication methimazole. Doses should be divided and taken after feedings, and the infants should be monitored for side effects.[2]

Women requiring higher doses of the antithyroid medication to control hyperthyroidism should not breastfeed.

Hypothyroidism

What Causes Hypothyroidism in Pregnancy?

Hypothyroidism in pregnancy is usually caused by Hashimoto disease and occurs in three to five out of every thousand pregnancies.[2] Hashimoto disease is a form of chronic inflammation of the thyroid gland.

Like Graves disease, Hashimoto disease is an autoimmune disorder. In Hashimoto disease, the immune system attacks the thyroid, causing inflammation and interfering with its ability to produce thyroid hormones.

Hypothyroidism in pregnancy can also result from existing hypothyroidism that is inadequately treated or from prior destruction or removal of the thyroid as a treatment for hyperthyroidism.

How Does Hypothyroidism Affect the Mother and Baby?

Some of the same problems caused by hyperthyroidism can occur with hypothyroidism. Uncontrolled hypothyroidism during pregnancy can lead to the following:

- Preeclampsia

- Anemia—too few red blood cells in the body, which prevents the body from getting enough oxygen

- Miscarriage
- Low birth weight
- Stillbirth
- Congestive heart failure, rarely

Because thyroid hormones are crucial to fetal brain and nervous system development, uncontrolled hypothyroidism—especially during the first trimester—can affect the baby's growth and brain development.

How Is Hypothyroidism in Pregnancy Diagnosed?

Like hyperthyroidism, hypothyroidism is diagnosed through a careful review of symptoms and measurement of TSH and T4 levels.

Symptoms of hypothyroidism in pregnancy include extreme fatigue, cold intolerance, muscle cramps, constipation, and problems with memory or concentration. High levels of TSH and low levels of free T4 generally indicate hypothyroidism. Because of normal pregnancy-related changes in thyroid function, test results must be interpreted with caution.

The TSH test can also identify subclinical hypothyroidism—a mild form of hypothyroidism that has no apparent symptoms. Subclinical hypothyroidism occurs in 2 to 3 percent of pregnancies.[2] Test results will show high levels of TSH and normal free T4.

Experts differ in their opinions as to whether asymptomatic pregnant women should be routinely screened for hypothyroidism. But if subclinical hypothyroidism is discovered during pregnancy, treatment is recommended to help ensure a healthy pregnancy.

How Is Hypothyroidism Treated During Pregnancy?

Hypothyroidism is treated with synthetic thyroid hormone called thyroxine—a medication which is identical to the T4 made by the thyroid. Women with preexisting hypothyroidism will need to increase their prepregnancy dose of thyroxine to maintain normal thyroid function. Thyroid function should be checked every six to eight weeks during pregnancy. Synthetic thyroxine is safe and necessary for the well-being of the fetus if the mother has hypothyroidism.

Eating, Diet, and Nutrition

During pregnancy, the body requires higher amounts of some nutrients to support the health of the mother and growing baby. Experts recommend pregnant women maintain a balanced diet and take a prenatal multivitamin and mineral supplement containing iodine to receive most nutrients necessary for thyroid health.

Dietary Supplements

Because the thyroid uses iodine to make thyroid hormone, iodine is an important mineral for a mother during pregnancy. During pregnancy, the baby gets iodine from the mother's diet. Women need more iodine when they are pregnant—about 250 micrograms a day. In the United States, about 7 percent of pregnant women may not get enough iodine in their diet or through prenatal vitamins.[3] Choosing iodized salt—salt supplemented with iodine—over plain salt and prenatal vitamins containing iodine will ensure this need is met.

However, people with autoimmune thyroid disease may be sensitive to harmful side effects from iodine. Taking iodine drops or eating foods containing large amounts of iodine—such as seaweed, dulse, or kelp—may cause or worsen hyperthyroidism and hypothyroidism.

To help ensure coordinated and safe care, people should discuss their use of dietary supplements with their health care provider.

Postpartum Thyroiditis

What Is Postpartum Thyroiditis?

Postpartum thyroiditis is an inflammation of the thyroid that affects about 4 to 10 percent of women during the first year after giving birth.[2] Thyroiditis causes stored thyroid hormone to leak out of the inflamed thyroid gland and raise hormone levels in the blood.

Postpartum thyroiditis is believed to be an autoimmune condition and causes mild hyperthyroidism that usually lasts one to two months. Many women then develop hypothyroidism lasting six to twelve months before the thyroid regains normal function. In some women, the thyroid is too damaged to regain normal function and their hypothyroidism is permanent, requiring lifelong treatment with synthetic thyroid hormone. Postpartum thyroiditis is likely to recur with future pregnancies.

Postpartum thyroiditis often goes undiagnosed because the symptoms are mistaken for postpartum blues—the exhaustion and moodiness that sometimes follow delivery. If symptoms of fatigue and lethargy do not go away within a few months or a woman develops postpartum depression, she should talk with her health care provider. If the hypothyroid symptoms are bothersome, thyroid medication can be given.

Points to Remember

- Thyroid disease is a disorder that results when the thyroid gland produces more or less thyroid hormone than the body needs.

- Pregnancy causes normal changes in thyroid function but can also lead to thyroid disease.

- Uncontrolled hyperthyroidism during pregnancy can lead to serious health problems in the mother and the unborn baby.

- During pregnancy, mild hyperthyroidism does not require treatment. More severe hyperthyroidism is treated with antithyroid medications, which act by interfering with thyroid hormone production.

- Uncontrolled hypothyroidism during pregnancy can lead to serious health problems in the mother and can affect the unborn baby's growth and brain development.

- Hypothyroidism during pregnancy is treated with synthetic thyroid hormone, thyroxine (T4).

- Postpartum thyroiditis—inflammation of the thyroid gland— causes a brief period of hyperthyroidism, often followed by hypothyroidism that usually goes away within a year. Sometimes the hypothyroidism is permanent.

Hope through Research

The National Institute of Diabetes and Digestive and Kidney Diseases (NIDDK) conducts and supports research into many kinds of disorders, including thyroid disease. Researchers are investigating the development, signs and symptoms, and genetics of thyroid function disorders to further understand thyroid diseases. Scientists continue to study treatment options for pregnant women with thyroid disorders, as well as long-term outcomes for mothers and their children.

Participants in clinical trials can play a more active role in their own health care, gain access to new research treatments before they are widely available, and help others by contributing to medical research.

Notes

1. Komal PS, Mestman JH. Graves hyperthyroidism and pregnancy: a clinical update. *Endocrine Practice*. 2010;16(1):118–29.

2.   Ogunyemi DA. Autoimmune thyroid disease and pregnancy. eMedicine website. www.emedicine.medscape.com/article/261913-overview. Updated April 23, 2010. Accessed August 11, 2011.

3.   Zimmerman MB. Iodine deficiency in pregnancy and the effects of maternal iodine supplementation on the offspring: a review. *American Journal of Clinical Nutrition.* 2009;89(2):668S–672S.

Chapter 9

Infectious Diseases with Adverse Fetal Effects

Chapter Contents

Section 9.1

Chickenpox and Pregnancy

Excerpted from Centers for Disease
Control and Prevention, May 31, 2011.

Pregnant women who get chickenpox are at risk for serious complications. For example, 10 to 20 percent of pregnant women who get chickenpox develop pneumonia, with the chance of death as high as 40 percent.

If a pregnant woman gets chickenpox while in the first or early second trimester of pregnancy, there is a small chance (0.4 to 2.0 percent) that the baby could be born with birth defects known as "congenital varicella syndrome." Babies born with congenital varicella syndrome may be of low birth weight and have scarring of the skin and problems with arms, legs, brain, and eyes.

Newborns whose mothers develop chickenpox rash from five days before to two days after delivery are at risk for chickenpox shortly after birth, with the chance of death as high as 30 percent.

Prevention

- All pregnant women should talk to a health care provider to determine if they are protected against chickenpox. For pregnant women, any of the following are evidence of protection against chickenpox:

  - Documentation of two doses of varicella vaccine

  - Blood test showing immunity to varicella

  - Diagnosis or verification by a health care provider of a history of chickenpox or herpes zoster, also known as shingles

- If a pregnant woman has never had the chickenpox, the best way to protect against chickenpox is to get the chickenpox vaccine. However, women should not receive the chickenpox vaccine during pregnancy. As soon as a pregnant woman who is not protected against chickenpox delivers her baby, she should be vaccinated against chickenpox. The first dose of vaccine can be given before she leaves the hospital and the second dose at the six- to eight-week postpartum visit. The vaccine is safe even for mothers who are nursing.

- Women who are thinking about getting pregnant but are not protected against chickenpox should get vaccinated at least one to three months before becoming pregnant. Women should not get vaccinated during pregnancy or during the thirty days before becoming pregnant.

- If a pregnant woman is not protected against chickenpox, people who live with her should be protected. If close contacts have not already had chickenpox, vaccination of these contacts is the most effective way to protect a pregnant woman against chickenpox.

- Pregnant women should stay away from anyone who has chickenpox. This includes people who have been vaccinated and then get a very mild form of chickenpox, sometimes called "breakthrough" chickenpox (usually little or no fever and fewer than fifty skin lesions). "Breakthrough" chickenpox is still contagious.

- If a pregnant woman is not protected against chickenpox and finds out that she has been in contact with someone who has chickenpox, she should call her doctor immediately.

Symptoms

Chickenpox rash usually appears first on the face and top half of the body, but can spread over the entire body causing 250 to 500 itchy blisters in people who have never been vaccinated against chickenpox. In people who have been vaccinated, the rash can be quite mild, such as only a few spots that look like mosquito bites.

Chickenpox illness lasts about five to ten days. Other symptoms include high fever, severe itching, uncomfortable rash, dehydration from vomiting or diarrhea, headache, infected skin lesions, worsening of asthma or more serious complications such as pneumonia.

Certain groups of persons are more likely to have more serious illness with complications. These include adults, infants, adolescents, and people with weak immune systems from either illnesses or from medications, such a long-term use of steroids.

Serious complications from chickenpox include bacterial infections that can involve many sites of the body, including the skin, tissues under the skin, bone, lungs (pneumonia), joints, and blood. Other serious complications are due directly to the virus infection and include viral pneumonia, bleeding problems, and infection of the brain (encephalitis).

Section 9.2

Cytomegalovirus and Pregnancy

"Cytomegalovirus (CMV) and Pregnancy,"
Centers for Disease Control and Prevention, June 21, 2011.

CMV, or cytomegalovirus, is a common virus that infects people of all ages. Once CMV is in a person's body, it stays there for life. Most infections with CMV are "silent," meaning most people who are infected with CMV have no signs or symptoms. However, CMV can cause disease in unborn babies.

CMV is spread through:

- person-to-person contact (such as kissing, sexual contact, and getting saliva or urine on your hands and then touching your eyes, or the inside of your nose or mouth);

- Breast milk of an infected woman who is breast feeding;

- Infected pregnant women, who can pass the virus to their unborn babies;

- Blood transfusions and organ transplantations.

Prevention

Pregnant women may want to take steps to reduce their risk of exposure to CMV and so reduce the risk of CMV infection of their fetus. Here are a few simple steps you can take to avoid exposure to saliva and urine that might contain CMV:

- Wash your hands often with soap and water for fifteen to twenty seconds, especially after doing any of the following:
  - Changing diapers
  - Feeding a young child
  - Wiping a young child's nose or drool
  - Handling children's toys
- Do not share food, drinks, or eating utensils used by young children.

- Do not put a child's pacifier in your mouth.

- Do not share a toothbrush with a young child.

- Avoid contact with saliva when kissing a child.

- Clean toys, countertops, and other surfaces that come into contact with children's urine or saliva.

People who work closely with children in settings, such as child care facilities, may be at greater risk of CMV infection than persons who do not work in such settings. If you are pregnant and work with children, follow standard hand-washing procedures after contact with body fluids, such as urine and saliva, that could contain CMV.

Symptoms

Most healthy children and adults infected with CMV have no symptoms and may not even know that they have been infected. Others may develop a mild illness. Symptoms may include fever, sore throat, fatigue, and swollen glands. These symptoms are similar to those of other illnesses, so most people are not aware that they are infected with CMV.

Most babies born with CMV (in other words, "congenital" CMV) never develop symptoms or disabilities. When babies do have symptoms, some can go away but others can be permanent.

Examples of symptoms or disabilities caused by congenital (meaning present at birth) CMV are listed here.

Temporary symptoms include the following:

- Liver problems

- Spleen problems

- Jaundice (yellow skin and eyes)

- Purple skin splotches

- Lung problems

- Small size at birth

- Seizures

Permanent symptoms or disabilities include the following:

- Hearing loss

- Vision loss

149

- Mental disability
- Small head
- Lack of coordination
- Seizures
- Death

Treatment

Currently, no treatment is recommended for CMV infection in healthy pregnant women. Vaccines for preventing CMV infection are still in the research and development stage.

Section 9.3

Listeriosis and Pregnancy

Excerpted from "Listeriosis (Listeria) and Pregnancy,"
Centers for Disease Control and Prevention, December 1, 2011.

Listeria is a type of bacteria found in soil, water, and sometimes on plants. Though *Listeria* is all around our environment, most *Listeria* infections in people are from eating contaminated foods.

Listeriosis can be passed to an unborn baby through the placenta even if the mother is not showing signs of illness. This can lead to any of the following:

- Premature delivery
- Miscarriage
- Stillbirth
- Serious health problems for the newborn

Prevention

The U.S. Department of Agriculture's (USDA's) Food Safety and Inspection Service (FSIS) and the U.S. Food and Drug Administration (FDA) provide the following advice for pregnant women:

- Do not eat hot dogs, luncheon meats, or deli meats unless they are reheated until steaming hot.

- Avoid getting fluid from hot dog packages on other foods, utensils, and food preparation surfaces, and wash hands after handling hot dogs, luncheon meats, and deli meats.

- Do not eat soft cheeses such as feta, Brie, and Camembert, blue-veined cheeses, or Mexican-style cheeses such as queso blanco, queso fresco, and Panela, unless they have labels that clearly state they are made from pasteurized milk. It is safe to eat hard cheeses, semi-soft cheeses such as mozzarella, pasteurized processed cheese slices and spreads, cream cheese, and cottage cheese.

- Do not eat refrigerated pâté or meat spreads. It is safe to eat canned or shelf-stable pâté and meat spreads.

- Do not eat refrigerated smoked seafood unless it is an ingredient in a cooked dish such as a casserole. Examples of refrigerated smoked seafood include salmon, trout, whitefish, cod, tuna, and mackerel, which are most often labeled as "nova-style," "lox," "kippered," "smoked," or "jerky." This fish is found in the refrigerated section or sold at deli counters of grocery stores and delicatessens. It is safe to eat canned fish such as salmon and tuna or shelf-stable smoked seafood.

- Do not drink raw (unpasteurized) milk or eat foods that contain unpasteurized milk.

- Use all refrigerated perishable items that are precooked or ready-to-eat as soon as possible.

- Clean your refrigerator regularly.

- Use a refrigerator thermometer to make sure that the refrigerator always stays at 40 °F or below.

Symptoms

In pregnant women, listeriosis may cause flu-like symptoms:

- Fever
- Chills
- Muscle aches
- Diarrhea
- Upset stomach

If the infection spreads to the nervous system, the symptoms may include the following:

- Headache
- Stiff neck
- Confusion
- Loss of balance
- Convulsions

Consult a doctor or health care provider if you have these symptoms. A blood test can be performed to find out if your symptoms are caused by listeriosis.

Treatment

If you have eaten food contaminated with *Listeria* and do not have any symptoms, most experts believe you don't need any tests or treatment, even if you are pregnant.

However, you should tell your physician or health care provider if you are pregnant and have eaten the contaminated food, and within two months experience flu-like symptoms.

During pregnancy, antibiotics are given to treat listeriosis in the mother. In most cases, the antibiotics also prevent infection of the fetus or newborn. Antibiotics are also given to babies who are born with listeriosis.

Section 9.4

Lymphocytic Choriomeningitis Virus and Pregnancy

Excerpted from "Lymphocytic Choriomeningitis Virus (LCMV) and Pregnancy," Centers for Disease Control and Prevention, April 1, 2010.

Lymphocytic choriomeningitis virus (LCMV) is a virus that can cause infection in animals and humans. Wild mice can carry LCMV and infect pet rodents, such as hamsters, pet mice, and guinea pigs. People can be infected through contact with urine, blood, saliva, droppings, or nesting materials of infected rodents.

If a woman has an LCMV infection while pregnant the unborn baby can also become infected. LCMV infection can cause severe birth defects or loss of the pregnancy (miscarriage).

Prevention

The risk of LCMV infection is low. Women who are pregnant or planning to become pregnant should avoid contact with wild or pet rodents, such as hamsters, pet mice, and guinea pigs.

Here are some steps to reduce the risk of LCMV infection during pregnancy:

- If there might be mice in your home, call a professional pest control company to control them or have someone else remove them.

- Avoid vacuuming or sweeping rodent urine, droppings, or nesting materials.

- Ask a friend or family member who does not live within the house to care for pet rodents in his or her home while you are pregnant. If this is not possible, keep the pet rodent in a separate part of the home and have another family member or friend care for the pet and clean its cage. Avoid being in the same room where the rodent is kept.

- After contact with a wild rodent or its urine, droppings, or nesting materials, wash hands very well with soap and water afterwards.

Treatment

Currently, there is no treatment available for LCMV infection. Pregnant women who have come in contact with a rodent, or have fever or other symptoms during pregnancy, should contact the doctor.

A blood test is available to detect current or previous LCMV infection. Having had LCMV infection in the past is not a risk for current or future pregnancies.

Section 9.5

Rubella (German Measles) and Pregnancy

"Rubella (German Measles) and Pregnancy," excerpted from *Infectious Diseases in Childcare Settings and Schools Manual,* http://www.hennepin.us/childcaremanual, © 2012 Hennepin County Human Services and Public Health Department. Reprinted with permission.

What is rubella?

Rubella (German measles) is usually a mild viral infection. Symptoms include generalized skin rash, tiredness, headache, fever, and swollen glands in the area behind the ears and the neck (lymphadenopathy). It is estimated that 25 to 50 percent of persons infected with rubella may not have any symptoms.

What illness does rubella infection cause? Is this illness serious?

Rubella is usually a mild illness. However, there may be severe illness in adults who have not had the disease in the past or have not had the vaccine. Joint stiffness and/or joint pain may occur in up to 70 percent of adult women infected with rubella. Some of the other problems that may occur include a bleeding problem called thrombocytopenia and infection of the brain (encephalitis). If a woman gets rubella during her pregnancy, congenital rubella syndrome (CRS) may occur and result in miscarriage, stillbirth, and severe birth defects. A baby with CRS may have blindness, heart defects, deafness, and mental retardation.

I've been exposed to someone with rubella. How will this exposure affect my pregnancy?

It is recommended that all women be tested for rubella early in their pregnancy. An estimated 90 percent of young adults in the United States are immune to rubella (most likely through vaccination). If you are immune and have been exposed, there is no concern. However, about 25 percent of babies whose mothers get rubella during the first three months of her pregnancy are likely to develop a fetal infection and are likely to have congenital rubella syndrome (CRS) as described above. After the twentieth week of pregnancy if a woman develops rubella, most likely there will not be any problems for either the mother or the unborn baby.

What should I do about this exposure?

If you know that you are immune to rubella (have had a blood test to show that you have antibodies to rubella), you do not need to be concerned about the exposure. If you are not immune to rubella and have been exposed to someone with rubella or have developed a rash illness that might be rubella, you should call your health care provider. They will do a blood test to see if you have become infected with the virus.

I have had a blood test for rubella. What do the results of the blood test show?

The blood test for rubella may show that you:

- Are immune (had rubella disease or vaccine in the past) and have no sign of recent infection. You are protected from rubella.

- Are not immune and have not yet been infected. You may wish to avoid anyone with rubella during your pregnancy.

- Have or had a recent infection. You should discuss what the risks are based on your stage of pregnancy with your health care provider.

If I'm infected or have been exposed, what do I need to do about my pregnancy?

Talk to your health care provider. Recommendations will depend on the stage of your pregnancy.

155

Is there a way I can keep from being infected with rubella during my pregnancy?

If you are not pregnant and not immune, all adults working with children should know their vaccine history or immune status. If you are not immune, you should be vaccinated with MMR (measles, mumps, and rubella) vaccine.

When you are given the vaccine you should avoid becoming pregnant for at least one month after immunization. Rubella vaccine should not be given to pregnant women.

If you are pregnant, you should receive MMR vaccine after your baby is delivered.

Section 9.6

Sexually Transmitted Diseases (STDs) and Pregnancy

"STDs and Pregnancy: CDC Fact Sheet,"
Centers for Disease Control and Prevention, February 27, 2012.

Can pregnant women become infected with STDs?

Yes, women who are pregnant can become infected with the same sexually transmitted diseases (STDs) as women who are not pregnant. Pregnancy does not provide women or their babies any protection against STDs. The consequences of an STD can be significantly more serious, even life threatening, for a woman and her baby if the woman becomes infected with an STD while pregnant. It is important that women be aware of the harmful effects of STDs and know how to protect themselves and their children against infection.

How common are STDs in pregnant women in the United States?

Some STDs, such as genital herpes and bacterial vaginosis, are quite common in pregnant women in the United States. Other STDs, notably human immunodeficiency virus (HIV) and syphilis, are much less common in pregnant women. Table 9.1 shows the estimated number of pregnant women in the United States who are infected with specific STDs each year.

How do STDs affect a pregnant woman and her baby?

STDs can have many of the same consequences for pregnant women as for women who are not pregnant. STDs can cause cervical and other cancers, chronic hepatitis, pelvic inflammatory disease, infertility, and other complications. Many STDs in women are silent; that is, without signs or symptoms.

Table 9.1. Pregnant Women with Sexually Transmitted Diseases (U.S.)

STDs	Estimated Number of Pregnant Women Infected Each Year
Bacterial vaginosis	1,080,000
Herpes simplex virus 2	880,000
Chlamydia	100,000
Trichomoniasis	124,000
Gonorrhea	13,200
Hepatitis B	16,000
HIV	6,400
Syphilis	<1,000

STDs can be passed from a pregnant woman to the baby before, during, or after the baby's birth. Some STDs (like syphilis) cross the placenta and infect the baby while it is in the uterus (womb). Other STDs (like gonorrhea, chlamydia, hepatitis B, and genital herpes) can be transmitted from the mother to the baby during delivery as the baby passes through the birth canal. HIV can cross the placenta during pregnancy, can infect the baby during the birth process, and unlike most other STDs, can infect the baby through breastfeeding.

A pregnant woman with an STD may also have early onset of labor, premature rupture of the membranes surrounding the baby in the uterus, and uterine infection after delivery.

The harmful effects of STDs in babies may include stillbirth (a baby that is born dead), low birth weight (less than five pounds), conjunctivitis (eye infection), pneumonia, neonatal sepsis (infection in the baby's blood stream), neurologic damage, blindness, deafness, acute hepatitis, meningitis, chronic liver disease, and cirrhosis. Most of these problems can be prevented if the mother receives routine prenatal care, which includes screening tests for STDs starting early in pregnancy and repeated close to delivery, if necessary. Other problems can be treated if the infection is found at birth.

Should pregnant women be tested for STDs?

Yes, STDs affect women of every socioeconomic and educational level, age, race, ethnicity, and religion. The CDC 2010 Sexually Transmitted Diseases Treatment Guidelines recommend that pregnant women be screened on their first prenatal visit for STDs, which may include the following:

- Chlamydia
- Gonorrhea
- Hepatitis B
- HIV
- Syphilis

Pregnant women should ask their doctors about getting tested for these STDs, since some doctors do not routinely perform these tests. New and increasingly accurate tests continue to become available. Even if a woman has been tested in the past, she should be tested again when she becomes pregnant.

Can STDs be treated during pregnancy?

Chlamydia, gonorrhea, syphilis, trichomoniasis, and bacterial vaginosis (BV) can be treated and cured with antibiotics during pregnancy. There is no cure for viral STDs, such as genital herpes and HIV, but antiviral medication may be appropriate for pregnant women with herpes and definitely is for those with HIV. For women who have active genital herpes lesions at the time of delivery, a cesarean delivery (C-section) may be performed to protect the newborn against infection. C-section is also an option for some HIV-infected women. Women who test negative for hepatitis B may receive the hepatitis B vaccine during pregnancy.

How can pregnant women protect themselves against infection?

The surest way to avoid transmission of sexually transmitted diseases is to abstain from sexual contact, or to be in a long-term mutually monogamous relationship with a partner who has been tested and is known to be uninfected.

Latex condoms, when used consistently and correctly, are highly effective in preventing transmission of HIV, the virus that causes acquired immune deficiency syndrome (AIDS). Latex condoms, when used consistently and correctly, can reduce the risk of transmission of gonorrhea, chlamydia, and trichomoniasis Correct and consistent use of latex condoms can reduce the risk of genital herpes, syphilis, and chancroid only when the infected area or site of potential exposure is protected by the condom. Correct and consistent use of latex condoms may reduce the risk for genital human papillomavirus (HPV) and associated diseases (e.g., warts and cervical cancer).

Section 9.7

Toxoplasmosis and Pregnancy

Excerpted from "While You're Pregnant: Toxoplasma,"
U.S. Food and Drug Administration, October 25, 2011.

What Is Toxoplasma Gondii?

It's a parasite found in raw and undercooked meat, unwashed fruits and vegetables, water, dust, soil, dirty cat-litter boxes, and outdoor places where cat feces can be found. It can cause an illness called toxoplasmosis that can be particularly harmful to you and your unborn baby.

How Could I Get Toxoplasmosis?

You could get this illness by doing the following things:

- Eating raw or undercooked meat, especially pork, lamb, or venison, or by touching your hands to your mouth after handling undercooked meat.

- Using contaminated knives, utensils, cutting boards, and other foods that have had contact with raw meat.

- Drinking water contaminated with *T. gondii.*

- Accidentally ingesting contaminated cat feces, which can occur if you touch your hands to your mouth after gardening, cleaning a litter box, or touching anything that comes in contact with cat feces.

How Could Toxoplasmosis Affect Me?

Symptoms typically include: swollen glands, fever, headache, muscle pain, or a stiff neck. Toxoplasmosis can be difficult to detect. Some women infected with the parasite may not have noticeable symptoms, so a pregnant woman can easily expose her fetus to toxoplasmosis without even being aware that she's ill. That's why prevention of toxoplasmosis is very important. If you do experience any of the above symptoms, see your doctor or health care provider immediately.

How Can Toxoplasmosis Affect My Baby?

In babies, *T. gondii* can cause hearing loss, mental retardation, and blindness. Some children can develop brain or eye problems years after birth. Children born infected with *T. gondii* can also require years of special care, including special education and ophthalmology visits. Early identification and treatment of children infected with *T. gondii* is essential in order to minimize the parasite's effects.

How Can I Prevent Toxoplasmosis?

It's easy—you and your family should do the following things. Clean:

- Wash your hands with soap and warm water after touching soil, sand, raw meat, cat litter, or unwashed vegetables.

- Wash all cutting boards and knives thoroughly with soap and hot water after each use.

- Thoroughly wash and/or peel all fruits and vegetables before eating them.

Separate:

- Separate raw meat from other foods in your grocery shopping cart, refrigerator, and while preparing and handling foods at home.

Cook:

- Cook meat thoroughly. The internal temperature of the meat should reach 160° F (71° C). Use a food thermometer to check.
- Don't sample meat until it's cooked.

Don't Drink the Water!

Avoid drinking untreated water, particularly when traveling in less-developed countries.

For Cat Lovers

Don't give "Fluffy" away, but be aware that *T. gondii* infects essentially all cats that spend any time outdoors. Cats get this parasite by eating small animals or raw meat that's been infected. The parasite is then passed on through the cat's feces. It doesn't make the cat sick, so a pregnant woman may not know if her cat has it.

Follow these tips:

- If possible, have someone else change the litter box. If you have to clean it, wear disposable gloves and wash your hands thoroughly with soap and warm water afterwards.

- Change the litter box daily. The parasite doesn't become infectious until one to five days after it's shed in the feces.

- Wear gloves when gardening in a garden or handling sand from a sandbox because cats may have excreted feces in them. Be sure to wash your hands with soap and warm water afterwards.

- Cover outdoor sandboxes to prevent cats from using them as litter boxes.

- Feed your cat commercial dry or canned food. Never feed your cat raw meat because it can be a source of the *T. gondii* parasite.

- Keep indoor cats indoors. Be especially cautious if you bring outdoor cats indoors.

- Avoid stray cats, especially kittens.

- Don't get a new cat while you're pregnant.

Note: If you have a cat and are concerned about exposure to *Toxoplasma*, talk to your doctor or health care provider.

Chapter 10

Amniotic Fluid Disorders

Chapter Contents

Section 10.1

Amniotic Band Syndrome

"Amniotic Band Syndrome," by Dr. Mike (Emanuel) Vlastos, M.D., Director, St. Louis Fetal Care Institute. © 2013. All rights reserved. Reprinted with permission. To learn about the advanced diagnostic and treatment options available at St. Louis Fetal Care Institute for amniotic band syndrome and other fetal conditions and abnormalities, visit www.cardinalglennon.com/fetalcareinstitute.

What is amniotic band syndrome and what causes it?

Amnion is a membrane that surrounds the baby in utero. If it ruptures, strands of amnion can end up floating in the amniotic fluid. These strands can attach to the baby's developing body parts and cause injury. This is known as amniotic band syndrome.

Untreated, the bands become tighter around the body part they are attached to, which is why amniotic band syndrome often leads to amputation, severe deformity of limbs, webbed toes or fingers, or severe defects of the head, face, or spine. It is rare, occurring in one out of every one thousand to two thousand births.

No one knows for certain exactly what causes amniotic band syndrome, but many physicians and researchers agree that it starts with the rupture of the amnion (a thin sac that forms around the fetus that protects it) early in pregnancy. Bands of amnion then encircle parts of the fetus's body. The rupture of the amnion appears to be random and is not related to anything the mother did or did not do during pregnancy. Further, even if it has occurred in a previous pregnancy, it is unlikely to occur again in another pregnancy.

How is amniotic band syndrome diagnosed?

A routine prenatal ultrasound, as early as twelve weeks of gestation, can show the primary effects of the band on the affected extremity. Your doctor can then use Doppler blood flow studies to measure how severely the blood flow is restricted. The side effects can range from mild to severe, from swollen limbs to absent limbs or digits.

How is amniotic band syndrome managed and treated during pregnancy?

Your doctor will examine each case of amniotic band syndrome closely to confirm that the condition is actually amniotic band syndrome (ABS), and not a uterine fold. If your doctor finds an amniotic band, your doctor will find the best way to prevent progressive injury.

If the amniotic band is touching an area of the baby but not causing injury or cutting off blood flow, no surgery is necessary. If your doctor finds that the amniotic band is threatening the baby's life by impeding blood flow to a limb, entangling the umbilical cord, or threatening to cause a severe deforming or facial problem, he or she can do fetoscopic surgery.

During this surgery, the surgeon inserts a pencil-tip-sized telescope in the mother's uterus and uses a laser to cut the amniotic band. This procedure immediately reduces the pressure on the affected extremity and allows it to develop normally, without any further damage.

What happens after surgery?

After surgery, your doctor will follow the patient closely throughout the pregnancy to monitor the affected extremity. Fetal surgery does have risks, including preterm labor, infection, and bleeding, but your doctor can treat you with medications to reduce the risk of these complications.

After a baby with ABS is born, the affected body part will be examined by a plastic surgeon and orthopedic specialist to determine if any additional treatment is needed.

Section 10.2

Oligohydramnios

"Low Amniotic Fluid Levels: Oligohydramnios," © 2007 American Pregnancy Association (www.americanpregnancy.org). All rights reserved. Reprinted with permission. Reviewed by David A. Cooke, M.D., FACP, January 2013.

The amniotic fluid is part of the baby's life support system. It protects your baby and aids in the development of muscles, limbs, lungs, and digestive system. Amniotic fluid is produced soon after the amniotic sac forms at about twelve days after conception. It is first made up of water that is provided by the mother, and then around twenty weeks fetal urine becomes the primary substance. As the baby grows he or she will move and tumble in the womb with the help of the amniotic fluid. In the second trimester the baby will begin to breathe and swallow the amniotic fluid. In some cases the amniotic fluid may measure too low or too high. If the measurement of amniotic fluid is too low it is called oligohydramnios. If the measurement of amniotic fluid is too high it is called polyhydramnios.

What is oligohydramnios?

Oligohydramnios is the condition of having too little amniotic fluid. Doctors can measure the amount of fluid through a few different methods, most commonly through amniotic fluid index (AFI) evaluation or deep pocket measurements. If an AFI shows a fluid level of less than five centimeters (or less than the fifth percentile), the absence of a fluid pocket two to three centimeters in depth, or a fluid volume of less than 500mL at thirty-two to thirty-six weeks' gestation, then a diagnosis of oligohydramnios would be suspected. About 8 percent of pregnant women can have low levels of amniotic fluid, with about 4 percent being diagnosed with oligohydramnios. It can occur at any time during pregnancy, but it is most common during the last trimester. If a woman is past her due date by two weeks or more, she may be at risk for low amniotic fluid levels since fluids can decrease by half once she reaches forty-two weeks' gestation. Oligohydramnios can cause complications in about 12 percent of pregnancies that go past forty-one weeks.

What causes low amniotic fluid?

- **Birth defects:** Problems with the development of the kidneys or urinary tract which could cause little urine production, leading to low levels of amniotic fluid.

- **Placental problems:** If the placenta is not providing enough blood and nutrients to the baby, then the baby may stop recycling fluid.

- **Leaking or rupture of membranes:** This may be a gush of fluid or a slow constant trickle of fluid. This is due to a tear in the membrane. Premature rupture of membranes (PROM) can also result in low amniotic fluid levels.

- **Post-date pregnancy:** A post-date pregnancy (one that goes over forty-two weeks) can have low levels of amniotic fluid, which could be a result of declining placental function.

- **Maternal complications:** Factors such as maternal dehydration, hypertension, preeclampsia, diabetes, and chronic hypoxia can have an effect on amniotic fluid levels.

What are the risks of having low amniotic fluid?

The risks associated with oligohydramnios often depend on the gestation of the pregnancy. The amniotic fluid is essential for the development of muscles, limbs, lungs, and the digestive system. In the second trimester, the baby begins to breathe and swallow the fluid to help their lungs grow and mature. The amniotic fluid also helps the baby develop muscles and limbs by providing plenty of room to move around. If oligohydramnios is detected in the first half of pregnancy, the complications can be more serious and include:

- compression of fetal organs resulting in birth defects;

- increased chance of miscarriage or stillbirth.

If oligohydramnios is detected in the second half of pregnancy, complications can include:

- intrauterine growth restriction (IUGR);

- preterm birth;

- labor complications such as cord compression, meconium-stained fluid, and cesarean delivery.

What treatments are available if I am experiencing low amniotic fluid?

The treatment for low levels of amniotic fluid is based on gestational age. If you are not full term yet, your doctor will monitor you and your levels very closely. Tests such as nonstress and contraction stress test may be done to monitor your baby's activity. If you are close to full term, then delivery is usually what most doctors recommend in situations of low amniotic fluid levels. Other treatments that may be used include:

- Amnioinfusion during labor through an intrauterine catheter. This added fluid helps with padding around the umbilical cord during delivery and is reported to help lower the chances of a cesarean delivery.

- Injection of fluid prior to delivery through amniocentesis. The condition of oligohydramnios is reported to often return within one week of this procedure, but it can aid in helping doctors visualize fetal anatomy and make a diagnosis.

- Maternal rehydration with oral fluids or intravenous (IV) fluids has shown to help increase amniotic fluid levels.

Section 10.3

Polyhydramnios

Polyhydramnios is the presence of too much amniotic fluid around the fetus.

Causes of Polyhydramnios

- Polyhydramnios can sometimes mean that there is a birth defect or a medical problem.

- Birth defects that affect the baby's ability to swallow and process amniotic fluid may cause polyhydramnios. Most of these birth defects are rare, but it is important to perform a detailed ultrasound to make sure there is no evidence of these conditions. This ultrasound can detect between 50 and 75 percent of all birth defects.

- Polyhydramnios may also be seen in conditions that cause fetal anemia, such as isoimmunization (where the mother's immune system attacks the baby's red blood cells) or certain viral infections.

- Polyhydramnios may indicate that you have developed gestational diabetes (diabetes during pregnancy).

Diagnosing Polyhydramnios

- In early pregnancy, we can measure the depth of a pocket of amniotic fluid via ultrasound. It should be 3 to 8 centimeters deep.

- By about twenty-four weeks, the uterus has divided into four sections. We can measure the largest pocket of fluid in each section. Although a normal fluid level changes with gestational age, polyhdyramnios is typically defined as a total fluid volume of greater than 24 centimeters.

Impact on Pregnancy

• Most women with polyhydramnios will deliver healthy babies with no problems.

• If polyhydramnios is severe, it may make your uterus contract. You may also find it difficult to get comfortable in a chair or lying down.

Further Testing

• If you have not been checked recently for diabetes, your doctor can order a glucose screening test.

• You can have a detailed ultrasound.

• More frequent prenatal visits are often needed.

• You may need a nonstress test, which monitors the baby's heartbeat.

• Occasionally, amniocentesis is performed to remove some of the fluid and relieve discomfort, or to detect certain genetic conditions.

Chapter 11

Placental Disorders

Chapter Contents

Section 11.1

Placental Abruption

"What Is Placenta Abruption?" reprinted with permission from the
Utah Department of Health Maternal and Infant Health Program, http://
health.utah.gov/mihp. © 2012 Utah Department of Health.

Placental abruption is the early separation of the placenta (after-birth) from the wall of the uterus (womb). The placenta is an organ that grows inside the uterus during pregnancy to provide food and oxygen to the baby. Separation of the placenta before delivery occurs in about 1 in 120 births. It can occur any time after about the twentieth week of pregnancy, and occurs more often in the last three months.

Normally the placenta does not separate from the uterus until right after the birth of the baby. When placental abruption occurs, the placenta starts to come away from the uterus before the baby is born. This can cause serious problems for the baby and mother.

You are at a higher risk for placental abruption if you:

- smoke cigarettes;

- are thirty-five years of age or older;

- have had more than four or five children;

- are pregnant with twins or triplets;

- have high blood pressure;

- use cocaine or other illegal drugs;

- have diabetes;

- have had a previous abruption;

- have trauma to the uterus such as a car accident or a fall;

- have certain blood-clotting disorders;

- have a bag of water that breaks early in the pregnancy.

The symptoms of placental abruption may include:

- contractions (tightening of the uterus) that don't stop;

172

- severe back or abdominal pain;
- tenderness in the abdomen over the uterus;
- vaginal bleeding (sometimes).

How Is It Diagnosed?

The doctor or midwife will give you a physical exam, looking for signs of blood loss. These tests may be done:

- Blood tests
- Ultrasound scan to look for a blood clot behind the placenta
- Fetal monitoring to check the baby's heart rate and look for signs of distress in the baby

The abruption may be described as a Grade 1 (mild), Grade 2 (mild to moderate), or Grade 3 (moderate to severe).

How Is It Treated?

This will depend on many things, such as:

- how much of the placenta has separated from the uterus;
- how close the pregnancy is to full term (thirty-seven weeks or more);
- your health and whether you have other problems, such a high blood pressure;
- the amount of blood you have lost;
- the baby's health.

If the separation of the placenta is small, the baby isn't in distress, and your condition is stable, you may be able to go home and continue the pregnancy with frequent checkups. You may be advised to avoid sexual activity and some forms of physical activity.

If you are admitted to the hospital, you will be given intravenous (IV) fluids. A fetal monitor will be used to check the baby for signs of distress. Your blood pressure, pulse, and amount of bleeding will be closely checked. Blood tests will be done to check your iron level and blood clotting factors.

If the separation is moderate, the baby is not in distress, and your condition is stable, the doctor may induce labor and perform a vaginal delivery. If the baby is in distress or if you are losing a lot of blood, the doctor will deliver the baby immediately by cesarean section.

There is no treatment to stop the placenta from separating or to reattach it. The baby can survive when even up to one half of the placenta is separated from the uterus.

What Are the Effects?

Sometimes the separation and bleeding begins and then stops without treatment. As long as you and the baby are healthy, your pregnancy can continue with frequent checkups. A mild case will probably have no long-term effects on your health or your baby's health.

A moderate to severe separation of the placenta may have the following effects:

- A large blood loss may require blood transfusions and intensive care after delivery for the mother.

- The baby may be in distress until delivery and may need to be born prematurely. They may have problems with breathing and feeding. In severe cases the baby could have permanent problems or be stillborn.

The good news is that with quick attention and expert care, nearly all mothers and their babies survive.

Helping to Prevent Placental Abruption

Good prenatal care (beginning in the first thirteen weeks and continuing with regular visits) and a healthy diet may reduce the risk of high blood pressure during pregnancy. Prevention of high blood pressure decreases the risk of abruption.

If you smoke, decreasing the number of cigarettes and stopping smoking will decrease your risks of having a placental abruption.

Always use a seat belt in the car to minimize any potential trauma from a car accident. If an accident does occur, or if you have a fall, either call your provider or go to the hospital for further monitoring.

Abruption caused by the use of cocaine or amphetamines can be prevented if the mother stops using these drugs.

If you have had a placental abruption with a previous pregnancy and are pregnant again, be sure to report this to your care provider and immediately report any contractions or bleeding you might experience.

Section 11.2

Placenta Accreta, Increta, and Percreta

The placenta grows in your uterus (womb) and supplies the baby with food and oxygen through the umbilical cord. Normally, the placenta grows onto the upper part of the uterus and stays there until your baby is born. During the last stage of labor, the placenta separates from the wall of the uterus, and your contractions help push it into the vagina (birth canal). This is also called the afterbirth.

Sometimes the placenta attaches itself into the wall of the uterus too deeply. This can cause problems, including:

- **Placenta accreta:** The placenta attaches itself too deeply and too firmly into the uterus.

- **Placenta increta:** The placenta attaches itself even more deeply into the muscle wall of uterus.

- **Placenta percreta:** The placenta attaches itself and grows through the uterus, sometimes extending to nearby organs, such as the bladder.

In these conditions, the placenta doesn't completely separate from the uterus after you give birth. This can cause dangerous bleeding. These conditions happen in about 1 in 530 births each year.

What are the signs of these placental conditions?

Placental conditions often cause vaginal bleeding in the third trimester. Call your health care provider right away if you have vaginal bleeding anytime during your pregnancy. If the bleeding is severe, go to the hospital right away.

How are these placental conditions diagnosed?

These conditions usually are diagnosed using ultrasound. In some cases, your provider may use magnetic resonance imaging (MRI). MRI uses magnets and computers to make a clear picture that may be hard to see on an ultrasound. The test is painless and safe for you and your baby.

How are these placental conditions treated?

When these conditions are found before birth, your provider may recommend a cesarean section (also called c-section) immediately followed by a hysterectomy. This can help prevent bleeding from becoming life threatening. A c-section is surgery in which your baby is born through a cut that your provider makes in your belly and uterus. A hysterectomy is when your uterus is removed by surgery. Without a uterus, you can't get pregnant again in the future.

If you have a placental condition, the best time for you to have your baby is unknown. But your provider may recommend that you give birth at around thirty-four to thirty-eight weeks of pregnancy to help prevent dangerous bleeding. If you want to have future pregnancies, he or she may use special treatments before the c-section to try to control bleeding and save your uterus.

If your provider finds these conditions at birth, he or she may try to remove the placenta in surgery to stop the bleeding. However, a hysterectomy is often necessary.

What causes these placental conditions?

We don't know what causes these kinds of placental conditions. But they often happen where you have a scar from a surgery, like removing a fibroid or having a c-section. A fibroid is a tumor that grows in the wall of the uterus (womb). If you've had a c-section, you're more likely than if you had a vaginal birth to have these kinds of conditions. And the more c-sections you've had, the more likely you are to have these placental problems.

Things that may make you more likely to have these kinds of placental conditions include:

- smoking cigarettes;
- being thirty-five or older;
- being pregnant before;
- having placenta previa.

How can you reduce your risk for placental conditions?

One way to reduce your chances for having these kinds of placental conditions in future pregnancies is to have your babies by vaginal birth instead of c-section. Have a c-section only if there are health problems with you or your baby that make it medically necessary. For some moms and babies, health problems make c-section safer than vaginal birth. But if your pregnancy is healthy, it's best to stay pregnant until labor begins on its own. Don't schedule a c-section for nonmedical reasons, like wanting to have your baby on a certain day or because you're uncomfortable and want to have your baby earlier than your due date.

Even if you've already had a c-section, you may be able to have your next baby by vaginal birth. This is called vaginal birth after cesarean (VBAC). You may be able to have a VBAC depending on what kind of incision (cut) you had in your c-section and your overall pregnancy health. Talk to your provider if you think VBAC may be right for you.

What are some other placental problems?

In some cases, the placenta doesn't develop correctly or work as well as it should. It may be too thin, too thick, or have an extra lobe. The umbilical cord may not be attached correctly. Problems like infections, blood clots, and infarcts (an area of dead tissue, like a scar) can happen during pregnancy and damage the placenta.

Placental problems like these can lead to health risks for you and your baby. Some of these risks include:

- You may have a miscarriage.

- Your baby doesn't grow as well as he or she should during pregnancy.

- You may have bleeding at birth.

- You may have a premature birth. This is birth that happens too soon, before thirty-seven completed weeks of pregnancy.

- Your baby may have birth defects.

Your provider checks the placenta after birth. Sometimes the placenta is sent for testing in a lab, especially if the baby has certain health problems, like poor growth.

Section 11.3

Placental Insufficiency

© 2012 A.D.A.M., Inc. Reprinted with permission.

The placenta is the link between you and your baby. When the placenta does not work as well as it should, your baby can get less oxygen and nutrients from you. As a result, your baby may:

- not grow as well;
- show signs of fetal stress (this means the baby's heart does not work normally);
- have a harder time during labor.

Causes

The placenta may not work as well due to pregnancy problems or habits in the mother, such as:

- diabetes;
- going past your due date;
- high blood pressure during pregnancy (called preeclampsia);
- medical conditions that increase the mother's chances of blood clots;
- smoking;
- taking cocaine or other drugs.

Certain medications can also increase the risk of placenta insufficiency.

In some cases, the placenta:

- may have an abnormal shape;
- may not grow big enough (more likely if you are carrying twins or other multiples);
- does not attach correctly to the surface of the womb;
- breaks away from the surface of the womb or bleeds.

Symptoms

A woman with placental insufficiency usually does not have any symptoms.

Exams and Tests

The health care provider will measure the size of your growing womb (uterus) at each visit, starting about halfway through your pregnancy.

If your uterus is not growing as expected, a pregnancy ultrasound will be done. This test will measure your baby's size and growth, and assess the size and placement of the placenta.

Other times, problems with the placenta or your baby's growth may be found on a routine ultrasound that is done during your pregnancy.

Either way, your doctor will order tests to check how your baby is doing. The tests may show that your baby is active and healthy, and the amount of amniotic fluid is normal. Or, these tests can show that the baby is having problems.

If there is a problem with the placenta, you and your doctor must decide whether to induce labor.

You may be asked to keep a daily record of how often the baby moves or kicks.

Treatment

If your pregnancy is less than thirty-seven weeks and the tests show that your baby is not under too much stress, your doctor may decide to wait longer. Sometimes you may need to get increased rest on your side. You will have tests often to make sure your baby is doing well. Treating high blood pressure or diabetes may also help improve the baby's growth.

If your pregnancy is over thirty-seven weeks or tests show your baby is not doing well, your doctor may want to deliver your baby. He or she may induce labor, or you may need a cesarean section.

Outlook (Prognosis)

Problems with the placenta can affect the developing baby's growth. The baby cannot grow and develop normally in the womb if it does not get enough oxygen and nutrients.

When this occurs, it is called intrauterine growth restriction (IUGR). This increases the chances of complications during pregnancy and delivery.

Prevention

Getting prenatal care early in pregnancy will help make sure that the mother is as healthy as possible during the pregnancy.

Smoking, alcohol, and other illicit drugs can interfere with the baby's growth. Avoiding these substances may help prevent placental insufficiency and other pregnancy complications.

Section 11.4

Placenta Previa

© 2012 A.D.A.M., Inc. Reprinted with permission.

Placenta previa is a problem of pregnancy in which the placenta grows in the lowest part of the womb (uterus) and covers all or part of the opening to the cervix.

The placenta grows during pregnancy and feeds the developing baby. The cervix is the opening to the birth canal.

Causes

During pregnancy, the placenta moves as the womb stretches and grows. It is very common for the placenta to be low in the womb in early pregnancy. But as the pregnancy continues, the placenta moves to the top of the womb. By the third trimester, the placenta should be near the top of the womb, so the cervix is open for delivery.

Sometimes, the placenta partly or completely covers the cervix. This is called a previa.

There are different forms of placenta previa:

- **Marginal:** The placenta is next to cervix but does not cover the opening.
- **Partial:** The placenta covers part of the cervical opening.
- **Complete:** The placenta covers all of the cervical opening.

Placenta previa occurs in one out of two hundred pregnancies. It is more common in women who have:

- abnormally shaped uterus;
- many previous pregnancies;
- multiple pregnancy (twins, triplets, etc.);
- scarring on the lining of the uterus, due to history of surgery, cesarean section (c-section), previous pregnancy, or abortion.

Women who smoke or have their children at an older age may also have an increased risk.

Symptoms

The main symptom of placenta previa is sudden bleeding from the vagina. Some women have cramps, too. The bleeding often starts near the end of the second trimester or beginning of the third trimester.

Bleeding may be severe. It may stop on its own but can start again days or weeks later.

Labor sometimes starts within several days of heavy bleeding. Sometimes, bleeding may not occur until after labor starts.

Exams and Tests

Your health care provider can diagnose this condition with a pregnancy ultrasound.

Treatment

Your health care provider will carefully consider the risk of bleeding against early delivery of your baby. After thirty-six weeks, delivery of the baby may be the best treatment.

Nearly all women with placenta previa need a c-section. If the placenta covers all or part of the cervix, a vaginal delivery can cause severe bleeding. This can be deadly to both the mother and the baby.

If the placenta is near or covering a part of the cervix, your doctor may recommend:

- reducing your activities;
- bed rest;
- pelvic rest, which means no sex, no tampons, and no douching.

Nothing should be placed in the vagina.

You may need to stay in the hospital so your health care team can closely monitor you and your baby.

Other treatments you may receive:

- blood transfusions;

- medicines to prevent early labor;

- medicines to help pregnancy continue to at least thirty-six weeks;

- shot of special medicine called RhoGAM if your blood type is Rh-negative;

- steroid shots to help the baby's lungs mature.

An emergency c-section may be done if the bleeding is heavy and cannot be controlled.

Outlook (Prognosis)

The biggest risk is severe bleeding that can be life threatening to the mother and baby. If you have severe bleeding, you baby may need to be delivered early, before major organs, such as the lungs, have developed.

When to Contact a Medical Professional

Call your health care provider if you have vaginal bleeding during pregnancy. Placenta previa can be dangerous to both you and your baby.

Chapter 12

Umbilical Cord Abnormalities

The umbilical cord is a narrow tube-like structure that connects the developing baby to the placenta. The cord is sometimes called the baby's "supply line" because it carries the baby's blood back and forth between the baby and the placenta. It delivers nutrients and oxygen to the baby and removes the baby's waste products.

The umbilical cord begins to form at five weeks after conception. It becomes progressively longer until twenty-eight weeks of pregnancy, reaching an average length of twenty-two to twenty-four inches.[1] As the cord gets longer, it generally coils around itself. The cord contains three blood vessels: two arteries and one vein:

- The vein carries oxygen and nutrients from the placenta (which connects to the mother's blood supply) to the baby.

- The two arteries transport waste from the baby to the placenta (where waste is transferred to the mother's blood and disposed of by her kidneys).

A gelatin-like tissue called Wharton's jelly cushions and protects these blood vessels.

A number of abnormalities can affect the umbilical cord. The cord may be too long or too short. It may connect improperly to the placenta or become knotted or compressed. Cord abnormalities can lead to problems during pregnancy or during labor and delivery.

In some cases, cord abnormalities are discovered before delivery during an ultrasound. However, they usually are not discovered until after delivery when the cord is examined directly. The following are the most frequent cord abnormalities and their possible effects on mother and baby.

What is single umbilical artery?

About 1 percent of singleton and about 5 percent of multiple pregnancies (twins, triplets, or more) have an umbilical cord that contains only two blood vessels, instead of the normal three. In these cases, one artery is missing.[2] The cause of this abnormality, called single umbilical artery, is unknown.

Studies suggest that babies with single umbilical artery have an increased risk for birth defects, including heart, central nervous system, and urinary-tract defects and chromosomal abnormalities.[2,3] A woman whose baby is diagnosed with single umbilical artery during a routine ultrasound may be offered certain prenatal tests to diagnose or rule out birth defects. These tests may include a detailed ultrasound, amniocentesis (to check for chromosomal abnormalities), and in some cases, echocardiography (a special type of ultrasound to evaluate the fetal heart). The provider also may recommend that the baby have an ultrasound after birth.

What is umbilical cord prolapse?

Umbilical cord prolapse occurs when the cord slips into the vagina after the membranes (bag of waters) have ruptured, before the baby descends into the birth canal. This complication affects about one in three hundred births.[1] The baby can put pressure on the cord as he passes through the cervix and vagina during labor and delivery. Pressure on the cord reduces or cuts off blood flow from the placenta to the baby, decreasing the baby's oxygen supply. Umbilical cord prolapse can result in stillbirth unless the baby is delivered promptly, usually by cesarean section.

If the woman's membranes rupture and she feels something in her vagina, she should go to the hospital immediately or, in the United States, call 911. A health care provider may suspect umbilical cord prolapse if the bay develops heart rate abnormalities after the membranes have ruptured. The provider can confirm a cord prolapse by doing a pelvic examination. Cord prolapse is an emergency. Pressure on the cord must be relieved immediately by lifting the presenting fetal part away from the cord while preparing the woman for prompt cesarean delivery.

The risk of umbilical cord prolapse increases if:

- the baby is in a breech (foot-first) position;

- the woman is in preterm labor;

- the umbilical cord is too long;

- there is too much amniotic fluid;

- the provider ruptures the membranes to start or speed up labor;

- the woman is delivering twins vaginally. The second twin is more commonly affected.

What is vasa previa?

Vasa previa occurs when one or more blood vessels from the umbilical cord or placenta cross the cervix underneath the baby. The blood vessels, unprotected by the Wharton's jelly in the umbilical cord or the tissue in the placenta, sometimes tear when the cervix dilates or the membranes rupture. This can result in life-threatening bleeding in the baby. Even if the blood vessels do not tear, the baby may suffer from lack of oxygen due to pressure on the blood vessels. Vasa previa occurs in 1 in 2,500 births.[4]

When vasa previa is diagnosed unexpectedly at delivery, more than half of affected babies are stillborn.[4] However, when vasa previa is diagnosed by ultrasound earlier in pregnancy, fetal deaths generally can be prevented by delivering the baby by cesarean section at about thirty-five weeks of gestation.[4]

Pregnant women with vasa previa sometimes have painless vaginal bleeding in the second or third trimester. A pregnant woman who experiences vaginal bleeding should always report it to her health care provider so that the cause can be determined and any necessary steps taken to protect the baby.

A pregnant woman may be at increased risk for vasa previa if she:

- has a velamentous insertion of the cord (the umbilical cord inserts abnormally into the fetal membranes, instead of the center of the placenta);

- has placenta previa (a low-lying placenta that covers part or all of the cervix) or certain other placental abnormalities;
- is expecting more than one baby.

What is a nuchal cord?

About 25 percent of babies are born with a nuchal cord (the umbilical cord wrapped around the baby's neck).[1] A nuchal cord, also called nuchal loops, rarely causes any problems. Babies with a nuchal cord are generally healthy.

Sometimes fetal monitoring shows heart rate abnormalities during labor and delivery in babies with a nuchal cord. This may reflect pressure on the cord. However, the pressure is rarely serious enough to cause death or any lasting problems, although occasionally a cesarean delivery may be needed.

Less frequently, the umbilical cord becomes wrapped around other parts of the baby's body, such as a foot or hand. Generally, this doesn't harm the baby.

What are umbilical cord knots?

About 1 percent of babies are born with one or more knots in the umbilical cord.[1] Some knots form during delivery when a baby with a nuchal cord is pulled through the loop. Others form during pregnancy when the baby moves around. Knots occur most often when the umbilical cord is too long and in identical-twin pregnancies. Identical twins share a single amniotic sac, and the babies' cords can become entangled.

As long as the knot remains loose, it generally does not harm the baby. However, sometimes the knot or knots can be pulled tight, cutting off the baby's oxygen supply. Cord knots result in miscarriage or stillbirth in 5 percent of cases.[1] During labor and delivery, a tightening knot can cause the baby to have heart rate abnormalities that are detected by fetal monitoring. In some cases, a cesarean delivery may be necessary.

What is an umbilical cord cyst?

Umbilical cord cysts are outpockets in the cord. They are found in about 3 percent of pregnancies.[2]

There are true and false cysts:

- True cysts are lined with cells and generally contain remnants of early embryonic structures.

- False cysts are fluid-filled sacs that can be related to a swelling of the Wharton's jelly.

Studies suggest that both types of cysts are sometimes associated with birth defects, including chromosomal abnormalities and kidney and abdominal defects.[2] When a cord cyst is found during an ultrasound, the provider may recommend additional tests, such as amniocentesis and a detailed ultrasound, to diagnose or rule out birth defects.

Does the March of Dimes support research on umbilical cord abnormalities?

The March of Dimes continues to support research aimed at preventing umbilical cord abnormalities and the complications they cause. One grantee is studying the development of blood vessels in the umbilical cord for insight into the causes of single umbilical artery and other cord abnormalities. The goals of this study are to:

- develop a better understanding of the causes of birth defects;

- develop treatments to help prevent oxygen deprivation before and during delivery, which may contribute to cerebral palsy and other forms of brain damage.

References

1. Cruikshank, D.W. Breech, Other Malpresentations, and Umbilical Cord Complications, in: Scott, J.R., et al. (eds.), *Danforth's Obstetrics and Gynecology, 9th Edition*. Philadelphia, Lippincott Williams and Wilkins, 2003, pages 381–95.

2. Morgan, B.L.G. and Ross, M.G. Umbilical Cord Complications. emedicine.com, March 1, 2006.

3. Gossett, D.R., et al. Antenatal Diagnosis of Single Umbilical Artery: Is Fetal Echocardiography Warranted? *Obstetrics and Gynecology*, volume 100, number 5, November 2002, pages 903–8.

4. Oyelese, Y. and Smulian, J.C. Placenta Previa, Placenta Accreta, and Vasa Previa. *Obstetrics and Gynecology*, volume 107, number 4, April 2006, pages 927–41.

Chapter 13

Other Pregnancy Complications

Chapter Contents

Section 13.1

Intrauterine Growth Restriction

Babies come in all sizes. Some are just naturally larger or smaller than others.

But in certain cases, babies in the womb are smaller than they should be. When this happens, it could be due to a condition known as intrauterine growth restriction, or IUGR.

About IUGR

The term IUGR refers to a condition in which a baby in the womb fails to grow at the expected rate during the pregnancy. In other words, at any point in the pregnancy, the baby is not as big as would be expected for how far along the mother is in her pregnancy (this timing is referred to as an unborn baby's "gestational age").

Babies who have IUGR often have a low weight at birth. If the weight is below the tenth percentile for a baby's gestational age (meaning that 90 percent of babies that age weigh more), the baby is also referred to as "small for gestational age," or SGA.

It's important to note that not all babies who are small for gestational age had IUGR while in the womb. Some are healthy babies who are just born smaller than average because their parents are small in stature.

The two types of IUGR are:

1. In symmetrical IUGR, a baby's body is proportionally small. That means that all parts of the baby's body are similarly small in size.

2. In asymmetrical IUGR, the baby has a normal-size head and brain but the rest of the body is small.

Causes

In many cases, IUGR is the result of a problem that prevents a baby from getting enough oxygen and nutrients. This lack of nourishment slows the baby's growth. It can happen for a number of reasons. A common cause is placental insufficiency, in which the tissue that delivers oxygen and nutrients to the baby is not attached properly or isn't working correctly.

Other possible causes during a woman's pregnancy include:

- certain behaviors, such as smoking, drinking alcohol, or abusing drugs;
- exposure to infections (passed from the mother), such as cytomegalovirus, German measles (rubella), toxoplasmosis, and syphilis;
- taking certain medications;
- high blood pressure;
- genetic disorders or birth defects;
- living in high altitudes.

Risk Factors

IUGR is more likely to occur in women who are carrying more than one baby or who had a previous baby who was SGA or had IUGR. Certain medical conditions, such as heart, lung, blood, or autoimmune disease, and high blood pressure or anemia, can also increase a woman's risk of developing IUGR. So can eating poorly or being underweight before or during pregnancy.

Diagnosis

Since not all babies who are small have IUGR, an accurate diagnosis is important. Initially, this diagnosis relies on correctly determining the baby's age by accurately dating the pregnancy.

Gestational age is initially estimated using the first day of a woman's last menstrual period. Later in the pregnancy (usually between weeks eight and thirteen), it is confirmed through an ultrasound. Once a baby's gestational age is known, doctors use it to monitor the baby's growth and compare it with the expected growth rate. If the baby is growing more slowly than expected (sometimes referred to as "small for dates"), doctors will continue to monitor the baby's growth and may perform more tests to determine whether the baby has IUGR.

Monitoring of growth is done in several ways. A measurement called the uterine fundal height helps estimate a baby's size by measuring a mother's belly from the top of the pubic bone to the uterus. Another way to monitor a baby's growth is by using ultrasounds. In fact, IUGR is usually diagnosed through an ultrasound examination.

During an ultrasound, a technician coats the woman's belly with a gel and then moves a probe (wand-like instrument) over it. High-frequency sound waves "echo" off the body and create pictures of the baby on a computer screen. These pictures can be used to estimate the baby's size and weight.

Although these estimates might not be exactly correct, they help health care providers track the baby's growth and determine whether a problem exists. Ultrasounds also can help identify other potential troubles, such as problems with the placenta or low amniotic fluid levels.

Health care providers might also perform some additional tests to diagnose IUGR, such as:

- fetal monitoring to track the baby's heart rate and movements;

- screenings for infections;

- amniocentesis to help determine the cause of IUGR.

If a Baby Has IUGR

Once IUGR has been diagnosed, treatment is individualized for each patient depending on the baby's condition and the woman's month of pregnancy.

The baby will be closely monitored, usually with frequent prenatal visits and ultrasounds, to keep track of growth and watch for other potential problems. In some cases, health care providers will recommend inducing labor and delivery early if monitoring shows that a baby has stopped growing or has other problems.

A cesarean section (C-section) might be done if the stress of a vaginal delivery is considered too risky for the baby. Although early delivery might be necessary, the goal is to keep the baby safe in the womb for as long as possible. Sometimes amniocentesis can help determine lung maturity and whether the baby is likely to be able to breathe on his or her own.

Treatment for IUGR also includes addressing the possible causes, including managing any maternal illness and ensuring that the mother eats a healthy and nutritious diet and gains the appropriate amount of weight. Some women are told to avoid aerobic exercise and some are placed on bed rest to improve blood flow to the baby.

Outlook

Unfortunately, babies with IUGR are more likely to have health problems both before and after birth. Those who are born prematurely or are very small at birth are more likely to have problems that result in longer hospital stays. They might also need to receive special care after birth, such as help breathing or medicine to prevent infections.

Other problems that can be associated with IUGR include:

- decreased tolerance for birth, resulting in increased likelihood of C-section delivery;

- problems with breathing and feeding;

- trouble maintaining body temperature;

- abnormal blood cell counts;

- low blood sugar level (hypoglycemia);

- decreased ability to fight infection;

- increased likelihood of neurological problems;

- increased likelihood of stillbirth (dying in the womb before birth).

The long-term effects of IUGR may depend on the condition that caused the problem in the first place.

Coping

When a woman learns that her baby has or might have IUGR, the best thing she can do is to keep all of her prenatal visits and testing appointments and follow her health care provider's recommendations. She also should take care of herself by eating a healthy diet, getting enough rest, and avoiding alcohol, drugs, and tobacco.

Section 13.2

Preeclampsia and Eclampsia

National Institute of Child Health and Human Development,
National Institutes of Health, September 10, 2006. Updated by
David A. Cooke, M.D., FACP, December 2012.

What are preeclampsia and eclampsia?

Preeclampsia is a syndrome marked by a sudden increase in the blood pressure of a pregnant woman after the twentieth week of pregnancy. It can affect the mother's kidney, liver, and brain. If left untreated, the condition can be fatal for the mother and/or the baby and can lead to long-term health problems.

Eclampsia is a more severe form of preeclampsia that can cause seizures and coma in the mother.

Physicians have known about preeclampsia for a very long time, but the disease is only now beginning to be understood. Current evidence suggests an abnormality in the growth of blood vessels in the placenta leads to excessive release of cell chemicals that affect the cardiovascular system. Widespread changes in response to these chemicals can lead to the high blood pressure and organ damage that may accompany preeclampsia.

What are the symptoms of preeclampsia?

Possible signs of preeclampsia include the following:

- High blood pressure

- Too much protein in the urine

- Swelling in a woman's face and hands (a woman's feet might swell too, but swollen feet are common during pregnancy and may not signal a problem)

- Systemic problems, such as headache, blurred vision, and abdominal pain

What is the treatment for preeclampsia?

The only cure for preeclampsia is delivering the fetus. Medications for high blood pressure and intravenous (IV) magnesium are sometimes used in treatment of preeclampsia, but they do not cure the condition.

If preeclampsia develops, the health care provider may develop a plan to try to prolong the pregnancy to give the fetus more time to grow and mature. At the same time, the health care provider will closely watch the health of the mother for signs that the fetus needs to be delivered right away, even prematurely, if necessary. If the preeclampsia is severe enough and the fetus is not delivered, the mother could die. Health care providers will take steps to prevent the condition from being fatal for mother and baby.

If you have questions about preeclampsia and delivery, talk to your health care provider.

What are the risk factors for preeclampsia?

There is no proven way to prevent preeclampsia. But some women are more likely to develop it, including the following:

- Women who have high blood pressure before becoming pregnant

- Women who had high blood pressure or preeclampsia in previous pregnancies

- Women who are obese

- Women younger than age twenty or older than age forty

- Women who are pregnant with more than one baby

- Women with certain health conditions, such as diabetes or kidney disease

Data suggest that taking low-dose aspirin during early pregnancy may reduce risk of developing preeclampsia or eclampsia. However, there is disagreement among experts as to whether women at risk should take aspirin, and if so, which women. Aspirin use during pregnancy can cause serious complications, so it should be taken only if specifically recommended by your doctor.

Recent improvements in the scientific understanding of what actually occurs in preeclampsia may lead to better ways to diagnose it early, or perhaps prevent it entirely.

A number of blood tests are being tested to determine whether they can accurately predict development of preeclampsia. Initial results are promising, but the tests are not ready for general use. There is also some data suggesting that ultrasound measurement of placental blood flow during early pregnancy may predict which women will develop preeclampsia. However, this approach is also considered experimental.

Section 13.3

Rh Incompatibility

© 2012 A.D.A.M., Inc. Reprinted with permission.

Rh incompatibility is a condition that develops when a pregnant woman has Rh-negative blood and the baby in her womb has Rh-positive blood.

Causes

During pregnancy, red blood cells from the unborn baby can cross into the mother's bloodstream through the placenta.

If the mother is Rh-negative, her immune system treats Rh-positive fetal cells as if they were a foreign substance and makes antibodies against the fetal blood cells. These anti-Rh antibodies may cross back through the placenta into the developing baby and destroy the baby's circulating red blood cells.

When red blood cells are broken down, they make bilirubin. This causes an infant to become yellow (jaundiced). The level of bilirubin in the infant's bloodstream may range from mild to dangerously high.

Because it takes time for the mother to develop antibodies, firstborn infants are often not affected unless the mother had past miscarriages or abortions that sensitized her immune system. However, all children she has afterwards who are also Rh-positive may be affected.

Rh incompatibility develops only when the mother is Rh-negative and the infant is Rh-positive. Thanks to the use of special immune globulins called RhoGAM, this problem has become uncommon in the United States and other places that provide access to good prenatal care.

Symptoms

Rh incompatibility can cause symptoms ranging from very mild to deadly. In its mildest form, Rh incompatibility causes the destruction of red blood cells.

After birth, the infant may have:

- yellowing of the skin and whites of the eyes (jaundice);

- low muscle tone (hypotonia) and lethargy.

Exams and Tests

Before delivery, the mother may have an increased amount of amniotic fluid around her unborn baby (polyhydramnios).

There may be:

- a positive direct Coombs test result;

- higher-than-normal levels of bilirubin in the baby's umbilical cord blood;

- signs of red blood cell destruction in the infant's blood.

Treatment

Because Rh incompatibility is preventable with the use of RhoGAM, prevention remains the best treatment. Treatment of an infant who is already affected depends on the severity of the condition.

Infants with mild Rh incompatibility may be treated with:

- feeding and fluids (hydration);

- phototherapy using bilirubin lights.

Outlook (Prognosis)

Full recovery is expected for mild Rh incompatibility.

Possible Complications

Possible complications include:

- brain damage due to high levels of bilirubin (kernicterus);

- fluid buildup and swelling in the baby (hydrops fetalis);

- problems with mental function, movement, hearing, speech, and seizures.

When to Contact a Medical Professional

Call your health care provider if you think or know you are pregnant and have not yet seen a doctor.

Prevention

Rh incompatibility is almost completely preventable. Rh-negative mothers should be followed closely by their obstetricians during pregnancy.

Special immune globulins, called RhoGAM, are now used to prevent RH incompatibility in mothers who are Rh-negative.

If the father of the infant is Rh-positive or if his blood type cannot be confirmed, the mother is given an injection of RhoGAM during the second trimester. If the baby is Rh-positive, the mother will get a second injection within a few days after delivery.

These injections prevent the development of antibodies against Rh-positive blood. However, women with Rh-negative blood type must receive injections:

- during every pregnancy;

- if they have a miscarriage or abortion;

- after prenatal tests such as amniocentesis and chorionic villus biopsy;

- after injury to the abdomen during pregnancy.

Alternative Names

Rh-induced hemolytic disease of the newborn

References

Stoll BJ. Blood disorders. In: Kliegman RM, Behrman RE, Jenson HB, Stanton BF, eds. *Nelson Textbook of Pediatrics. 18th ed.* Philadelphia, Pa: Saunders Elsevier; 2007:chap 103.

Chapter 14

Fetal Surgery and Other Fetal Treatment Techniques

Fetal Intervention

Fetal intervention refers to the techniques used to treat a fetus inside the uterus. Although many diseases and conditions can be diagnosed before birth with imaging and genetic tests, very few actually require intervention. If your doctor determines that your baby would benefit from intervention, your doctor will explain all of the options and their benefits and risks.

If you decide to have fetal intervention, your doctor's most important consideration becomes your health. While the goal of any fetal intervention is to treat the fetus, to do so requires access to the uterus and this may present varying degrees of risk for you. If the uterus is accessed through surgery, particularly open fetal surgery where an incision is made, there are anesthetic and surgical risks. If the uterus is accessed through a needle or other fine instrument, the risks are much lower. It's your doctor's responsibility to ensure your well being first.

There are three fetal intervention techniques:

- **Fetal image guided surgery:** Fetal image guided surgery (FIGS) uses sonogram imaging to guide intervention to the fetus, without an incision or endoscopic view inside the uterus. FIGS is performed through the skin or, in some cases, through

This chapter includes "Fetal Intervention" and "EXIT Procedure," © 2013 Fetal Treatment Program of New England. All rights reserved. Reprinted with permission. For additional information, visit www.fetal-treatment.org.

a small opening in the abdomen. Performed under regional or local anesthesia, FIGS is the least invasive intervention technique, requiring less time in the hospital and causing little discomfort. However, because the uterus membrane is punctured as part of the procedure, there is a risk of preterm labor, so monitoring and medications are often needed until delivery. FIGS is typically an outpatient procedure but may require overnight admittance to monitor for preterm labor.

- **Fetoscopic surgery:** This type of intervention (also called "Fetendo") was developed to avoid making an incision in the uterus, and thereby minimizing preterm labor. Fetendo is performed through either the skin or a small opening in the abdomen, and uses endoscopic and sonographic-guided images to visualize the fetus. Performed under regional or general anesthesia, this procedure is less invasive than open surgery, resulting in easier postoperative recovery. Preterm labor is a risk, so monitoring and medications are still necessary. Recovery typically requires a one- to two-day hospital stay.

- **Open fetal surgery:** Open fetal surgery is the most invasive type of intervention. Performed while the mother is under general anesthesia, an incision is made into the lower abdomen to expose the uterus, which is then opened with a stapling device used to prevent bleeding. Once the surgical repair of the fetus is complete, the uterus and maternal abdominal wall are closed and the mother is awakened. Open fetal surgery is major surgery and no different than any intro-abdominal operation, such as the removal of a gall bladder or a Cesarean section, except that the mother remains pregnant at the end of the operation. The surgery and recovery require hospitalization for up to a week, as well as Cesarean delivery of this and future pregnancies. Because an incision has been made in the uterus itself mid-gestation, open fetal surgery can lead to preterm delivery, so the mother will require close monitoring and medications to manage preterm labor.

EXIT Procedure

An ex utero intrapartum (EXIT) procedure is a specialized delivery, much like a Cesarean section, that is planned when there is a possibility that the newborn baby will not be able to breathe on his or her own after birth—and that it will be very difficult or impossible to insert a breathing tube. Many things can cause a newborn's airway to be compressed, such as a number of rare congenital disorders; a mass or tumor; or in cases of fetal tracheal occlusion. Airway compression discovered at birth is a medical emergency; however, it is often discovered during prenatal ultrasound, allowing your doctor to plan a safe delivery using the EXIT procedure.

How Does It Work?

The fetus receives oxygen from the placenta, through the umbilical cord. Normally at birth, the cord is clamped and the baby takes his or her first breath. In an EXIT procedure, your doctor delivers the neck and head of the baby, while the rest of the body and umbilical cord remain inside the uterus. This allows your doctor to try to open the baby's airway while he or she is still receiving oxygen through the umbilical cord.

How Is It Performed?

While you are under general anesthesia, an incision will be made on the midline of your abdomen and uterus. Your doctor partially delivers the baby through the opening, while a pediatric head and neck surgeon establishes an airway so the fetus can breathe. This is done by inserting a breathing tube through the mouth or, if possible, by making a small incision in the neck and going directly into the windpipe.

An EXIT procedure provides up to thirty to forty-five minutes to secure a safe access to the airway; however, the uterus and umbilical cord must stay relaxed. At birth, there is a natural tendency for the baby to come out, the umbilical cord to close, the placenta to detach, and the uterus to contract. Your anesthesiologists and surgeons work to slow this process and to keep the uterus as relaxed as possible, which requires a delicate balance of medication and surgical maneuvers. Once the EXIT is complete, the umbilical cord is cut and clamped and the infant is fully delivered.

Part Two

Prematurity and
Other Birth Complications

Chapter 15

Premature Labor

Pregnancy is normally a time of happiness and anticipation, but it can also be a time of uncertainty. Many women have concerns about what is happening with their baby and wonder, "Is everything okay"? Some women have concerns about going into labor early. Premature labor occurs in about 12 percent of all pregnancies. However, by knowing the symptoms and avoiding particular risk factors, a woman can reduce her chance of going into labor prematurely.

What is premature labor?

A normal pregnancy lasts about forty weeks. Occasionally, labor begins prematurely, before the thirty-seventh week of pregnancy. This happens because uterine contractions cause the cervix to open earlier than normal. Consequently, the baby is born premature and can be at risk for health problems. Fortunately, research, technology, and medicine have helped improve the health of premature babies.

What risk factors place me at a high risk for premature labor?

Although the specific causes of premature labor are not yet known, certain factors may increase a woman's risk of having premature labor.

However, having a specific risk factor does not mean a woman will experience premature labor. A woman might have premature labor for no apparent reason. If you have any of the following risk factors, it is important to know the symptoms of premature labor and what to do if it occurs.

Women are at greatest risk for premature labor if:

- they are pregnant with multiples;

- they have had a previous premature birth;

- they have certain uterine or cervical abnormalities.

Medical risk factors include:

- recurring bladder and/or kidney infections;

- urinary tract infections, vaginal infections, and sexually transmitted infections;

- infection with fever greater than 101 degrees F during pregnancy;

- unexplained vaginal bleeding after twenty weeks of pregnancy;

- chronic illness such as high blood pressure, kidney disease, or diabetes;

- multiple first-trimester abortions or one or more second-trimester abortions;

- underweight or overweight before pregnancy;

- clotting disorder (thrombophilia);

- being pregnant with a single fetus after in vitro fertilization (IVF);

- short time between pregnancies (less than six to nine months between birth and beginning of the next pregnancy).

Lifestyle risks for premature labor include:

- little or no prenatal care;

- smoking;

- drinking alcohol;

- using illegal drugs;

- domestic violence, including physical, sexual, or emotional abuse;

- lack of social support;

- high levels of stress;

- low income;

- long working hours with long periods of standing.

What are warning signs of premature labor?

It may be possible to prevent a premature birth by knowing the warning signs and calling your health care provider if you think you might be having premature labor. Warning signs and symptoms of premature labor include:

- a contraction every ten minutes or more frequently within one hour (five or more uterine contractions in an hour);

- watery fluid leaking from your vagina (this could indicate that your bag of water is broken);

- menstrual-like cramps in the lower abdomen that can come and go or be constant;

- low, dull backache felt below the waistline that may come and go or be constant;

- pelvic pressure that feels like your baby is pushing down;

- abdominal cramps that may occur with or without diarrhea;

- increase or change in vaginal discharge.

What does a contraction feel like?

As the muscles of your uterus contract, you will feel your abdomen harden. As the contraction goes away, your uterus becomes soft. Throughout pregnancy, the layers of your uterus will tighten irregularly which are usually not painful. These are known as Braxton Hicks contractions and are usually irregular and do not open the cervix. If these contractions become regular or more frequent such as one every ten to twelve minutes for at least an hour, they may be premature labor contractions, which can cause the cervix to open. If this happens, it is important to contact your health care provider as soon as possible.

How can I check for contractions?

While lying down, use your fingertips to feel your uterus tighten and soften. This is called "palpation." During a contraction your abdomen will feel hard all over, not just in one area. However, as your baby grows you may feel your abdomen become firmer in one area and then become soft again.

What should I do if I think I am experiencing premature labor?

If you think you are showing signs and symptoms of premature labor, call your health care provider immediately. It is natural to be a bit anxious during this time but by becoming aware of the symptoms and taking the following steps, you can help prevent premature labor:

- Empty your bladder.

- Lie down tilted towards your left side; this may slow down or stop signs and symptoms.

- Avoid lying flat on your back; this may cause contractions to increase.

- Drink several glasses of water because dehydration can cause contractions.

- Monitor contractions for one hour by counting the minutes from the beginning of one contraction to the beginning of the next.

If symptoms worsen or don't disappear after one hour, call your health care provider again or go to the hospital. When you call your health care provider, be sure to tell them that you are concerned that you might have started premature labor. The only sure way to know if you are in premature labor is by examination of your cervix. If your cervix is opening up, premature labor could be the cause.

What is the treatment to prevent premature labor from starting or continuing?

Magnesium sulfate is a medication given through an intravenous (IV) line, which may cause nausea temporarily. A large dose is given initially and then a smaller continuous dose is given for twelve to twenty-four hours or more.

Corticosteroid is a medication given twenty-four hours before birth to help accelerate the baby's lung and brain maturity.

Oral medications are sometimes used to decrease the frequency of contractions, and may make women feel better.

What impact does premature labor have on my pregnancy?

The longer your baby is in the womb, the better the chance he or she will be healthy. Babies who are born prematurely are at higher risk of brain and other neurological complications, as well as breathing and digestive problems. Some premature babies grow up with a developmental delay and/or have learning difficulties in school. The earlier in pregnancy a baby is born, the more health problems are likely to develop.

Premature labor does not always result in premature delivery. Some women with premature labor and early dilation of the cervix are put on bed rest until the pregnancy progresses.

Most babies born prior to twenty-four weeks have little chance of survival. Only about 50 percent will survive and the other 50 percent may die or have permanent problems. However, babies born after thirty-two weeks have a very high survival rate and usually do not have long-term complications.

Premature babies born at hospitals with neonatal intensive care units (NICU) have the best results. If you deliver at a hospital that does not have a NICU, you might be transferred to a nearby hospital.

Chapter 16

Complications of Prematurity

Chapter Contents

Section 16.1

Apnea of Prematurity

After they're born, babies must breathe continuously to get oxygen. In a premature baby, the part of the central nervous system (brain and spinal cord) that controls breathing is not yet mature enough to allow nonstop breathing. This causes large bursts of breath followed by periods of shallow breathing or stopped breathing. The medical term for this is apnea of prematurity, or AOP.

About Apnea of Prematurity

Apnea of prematurity is fairly common in preemies. Doctors usually diagnose the condition before the mother and baby are discharged from the hospital, and the apnea usually goes away on its own as the infant matures. Once apnea of prematurity goes away, it does not come back. But no doubt about it—it's frightening while it's happening.

Apnea is a medical term that means a baby has stopped breathing. Most experts define apnea of prematurity as a condition in which premature infants stop breathing for fifteen to twenty seconds during sleep.

Generally, babies who are born at less than thirty-five weeks' gestation have periods when they stop breathing or their heart rates drop. (The medical name for a slowed heart rate is bradycardia.) These breathing abnormalities may begin after two days of life and last for up to two to three months after the birth. The lower the infant's weight and level of prematurity at birth, the more likely he or she will have AOP.

Although it's normal for all infants to have pauses in breathing and heart rates, those with AOP have drops in heart rate below eighty beats per minute, which causes them to become pale or bluish. They may also appear limp and their breathing may be noisy. They then either start breathing again by themselves or require help to resume breathing.

AOP should not be confused with periodic breathing, which is also common in premature newborns. Periodic breathing is marked by a pause in breathing that lasts just a few seconds and is followed by several rapid and shallow breaths. Periodic breathing is not accompanied by a change in facial color (such as blueness around the mouth) or a drop in heart rate. A baby who has periodic breathing resumes regular breathing on his or her own. Although it can be frightening, periodic breathing typically causes no other problems in newborns.

Treatment

Most of the time, premature infants (especially those less than thirty-four weeks' gestation at birth) will receive medical care for apnea of prematurity in the hospital's neonatal intensive care unit (NICU). When they are first born, many of these premature infants must get help breathing because their lungs are too immature to allow them to breathe on their own.

Medications

Many babies with AOP are given oral or intravenous (IV) caffeine medication to stimulate their breathing. Like the caffeine in coffee or soft drinks, a low dose of caffeine helps keep infants alert and breathing regularly. Most infants are taken off the caffeine while still in the NICU, although a small number will be discharged on the medication.

Monitoring Breathing

Babies are monitored continuously for any evidence of apnea. The cardiorespiratory monitor (also known as an apnea and bradycardia, or A/B, monitor) also tracks the infant's heart rate. An alarm on the monitor sounds if there's no breath for a set number of seconds. When the monitor sounds, a nurse immediately checks the baby for signs of distress. False alarms are not uncommon.

If a baby doesn't begin to breathe again within fifteen seconds, a nurse will rub the baby's back, arms, or legs to stimulate the breathing. Most of the time, babies with apnea of prematurity spells will begin breathing again on their own with this kind of stimulation.

However, if the nurse handles the baby, and the baby still hasn't begun breathing unassisted and becomes pale or bluish in color, oxygen may be administered with a handheld bag and mask. The nurse or doctor will place the mask over the infant's face and use the bag to slowly pump a few breaths into the lungs. Usually only a few breaths are needed before the baby begins to breathe again on his or her own.

AOP can happen once a day or many times a day. Doctors will closely evaluate your infant to make sure the apnea isn't due to another condition, such as infection.

When Your Baby Is on a Home Apnea Monitor

Although apnea spells are usually resolved by the time most preemies go home, a few will continue to have them. In these cases, if the doctor thinks it's necessary, the baby will be discharged from the NICU with an apnea monitor. Your baby may also need to take caffeine medication for a short time at home.

An apnea monitor has two main parts: a belt with sensory wires that a baby wears around the chest and a monitoring unit with an alarm. The sensors measure the baby's chest movement and breathing rate while the monitor continuously records these rates.

Before your baby leaves the hospital, the NICU staff will thoroughly review the monitor with you and give you detailed instructions on how and when to use it, as well as how to respond to an alarm. Parents and caregivers will also be trained in infant cardiopulmonary resuscitation (CPR), even though it's unlikely they'll ever have to use it.

If your baby isn't breathing or his or her face seems pale or bluish, follow the instructions given to you by the NICU staff. Usually, your response will involve some gentle stimulation techniques and, if these don't work, starting CPR and calling 911. Remember, never shake your baby to wake him or her.

It can be very stressful to have a baby at home on an apnea monitor. Some parents find themselves watching the monitor, afraid even to take a shower or run to the mailbox. This usually becomes easier with time. If you're feeling this way, it can help to share your feelings with the NICU staff. They may be able to reassure you and even put you in touch with other parents of preemies who have gone through the same thing.

Your doctor will determine how long your baby wears the monitor, so be sure to ask if you have any questions or concerns.

Caring for Your Baby

Apnea of prematurity usually resolves on its own with time. For most preemies, this means AOP stops around forty-four weeks of postconceptional age. Postconceptional age is defined as the gestational age (how many weeks of pregnancy at the time of birth) plus the postnatal age (weeks of age since birth). In rare cases, AOP continues for a few weeks longer.

Healthy infants who have had AOP usually do not go on to have more health or developmental problems than other babies. The apnea of prematurity does not cause brain damage. A healthy baby who is apnea free for a week will probably never have AOP again.

Although sudden infant death syndrome (SIDS) does occur more often in premature infants, no relationship between AOP and SIDS has ever been proved.

Aside from AOP, other complications with your premature baby may limit the time and interaction that you can have with your little one. Nevertheless, you can bond with your baby in the NICU. Talk to the NICU staff about what type of interaction would be best for your baby, whether it's holding, feeding, caressing, or just speaking softly. The NICU staff is not only trained to care for premature babies, but also to reassure and support their parents.

Section 16.2

Bronchopulmonary Dysplasia

Excerpted from "Bronchopulmonary Dysplasia,"
© 2012 A.D.A.M., Inc. Reprinted with permission.

Bronchopulmonary dysplasia (BPD) is a chronic lung condition that affects newborn babies who were either put on a breathing machine after birth or were born very early (prematurely).

Causes

Bronchopulmonary dysplasia (BPD) occurs in severely ill infants who have received high levels of oxygen for long periods of time or who have been on a breathing machine (ventilator).

It is more common in infants born early (prematurely), whose lungs were not fully developed at birth.

Risk factors include:

- congenital heart disease;

- prematurity, usually in infants born before thirty-two weeks gestation;

- severe respiratory or lung infection.

The risk of severe BPD has decreased in recent years.

Symptoms

- Bluish skin color (cyanosis)
- Cough
- Rapid breathing
- Shortness of breath

Exams and Tests

- Arterial blood gas
- Chest computed tomography (CT) scan
- Chest x-ray
- Pulse oximetry

Treatment

In the Hospital

A breathing machine (ventilator) is usually needed to send pressure to the lungs to keep the baby's lung tissue inflated and to deliver more oxygen. Pressures and oxygen levels are slowly reduced. After being weaned from the ventilator, the infant may continue to get oxygen by a mask or nasal tube for several weeks or months.

Infants with BPD are usually fed by tubes inserted into the stomach (nasogastric [NG] tube). These babies need extra calories due to the effort of breathing. Infants may need to limit fluids, and may be given medications that remove water from the body (diuretics) to keep the lungs from filling with fluid. Other medications can include corticosteroids, bronchodilators, and surfactant.

Parents of these infants need emotional support, because it can take time for the disease to get better, and the infant may need to stay in the hospital for a long time.

At Home

Infants with BPD may need oxygen therapy for weeks to months after leaving the hospital. It is very important for all infants with chronic lung disease to receive enough calories as they recover. Many will need tube feedings or special formulas.

It is very important to prevent your child from getting colds and other respiratory infections, such as respiratory syncytial virus (RSV).

A simple way to help prevent RSV infection is to wash your hands often, especially before touching your baby. It's important to make certain that other people, especially caregivers, take precautions to avoid giving RSV to your baby. The following simple steps can help protect your baby:

- Insist that others wash their hands with warm water and soap before touching your baby.

- Have others avoid contact with your baby if they have a cold or fever. If necessary, it may be helpful for them to wear a mask.

- Be aware that kissing your baby can spread RSV infection.

- Try to keep young children away from your baby. RSV is very common among young children and easily spreads from child to child.

- Do not smoke inside your house, car, or anywhere near your baby. Exposure to tobacco smoke increases the risk of RSV illness.

Parents with high-risk infants should avoid crowds during outbreaks of RSV. Moderate-to-large outbreaks are often reported in the local news and newspapers to provide parents with an opportunity to avoid exposure.

The drug palivizumab (Synagis) is approved for the prevention of RSV disease in children younger than twenty-four months who are at high risk for serious RSV disease. Ask your doctor whether your child is at high risk for RSV and if he or she needs this medicine.

Outlook (Prognosis)

Babies with BPD get better slowly over time. It's possible for infants to need oxygen therapy for many months. Some infants with this condition might not survive. Some children are left with long-term lung damage.

Possible Complications

Babies who have had BPD are at greater risk for repeated respiratory infections, such as pneumonia, bronchiolitis, and respiratory syncytial virus (RSV), that require a hospital stay. Many of the airway (bronchiole) changes in babies with BPD will not go away.

Other potential complications in babies who have had BPD are:

- developmental problems;

- poor growth;

- pulmonary hypertension.

Prevention

To help prevent BPD:

- Prevent premature delivery whenever possible. Certain pregnant women can take the medication betamethasone to help prevent RSV in their newborns.

- The health care provider should take the baby off breathing assistance early, if possible, and use a substance that helps open the baby's lungs (surfactant).

Section 16.3

Intraventricular Hemorrhage of the Newborn

"Intraventricular Hemorrhage (IVH) in Premature Babies," reprinted with permission from the Children's Hospitals and Clinics of Minnesota, © 2013. All rights reserved. For additional information, visit http://www .childrensmn.org.

What is intraventricular hemorrhage?

The ventricles (ven-trih-kuhls) are spaces in the brain that contain cerebrospinal fluid. Intraventricular hemorrhage (in-trah-ven-trik-yu-lar hem-or-age, or IVH) is bleeding in or near the ventricles. It is sometimes called a "bleed."

What causes IVH?

A preterm baby's brain has many tiny, fragile blood vessels. After birth, the premature baby's brain is exposed to changes in blood flow and oxygen levels. This may cause the blood vessels to break and bleeding to occur. It happens mostly in babies who are extremely premature or who have medical problems during or after birth.

What are the signs of IVH?

Many babies do not have any symptoms at the time the bleeding occurs. Some babies do have symptoms such as: apnea (pauses in breathing), bradycardia (low heart rate), anemia, seizures, poor muscle tone, decreased activity, and bulging fontanel (the soft spot on the top of the baby's head).

How is IVH diagnosed?

Babies at risk for IVH will have an ultrasound of the head to check for bleeding in the first days after birth. This test is done at the baby's bedside and uses sound waves to give a picture of the baby's brain. The picture will show the size of the ventricles and any areas of bleeding in the brain tissue.

219

IVH is graded on a scale of one to four, with grade IV being most severe (see Figure 16.1).

Grade I: bleeding near ventricle

Grade II: Blood in ventricle

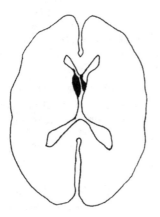
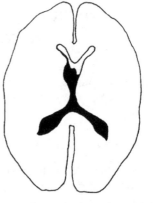

Grade III: Enlarged ventricle

Grade IV: Enlarged ventricle with blood in brain tissue

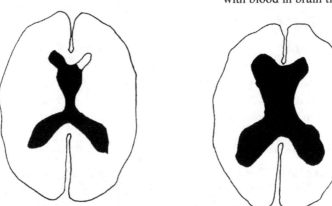

Figure 16.1. Grades of intraventricular hemorrhage (cross-section view of the brain): Grade I: bleeding near ventricle; Grade II: Blood in ventricle; Grade III: Enlarged ventricle; Grade IV: Enlarged ventricle with blood in brain tissue.

What happens to babies who have an IVH?

As many as 30 percent of babies born weighing less than 1,000 grams (about 2 pounds, 4 ounces) have intraventricular hemorrhages.

Most of these bleeds are mild (grade I or II), and about 90 percent resolve with few or no problems. In mild cases, the body absorbs the blood. Usually the follow-up head ultrasound is normal. The baby's development is most often typical for a preterm baby.

In more severe bleeds (grade III or IV), as blood absorbs there can be damage to the brain tissue. These bleeds (especially grade IV) may result in more problems. Short-term problems include enlarged ventricles and hydrocephalus.

Long-term problems include cerebral palsy (spasticity), hearing loss, vision problems, and learning disabilities.

How will I know if my baby will have long-term problems?

This can only be determined over time by monitoring the baby's development. For this reason, it is important to have your baby's progress followed after discharge from the hospital.

Section 16.4

Jaundice and Kernicterus

Excerpted from "Facts about Jaundice and Kernicterus,"
Centers for Disease Control and Prevention, March 30, 2011.

Jaundice is the yellow color seen in the skin of many newborns. Jaundice happens when a chemical called bilirubin builds up in the baby's blood. During pregnancy, the mother's liver removes bilirubin for the baby, but after birth the baby's liver must remove the bilirubin. In some babies, the liver might not be developed enough to efficiently get rid of bilirubin. When too much bilirubin builds up in a new baby's body, the skin and whites of the eyes might look yellow. This yellow coloring is called jaundice.

When severe jaundice goes untreated for too long, it can cause a condition called kernicterus. Kernicterus is a type of brain damage that can result from high levels of bilirubin in a baby's blood. It can cause athetoid cerebral palsy and hearing loss. Kernicterus also causes problems with vision and teeth and sometimes can cause intellectual disabilities. Early detection and management of jaundice can prevent kernicterus.

Signs and Symptoms

Jaundice usually appears first on the face and then moves to the chest, belly, arms, and legs as bilirubin levels get higher. The whites of the eyes can also look yellow. Jaundice can be harder to see in babies with darker skin color. The baby's doctor or nurse can test how much bilirubin is in the baby's blood.

See your baby's doctor the same day if your baby:

• is very yellow or orange (skin color changes start from the head and spread to the toes);

• is hard to wake up or will not sleep at all;

• is not breastfeeding or sucking from a bottle well;

• is very fussy;

• does not have enough wet or dirty diapers.

Get emergency medical help if your baby:

- is crying inconsolably or with a high pitch;
- is arched like a bow (the head or neck and heels are bent backward and the body forward);
- has a stiff, limp, or floppy body;
- has strange eye movements.

Diagnosis

Before leaving the hospital with your newborn, ask the doctor or nurse about a jaundice bilirubin test.

A doctor or nurse may check the baby's bilirubin using a light meter that is placed on the baby's head. This results in a transcutaneous bilirubin (TcB) level. If it is high, a blood test will likely be ordered.

The best way to accurately measure bilirubin is with a small blood sample from the baby's heel. This results in a total serum bilirubin (TSB) level. If the level is high, based upon the baby's age in hours and other risk factors, treatment will likely follow. Repeat blood samples will also likely be taken to ensure that the TSB decreases with the prescribed treatment.

Bilirubin levels are usually the highest when the baby is three to five days old. At a minimum, babies should be checked for jaundice every eight to twelve hours in the first forty-eight hours of life and again before five days of age.

Treatment

No baby should develop brain damage from untreated jaundice.

When being treated for high bilirubin levels, the baby will be undressed and put under special lights. The lights will not hurt the baby. This can be done in the hospital or even at home. The baby's milk intake may also need to be increased. In some cases, if the baby has very high bilirubin levels, the doctor will do a blood exchange transfusion. Jaundice is generally treated before brain damage is a concern.

Putting the baby in sunlight is not recommended as a safe way of treating jaundice.

Risk Factors

About 60 percent of all babies have jaundice. Some babies are more likely to have severe jaundice and higher bilirubin levels than others.

Babies with any of the following risk factors need close monitoring and early jaundice management:

Preterm babies: Babies born before thirty-seven weeks, or 8½ months, of pregnancy might have jaundice because their liver is not fully developed. The young liver might not be able to get rid of so much bilirubin.

Babies with darker skin color: Jaundice may be missed or not recognized in a baby with darker skin color. Checking the gums and inner lips may detect jaundice. If there is any doubt, a bilirubin test should be done.

East Asian or Mediterranean descent: A baby born to an East Asian or Mediterranean family is at a higher risk of becoming jaundiced. Also, some families inherit conditions (such as G6PD deficiency), and their babies are more likely to get jaundice.

Feeding difficulties: A baby who is not eating, wetting, or stooling well in the first few days of life is more likely to get jaundice.

Sibling with jaundice: A baby with a sister or brother that had jaundice is more likely to develop jaundice.

Bruising: A baby with bruises at birth is more likely to get jaundice. A bruise forms when blood leaks out of a blood vessel and causes the skin to look black and blue. The healing of large bruises can cause high levels of bilirubin, and your baby might get jaundice.

Blood type: Women with an O blood type or Rh-negative blood factor might have babies with higher bilirubin levels. A mother with Rh incompatibility should be given RhoGAM.

If You're Concerned

If you think your baby has jaundice, you should call and visit your baby's doctor right away. Ask your baby's doctor or nurse about a jaundice bilirubin test.

If your baby does have jaundice, it is important to take jaundice seriously and stick to the follow-up plan for appointments and recommended care.

Section 16.5

Necrotizing Enterocolitis

About Necrotizing Enterocolitis

As if the birth of a premature baby isn't stressful enough, premature babies can experience a number of diseases within the first weeks of life.

Necrotizing enterocolitis (NEC) is one of them. "Necrotizing" means the death of tissue, "entero" refers to the small intestine, "colo" to the large intestine, and "itis" means inflammation. But knowing what the words mean is only the start of understanding this infant disease.

A gastrointestinal disease that mostly affects premature infants, NEC involves infection and inflammation that causes destruction of the bowel (intestine) or part of the bowel. Although it affects only one in two thousand to four thousand births, or between 1 and 5 percent of neonatal intensive care unit (NICU) admissions, NEC is the most common and serious gastrointestinal disorder among hospitalized preterm infants.

NEC usually occurs within the first two weeks of life, usually after milk feeding has begun (at first, feedings are usually given through a tube that goes directly to the baby's stomach). About 10 percent of babies weighing less than 3 pounds, 5 ounces (1,500 grams) experience NEC. These premature infants have immature bowels, which are sensitive to changes in blood flow and prone to infection. They may have difficulty with blood and oxygen circulation and digestion, which increases their chances of developing NEC.

Causes

The exact cause of NEC is unknown, but one theory is that the intestinal tissues of premature infants are weakened by too little oxygen or blood flow. So when feedings are started, the added stress of food moving through the intestine allows bacteria normally found in the intestine to invade and damage the wall of the intestinal tissues. The damage may affect only a short segment of the intestine or can progress quickly to involve a much larger portion.

The infant is unable to continue feedings and starts to appear ill if bacteria continue to spread through the wall of the intestines and sometimes into the bloodstream. He or she may also develop imbalances in the minerals in the blood.

In severe cases of NEC, a hole (perforation) may develop in the intestine, allowing bacteria to leak into the abdomen and cause life-threatening infection (peritonitis). Because the infant's body systems are immature, even with quick treatment for NEC there may be serious complications.

Other factors seem to increase the risk of developing NEC. Some experts believe that the makeup of infant formula, the rate of delivery of the formula, or the immaturity of the mucous membranes in the intestines can cause NEC. (Babies who are fed breast milk can also develop NEC, but their risk is lower.)

Another theory is that babies born through difficult deliveries with lowered oxygen levels can develop NEC. When there isn't enough oxygen, the body sends the available oxygen and blood to vital organs instead of the gastrointestinal tract, and NEC can result.

Babies with an increased number of red blood cells (polycythemia) in circulation also seem to be at higher risk for NEC. Too many red blood cells thicken the blood and hinder the transport of oxygen to the intestines.

NEC sometimes seems to occur in "epidemics," affecting several infants in the same nursery. Although this may be due to coincidence, it suggests the possibility that it could in some cases be spread from one baby to another, despite the fact that all nurseries have very strict precautions to prevent the spread of infection.

Signs and Symptoms

The symptoms of NEC can resemble those of other digestive conditions, and may vary from infant to infant. Common symptoms include:

- poor tolerance to feedings;
- feedings stay in stomach longer than expected;
- decreased bowel sounds;
- abdominal distension (bloating) and tenderness;

- greenish (bile-colored) vomit;
- redness of the abdomen;
- increase in stools, or lack of stools;
- bloody stools.

More subtle signs of NEC might include apnea (periodic stoppage of breathing), bradycardia (slowed heart rate), diarrhea, lethargy, and fluctuating body temperature. Advanced cases may show fluid in the peritoneal (abdominal) cavity, peritonitis (infection of the membrane lining the abdomen), or shock.

Diagnosis and Treatment

The diagnosis of NEC is usually confirmed by the presence of an abnormal gas pattern as seen on an x-ray. This is indicated by a "bubbly" appearance of gas in the walls of the intestine, large veins of the liver, or the presence of air outside of the intestines in the abdominal cavity. A surgeon may insert a needle into the abdominal cavity to withdraw fluid to determine whether there is a hole in the intestines.

Most infants with NEC are treated medically, and symptoms end without the need for surgery. Treatment includes:

- stopping feedings;
- nasogastric drainage (inserting a tube through the nasal passages down to the stomach to remove air and fluid from the stomach and intestine);
- intravenous (IV) fluids for fluid replacement and nutrition;
- antibiotics for infection;
- frequent examinations and x-rays of the abdomen.

The baby's belly size is measured and watched carefully, and periodic blood samples are taken to look for bacteria. Stools are also checked for blood. If the abdomen is so swollen that it interferes with breathing, extra oxygen or mechanically assisted breathing (a ventilator) is used to help the baby breathe.

A baby who responds favorably may be back on regular feedings within seventy-two hours, although in most cases feedings are withheld and antibiotics are continued for seven to ten days. If the bowel perforates (tears) or the condition worsens, surgery may be indicated.

Severe cases of NEC may require removal of a segment of intestine. Sometimes after removal of diseased bowel, the healthy areas can be sewn back together. Other times, especially if the baby is very ill or there is spillage of stool in the abdomen, the surgeon will bring an area of the intestine or bowel to an opening on the abdomen (called an ostomy).

Most infants who develop NEC recover fully and do not have further feeding problems. In some cases, scarring and narrowing of the bowel may occur and can cause future intestinal obstruction or blockage.

Another residual problem may be malabsorption (the inability of the bowel to absorb nutrients normally). This is more common in children who required surgery for NEC and had part of their intestine removed.

Caring for Your Child

NEC can be extremely frightening to parents. Parents who are deprived of the experience of feeding their babies will certainly feel frustrated—their infant is so small, it just doesn't feel right to stop feedings. As important as it is to be able to hold and bond with your baby, this may not be possible while the baby is in critical condition.

Listen to and take comfort from the NICU staff—they are trained and eager to support parents of preemies as well as the preemies themselves. Remember that there's a good chance that your baby will be back on regular feedings within a short time.

Section 16.6

Persistent Pulmonary Hypertension of the Newborn

Persistent pulmonary hypertension of the newborn, or PPHN, occurs when a newborn's circulation system doesn't adapt to breathing outside the womb.

While in the womb, the fetus receives oxygen through the umbilical cord, so the lungs need little blood supply. There is high blood pressure in the lungs, so blood in the pulmonary artery is sent away from the lungs to the other organs through a fetal blood vessel, called the ductus arteriosus.

Normally, when a baby's born and begins breathing, the blood pressure in the lungs falls and blood flow to the lungs increases. Oxygen and carbon dioxide are exchanged in the lungs, then the blood is returned to the heart and pumped back out to the body. The ductus arteriosus constricts and permanently closes in the first day of life.

In babies with PPHN, the pressure in the lungs stays high and the ductus arteriosus remains open, allowing blood to be directed away from the lungs. PPHN is a rare but life-threatening condition that appears most often in full-term or post-term babies who have had a difficult birth or conditions such as infection or birth asphyxia.

Signs and Symptoms

The signs and symptoms of persistent pulmonary hypertension of the newborn may include:

- rapid breathing, also called tachypnea;

- rapid heart rate;

- respiratory distress, including signs such as flaring nostrils and grunting;

- cyanosis, a condition in which the baby's skin has a bluish tint even while he or she is receiving extra oxygen;

- heart murmur, where a baby has an extra or abnormal heart sound;

- low oxygen levels (a baby with PPHN may continue to have low oxygen levels in the blood even while receiving 100 percent oxygen).

Diagnosis

Various imaging and laboratory tests can help determine if a baby has persistent pulmonary hypertension of the newborn. These may include:

- chest x-rays to determine if the baby has lung disease or an enlarged heart;

- echocardiogram—an ultrasound of the heart—to determine if the baby has heart or lung disease and evaluate blood flow in those organs;

- ultrasound of the head to look for bleeding in the brain;

- arterial blood gas (ABG) to determine how well oxygen is being delivered to the body;

- complete blood count (CBC) to measure the number of oxygen-carrying red blood cells, white blood cells, and platelets;

- serum electrolyte tests to evaluate the balance of minerals in the blood;

- lumbar puncture, also called a spinal tap, and blood tests to help determine whether the baby has an infection;

- pulse oximetry, which measures oxygen levels in the blood, to help monitor whether the baby's tissues are receiving enough oxygen.

Treatment

In treatment for PPHN, the main goal is to increase oxygen flow to the baby's organs to prevent serious health problems. Treatment may include a wide range of mechanical ventilation and respiratory therapy options such as:

- **Oxygen:** One hundred percent supplemental oxygen may be given to your baby through a mask or plastic hood.

- **Assisted ventilation:** During this procedure, a tube is inserted into your baby's windpipe, a ventilator takes over your baby's breathing, and oxygen is given.

- **Nitric oxide:** Research has shown that this gas is effective in treating PPHN because it relaxes contracted lung blood vessels and improves blood flow to the lungs. It is given through the ventilator.

- **High frequency oscillatory ventilation:** This type of ventilation may improve the oxygen level in the blood if other types of ventilation aren't effective.

Extracorporeal Membrane Oxygenation (ECMO)

In addition, an extracorporeal membrane oxygenation (ECMO) machine may be used for babies who are experiencing serious heart or lung failure. The ECMO delivers oxygen to the brain and body as temporary support while the PPHN resolves. ECMO is similar to a heart-lung bypass machine, which takes over your baby's heart and lung functions with an external pump and oxygenator. Blood is drained from the baby to an artificial lung, where oxygen is added and carbon dioxide is removed, then the blood is pumped back into your child.

Section 16.7

Respiratory Distress Syndrome

Excerpted from "Neonatal Respiratory Distress Syndrome,"
© 2012 A.D.A.M., Inc. Reprinted with permission.

Neonatal respiratory distress syndrome (RDS) is most commonly seen in premature infants. The condition makes it difficult to breathe.

Causes

Neonatal RDS occurs in infants whose lungs have not yet fully developed.

The disease is mainly caused by a lack of a slippery, protective substance called surfactant, which helps the lungs inflate with air and keeps the air sacs from collapsing. This substance normally appears in fully developed lungs.

Neonatal RDS can also be the result of genetic problems with lung development.

The earlier a baby is born, the less developed the lungs are and the higher the chance of neonatal RDS. Most cases are seen in babies born before twenty-eight weeks. It is very uncommon in infants born full-term (at forty weeks).

In addition to prematurity, the following increase the risk of neonatal RDS:

- A brother or sister who had RDS

- Diabetes in the mother

- Cesarean delivery

- Delivery complications that reduce blood flow to the baby

- Multiple pregnancy (twins or more)

- Rapid labor

The risk of neonatal RDS may be decreased if the pregnant mother has chronic, pregnancy-related high blood pressure or prolonged rupture of membranes, because the stress of these situations can cause the infant's lungs to mature sooner.

Symptoms

The symptoms usually appear within minutes of birth, although they may not be seen for several hours. Symptoms may include:

- bluish color of the skin and mucus membranes (cyanosis);
- brief stop in breathing (apnea);
- decreased urine output;
- grunting;
- nasal flaring;
- rapid breathing;
- shallow breathing;
- shortness of breath and grunting sounds while breathing;
- unusual breathing movement—drawing back of the chest muscles with breathing.

Exams and Tests

A blood gas analysis shows low oxygen and excess acid in the body fluids.

A chest x-ray shows the lungs have a characteristic "ground glass" appearance, which often develops six to twelve hours after birth.

Lab tests are done to rule out infection and sepsis as a cause of the respiratory distress.

Treatment

High-risk and premature infants require prompt attention by a neonatal resuscitation team.

Despite greatly improved RDS treatment in recent years, many controversies still exist. Delivering artificial surfactant directly to the infant's lungs can be enormously important, but how much should be given and who should receive it and when is still under investigation.

Infants will be given warm, moist oxygen. This is critically important, but needs to be given carefully to reduce the side effects associated with too much oxygen.

A breathing machine can be lifesaving, especially for babies with the following:

• High levels of carbon dioxide in the arteries

• Low blood oxygen in the arteries

• Low blood pH (acidity)

It can also be lifesaving for infants with repeated breathing pauses. There are a number of different types of breathing machines available. However, the devices can damage fragile lung tissues, and breathing machines should be avoided or limited when possible.

A treatment called continuous positive airway pressure (CPAP) that delivers slightly pressurized air through the nose can help keep the airways open and may prevent the need for a breathing machine for many babies. Even with CPAP, oxygen and pressure will be reduced as soon as possible to prevent side effects associated with excessive oxygen or pressure.

A variety of other treatments may be used, including:

• extracorporeal membrane oxygenation (ECMO) to directly put oxygen in the blood if a breathing machine can't be used;

• inhaled nitric oxide to improve oxygen levels.

It is important that all babies with RDS receive excellent supportive care, including the following, which help reduce the infant's oxygen needs:

• Few disturbances

• Gentle handling

• Maintaining ideal body temperature

Infants with RDS also need careful fluid management and close attention to other situations, such as infections, if they develop.

Outlook (Prognosis)

The condition often worsens for two to four days after birth with slow improvement thereafter. Some infants with severe respiratory distress syndrome will die, although this is rare on the first day of life. If it occurs, it usually happens between days two and seven.

Long-term complications may develop as a result of too much oxygen, high pressures delivered to the lungs, the severity of the condition itself, or periods when the brain or other organs did not receive enough oxygen.

Possible Complications

Air or gas may build up in:

- the space surrounding the lungs (pneumothorax);
- the space in the chest between the lungs (pneumomediastinum);
- the area between the heart and the thin sac that surrounds the heart (pneumopericardium).

Other complications may include:

- bleeding into the brain (intraventricular hemorrhage of the newborn);
- bleeding into the lung (sometimes associated with surfactant use);
- blood clots due to an umbilical arterial catheter;
- bronchopulmonary dysplasia;
- delayed mental development and mental retardation associated with brain damage or bleeding;
- retinopathy of prematurity and blindness.

Prevention

Preventing prematurity is the most important way to prevent neonatal RDS. Ideally, this effort begins with the first prenatal visit, which should be scheduled as soon as a mother discovers that she is pregnant. Good prenatal care results in larger, healthier babies and fewer premature births.

Avoiding unnecessary or poorly timed cesarean sections can also reduce the risk of RDS.

If a mother does go into labor early, a lab test will be done to determine the maturity of the infant's lungs. When possible, labor is usually halted until the test shows that the baby's lungs have matured. This decreases the chances of developing RDS.

In some cases, medicines called corticosteroids may be given to help speed up lung maturity in the developing baby. They are often given to pregnant women between twenty-four and thirty-four weeks of pregnancy who seem likely to delivery in the next week. The therapy can reduce the rate and severity of RDS, as well as the rate of other complications of prematurity, such as intraventricular hemorrhage, patent ductus arteriosus, and necrotizing enterocolitis. It is not clear if additional doses of corticosteroids are safe or effective.

Section 16.8

Retinopathy of Prematurity

Excerpted from "Facts about Retinopathy of Prematurity,"
National Eye Institute, National Institutes of Health, October 2009.

What Is Retinopathy of Prematurity?

Retinopathy of prematurity (ROP) is a potentially blinding eye disorder that primarily affects premature infants weighing about 2.75 pounds (1250 grams) or less that are born before thirty-one weeks of gestation (A full-term pregnancy has a gestation of thirty-eight to forty-two weeks). The smaller a baby is at birth, the more likely that baby is to develop ROP. This disorder—which usually develops in both eyes—is one of the most common causes of visual loss in childhood and can lead to lifelong vision impairment and blindness. ROP was first diagnosed in 1942.

Frequently Asked Questions about Retinopathy of Prematurity

Are There Different Stages of ROP?

Yes. ROP is classified in five stages, ranging from mild (stage I) to severe (stage V):

- **Stage I:** Mildly abnormal blood vessel growth. Many children who develop stage I improve with no treatment and eventually develop normal vision. The disease resolves on its own without further progression.

- **Stage II:** Moderately abnormal blood vessel growth. Many children who develop stage II improve with no treatment and eventually develop normal vision. The disease resolves on its own without further progression.

- **Stage III:** Severely abnormal blood vessel growth. The abnormal blood vessels grow toward the center of the eye instead of following their normal growth pattern along the surface of the retina.

Some infants who develop stage III improve with no treatment and eventually develop normal vision. However, when infants have a certain degree of Stage III and "plus disease" develops, treatment is considered. "Plus disease" means that the blood vessels of the retina have become enlarged and twisted, indicating a worsening of the disease. Treatment at this point has a good chance of preventing retinal detachment.

- **Stage IV:** Partially detached retina. Traction from the scar produced by bleeding and abnormal vessels pulls the retina away from the wall of the eye.

- **Stage V:** Completely detached retina and the end stage of the disease. If the eye is left alone at this stage, the baby can have severe visual impairment and even blindness.

Most babies who develop ROP have stages I or II. However, in a small number of babies, ROP worsens, sometimes very rapidly. Untreated ROP threatens to destroy vision.

Can ROP Cause Other Complications?

Yes. Infants with ROP are considered to be at higher risk for developing certain eye problems later in life, such as retinal detachment, myopia (nearsightedness), strabismus (crossed eyes), amblyopia (lazy eye), and glaucoma. In many cases, these eye problems can be treated or controlled.

Causes and Risk Factors

What Causes ROP?

ROP occurs when abnormal blood vessels grow and spread throughout the retina, the tissue that lines the back of the eye. These abnormal blood vessels are fragile and can leak, scarring the retina and pulling it out of position. This causes a retinal detachment. Retinal detachment is the main cause of visual impairment and blindness in ROP.

Several complex factors may be responsible for the development of ROP. The eye starts to develop at about sixteen weeks of pregnancy, when the blood vessels of the retina begin to form at the optic nerve in the back of the eye. The blood vessels grow gradually toward the edges of the developing retina, supplying oxygen and nutrients. During the last twelve weeks of a pregnancy, the eye develops rapidly. When a baby is born full-term, the retinal blood vessel growth is mostly complete (The retina usually finishes growing a few weeks to a month after birth). But if a baby is born prematurely, before these blood vessels have reached the edges of the retina, normal vessel growth may stop. The edges of the retina—the periphery—may not get enough oxygen and nutrients.

Scientists believe that the periphery of the retina then sends out signals to other areas of the retina for nourishment. As a result, new abnormal vessels begin to grow. These new blood vessels are fragile and weak and can bleed, leading to retinal scarring. When these scars shrink, they pull on the retina, causing it to detach from the back of the eye.

Are There Other Risk Factors for ROP?

In addition to birth weight and how early a baby is born, other factors contributing to the risk of ROP include anemia, blood transfusions, respiratory distress, breathing difficulties, and the overall health of the infant.

An ROP epidemic occurred in the 1940s and early 1950s when hospital nurseries began using excessively high levels of oxygen in incubators to save the lives of premature infants. During this time, ROP was the leading cause of blindness in children in the United States. In 1954, scientists funded by the National Institutes of Health determined that the relatively high levels of oxygen routinely given to premature infants at that time were an important risk factor, and that reducing the level of oxygen given to premature babies reduced the incidence of ROP. With newer technology and methods to monitor the oxygen levels of infants, oxygen use as a risk factor has diminished in importance.

Although it had been suggested as a factor in the development of ROP, researchers supported by the National Eye Institute (NEI) determined that lighting levels in hospital nurseries has no effect on the development of ROP.

Treatment

How Is ROP Treated?

The most effective proven treatments for ROP are laser therapy or cryotherapy. Laser therapy "burns away" the periphery of the retina, which has no normal blood vessels. With cryotherapy, physicians use an instrument that generates freezing temperatures to briefly touch spots on the surface of the eye that overlie the periphery of the retina. Both laser treatment and cryotherapy destroy the peripheral areas of the retina, slowing or reversing the abnormal growth of blood vessels. Unfortunately, the treatments also destroy some side vision. This is done to save the most important part of our sight—the sharp, central vision we need for "straight ahead" activities such as reading, sewing, and driving.

Both laser treatments and cryotherapy are performed only on infants with advanced ROP, particularly stage III with "plus disease." Both treatments are considered invasive surgeries on the eye, and doctors don't know the long-term side effects of each.

In the later stages of ROP, other treatment options include the following:

- **Scleral buckle:** This involves placing a silicone band around the eye and tightening it. This keeps the vitreous gel from pulling on the scar tissue and allows the retina to flatten back down onto the wall of the eye. Infants who have had a scleral buckle need to have the band removed months or years later, since the eye continues to grow; otherwise they will become nearsighted. Scleral buckles are usually performed on infants with stage IV or V.

- **Vitrectomy:** Vitrectomy involves removing the vitreous and replacing it with a saline solution. After the vitreous has been removed, the scar tissue on the retina can be peeled back or cut away, allowing the retina to relax and lay back down against the eye wall. Vitrectomy is performed only at stage V.

What Happens If Treatment Does Not Work?

While ROP treatment decreases the chances for vision loss, it does not always prevent it. Not all babies respond to ROP treatment, and the disease may get worse. If treatment for ROP does not work, a retinal detachment may develop. Often, only part of the retina detaches (stage IV). When this happens, no further treatments may be needed, since a partial detachment may remain the same or go away without treatment. However, in some instances, physicians may recommend treatment to try to prevent further advancement of the retinal detachment (stage V). If the center of the retina or the entire retina detaches, central vision is threatened, and surgery may be recommended to reattach the retina.

Current Research

What Research Is Being Done?

The NEI-supported clinical studies on ROP include the following:

- The Cryotherapy for Retinopathy of Prematurity (CRYO-ROP)-Outcome Study of Cryotherapy for Retinopathy of Prematurity Study examined the safety and effectiveness of cryotherapy (freezing treatment) of the peripheral retina in reducing the risk of blindness in certain low birth-weight infants with ROP. Follow-up results confirm that applying a freezing treatment to the eyes of premature babies with ROP helps save their sight. The follow-up results also give researchers more information about how well the babies can see in the years after cryotherapy.

- The Effects of Light Reduction on Retinopathy of Prematurity (Light-ROP) Study evaluated the effect of ambient light reduction on the incidence of ROP. The study determined that light reduction has no effect on the development of a potentially blinding eye disorder in low birth weight infants. The study determined that light reduction in hospital nurseries has no effect on the development of ROP.

- The Supplemental Therapeutic Oxygen for Prethreshold Retinopathy of Prematurity (the STOP-ROP) Multicenter Trial tested the efficacy, safety, and costs of providing supplemental oxygen in moderately severe retinopathy of prematurity (prethreshold ROP). Results showed that modest supplemental oxygen given to premature infants with moderate cases of ROP may not significantly improve ROP, but definitely does not make it worse.

- The Early Treatment for Retinopathy of Prematurity Study (ETROP) is designed to determine whether earlier treatment in carefully selected cases of ROP will result in an overall better visual outcome than treatment at the conventional disease threshold point used in the CRYO-ROP study.

Section 16.9

Transient Tachypnea of the Newborn

Some newborns' breathing during the first hours of life is more rapid and labored than normal because of a lung condition called transient tachypnea of the newborn (TTN).

About 1 percent of all newborns develop TTN, which usually eases after a few days with treatment. Babies born with TTN need special monitoring and treatment while in the hospital, but afterwards most make a full recovery, with no lasting effect on growth and development.

About TTN

Before birth, a fetus's lungs are filled with fluid. While inside the mother, a fetus does not use the lungs to breathe—all oxygen comes from the blood vessels of the placenta.

As the due date nears, the baby's lungs begin to clear the fluid in response to hormonal changes. Some fluid may also be squeezed out during the birth, as a baby passes through the birth canal. After the birth, as a newborn takes those first breaths, the lungs fill with air and more fluid is pushed out of the lungs. Any remaining fluid is then coughed out or gradually absorbed into the body through the bloodstream and lymphatic system.

In infants with TTN, however, extra fluid in the lungs remains or the fluid is cleared too slowly. So it is more difficult for the baby to inhale oxygen properly, and the baby breathes faster and harder to get enough oxygen into the lungs.

Causes of TTN

TTN, also called "wet lungs" or type II respiratory distress syndrome, usually can be diagnosed in the hours after birth. It's not possible to detect before the birth whether a child will have it.

TTN can occur in both preemies (because their lungs are not yet fully developed) and full-term babies.

Newborns at higher risk for TTN include those who are:

- delivered by cesarean section (C-section);

- born to mothers with diabetes;

- born to mothers with asthma;

- small for gestational age (small at birth).

During vaginal births, especially with full-term babies, the pressure of passing through the birth canal squeezes some of the fluid out of the lungs. Hormonal changes during labor may also lead to absorption of some of the fluid.

Babies who are small or premature or who are delivered via rapid vaginal deliveries or C-section don't undergo the usual squeezing and hormone changes of a vaginal birth. So they tend to have more fluid than normal in their lungs when they take their first breaths.

Signs and Symptoms of TTN

Symptoms of TTN include:

- rapid, labored breathing (tachypnea) of more than sixty breaths a minute;

- grunting or moaning sounds when the baby exhales;

- flaring nostrils or head bobbing;

- retractions (when the skin pulls in between the ribs or under the ribcage during rapid or labored breathing);

- cyanosis (when the skin turns a bluish color) around the mouth and nose.

Other than the above symptoms, infants with TTN will look fairly healthy.

Diagnosis

Because TTN has symptoms that are initially similar to more severe newborn respiratory problems (such as pneumonia or persistent pulmonary hypertension), doctors may use chest x-rays in addition to physical examination to make a diagnosis.

Other indicators used to make a diagnosis of TTN:

- If an infant has TTN, the x-ray picture of the lungs will appear streaked and fluid may be seen. The x-ray will otherwise appear fairly normal.

- Pulse-oximetry monitoring, which is when a small piece of tape containing an oxygen sensor is placed around a baby's foot or hand and connected to a monitor. This tells doctors how well the lungs are sending oxygen to the blood and is also useful in monitoring TTN. Sometimes oxygen levels need to be checked with a blood test.

- A complete blood count (CBC) may also be drawn from one of the baby's veins or a heel to check for signs of infection.

Treating TNN

As with any newborn who has a breathing problem, infants with TTN are closely watched. Sometimes they'll be admitted to the neonatal intensive care unit (NICU) for extra care. Monitors will measure heart rate, breathing rate, and oxygen levels.

Some are simply monitored to ensure that their breathing rates slow down and their oxygen levels remain normal. Others might need to receive extra oxygen through a mask, a small tube under the nose, or under a plastic oxygen hood (sometimes called a "headbox").

If a baby is still struggling to breathe, even when oxygen is given, continuous positive airway pressure (CPAP) might be used to keep air flowing through the lungs. With CPAP, a baby wears a special oxygen cannula (a type of tubing placed directly into the nose) and a machine continuously pushes a stream of pressurized air into the baby's nose to help keep the lungs open during breathing.

In the most severe cases of TTN, a baby would need ventilator support, but this is rare.

Nutrition can be a problem if an infant is breathing so fast that he or she can't suck, swallow, and breathe simultaneously. In that case, intravenous (IV) fluids provide hydration and will prevent the infant's blood sugar from dipping to dangerously low levels.

If your baby has TTN and you want to breastfeed, talk to your doctor or a nurse about maintaining your milk supply by using a breast pump while your infant receives IV fluids.

Within twenty-four to forty-eight hours, the breathing of infants with TTN usually improves and returns to normal, and within seventy-two hours, all symptoms of TTN end.

If fluid stays in a baby's lungs beyond that, or if an infant is not improving, doctors will look for other medical problems.

Bringing Your Baby Home

After babies with TTN receive special monitoring and treatment in the hospital, they usually recover fully. Even after TTN resolves, watch for signs of respiratory distress and call your doctor if you suspect a problem.

If your baby has trouble breathing, appears blue, or if the skin pulls in between the ribs or under the ribcage during rapid or labored breathing, call your doctor or emergency services (911) right away.

Chapter 17

Pregnancy Concerns with Twins and Other Multiple Births

Chapter Contents

Section 17.1

Twins, Triplets, and Other Multiples

U.S. Department of Health and Human
Services Office on Women's Health, September 27, 2010.

If you are pregnant with more than one baby, you are far from alone. In the past two decades, the number of multiple births has climbed way up in the United States. In 2005, 133,122 twin babies and 6,208 triplet babies were born in the United States. In 1980 there were only 69,339 twin and 1,337 triplet births.

Why the increase? For one, more women are having babies after age thirty. Women in their thirties are more likely than younger women to conceive more than one baby naturally. Another reason is that more women are using fertility treatments to help them conceive. Fertility treatments can increase the likelihood of multiple births.

How Twins Are Formed

Twins form in one of two ways.

Identical twins occur when a single fertilized egg splits into two. Identical twins look almost exactly alike and share the exact same genes. Most identical twins happen by chance.

Fraternal twins occur when two separate eggs are fertilized by two separate sperm. Fraternal twins do not share the exact same genes— they are no more alike than they are to their siblings from different pregnancies. Fraternal twins tend to run in some families.

Multiple births can be fraternal, identical, or a combination. Multiples associated with fertility treatments are mainly fraternal.

Pregnancy with Multiples

Years ago, most twins came as a surprise. Now, thanks to advances in prenatal care, most women learn about a multiple pregnancy early. You might suspect you are pregnant with multiples if you have more severe body changes, including the following:

- Rapid weight gain in the first trimester
- Intense nausea and vomiting
- Extreme breast tenderness

Your doctor can confirm whether you are carrying more than one baby through ultrasound. If you are pregnant with twins or other multiples, you will need to see your doctor more often than women who are carrying only one baby because your risk of complications is greater. Women carrying more than one baby are at higher risk of the following:

- Preterm birth
- Low birth weight
- Preeclampsia
- Gestational diabetes
- Cesarean birth

More frequent prenatal visits help your doctor to monitor your and your babies' health. Your doctor will also tell you how much weight to gain, if you need to take extra vitamins, and how much activity is safe. With close monitoring, your babies will have the best chance of being born near term and at a healthy weight.

After delivery and once your babies come home, you may feel overwhelmed and exhausted. Ask for help from your partner, family, and friends. Volunteer help and support groups for parents of multiples also can ease the transition.

Section 17.2

Twin Reversed Arterial Perfusion (TRAP) Sequence

Acardiac twins, otherwise known as twin reversed-arterial perfusion (TRAP) sequence, is a rare and serious complication of monochorionic (one placenta) twins. Although the cause for the syndrome is not completely understood, it has been hypothesized that large vessels on the surface of the common placenta are responsible. Blood is perfused from one twin ("pump" twin) to the other twin ("acardiac" twin) by retrograde (backward) flow. Thus, the acardiac twin receives deoxygenated (oxygen-depleted) arterial blood from the pump twin in the wrong direction.

The inadequate perfusion of the acardiac twin is responsible for a spectrum of lethal anomalies, including acardia (absent heart), acephalus (absent skull), severe maldevelopment of the upper body, and a relative excess of edematous (excess fluid) connective tissue. Although the pump twin is structurally normal, there is an increased risk of death (up to 50 to 75 percent) for that twin. This is due to two important factors. First, the pump twin's heart has to work to support the perfusion (pumping of blood) of both the pump twin and the acardiac twin. Eventually, the strain to the pump twin's heart may be too great, resulting in high-output heart failure. Second, premature delivery or miscarriage may occur due to the polyhydramnios (excess amniotic fluid volume) and/or rapid growth of the acardiac twin.

Risk factors associated with pregnancy loss include polyhydramnios (defined as a maximum vertical pocket of amniotic fluid greater than or equal to 8.0 centimeters), large TRAP twin (estimated fetal weight of the acardiac twin is 50 percent or greater than that of the pump twin), evidence of heart failure in the pump twin (hydrops), or critically abnormal blood flow patterns identified on Doppler ultrasound. Because of the high risk of pregnancy loss in pregnancies complicated by acardiac/TRAP sequence in the setting of these risk factors, surgical treatment in the womb to separate the circulatory systems of the twins has been proposed.

Frequency

One in thirty-five thousand births.

Diagnosis

The diagnosis of acardiac twins or TRAP sequence is suggested by the presence of a monochorionic (single placenta) twin pregnancy in which one twin (the pump twin) appears structurally normal (no ultrasound findings consistent with birth defects), while the other twin (the acardiac/TRAP twin) has multiple profound birth defects (as listed in the background section above) which are not compatible with life.

The diagnosis is confirmed with the use of combined pulsed and color Doppler ultrasound studies. This method allows for the documentation of the arterial blood flow perfusing the acardiac/TRAP twin in a retrograde fashion, thus securing the diagnosis.

Once the diagnosis is established, further ultrasound studies must be performed to assess whether that individual pregnancy is in the high-risk category for pregnancy loss. These findings are summarized in the section below titled, "Candidacy for Surgical Treatment."

Management Options and Outcomes

The following management options and corresponding expected outcomes are listed below for pregnancies complicated by acardiac twins (TRAP sequence) with a high-risk factor, thus meeting criteria for fetal surgery:

1. **Expectant management:** This means that your pregnancy will be watched closely by frequent ultrasounds and other methods, with the delivery timed to prevent the death of the pump twin in the womb. This is associated with a 50 to 75 percent risk of pregnancy loss or extreme prematurity.

2. **Umbilical cord occlusion:** There is approximately a 66 percent chance that the pump twin will survive, with a 5 percent risk of neurologic injury.

General Candidacy for Surgical Treatment

The inclusion and exclusion criteria for consideration of surgical intervention to separate the circulatory system of the acardiac twin from the pump twin are listed below. The goal of surgical treatments for TRAP is to stop the flow of blood to the acardiac twin, thus relieving the strain on the pump twin.

Inclusion Criteria

All pregnancies must be between sixteen and twenty-six weeks' gestation. Once the diagnosis of acardiac/TRAP sequence has been confirmed, at least one of the following must be present to be considered a candidate for surgical treatment:

1. Size of acardiac twin exceeds the pump twin (abdominal circumference of acardiac twin larger than that of pump twin)

2. Polyhydramnios (maximum vertical pocket [MVP] > 8cm)

3. Critically abnormal Doppler in the pump twin (persistent absent or reversed diastolic flow in the umbilical artery, pulsatile flow in the umbilical vein, and/or reversed flow in the ductus venosus)

4. Fetal hydrops of the pump twin

5. Monochorionic-monoamniotic twins

6. The presence of a short cervix is a relative indication, and will be addressed on an individual basis

Exclusion Criteria

1. Presence of major congenital anomalies of the pump twin

2. Abnormal karyotype (characteristics of cell chromosomes)

3. Ruptured membranes (broken bag of waters)

4. Chorioamnionitis (infection in the womb)

Details of Procedures

Because of the peculiarities of each pregnancy complicated by acardiac/TRAP sequence, it is very important to stress that a single surgical approach is inadequate to provide optimal treatment. Each pregnancy must be individually assessed, and the type of fetal surgery must be tailored to the specifics of each case. Important considerations include surgical access (it is preferable to enter the sac of the acardiac/TRAP twin if possible), the size and position of the acardiac twin, the length of the umbilical cord, and the location and length of the placental vascular connections.

Using the above-mentioned considerations, the following surgical approaches are recommended. Note that most surgeries are performed under local anesthesia with intravenous sedation. About a 2- to 3-millimeter (one-tenth of an inch) incision is made on the abdomen to allow the insertion of the microsurgical instruments into the womb. Antibiotics are given to the mother.

Fetal Surgery Techniques

1. **Radiofrequency ablation:** Radiofrequency ablation is done with a very thin needle that is inserted where the blood vessels flow into the acardiac twin. Then, guided by ultrasound, a radiofrequency device is used to destroy the blood vessels in order to stop the blood flow. This is all done without any incisions, which makes the pain and recovery very similar to an amniocentesis.

2. **Umbilical cord ligation (UCL):** Suture ligature is tied around the umbilical cord of the acardiac/TRAP twin. The procedure could be carried out by ultrasound alone or by combined ultrasound-endoscopy. Some cases do require a second port (incision).

3. **Laser therapy of the placental vessels (L-AAVV):** Using the techniques originally developed for the treatment of twin-twin transfusion syndrome (TTTS), the communicating vessels on the placental surface are sealed by laser energy.

4. **Laser umbilical cord occlusion (L-UCO):** The umbilical cord artery then vein is laser occluded using laser energy guided through an operating endoscope.

5. **Transection (cutting across) of the umbilical cord of the acardiac/TRAP twin:** This technique is reserved for those cases with monoamniotic twins or where dividing amniorrhexis was performed.

Postoperative Care

Typically, you will remain in the hospital for one to two days after surgery. You will then be sent home to the care of your primary obstetrician and perinatologist. Weekly ultrasound is recommended for the four weeks after surgery. Then, depending on the clinical circumstances, follow up ultrasounds may be performed every three to four weeks for the duration of the pregnancy.

Section 17.3

Twin-Twin Transfusion Syndrome

TTTS, or twin-to-twin transfusion syndrome is a disease of the placenta. It affects pregnancies with monochorionic (shared-placenta) multiples when blood passes disproportionately from one baby to the other
through connecting blood vessels within their shared placenta. One baby,
the recipient twin, gets too much blood overloading his or her cardiovascular system, and may die from heart failure. The other baby, the donor
twin or stuck twin, does not get enough blood and may die from severe
anemia. Left untreated, mortality rates are near 100 percent.

The cause of TTTS is attributed to unbalanced flow of blood through
vascular channels that connect the circulatory systems of each twin
via the common placenta. The shunting of blood through the vascular
communications leads to a net flow of blood from one twin (the donor)
to the other twin (the recipient). The donor twin develops oligohydramnios (low amniotic fluid) and poor fetal growth, while the recipient
twin develops polyhydramnios (excess amniotic fluid), heart failure,
and hydrops. If left untreated, the pregnancy may be lost due to lack
of blood getting to the smaller twin, fluid overload and heart failure
in the larger twin, and/or preterm (early) labor leading to miscarriage
of the entire pregnancy.

Some general treatment approaches consist of using laser energy
to seal off the blood vessels that shunt blood between the fetuses.
Because the surgical approach is via an operative fetoscope, there is
minimal risk to the mother. Laser therapy for TTTS has been shown
to provide improved pregnancy outcomes compared to alternative
therapies, although all treatment options should be discussed with
your fetal surgeon.

Frequency

One in seven monochorionic pregnancies are afflicted with TTTS.

Diagnosis and Staging

The in utero diagnosis of TTTS is established by ultrasound. First, the presence of a shared placenta (monochorionic) is confirmed. Ultrasounds performed earlier in the pregnancy may be useful in establishing the chorionicity (number of placentas). Ultrasound findings such as a single placenta, same fetal sex, and a "T-sign" in which the dividing membrane inserts perpendicular to the placenta are helpful in diagnosing a monochorionic twin gestation.

TTTS is then diagnosed simply by assessing the discordance of amniotic fluid volume on either side of the dividing fetal membranes. The maximum vertical pocket (MVP) of amniotic fluid volume must be greater than or equal to 8.0 centimeters in the recipient's sac, and less than or equal to 2.0 centimeters in the donor's sac.

Although TTTS is diagnosed via ultrasound, women with a monochorionic or monoamniotic pregnancy can be alerted to certain symptoms that may require medical attention. Symptoms may include a sudden increase in the size of the pregnant belly, a sudden increase in fatigue or pressure in the belly or back, and/or sudden unexplained increase in weight (e.g., seven lbs in a week or less).

Once the diagnosis of TTTS is established, the severity of the condition may be assessed using the Quintero Staging System, as listed below. This staging system is based on the observations of several hundred patients with TTTS. Not only does this staging system mirror the progression of disease, but it has also been shown to be important in establishing the prognosis. An atypical presentation of TTTS may occur if the fetal bladder of the donor twin remains visible despite the presence of critically abnormal fetal Dopplers or hydrops.

Quintero Staging System

- **Stage I:** The fetal bladder of the donor twin remains visible sonographically.

- **Stage II:** The bladder of the donor twin is collapsed and not visible by ultrasound.

- **Stage III:** Critically abnormal fetal Doppler studies noted. This may include absent or reversed end-diastolic velocity (flow) in the umbilical artery, absent or reverse flow in the ductus venosus (liver), or pulsatile flow in the umbilical vein.

- **Stage IV:** Fetal hydrops present.

- **Stage V:** Demise of either twin.

Management Options and Outcomes

Untreated, TTTS that presents before twenty-eight weeks' gestation is associated with approximately a 90 percent mortality rate. Because of the dismal prognosis of TTTS, various treatment methods have been advocated. Recent studies have shown improved outcomes in patients treated with laser therapy compared to the traditional method of serial amnioreductions (Quintero, *AJOG*, 2003; Senat, *NEJM*, 2004). In the European randomized trial, the study was interrupted prematurely because statistical improvement in pregnancy outcome in the laser therapy group was achieved at the time of an interval analysis (Senat, *NEJM*, 2004).

Treatment Options

1. **Laser surgery:** This surgical approach utilizes an operative fetoscope to deliver laser energy that then seals off the offending blood vessels on the surface of the common placenta. Because the vascular connections between the two fetuses are sealed, no further blood exchange between the fetuses takes place, thus eliminating the syndrome. Pregnancy outcomes after laser therapy for TTTS is as follows: approximately 85 percent of patients will have at least one fetus survive, 50 percent will have both survive, with a 5 percent risk of neurologic sequelae such as cerebral palsy. These results remain consistent regardless of Quintero stage (i.e., severity).

2. **Expectant management:** In this option the pregnancy would be followed with serial ultrasound examinations. There is approximately a 90 percent pregnancy loss rate in cases of TTTS diagnosed before twenty-eight weeks' gestation.

3. **Amnioreduction:** The purpose of this procedure is to remove excess amniotic fluid from the recipient's sac in order to prevent premature birth or miscarriage. This procedure is done via a needle placed using ultrasound guidance. Because this approach does not treat the underlying cause of TTTS, amniotic fluid excess may recur, resulting in the need for multiple amnioreductions. Overall, the success rate of this treatment approach is approximately 66 percent chance of at least one fetal survivor, with an incidence of 15 percent chance of brain damage. Unlike laser therapy, the risk of fetal death and neurologic sequelae increases with increasing Quintero stage.

4. **Fetal septostomy:** This has been suggested as a treatment option for TTTS. This procedure entails the purposeful needling of the dividing membrane in the hopes to equalize the amniotic fluid within each sac. Studies have not shown improved outcomes using this approach. Moreover, the disruption of the dividing membrane may result in cord entanglement, which may be an additional cause of fetal death. Generally this procedure is not advised.

5. **Umbilical cord occlusion:** This procedure utilizes an operative fetoscope to interrupt the flow of blood through the umbilical cord of one of the fetuses. This fetus dies and remains inside the uterus for the duration of the pregnancy. The remaining twin will have an 85 percent chance of survival, and 5 percent risk of brain damage. Because the risks of this procedure are similar to laser therapy, but laser therapy provides the additional benefit of the chance of survival for both twins, this procedure is generally not offered for the treatment of TTTS unless the demise of one twin is a foregone conclusion due to fetal anomalies and condition.

Candidacy for Laser Surgery

To generally qualify for laser surgery, the following criteria usually must be met:

Inclusion criteria:

1. Gestational age: sixteen weeks, zero days to twenty-six weeks, zero days.

2. Diagnosis of TTTS:

   - Single (shared placenta) with thin dividing membrane (or no dividing membrane in the case of monoamniotic twins).

   - Polyhydramnios: maximum vertical pocket of 8 centimeters or more in the recipient twin, prior to amnioreduction.

   - Oligohydramnios: maximum vertical pocket of 2 centimeters or less in the donor twin, prior to amnioreduction.

   - Same gender, if visible.

General exclusion criteria:

1. One or both babies have other major birth defects.

2. Genetic studies showing an uncompensated abnormality.

3. A hole in the dividing membrane that was intentionally made.

4. Ruptured fetal membranes (leakage of amniotic fluid from the vagina).

5. Chorioamnionitis (infection in the uterus).

6. Ultrasound evidence of brain damage of either fetus.

7. Placental abruption (separation of the placenta from the uterus).

8. Active labor.

Laser Surgery–Details of Procedure

Most surgeries are performed under local anesthesia with some intravenous sedation. A small incision (3 millimeters or about one-tenth of an inch) will be made and a trocar (small metal tube) will be inserted into the amniotic sac of the recipient twin. Amniotic fluid may be sent for genetic and microbiology studies. An endoscope (medical telescope) will be passed into the uterus. The blood vessels, which are visible on the surface of the placenta, will be analyzed, and all communicating vessels will be sealed off with laser energy. A second trocar may have to be inserted to complete the surgery, particularly if the placenta is anterior. At the conclusion of the surgery, the excess amniotic fluid may be drained from the sac of the recipient twin. You will be given antibiotics before and after surgery.

Laser Surgery—Postoperative Care

Typically, you will remain in the hospital for one to two days after surgery. You will then be sent home to the care of your primary obstetrician and perinatologist. Weekly ultrasound is recommended for the four weeks after surgery. Then, depending on the clinical circumstances, follow up ultrasounds generally should be performed every two to three weeks for the duration of the pregnancy (however, it is the recommendation of Fetal Hope to have weekly monitoring via ultrasound, nonstress tests (NSTs), or other appropriate means).

Additional Information (Nutrition)

If TTTS is diagnosed in its early stages some physicians will recommend a wait and see approach. Under this approach the mother is usually encouraged to consume increased amounts of protein, often through protein drinks like Boost or Ensure. Some physicians incorrectly indicate that TTTS can be "cured" by bed rest and proper nutrition (usually an increase in protein through protein drinks). Most studies indicate, regardless of a TTTS diagnosis, most pregnant women with multiples suffer malnutrition due to the nutritional needs of more than one fetus on the woman. Fetal Hope does promote proper nutrition including increase in nutritious foods such as fruit, vegetables, and an increase in protein via lean meats and/or protein supplements. Providing proper nutrition to the pregnant mother will only allow her to be stronger for the pregnancy and for her babies to have more than adequate nutrition for their growth.

Section 17.4

Unequal Placental Sharing

The Facts

Although most pregnancies with monochorionic twins (twins that share a common placenta) are uncomplicated, the presence of a common placenta does pose a relatively increased risk to the welfare of the fetuses. The single placenta contains blood vessels that link the blood flow between the twins. Unbalanced flow of blood from one twin to the other twin may lead to a cascade of events that result in twin-twin transfusion syndrome. Another potential problem that may occur in monochorionic twins is the disproportionate distribution of placental mass between the twins (unequal sharing of the placenta). This factor may result in poor nourishment of one of the twins, resulting in subsequent poor overall fetal growth. Because this problem typically affects only one of the fetuses, this condition has been coined selective intrauterine growth restriction (SIUGR). SIUGR is estimated to occur in approximately 10 percent of monochorionic twin pregnancies.

Severe cases of monochorionic twins with SIUGR show ultrasound evidence of abnormal blood flow through the umbilical artery of the poorly grown twin. In this circumstance, spontaneous death of this baby within the womb may occur in up to 40 percent of cases. Because of the blood vessels that link the twins' circulatory system together, death of one twin may result in severe drop in blood pressure of the other twin and subsequent brain damage (up to 30 percent) or death (up to 40 percent). This complication results from the hemorrhage of blood from the appropriately grown twin into the demised SIUGR twin.

Because the adverse effects to the appropriately grown twin are mediated through the blood vessels that link the circulations of the twins, it has been suggested that obliteration of these vascular communications may result in improved outcomes for the normally grown twin. Separation of the circulations may be done using the surgical techniques which were originally developed for the treatment of twin-twin transfusion syndrome.

Diagnosis

The in utero diagnosis of SIUGR is established by ultrasound. First, the presence of a shared placenta (monochorionic) should be confirmed. Usually ultrasounds performed earlier in the pregnancy may be useful in establishing the chorionicity (number of placentas). Ultrasound findings such as a single placenta, same fetal sex, and a "T-sign" in which the dividing membrane inserts perpendicular to the placenta are helpful in diagnosing a monochorionic twin gestation.

Once a monochorionic placentation has been established, the diagnosis of SIUGR requires the presence of three important ultrasound findings:

1. The estimated fetal weight (EFW) of one twin measures less than the tenth percentile for the assigned gestational age. The EFW is calculated by measuring standard fetal biometric components via ultrasound. Because prior studies have shown negligible difference between growth curves for singleton and twin gestations in the second trimester, standards as established by Hadlock (1991) for singletons are used to assign the growth percentile.

2. Persistent absent or reversed flow in the umbilical artery of the growth-restricted twin.

3. Finally, the diagnosis of twin-twin transfusion syndrome (TTTS) must be excluded. TTTS is diagnosed by assessing the discordance of amniotic fluid volume on either side of

the dividing fetal membranes; the maximum vertical pocket (MVP) of amniotic fluid volume must be greater than or equal to 8.0 centimeters in the recipient's sac, and less than or equal to 2.0 centimeters in the donor's sac to secure the diagnosis of TTTS.

Management Options and Outcomes

The treatment options along with expected pregnancy outcomes are listed below:

1. **Expectant management:** Prior to the development of the laser therapy outlined below, the treatment of this condition has been traditionally one of expectant management. This entails at least weekly ultrasound assessments of fetal well-being, amniotic fluid volume assessment, and Doppler studies of the umbilical artery, as well as sonograms to assess fetal growth about every three weeks. After twenty-four weeks' gestation, parents traditionally discuss with their physicians whether there is a need for increased fetal surveillance, such as fetal heart rate monitoring, and if a course of steroids is required for fetal maturation therapy. Early delivery may be decided if fetal status is deemed nonreassuring based on fetal heart rate monitoring or ultrasound parameters. The challenge that this condition presents to parents and physicians alike is in regards to the timing of delivery. On the one hand, delay of delivery will reduce the complications associated with premature birth. On the other hand, prolongation of the pregnancy in this setting, particularly if findings suggestive of a nonreassuring fetal status are present, may result in the demise of one twin in the womb. This may occur in up to 40 percent of monochorionic twins with SIUGR. As described above, the death of one twin while in the womb may result in the concomitant demise of the other twin in as high as 40 percent of cases. If the other twin does survive, there is up to a 30 percent risk of subsequent neurologic handicap. The demise of a twin results in these adverse effects on the other twin because of the blood vessels on the surface of the placenta that connect the circulatory systems of the babies—essentially linking the livelihoods of each baby to one another.

2. **Laser therapy:** This surgical approach utilizes an operative fetoscope to deliver laser energy that then seals off the offending blood vessels on the surface of the common placenta.

Because the vascular connections between the two fetuses are sealed, no further blood exchange between the fetuses takes place. It has been theorized that elimination of the vascular communications may decrease or prevent harm to the surviving twin in the case of the demise of one twin. The magnitude of this potential benefit is unknown.

Candidacy for Treatment

To qualify for treatment, generally the following conditions must be met.

Inclusion Criteria

1. Gestational age sixteen to twenty-six weeks.

2. Sonographic evidence of monochorionicity (shared placenta).

3. Diagnosis of IUGR present in one twin (fetal weight at or below the tenth percentile for gestational age [Hadlock et al. 1991]).

4. Absent or reverse-end diastolic flow in the umbilical artery in the SIUGR twin.

General Exclusion Criteria

1. Presence of twin-twin transfusion syndrome defined as a maximum vertical pocket (MVP) of ≤ 2 cm in one sac and MVP of ≥ 8 cm in the other sac.

2. Presence of major congenital anomalies (anencephaly, acardia, spina bifida) or intracranial findings in either twin: IVH, porencephalic cysts, ventriculomegaly, or other findings suggestive of brain damage.

3. Unbalanced chromosomal complement.

4. Ruptured or detached membranes.

5. Placental abruption.

6. Chorioamnionitis (infection in the uterus).

7. Triplets

Details of Surgical Procedure

Most surgeries are performed under local anesthesia with some intravenous sedation. A small incision (3 millimeters or about one-tenth of an inch) will be made and a trocar (small metal tube) will be inserted into the amniotic sac of the normally grown twin. Amniotic fluid may be sent for genetic and microbiology studies. An endoscope (medical telescope) will be passed into the uterus. The blood vessels, which are visible on the surface of the placenta, will be analyzed, and all communicating vessels will be sealed off with laser energy. A second trocar may have to be inserted to complete the surgery, particularly if the placenta is anterior. You will be given antibiotics before and after surgery.

Postoperative Care

Typically, you will remain in the hospital for one to two days after surgery. You will then be sent home to the care of your primary obstetrician and perinatologist. Follow-up ultrasounds will be scheduled every week for the first month to detect possible intrauterine fetal demise, and monthly thereafter. Delivery will be decided based on obstetrical indications (however, it is the recommendation of Fetal Hope to have weekly monitoring via ultrasound, nonstress tests [NSTs], or other appropriate means.).

Section 17.5

Vanishing Twin Syndrome

Vanishing twin syndrome was first recognized in 1945. Vanishing twin syndrome is when one of a set of twin/multiple fetuses disappears in the uterus during pregnancy. This is the result of a miscarriage of one twin/multiple. The fetal tissue is absorbed by the other twin/multiple, the placenta, or the mother. This gives the appearance of a "vanishing twin."

How is vanishing twin syndrome identified?

Before the use of ultrasound, the diagnosis of the death of a member of a multiple pregnancy was made through an examination of the placenta after delivery. Today, with the availability of early ultrasounds, the presence of twins or multiple fetuses can be detected during the first trimester. A follow-up ultrasound may reveal the "disappearance" of a twin.

For example, a woman may have an ultrasound at six or seven weeks' gestation. The doctor identifies two fetuses and the woman is told she is having twins. When the woman returns for her next visit, only one heartbeat can be heard with Doppler. A second ultrasound is conducted and only one fetus is observed.

Sometimes a woman may have symptoms that would indicate a miscarriage, yet, with an ultrasound, a single baby is found in her uterus.

Vanishing twin syndrome has been diagnosed more frequently since the use of ultrasonography in early pregnancy. A conservative estimate of frequency is that vanishing twin syndrome occurs in 21 to 30 percent of multifetal pregnancies.

What is the cause of vanishing twin syndrome?

The cause of vanishing twin syndrome is frequently unknown. Abnormalities that result in the vanishing twin appear to be present from early in development rather than from a sudden occurrence. Analysis of the placenta and/or fetal tissue frequently reveals chromosomal abnormalities, while the surviving twin is usually normal. Improper cord implantation may also be a cause.

What are the effects of vanishing twin syndrome on the mother and surviving twin?

If the loss occurs within the first trimester, neither the remaining fetus nor the mother has clinical signs or symptoms. The prognosis of the surviving twin is usually excellent, but it depends on the factors that contributed to the death of the other twin. If the twin dies in the second or third trimester, there are increased risks to the surviving fetus. This could include a higher rate of cerebral palsy and a threat to the continuation of the pregnancy.

When a twin dies after the embryonic period of gestation (eight weeks), the water within the twin's tissues, the amniotic fluid, and the placental tissue may be reabsorbed. This results in the flattening of the deceased twin from the pressure of the surviving twin. At delivery, the deceased fetus may be identified as fetus compressus (compressed enough to be noticed) or as fetus papyraceous (flattened remarkably through loss of fluid and most of the soft tissue).

What are the signs of a possible vanishing twin syndrome?

Research indicates more cases in women over the age of thirty years.

Problems will usually begin early in the first trimester. The most common symptoms include bleeding, uterine cramps, and pelvic pain.

What medical care is recommended for vanishing twin syndrome?

No special medical care is necessary with an uncomplicated vanishing twin in the first trimester. Neither the surviving twin nor the mother would require medical treatment. If the fetal death is in the second or third trimester, the pregnancy may be treated as high-risk. Cerebral palsy may result in the surviving twin.

Pregnant women should seek medical care if they are experiencing bleeding, cramping, and pelvic pain. They should be evaluated at a place with ultrasound capabilities. The use of an ultrasound is important to determine that no viable fetus remains before deciding if a dilation and curettage (D&C) might be indicated. The woman can choose to wait for a natural miscarriage in many cases.

Chapter 18

Labor and Delivery Concerns in Complicated Pregnancies

Chapter Contents

Section 18.1

What to Expect in Labor and Delivery When Your Baby Has a Health Problem

"When Your Baby Is Born with a Health Problem," April 2009, reprinted with permission from www.kidshealth.org. This information was provided by KidsHealth®, one of the largest resources online for medically reviewed health information written for parents, kids, and teens. For more articles like this, visit www.KidsHealth.org, or www.TeensHealth.org. Copyright © 1995–2012 The Nemours Foundation. All rights reserved.

If you're expecting a baby, you're probably learning all you can about how to make your pregnancy, labor, and delivery go smoothly and leave you and your baby in good health. But it's also important to understand that certain health problems and complications can't be prevented, no matter how smoothly the pregnancy goes.

There's no way to be completely prepared for complications during delivery or for the discovery that your child has a birth defect or medical problem. But understanding common newborn health problems and how they're treated might reduce anxiety about the potential that something might go wrong.

Before Your Baby Is Born

With prenatal tests, doctors often can detect certain birth defects, such as spina bifida, Down syndrome, congenital heart disease, exposed bowel, or cleft lip, before the baby is born.

Other birth defects can't be discovered until after the baby is born. Delivery complications such as meconium aspiration (when a newborn inhales a mixture of meconium—the baby's first feces, ordinarily passed after birth—and amniotic fluid during labor and delivery) can occur.

If a birth defect is discovered prenatally, your doctor may discuss what will happen in the time right after you deliver the baby. You and your doctor should discuss which hospital is best prepared to care for your baby so that you can plan to deliver there.

You might want to ask if you can tour the intensive or special care unit at the hospital to become familiar with it and meet the team of health care professionals who may care for your baby. This team may include neonatologists, pediatric anesthesiologists, pediatric surgeons, neonatal nurses, nurse practitioners, and doctors in training (like fellows and residents).

Common Newborn Problems

It is very common for infants, particularly those born prematurely, to have jaundice or breathing problems.

Many preemies and even full-term infants can develop jaundice if their immature liver initially can't get rid of excess bilirubin (a yellow pigment produced by the normal breakdown of red blood cells) in the blood. Jaundice can make a baby's skin and whites of the eyes appear yellowish.

If your baby has jaundice, the doctor may order blood tests to measure the bilirubin levels and determine if treatment is necessary. Usually, jaundice is treated by exposing the baby to special lights that help break down the extra bilirubin so the baby's body can process it.

Immature lungs, another common problem, occurs when a baby's lungs lack sufficient surfactant, a chemical that prevents the air sacs from collapsing during breathing. Surfactant isn't usually fully in the fetal lungs until after thirty-four weeks' gestational age, so many preemies need help with their breathing. Ventilators, machines that are hooked up to a small plastic tube that goes into the baby's windpipe, are often used to aid in breathing.

Synthetic surfactant is now routinely given (down a breathing tube) to very premature babies soon after birth. Premature babies do not have enough of their own surfactant to keep their lungs expanded. Giving extra surfactant allows infants to breathe on their own much sooner than in the past, and they sustain less lung damage because they don't need long-term ventilator use.

In the Delivery Room

Most babies are born in a labor and delivery room. But if there are complications, the mother may be transferred to a delivery room with additional medical equipment. Besides the obstetrician, midwife, or family doctor, there might also be nurses, neonatologists, or other specialists on hand to provide special medical attention the baby might need.

For example, if a newborn has spina bifida (exposed spinal structures) or hydrocephalus (excess fluid inside of or surrounding the brain), the doctors will take special care to support the head or cover the opening in the spine. For a newborn with an exposed bowel, the intestines are covered to protect them from infection and from heat and fluid losses.

In the case of meconium aspiration, usually the doctor tries to clear the baby's airways with suction to draw out any fluid interfering with breathing. A baby who continues to have trouble breathing or is very premature may need a breathing tube.

Whenever there is a problem, the medical staff, including a pediatrician or neonatologist, will monitor the baby's breathing and heart rate and make sure that the infant is kept warm. If necessary, they will perform a special kind of cardiopulmonary resuscitation (CPR) for newborns. When stable enough to be moved, the baby is likely to be taken directly to the neonatal intensive care unit (NICU) for further treatment.

The obstetrics (OB) team will stay with the mother while the baby is being treated, providing any medical care she needs. The OB team makes sure that the mother delivers the placenta, that she receives any needed stitches, and in the case of cesarean delivery, completes the surgery.

Communicating with the Doctor

Ask the medical team caring for your baby in the NICU to communicate with you about your baby's condition. If your baby has a condition that was diagnosed before birth, the doctor will explain any changes from the original plan and update you on the baby's progress. When a problem is unanticipated, the doctor or nurse will explain what is going on. In an emergency, the medical staff may not be able to explain things right away, but will do so as soon as things calm down.

Beyond the Delivery Room

Once out of the delivery room, the baby might need intravenous (IV) medications or fluids. And because babies lose heat quickly, your newborn will be put in an incubator or radiant warmer to maintain proper body temperature.

If the baby's breathing is too fast or labored, the medical team may order chest x-rays to determine its cause. Sometimes, blood tests or a foot or hand oxygen monitor can tell the doctor how much help breathing the baby needs. The team may need to give the baby a little extra oxygen or put the baby on a ventilator to assist with breathing.

When the baby's breathing and heartbeat are stabilized, treatment for any birth defects may begin. This evaluation and treatment period can last days or weeks, depending on the baby's condition.

Doctors may also want to take blood tests to rule out any other problems and measure such things as the baby's blood count and blood sugar levels. Some blood tests can take blood from the baby's heel, while others must draw it directly from a vein in the baby's arm.

Getting the Care You Need

Time apart from a newborn is extremely difficult for the family— particularly the parents.

It's common to feel disappointment and even guilt. It can help to talk about these feelings with a member of the medical team or a hospital social worker. And getting as much information as possible about your baby's medical problem might help ease feelings of anxiety and powerlessness.

Most hospitals encourage parents to spend as much time as they can with their babies. If the baby is transferred to a hospital with a special neonatal care unit, consider asking if the mother can get necessary postpartum care there, too, so that they can recover together.

Sometimes it is necessary for babies to stay in the hospital after the mother has gone home. It's hard for new moms to leave without their babies, but it can help to talk about your feelings with friends, family, and the medical staff.

And parents should get plenty of rest and regular exercise and be sure to eat well during this time. If the mother wants to breastfeed, talk with a nurse or lactation consultant about using a breast pump so she can freeze breast milk for when the baby is ready for it.

If your baby is born with a health problem, you have many options for information and support. Start by asking your doctors for information on hospital- or community-based resources. Support groups, both in person and online, are available for many disorders and conditions.

Section 18.2

Cesarean Section

Every pregnant woman hopes for a short labor and delivery with no complications—manageable contractions, some pushing, then a beautiful baby—but it doesn't always work out that way.

These days, about 30 percent of all babies in the United States are delivered via cesarean section (C-section).

Even if you're envisioning a traditional vaginal birth, it may help to ease some fears to learn why and how C-sections are performed, just in case everything doesn't go as planned.

What Is a C-Section?

A C-section is the surgical delivery of a baby that involves making incisions in the mother's abdominal wall and uterus. Generally considered safe, C-sections do have more risks than vaginal births. Plus, you can come home sooner and recover quicker after a vaginal delivery.

However, C-sections can help women at risk for complications avoid dangerous delivery-room situations and can save the life of the mother and/or baby when emergencies occur.

C-sections are done by obstetricians (doctors who care for pregnant women before, during, and after birth) and some family physicians. Although more and more women are choosing midwives to deliver their babies, midwives of any licensing degree cannot perform C-sections.

Why They're Needed

Some C-sections are scheduled if the doctor is aware of certain factors that would make a vaginal birth risky. That means some women know ahead of time that they will be delivering via C-section and are able to schedule their baby's "birth day" well in advance. This allows them to prepare themselves emotionally and mentally for the birth—which can help to lessen the feelings of disappointment that many mothers who are unable to deliver vaginally experience.

So what determines if a woman is scheduled for a C-section? A doctor may schedule one if:

- the baby is in breech (feet- or bottom-first) or transverse (sideways) position in the womb (although some babies can be turned before labor begins or delivered vaginally using forceps and anesthesia);

- the baby has certain birth defects (such as severe hydrocephalus);

- the mother has problems with the placenta, such as placenta previa (when the placenta sits too low in the uterus and covers the cervix);

- the mother has a medical condition that could make a vaginal delivery risky for herself or the baby (such as human immunodeficiency virus [HIV] or an active case of genital herpes);

- some multiple pregnancies;

- the mother previously had surgery on her uterus or a C-section (although many such women can safely have a vaginal birth after a C-section, called a VBAC).

Some C-sections are unexpected emergency deliveries performed when complications arise with the mother and/or baby during pregnancy or labor. An emergency C-section might be required if:

- labor stops or isn't progressing as it should (and medications aren't helping);

- the placenta separates from the uterine wall too soon (called placental abruption);

- the umbilical cord becomes pinched (which could affect the baby's oxygen supply) or enters the birth canal before the baby (called umbilical cord prolapse);

- the baby is in fetal distress—certain changes in the baby's heart rate may mean that the baby is not getting enough oxygen;

- the baby's head or entire body is too big to fit through the birth canal.

Of course, each woman's pregnancy and delivery is different. If your doctor has recommended a C-section and it's not an emergency, you can ask for a second opinion. In the end, you most often need to rely on the judgment of the doctors.

The Procedure

The thought of having surgery can be unnerving for any woman. Here's a quick look at what usually happens during a scheduled C-section.

Your labor coach can be right by your side, clad in a surgical mask and gown, during the entire delivery (although partners may not be allowed to stay during emergency C-sections). Before the procedure begins, an anesthesiologist will discuss your options.

To prepare for the delivery, you'll probably have:

- various monitors in place to keep an eye on your heart rate, breathing, and blood pressure;

- your mouth and nose covered with an oxygen mask or a tube placed in your nostrils to give you oxygen;

- a catheter (a thin tube) inserted into your bladder through your urethra (which may be uncomfortable when it is placed, but should not be painful);

- an IV in your arm or hand;

- your belly washed and any hair between the bellybutton and pubic bone shaved;

- a privacy screen put around your belly.

After being given anesthesia, the doctor makes an incision on the skin of the abdomen—either vertically (from the bellybutton down to the pubic hair line) or horizontally (one to two inches above the pubic hairline, sometimes called "the bikini cut").

The doctor then gently parts the abdominal muscles to get to the uterus, where he or she will make another incision in the uterus itself. This incision can also be vertical or horizontal. Doctors usually use a horizontal incision in the uterus, also called transverse, which heals better and makes a VBAC much more possible.

Once the uterine incision is made, the baby is gently pulled out. The doctor suctions the baby's mouth and nose, then clamps and cuts the umbilical cord. As with a vaginal birth, you should be able to see your baby right away. Then, the little one is handed over to the nurses and a pediatrician or other doctor who will be taking care of your newborn for a few minutes (or longer, if there are concerns).

The obstetrician then removes the placenta from the uterus, closes the uterus with dissolvable stitches, and closes the abdominal incision with stitches or surgical staples that are usually removed, painlessly, a few days later.

If the baby is ok, you can hold and/or nurse your newborn in the recovery room by lying on your side (since holding your baby will put too much pressure on your abdomen).

How You Might Feel

You won't feel any pain during the C-section, although you may feel sensations like pulling and pressure. With a planned C-section, the anesthesiologist will give you the option to be unconscious (or "asleep") during the delivery using general anesthesia or awake and simply numbed from the waist down using regional anesthesia (an epidural and/or a spinal block).

Many women want to be awake to see and hear their baby being born. A curtain will be over your abdomen during the surgery, but you may be able to take a peek as your baby is being delivered from your belly.

However, women who need to have an emergency C-section occasionally require general anesthesia, so they're unconscious during the delivery and won't remember anything or feel any pain.

Risks

C-sections today are, in general, safe for both mother and baby. However, there are risks with any kind of surgery. Potential C-section risks include:

- increased bleeding (that could, though rarely, result in a blood transfusion);

- infection (antibiotics are usually given to help prevent infection);

- bladder or bowel injury;

- reactions to medications;

- blood clots;

- death (very rare);

- possible injury to the baby.

Some of the regional anesthetic used during a C-section does reach the baby, but it's much less than what the newborn would get if the mother received general anesthesia (which sedates the baby as well as the mother). Babies born by C-section sometimes have breathing problems (transient tachypnea of the newborn) after birth since labor hasn't jump-started the clearance of fluid from their lungs. This usually gets better on its own within the first day or two of life.

Having a C-section may—or may not—affect future pregnancies and deliveries. Many women can have a successful and safe vaginal birth after cesarean but, in some cases, future births may have to be C-sections, especially if the incision on the uterus was vertical rather than horizontal. A C-section can also put a woman at increased risk of possible problems with the placenta during future pregnancies.

In the case of emergency C-sections, the benefits usually far outweigh the risks. A C-section could save your life or your baby's.

Recovery

As with any surgery, there's usually some degree of pain and discomfort after a C-section. The recovery period is also a little longer than for vaginal births. Women who've had C-sections usually remain in the hospital for about three or four days and need to stay in bed for at least a day after the delivery.

Right after, you may feel itchy, sick to your stomach, and sore—these are all normal reactions to the anesthesia and surgery. If you needed general anesthesia for an emergency C-section, you may feel groggy, confused, chilly, scared, alarmed, or even sad. Your doctor can give you medications to ease any discomfort or pain.

For the first few days and even weeks, you might:

- feel tired;

- have soreness around the incision (the doctor can prescribe medications and/or recommend over-the-counter pain relievers that are safe to take if you're breastfeeding);

- be constipated and gassy;

- have a hard time getting around and/or lifting your baby.

After about six to eight weeks, the uterus is usually healed and you can probably get back to your normal routine. At the beginning, you'll need to avoid driving or lifting anything heavy so that you don't put any unnecessary pressure on your incision. Check with your doctor about when you can get back to your usual activities. And as with a vaginal delivery, you should refrain from having sex until about six weeks after delivery and your doctor has given you the go-ahead.

Frequent and early walking may help ease some post-cesarean pains and discomfort. Among other things, it can help prevent blood clots and keep your bowels moving. But don't push yourself—take it easy and have someone help you get around, especially up and down stairs. Enlist friends, family, and neighbors to lend a helping hand with meals and housework for a while, especially if you have other children.

Although breastfeeding may also be a little painful at first, lying on your side to nurse or using the clutch (or football) hold can take the pressure off your abdomen.

Also, C-sections scars fade over time. They'll start to decrease in size and become a natural skin color in the weeks and months after delivery. And because incisions are often made in the "bikini" area, many C-section scars aren't even noticeable.

Call your doctor if you have:

- fever;

- signs of infection around your incision (swelling, redness, warmth, or pus);

- pain around your incision or in your abdomen that comes on suddenly or gets worse;

- foul-smelling vaginal discharge;

- heavy vaginal bleeding;

- leg pains, or swelling or redness of your legs;

- difficulty breathing or chest pain;

- feelings of depression;

- pain in one or both breasts.

Emotionally, you may feel a little disappointed if you'd been hoping for a vaginal birth or had gone through labor that ended in a C-section. Although it can be disheartening when the traditional way doesn't work for your delivery, having a C-section does not make the birth of your baby any less special or your efforts any less amazing. After all, you went through major surgery to deliver your baby! It might not be the birth experience you'd imagined, but you can finally meet the little one you've been nurturing all this time!

Chapter 19

Screening Tests for Newborns

Chapter Contents

Section 19.1

Newborn Screening Tests:
What You Need to Know

About Newborn Screening

Newborn screening is the practice of testing every newborn for certain harmful or potentially fatal disorders that aren't otherwise apparent at birth.

Many of these are metabolic disorders (often called "inborn errors of metabolism") that interfere with the body's use of nutrients to maintain healthy tissues and produce energy. Other disorders that screening can detect include problems with hormones or the blood.

In general, metabolic and other inherited disorders can hinder an infant's normal physical and mental development in a variety of ways. And parents can pass along the gene for a certain disorder without even knowing that they're carriers.

With a simple blood test, doctors often can tell whether newborns have certain conditions that eventually could cause problems. Although these conditions are considered rare and most babies are given a clean bill of health, early diagnosis and proper treatment can make the difference between lifelong impairment and healthy development.

Screening: Past, Present, and Future

In the early 1960s, scientist Robert Guthrie, Ph.D., developed a blood test that could determine whether newborns had the metabolic disorder phenylketonuria (PKU). People with PKU lack an enzyme needed to process the amino acid phenylalanine, which is necessary for normal growth in kids and for normal protein use throughout life.

However, if too much phenylalanine builds up, it damages brain tissue and eventually can cause substantial developmental delay.

If kids born with PKU are put on a special diet right away, they can avoid the developmental delay the condition caused in past generations and lead normal lives.

Since the development of the PKU test, researchers have developed additional blood tests that can screen newborns for other disorders that, unless detected and treated early, can cause physical problems, developmental delay, and in some cases, death.

The federal government has set no national standards, so screening requirements vary from state to state and are determined by individual state public health departments. Many states have mandatory new-born screening programs, but parents can refuse the testing for their infant if they choose.

Almost all states now screen for more than thirty disorders. One screening technique, the tandem mass spectrometry (or MS/MS), can screen for more than twenty inherited metabolic disorders with a single drop of blood.

Which Tests Are Offered?

Traditionally, state decisions about what to screen for have been based on weighing the costs against the benefits. "Cost" considerations include:

- the risk of false positive results (and the worry they cause);

- the availability of treatments known to help the condition;

- financial costs.

So what can you do? Your best strategy is to stay informed. Discuss this issue with both your obstetrician or health care provider and your future baby's doctor before you give birth. Know what tests are routinely done in your state and in the hospital where you'll deliver (some hospitals go beyond what's required by state law).

If your state isn't offering screening for the expanded panel of disorders, you may want to ask your doctors about supplemental screening, though you'll probably have to pay for additional tests yourself.

If you're concerned about whether your infant was screened for certain conditions, ask your child's doctor for information about which tests were done and whether further tests are recommended.

Newborn screening varies by state and is subject to change, especially given advancements in technology. However, the disorders listed here are the ones typically included in newborn screening programs.

PKU

When this disorder is detected early, feeding an infant a special formula low in phenylalanine can prevent mental retardation. A low-phenylalanine diet will need to be followed throughout childhood and adolescence and perhaps into adult life. This diet cuts out all high-protein foods, so people with PKU often need to take a special artificial formula as a nutritional substitute. Incidence: 1 in 10,000 to 25,000.

Congenital Hypothyroidism

This is the disorder most commonly identified by routine screening. Affected babies don't have enough thyroid hormone and so develop retarded growth and brain development. (The thyroid, a gland at the front of the neck, releases chemical substances that control metabolism and growth.)

If the disorder is detected early, a baby can be treated with oral doses of thyroid hormone to permit normal development. Incidence: 1 in 4,000.

Galactosemia

Babies with galactosemia lack the enzyme that converts galactose (one of two sugars found in lactose) into glucose, a sugar the body is able to use. As a result, milk (including breast milk) and other dairy products must be eliminated from the diet. Otherwise, galactose can build up in the system and damage the body's cells and organs, leading to blindness, severe mental retardation, growth deficiency, and even death.

Incidence: 1 in 60,000 to 80,000. Several less severe forms of galactosemia that may be detected by newborn screening may not require any intervention.

Sickle Cell Disease

Sickle cell disease is an inherited blood disease in which red blood cells mutate into abnormal "sickle" shapes and can cause episodes of pain, damage to vital organs such as the lungs and kidneys, and even death. Young children with sickle cell disease are especially prone to certain dangerous bacterial infections, such as pneumonia (inflammation of the lungs) and meningitis (inflammation of the brain and spinal cord).

Studies suggest that newborn screening can alert doctors to begin antibiotic treatment before infections occur and to monitor symptoms of possible worsening more closely. The screening test can also detect other disorders affecting hemoglobin (the oxygen-carrying substance in the blood).

Incidence: about 1 in every 500 African American births and 1 in every 1,000 to 1,400 Hispanic American births; also occurs with some frequency among people of Mediterranean, Middle Eastern, and South Asian descent.

Biotinidase Deficiency

Babies with this condition don't have enough biotinidase, an enzyme that recycles biotin (a B vitamin) in the body. The deficiency may cause seizures, poor muscle control, immune system impairment, hearing loss, mental retardation, coma, and even death. If the deficiency is detected in time, however, problems can be prevented by giving the baby extra biotin. Incidence: 1 in 72,000 to 126,000.

Congenital Adrenal Hyperplasia

This is actually a group of disorders involving a deficiency of certain hormones produced by the adrenal gland. It can affect the development of the genitals and may cause death due to loss of salt from the kidneys. Lifelong treatment through supplementation of the missing hormones manages the condition. Incidence: 1 in 12,000.

Maple Syrup Urine Disease (MSUD)

Babies with MSUD are missing an enzyme needed to process three amino acids that are essential for the body's normal growth. When not processed properly, these can build up in the body, causing urine to smell like maple syrup or sweet, burnt sugar. These babies usually have little appetite and are extremely irritable.

If not detected and treated early, MSUD can cause mental retardation, physical disability, and even death. A carefully controlled diet that cuts out certain high-protein foods containing those amino acids can prevent this. Like people with PKU, those with MSUD are often given a formula that supplies the necessary nutrients missed in the special diet they must follow. Incidence: 1 in 250,000.

Tyrosinemia

Babies with this amino acid metabolism disorder have trouble processing the amino acid tyrosine. If it accumulates in the body, it can cause mild retardation, language skill difficulties, liver problems, and even death from liver failure. Treatment requires a special diet and sometimes a liver transplant. Early diagnosis and treatment seem to offset long-term problems, although more information is needed. Incidence: not yet determined. Some babies have a mild self-limited form of tyrosinemia.

Cystic Fibrosis

Cystic fibrosis (CF) is a genetic disorder that particularly affects the lungs and digestive system and makes kids who have it more vulnerable to repeated lung infections. There is no known cure—treatment involves trying to prevent serious lung infections (sometimes with antibiotics) and providing adequate nutrition. Early detection may help doctors reduce the problems associated with CF, but the real impact of newborn screening has yet to be determined. Incidence: 1 in 2,000 Caucasian babies; less common in African Americans, Hispanics, and Asians.

Medium Chain Acyl CoA Dehydrogenase (MCAD) Deficiency

MCAD deficiency is a fatty acid metabolism disorder. Kids who have it are prone to repeated episodes of low blood sugar (hypoglycemia), which can cause seizures and interfere with normal growth and development. Treatment involves making sure kids don't fast (skip meals) and supplies extra nutrition (usually by intravenous nutrients) when they're ill. Early detection and treatment can help affected children live normal lives.

Toxoplasmosis

Toxoplasmosis is a parasitic infection that can be transmitted through the mother's placenta to an unborn child. The disease-causing organism can invade the brain, eye, and muscles, possibly resulting in blindness and mental retardation. The benefit of early detection and treatment is uncertain. Incidence: 1 in 1,000. But only one or two states screen for toxoplasmosis.

Hearing Screening

Most but not all states require newborns' hearing to be screened before they're discharged from the hospital. If your baby isn't examined then, be sure that he or she does get screened within the first three weeks of life.

Kids develop critical speaking and language skills in their first few years. A hearing loss that's caught early can be treated to help prevent interference with that development.

Should I Request Additional Tests?

If you answer "yes" to any of these questions, talk to your doctor and perhaps a genetic counselor about additional tests:

- Do you have a family history of an inherited disorder?

- Have you previously given birth to a child who's affected by a disorder?

- Did an infant in your family die because of a suspected metabolic disorder?

- Do you have another reason to believe that your child may be at risk for a certain condition?

How Screening Is Done

In the first two or three days of life, your baby's heel will be pricked to obtain a small blood sample for testing. Most states have a state or regional laboratory perform the analyses, although some use a private lab.

It's generally recommended that the sample be taken after the first twenty-four hours of life. Some tests, such as the one for PKU, may not be as sensitive if they're done too soon after birth. However, because mothers and newborns are often discharged within a day, some babies may be tested within the first twenty-four hours. If this happens, experts recommend that a repeat sample be taken no more than one to two weeks later. It's especially important that the PKU screening test be run again for accurate results. Some states routinely do two tests on all infants.

Getting the Results

Different labs have different procedures for notifying families and pediatricians of the results. Some may send the results to the hospital where your child was born and not directly to your child's doctor, which may mean a delay in getting the results to you.

And although some states have a system that allows doctors to access the results via phone or computer, others may not. Ask your doctor how you'll get the results and when you should expect them.

If a test result comes back abnormal, try not to panic. This does not necessarily mean that your child has the disorder in question. A screening test is not the same as a diagnostic test. The initial screening provides only preliminary information that must be followed up with more specific diagnostic testing.

If testing confirms that your child does have a disorder, your doctor may refer you to a specialist for further evaluation and treatment. Keep in mind that dietary restrictions and supplements, along with proper medical supervision, often can prevent most of the serious physical and mental problems that were associated with metabolic disorders in the past.

You also may wonder whether the disorder can be passed on to any future children. You'll want to discuss this with your doctor and perhaps a genetic counselor. Also, if you have other children who weren't screened for the disorder, consider having testing done. Again, speak with your doctor.

Know Your Options

Because state programs are subject to change, you'll want to find up-to-date information about your state's (and individual hospital's) program. Talk to your doctor or contact your state's department of health for more information.

Section 19.2

Apgar Score

About the Apgar Score

The Apgar score, the very first test given to your newborn, occurs in the delivery or birthing room right after your baby's birth. The test was designed to quickly evaluate a newborn's physical condition and to determine any immediate need for extra medical or emergency care.

Although the Apgar score was developed in 1952 by an anesthesiologist named Virginia Apgar, you may have also heard it referred to as an acronym for: appearance, pulse, grimace, activity, and respiration.

The Apgar test is usually given to a baby twice: once at one minute after birth, and again at five minutes after birth. Sometimes, if there are concerns about the baby's condition or the score at five minutes is low, the test may be scored for a third time at ten minutes after birth.

Five factors are used to evaluate the baby's condition and each factor is scored on a scale of 0 to 2, with 2 being the best score:

1. Appearance (skin coloration)

2. Pulse (heart rate)

3. Grimace response (medically known as "reflex irritability")

4. Activity and muscle tone

5. Respiration (breathing rate and effort)

Doctors, midwives, or nurses add these five factors together to calculate the Apgar score. Scores obtainable are between 10 and 0, with 10 being the highest possible score.

What Apgar Scores Mean

A baby who scores an 8 or above on the test is generally considered in good health. However, a lower score doesn't mean that your baby is unhealthy or abnormal. But it may mean that your baby simply needs some special immediate care, such as suctioning of the airways or oxygen to help him or her breathe, after which your baby may improve.

At five minutes after birth, the Apgar score is recalculated. If your baby's score was low at first and hasn't improved, or there are other concerns, the doctors and nurses will continue any necessary medical care and will closely monitor your baby. Some babies are born with conditions that require extra medical care; others just take a little longer than usual to adjust to life outside the womb. Most newborns with initial Apgar scores that are a little low will eventually do just fine.

It's important for new parents to keep their baby's Apgar score in perspective. The test was designed to help health care providers assess a newborn's overall physical condition so that they could quickly determine whether the baby needed immediate medical care. It was not designed to predict a baby's long-term health, behavior, intellectual status, personality, or outcome. Very few babies score a perfect 10, since their hands and feet usually remain blue until they have warmed up. And perfectly healthy babies sometimes have a lower-than-usual score, especially in the first few minutes after birth.

Table 19.1. Apgar Scoring

Apgar Sign	2	1	0
Heart Rate (pulse)	Normal (above 100 beats per minute)	Below 100 beats per minute	Absent (no pulse)
Breathing (rate and effort)	Normal rate and effort, good cry	Slow or irregular breathing, weak cry	Absent (no breathing)
Grimace (responsiveness or "reflex irritability")	Pulls away, sneezes, coughs, or cries with stimulation	Facial movement only (grimace) with stimulation	Absent (no response to stimulation)
Activity (muscle tone)	Active, spontaneous movement	Arms and legs flexed with little movement	No movement, "floppy" tone
Appearance (skin coloration)	Normal color all over (hands and feet are pink)	Normal color (but hands and feet are bluish)	Bluish-gray or pale all over

Keep in mind that a slightly low Apgar score (especially at one minute) is common for some newborns, especially those born after a high-risk pregnancy, cesarean section, or a complicated labor and delivery. Lower Apgar scores are also seen in premature babies, who usually have less muscle tone than full-term newborns and who, in many cases, will require extra monitoring and breathing assistance because of their immature lungs.

If your doctor or midwife is concerned about your baby's score, he or she will let you know and will explain how your baby is doing, what might be causing problems, if any, and what care is being given.

With time to adjust to the new environment, and with any necessary medical care, most babies do very well. So rather than focusing on a number, just enjoy your new baby!

Section 19.3

Newborn Hearing Screening

"It's Important to Have Your Baby's Hearing Screened,"
National Institute on Deafness and Other Communication
Disorders, National Institutes of Health, May 2011.

Most children hear and listen to sounds from birth. They learn to talk by imitating the sounds around them and the voices of their parents and caregivers. But that's not true for all children. In fact, about two or three out of every one thousand children in the United States are born deaf or hard-of-hearing. More lose their hearing later during childhood. Many of these children may need to learn speech and language differently, so it's important to detect deafness or hearing loss as early as possible. For this reason, universal newborn hearing screening programs currently operate in all U.S. states and most of the territories. With help from the federal government, every state has established an Early Hearing Detection and Intervention program as part of its public health system. As a result, more than 95 percent of babies have their hearing screened soon after they are born.

When will my baby's hearing be screened?

Your baby's hearing should be screened before he or she leaves the hospital or birthing center. If you and your baby are already home and you haven't been told the results of the hearing screening, ask your doctor. If the results indicate your baby may have hearing loss, it's important to work with your doctor to make an appointment with a hearing expert, called an audiologist, to perform a more thorough hearing test before your baby is three months old.

How will my baby's hearing be screened?

Two different tests are used to screen for hearing loss in babies. In both tests, no activity is required from your child other than lying still.

The otoacoustic emissions (OAE) test shows whether parts of the ear respond properly to sound. During this test, a soft sponge earphone is inserted into your baby's ear canal and emits a series of sounds to measure an "echo" response that occurs in normal hearing ears. If there is no echo, it could indicate hearing loss.

The auditory brain stem response (ABR) test checks how the auditory brain stem (the part of the nerve that carries sound from the ear to the brain) and the brain respond to sound by measuring their electrical activity as your child listens. During this test, your baby wears small earphones in the ears and electrodes on the head. Your baby might be given a mild sedative to keep him or her calm and quiet during the test. If your child doesn't respond consistently to the sounds presented during either of these tests, your doctor will suggest a follow-up hearing screening and a referral to an audiologist for a more comprehensive hearing evaluation. If hearing loss is confirmed, it's important to consider the use of hearing devices and other communication options before your baby is six months old.

Why is it important to have my baby's hearing screened early?

The most important time for a child to learn language is in the first three years of life. In fact, children begin learning speech and language in the first six months of life. Research suggests that children with hearing loss who get help early develop better language skills than those who don't. The earlier you know about a child's hearing loss, the sooner you can make sure your child benefits from strategies that will help him or her learn to successfully communicate.

How can I recognize if my child develops hearing loss later in childhood?

Even though the screening tests are designed to detect hearing loss as early as possible, some children may not develop hearing loss until later in childhood. In those instances, parents, caregivers, or grandparents are often the first to notice. This means that, even if your baby has passed the hearing screening, you should still continue to look for signs that your baby is hearing well.

For example, during the first year, notice whether your baby reacts to loud noises, imitates sounds, and begins to respond to his or her name. When your child is age two, ask yourself whether he or she makes playful sounds with his or her voice, imitates simple words, and enjoys games like peek-a-boo and pat-a-cake. Is he or she using two-word sentences to talk about and ask for things? When your child is age three, notice whether he or she begins to understand "not now" and "no more" and follows simple directions. If for any reason you think your child is not hearing well, talk to your doctor.

If my child has hearing loss, can hearing be improved?

A variety of assistive devices and strategies are helpful for children who are hard-of-hearing. Some examples of these devices are listed here. An audiologist can help you determine whether these or other devices will help your child.

Hearing aids are devices that make sounds louder. They are worn in or behind the ear and come in several different shapes and sizes. Hearing aids can be used for varying degrees of hearing loss from mild to severe. An audiologist will fit a hearing aid that will work best for your child's degree of loss. Hearing aids can be expensive, so you'll want to find out whether they have a warranty or trial period. You'll also want to talk with your insurance provider to understand what, and how much, it will pay for.

Cochlear implants are small electronic devices that help provide a sense of sound to people who are profoundly deaf or hard-of-hearing. They consist of a microphone worn just behind the ear, which picks up sound from the environment; a speech processor, which selects and arranges the sounds; a transmitter and receiver/stimulator, which receive signals from the speech processor and convert them into electric impulses; and an implanted electrode array, which collects the impulses from the stimulator and sends them to the auditory nerve.

Not all children who have hearing loss should get cochlear implants. Doctors and hearing experts think they're best for children who have such severe hearing loss that they can't benefit from hearing aids. Some doctors now recommend the use of two cochlear implants, one for each ear, to help children identify the directions of sounds.

As children get older, many other devices are available to help their hearing. Some devices help children hear better in a classroom. Others make talking on the phone or watching television easier. For example, induction loop systems and frequency modulated (FM) systems can help eliminate or reduce distracting noises and make it easier to hear individual voices in a crowded room or group setting. Others, such as personal amplifiers, are better for one-on-one conversations.

How can I help my child communicate?

There are a variety of ways to help children with hearing loss express themselves and interact with others. The main options are listed below. The option you choose will depend on what you think is best for your child. Find out as much as you can about all of the choices, and ask your doctor to refer you to experts if you want to know more.

Auditory-oral and auditory-verbal options combine natural hearing ability and hearing devices such as hearing aids and cochlear implants with other strategies to help children develop speech and English-language skills. Auditory-oral options use visual cues such as lip-reading and sign language, while auditory-verbal options work to strengthen listening skills.

American Sign Language (ASL) is a language used by some children who are deaf and their families. ASL consists of hand signs, body movements, and facial expressions. ASL has its own grammar and syntax, which are different from English, but it has no written form.

Cued speech is a system that uses hand shapes along with natural mouth movements to represent speech sounds. Watching the mouth movements and the hand shapes can help some children learn to speech-read English; this is especially important in discriminating between sounds that look the same on the lips.

Signed English is a system that uses signs to represent words or phrases in English. Signed English is designed to enhance the use of both spoken and written English.

Combined options use portions of the various methods listed above. For example, some deaf children who use auditory-oral options also learn sign language. Children who use ASL also learn to read and write in English. Combined options can expose children who are deaf or hard-of-hearing to many different ways to communicate with others.

Section 19.4

Pulse Oximetry Screening for Critical Congenital Heart Defects

Centers for Disease Control and Prevention, January 23, 2012.

In the United States, about 4,800 (or 11.6 per 10,000) babies born each year have one of seven critical congenital heart defects (CCHDs).[1] Learn more about how pulse oximetry screening potentially can identify these babies soon after birth.

What are critical congenital heart defects?

The seven defects classified as critical congenital heart defects (CCHDs) are hypoplastic left heart syndrome, pulmonary atresia (with intact septum), tetralogy of Fallot, total anomalous pulmonary venous return, transposition of the great arteries, tricuspid atresia, and truncus arteriosus. Babies with one of these CCHDs are at significant risk for death or disability if their heart defect is not diagnosed and treated soon after birth. These seven CCHDs among some babies potentially can be detected using pulse oximetry screening, which is a test to determine the amount of oxygen in the blood and pulse rate. Certain hospitals routinely screen all newborns using pulse oximetry screening. However, pulse oximetry screening is not currently included in newborn screening in most states.

Other heart defects can be just as severe as these seven CCHDs and also require treatment soon after birth. However, pulse oximetry screening may not detect these heart defects as consistently as the seven disorders listed as CCHDs.

Why is screening for critical congenital heart defects important?

Some babies born with a heart defect can appear healthy at first and can be sent home with their families before their heart defect is detected. It has been estimated that at least 280 infants with an unrecognized CCHD are discharged each year from newborn nurseries

291

in the United States.[2] These babies are at risk for having serious problems within the first few days or weeks of life and often require emergency care.

Pulse oximetry newborn screening can identify some infants with a CCHD before they show any signs. Once identified, babies with a CCHD can be seen by cardiologists (heart doctors) and can receive specialized care and treatment that could prevent death or disability early in life. Treatment can include medications and surgery.

How are babies screened?

Pulse oximetry is a simple bedside test to determine the amount of oxygen in a baby's blood and the baby's pulse rate. Low levels of oxygen in the blood can be a sign of a CCHD. The test is done using a machine called a pulse oximeter, with sensors placed on the baby's skin. The test is painless and takes only a few minutes. Pulse oximetry screening does not replace a complete history and physical examination, which sometimes can detect a CCHD before oxygen levels in the blood become low. Pulse oximetry screening, therefore, should be used along with the physical examination.

When are babies screened?

Screening is done when a baby is twenty-four to forty-eight hours of age. If the baby is to be discharged from the hospital before he or she is twenty-four hours of age, screening should be done as late as possible before discharge. Pulse oximetry screening is not currently included in newborn screening in most states.

What are pulse oximetry screening results?

If the results are "negative" (in-range result), it means that the baby's test results did not show signs of a CCHD. This type of screening test does not detect all CCHDs, so it is possible to still have a critical or other heart defect with a negative screening result. If the results are "positive" (out-of-range result), it means that the baby's test results showed low levels of oxygen in the blood. This can be a sign of a CCHD. This does not always mean that the baby has a CCHD. It just means that more testing is needed.

The baby's doctor might recommend that the infant get screened again or have more specific tests, like an echocardiogram (an ultrasound picture of the heart), to diagnose a CCHD. Babies who are found to have a CCHD also might be evaluated by a clinical geneticist. This could help identify genetic syndromes associated with these heart defects and inform families about future risks.

What is the Centers for Disease Control and Prevention (CDC) doing?

The CDC is part of the U.S. Department of Health and Human Services (HHS) Secretary's Advisory Committee on Heritable Disorders in Newborns and Children (SACHDNC). SACHDNC was authorized by Congress to provide guidance to the HHS secretary about which conditions should be included in newborn and childhood screening programs. SACHDNC also advises the secretary on how systems should be developed to ensure that all newborns and children are screened and, when necessary, receive appropriate follow-up care. SACHDNC recommended that the HHS secretary add pulse oximetry screening for CCHDs to the Recommended Uniform Screening Panel. In September 2011, HHS Secretary Sebelius approved adding screening for CCHDs to the Recommended Uniform Screening Panel and outlined specific tasks assigned to National Institutes of Health (NIH), CDC, and Health Resources and Services Administration (HRSA).

References

1. Adapted from Reller, MD, Strickland, MJ, Riehle-Colarusso, TJ, Mahle, WT, Correa, A. Prevalence of congenital heart defects in metropolitan Atlanta, 1998–2005. *J Pediatr.* 2008;153:807–13.

2. Adapted from Knapp, AA, Metterville, DR, Kemper, AR, Prosser, L, Perrin, JM. Evidence review: Critical congenital cyanotic heart disease, Final Draft, September 3, 2010. Prepared for the Maternal and Child Health Bureau, Health Resources and Services Administration.

Chapter 20

Perinatal Infections

Chapter Contents

Section 20.1

Group B Streptococcal Infection

Excerpted from "Group B Strep: What You Need to Know," Centers for Disease Control and Prevention, May 2007. Reviewed by David A. Cooke, M.D., FACP, December 2012.

What is group B strep?

Group B strep (streptococcus) is a type of bacteria that can cause serious illness and death in newborns. Until recent prevention efforts, hundreds of babies died from group B strep every year. This type of bacteria can also cause illness in adults, especially the elderly, but it is most common in newborns.

Why do I need to get tested for group B strep during each pregnancy?

Group B strep bacteria can be passed from a mom who is a carrier for the bacteria (tests positive) to her baby during labor. Since the bacteria can come and go in your body, you need to be tested for group B strep every time you are pregnant, whether you tested negative or positive during the last pregnancy.

Toward the end of pregnancy (thirty-five to thirty-seven weeks), the doctor will swab your vagina and rectum. This is sent to a lab, where they test for group B strep bacteria. The bacteria take a few days to grow, and the results are sent to your doctor.

What happens to babies born with the group B strep bacteria?

Group B strep is the most common cause of sepsis (blood infection) and meningitis (infection of the fluid and lining around the brain) in newborns. Most newborn disease happens within the first week of life, called "early-onset" disease.

How can group B strep disease in babies be prevented?

Most early-onset group B strep disease in newborns can be prevented by giving antibiotics (medicine) through an intravenous (IV) line during labor to women who tested positive during their pregnancy. Because the bacteria can grow quickly, giving antibiotics before labor has started does not prevent the problem. Any woman who has a positive test for group B strep during this pregnancy should get antibiotics. Also, any pregnant woman who has had a baby in the past with group B strep disease, or who now has a bladder (urinary tract) infection caused by group B strep should get antibiotics during labor.

How does someone get group B strep?

Anyone can be a "carrier" for group B strep. The bacteria are found in the gastrointestinal tract (guts) and may move into the vagina and/or rectum. It is not a sexually transmitted disease (STD). About one in four women carry these bacteria. Most women would never have symptoms or know that they had these bacteria without a test during pregnancy.

What do I need to do during pregnancy or labor if I'm group B strep positive?

Talk with your doctor and create a labor plan that includes getting antibiotics for group B strep prevention in your newborn. When your water breaks, or when you go into labor, make sure to get to the hospital at least four hours before delivery to make sure there is enough time for the antibiotics to work. When you get to the hospital, remind the staff that you are group B strep positive.

Section 20.2

Hepatitis B

Excerpted from "Protect Your Baby for Life:
When a Pregnant Woman Has Hepatitis B," Centers for
Disease Control and Prevention, October 2010.

What is hepatitis B?

"Hepatitis" means inflammation of the liver. Hepatitis B is a contagious liver disease that results from infection with the hepatitis B virus. When a person becomes infected, the hepatitis B virus can stay in the person's body for the rest of his or her life and cause serious liver problems.

Can hepatitis B be spread to babies?

Yes. The hepatitis B virus can be spread to a baby during childbirth. This can happen during a vaginal delivery or a cesarean section.

How serious is hepatitis B?

When babies become infected with hepatitis B, they have a 90 percent chance of developing a lifelong, chronic infection. As many as one in four people with chronic hepatitis B develop serious health problems. Hepatitis B can cause liver damage, liver disease, and liver cancer.

Can doctors prevent a baby from getting hepatitis B?

Yes. Babies born to women with hepatitis B get two shots soon after birth. One is the first dose of the hepatitis B vaccine and the other shot is called HBIG. The two shots help prevent the baby from getting hepatitis B. The shots work best when they are given within twelve hours after being born.

What is HBIG?

HBIG is a medicine that gives a baby's body a "boost" or extra help to fight the virus as soon as he or she is born. The HBIG shot is only given to babies of mothers who have hepatitis B.

How many hepatitis B shots does my baby need?

Your baby will get three or four shots, depending on which brand of vaccine is used. After the first dose is given in the hospital, the next dose is given at one to two months of age. The last dose is usually given by the time your baby is one year old. Ask your doctor or nurse when your baby needs to come back for each shot.

Does my baby need all the shots?

All the hepatitis B shots are necessary to help keep your baby from getting hepatitis B.

How do I know my baby is protected?

After your baby has had all the hepatitis B shots, your doctor will test your baby's blood. The blood test tells you and your doctor that your baby is protected and does not have hepatitis B. The blood test is usually done one to two months after the last shot. Be sure to bring your baby back to your doctor for this important blood test.

Section 20.3

Human Immunodeficiency Virus (HIV)

"Women Infected with HIV and Their Babies After Birth,"
AIDSinfo.gov, February 2012.

I am human immunodeficiency virus (HIV) infected and pregnant. What are the chances my baby will be born with HIV?

In the United States and Europe, fewer than two babies in one hundred born to mothers infected with HIV are infected with the virus. This is because most women infected with HIV and their babies receive anti-HIV medications to prevent mother-to-child transmission of HIV and do not breastfeed. If you take anti-HIV medications during pregnancy and labor and delivery, if your baby receives anti-HIV medications after birth, and if you do not breastfeed your baby, the risk of passing HIV to your baby is very low.

Will my newborn baby receive anti-HIV medications?

Yes. Within six to twelve hours after delivery, babies born to women infected with HIV receive an anti-HIV medication called azidothymidine (AZT). AZT helps prevent mother-to-child transmission of HIV. The babies receive AZT for six weeks. (In certain situations, some babies may receive other anti-HIV medications in addition to AZT.)

When will my baby be tested for HIV?

HIV testing for babies born to women with known HIV infection is recommended at fourteen to twenty-one days, at one to two months, and again at four to six months. Testing for babies is done using a virologic HIV test. Virologic HIV tests look directly for the presence of HIV in the blood:

- To be diagnosed with HIV, a baby must have positive results from two virologic HIV tests.

- To know for certain that a baby is not infected with HIV, the baby must have two negative virologic HIV tests, the first at one month of age or older, and the second at least one month later.

Babies who are HIV-infected receive a combination of anti-HIV medications to treat HIV. At four to six weeks of age, babies infected with HIV also start a medication called Bactrim. (Bactrim is also given as a precaution when it's not known if a baby is HIV infected or not.) Bactrim helps prevent *Pneumocystis jiroveci* pneumonia (PCP), a type of pneumonia that can develop in people with advanced HIV.

What is the best way to feed my baby?

Because HIV can be transmitted through breast milk, women infected with HIV who live in the United States should not breastfeed. In the United States, infant formula is a safe and healthy alternative to breast milk. Although the risk is very low, HIV can be transmitted to a baby through food that was previously chewed (pre-chewed) by a mother or caretaker infected with HIV. To be safe, babies should not be fed pre-chewed food.

Will my anti-HIV medications change after I give birth?

After your baby is born, you and your health care provider may decide to stop or change your anti-HIV regimen. The decision to continue, change, or stop your anti-HIV medications will depend on several factors:

- Current expert recommendations on the use of anti-HIV medications

- Your CD4 count and viral load

- Issues that make it hard to take medications exactly as directed

- Whether or not your partner is infected with HIV

- The preferences of you and your health care provider

Don't stop taking any of your anti-HIV medications without first talking to your health care provider. Stopping your medications may limit the number of anti-HIV medications that will work for you and may cause your HIV infection to worsen.

Having a new baby is exciting! However, caring for a new baby while dealing with the physical and emotional changes that follow childbirth

301

can be stressful. It may be difficult to take your anti-HIV medications exactly as directed. If you feel sad or overwhelmed or have concerns about taking your medications, talk to your health care provider. Together you can make a plan to keep you and your baby healthy.

Chapter 21

What to Expect When Your Baby Is in the Neonatal Intensive Care Unit (NICU)

New parents eagerly look forward to bringing their baby home, so it can be frightening if your newborn needs to be admitted to the neonatal intensive care unit (NICU). At first it may seem like a foreign place, but understanding the NICU and what goes on there can help reduce your fears and let you better help your baby.

About the NICU

If your baby is sent to the NICU, your first question probably will be: What is this place? With equipment designed for infants and a hospital staff who have special training in newborn care, the NICU is an intensive care unit created for sick newborns who need specialized treatment.

Sometimes the NICU is also called:

- a special care nursery;

- an intensive care nursery;

- newborn intensive care.

"When Your Baby's in the NICU," October 2011, reprinted with permission from www.kidshealth.org. This information was provided by KidsHealth®, one of the largest resources online for medically reviewed health information written for parents, kids, and teens. For more articles like this, visit www.Kids Health.org, or www.TeensHealth.org. Copyright © 1995–2012 The Nemours Foundation. All rights reserved.

Babies who need to go to the unit are often admitted within the first twenty-four hours after birth. Babies may be sent to the NICU if:

- they're born prematurely;

- difficulties occur during their delivery;

- they show signs of a problem in the first few days of life.

Only very young babies (or babies with a condition linked to being born prematurely) are treated in the NICU—they're usually infants who haven't gone home from the hospital yet after being born. How long they'll remain in the unit depends on the severity of their illness.

Who Will Be Taking Care of My Baby?

Although many people help care for babies in the NICU, those most responsible for day-to-day care are nurses. You might come to know them very well and rely on them for information and reassurances about your baby.

The nurses you might interact with include a:

- **charge nurse:** the nurse in charge of the shift;

- **primary nurse:** the one assigned to your baby;

- **neonatal nurse practitioner:** someone with additional training in neonatology care.

Other people who may help care for your baby include:

- **a neonatologist**: a doctor specializing in newborn intensive care who heads up the medical team;

- **neonatology fellows, medical residents, and medical students:** all pursuing their training at different levels;

- **pediatric hospitalist:** a pediatrician who works solely in the hospital setting;

- **various specialists:** such as a neurologist, a cardiologist, or a surgeon to treat specific issues with the brain, heart, etc.;

- **a respiratory therapist:** who helps administer treatments that help with breathing;

- **a nutritionist:** who can determine what babies receiving intravenous (IV) nutrition need;

- **a physical therapist and/or occupational therapist:** who work with feeding and movement issues with the infants and their parents;

- **a pharmacist:** who helps manage a baby's medications;

- **lab technicians:** who process the laboratory tests (e.g., urine, blood) taken;

- **a chaplain:** who can counsel you and try to provide comfort; chaplains may be interfaith or of a particular religious affiliation but they're there to support anyone looking for a spiritual/ religious connection;

- **a social worker:** who helps you get the services you need and also lends emotional support by connecting you to other families and therapists, if needed.

Questions to Ask the Neonatologist or the Nurses

To better help you help your baby during a stay in intensive care, it's wise to get as much information as possible about what to expect. If you have questions, talk to the neonatologist or the nurses.

The nurses see your baby every day, so they can give you frequent updates on your little one. The plan of care for your infant is discussed on "rounds" every day. Nurses can help you to understand the diagnosis and treatment plan, but it's also helpful to discuss these issues with other members of the medical team, including:

- the attending neonatologist;

- the neonatal fellow;

- the neonatal nurse practitioner;

- the residents who are caring for your baby.

All of these health professionals are involved in determining the best plan of care for your baby.

You might want to ask the neonatologist and other doctors and/or the nurses:

- How long will my baby be in the unit?

- What, specifically, is the problem?

- What will be involved in my baby's treatment and daily care?

- What medicines will my baby have to take?

- What types of tests will be done?
- What can my baby eat and when?
- Will I be able to nurse or bottle-feed my baby—if so, when and how?
- Will someone help me learn how to nurse my baby?
- What can I do to help my baby?
- Will I be able to hold or touch my baby?
- How often and for how long can I stay in the unit? Can I sleep there?
- What sort of care will my baby need when we get home?
- Is there someone who can help us through the process?

You may also want to talk to the nurses in more detail about your baby's daily care and what to expect when you spend time with your little one. You should also learn the visiting schedule and any rules of the NICU so you'll know which family members can see the baby and when they can visit.

Questions to Ask the Social Worker

You might want to ask the social worker:

- Where can we get food when we're here?
- Can we eat in the NICU?
- Are cots or recliners available if we're allowed to stay overnight? What about blankets and pillows?
- Is nearby temporary housing available (such as through a Ronald McDonald House)?
- If so, how do we get a room?
- Is the room free? If not, is the cost low and/or covered by our health insurance?
- Are computers with internet access available for doing work or e-mailing friends and loved ones about our baby's progress?
- Are phones available in or around the NICU?
- Can we use our cell phones in the NICU? If not, can we be reached in the NICU?

- Is there a support group or other parents of children in the NICU we can talk to?

What to Expect in the NICU

Walking into the NICU can feel like stepping onto another planet—the environment is probably unlike anything you've experienced. The unit is often busy, with lots of activity, people moving around, and beeping monitors.

Once settled in the unit, your baby will receive care tailored to your little one's specific needs. Most NICU babies are on special feeding schedules, depending on their level of development or any problems they have. For instance, some infants are too premature or too sick to eat on their own, so they have a feeding tube that runs through the mouth and into the stomach. Others need high-calorie diets to help them grow.

Medications are another crucial part of NICU care—your child may take antibiotics, medicine to stimulate breathing, or something to help his or her blood pressure or heart rate, for example.

To ensure that your baby's care stays on track, the doctors also will order various tests, possibly including periodic blood and urine tests, x-rays, and ultrasounds. For infants whose care is complicated and involved, the doctors or nurses will place a line into an artery or vein so they can draw blood without having to repeatedly stick the baby.

NICU staff try to make the infants' stay in the nursery as comforting as possible for the infant as well as the families. The nurses can explain what all of the monitors, tubes, tests, and machines do, which will go a long way toward demystifying the NICU.

NICU Equipment

Here's a brief look at what some of the unfamiliar equipment does and how it may help your baby, depending on your little one's condition and diagnosis.

Feeding tubes: Often, NICU babies cannot get as many calories as they need through regular feeding from a bottle, so the nurses will use a small feeding tube to deliver formula or breast milk (that the mother pumps). The tube is placed into the baby's stomach through the mouth or through the nose.

If an infant is able to take some milk from the bottle, the nurse will just give the rest through the feeding tube. Sometimes, the babies get all their nutrition through the feeding tube so that they don't use excess energy trying to feed from the bottle.

The feeding tubes shouldn't be painful—they're taped in place so they won't move around and cause friction. However, if they're in place for a long time they can cause erosions in the stomach or nose where they rub, so are changed routinely to avoid this.

Infant warmers: These are beds with radiant heaters over them. Parents can touch their babies in the warmers, but it's always a good idea to talk to the NICU staff about it at first, just in case.

Isolettes: These are small beds enclosed by clear, hard plastic. The temperature of the isolette is controlled and closely monitored because premature infants frequently have difficulty maintaining their body temperature. Holes in the isolettes allow access to the infants so the nurses and doctors can examine the infants and parents can touch their babies.

IVs and lines: An intravenous catheter (or IV) is a thin flexible tube inserted into the vein with a small needle. Once in the vein, the needle is removed, leaving just the soft plastic tubing.

Almost all babies in the NICU have an IV for fluids and medications—usually in the hands or arms, but sometimes in the feet, legs, or even scalp. At first, the IV may be inserted in the baby's umbilical cord. In the first hours after delivery, the umbilical cord provides a way for the doctors to insert arterial or venous lines without having to use a needle through the skin.

Instead of giving your baby injections every few hours, IVs allow certain medications to be given continuously, several drops at a time. These are known as drips or infusions. Doctors may use these medications to help with heart function, blood pressure, or pain relief.

Some situations require larger IVs to deliver greater volumes of fluids and medications. These special IVs are known as central lines because they're inserted into the larger, more central veins of the chest, neck, or groin, as opposed to the hands and feet. They're inserted by a specially trained pediatric surgeon.

Arterial lines are very similar to IVs, but they're placed in arteries, not veins, and are used to monitor blood pressure and oxygen levels in the blood (although some babies may simply have blood pressure cuffs instead).

Monitors: Infants in the NICU are attached to monitors so the NICU staff are constantly aware of their vital signs. The nurses will often place the infants in positions that seem the most soothing, like on their tummies or on their sides.

The single monitor (which picks up and displays all the necessary information in one place) is secured to your baby's body with chest leads, which are small painless stickers connected to wires. The chest leads can count your child's heart rate and breathing rate. A pulse oximetry (or pulse ox) machine also may display your baby's blood oxygen levels on the monitor. Also painless, the pulse ox is taped to your baby's fingers or toes like a small bandage and emits a soft red light.

A temperature probe, a coated wire adhered to your baby's skin with a patch, can track your little one's temperature and display it on the monitor. And unless blood pressure is being directly monitored through an arterial line, your baby will usually have a blood pressure cuff in place.

Phototherapy: Often, premature infants or those with infections also have jaundice (a common newborn condition in which the skin and whites of the eyes turn yellow). Phototherapy is used to help get rid of the bilirubin that causes jaundice. The infants might lie on a special light therapy blanket and have lights attached to their beds or isolettes. Usually, they only need phototherapy for a few days.

Ventilators: Babies in the NICU sometimes need extra help to breathe. An infant is connected to the ventilator (or breathing machine) via an endotracheal tube (a plastic tube placed into the windpipe through the mouth or nose).

Babies who've been in the NICU for a prolonged stay—months at a time—may have a tracheostomy (a plastic tube inserted directly into the trachea) that's connected to the ventilator on the other end.

There are many different kinds of ventilators—different situations call for different machines—but they all accomplish the same basic purpose: to help a baby breathe.

Bonding with Your Baby in the NICU

All the machines may seem overwhelming, but don't let them keep you from interacting with your baby. Bonding with a baby in the NICU is as important as bonding with any newborn, sometimes even more so. You simply have to learn the best way to do it.

Parents can visit and spend time with their NICU babies. The number of people who can visit a baby in the NICU may be limited, but parents are usually allowed to stay most of the day (except when the medical team performs its daily examination and evaluation). Ask the NICU's social worker about what accommodations are available for parents—cots, recliners, or nearby housing such as through the Ronald McDonald House charities.

Other family members can visit only during specified hours and only a few at a time. And siblings may not be allowed in the NICU because children have a greater risk of introducing an infection. Check with the hospital staff about which family members can see your baby.

Depending on how sick your child is, you might be able to hold your little one even if he or she is on a ventilator or has an IV. If the doctors feel that would be too much for your baby, you can still hold his or her hand, stroke his or her head, and talk and sing to him or her. A gentle, consistent touch will be the most reassuring.

But for some very premature infants, touching is extremely stressful (if they were still in the womb, they would have little tactile stimulation). In these cases, doctors may suggest that you minimize physical contact but still spend as much time as possible with your baby. Check with the doctor or nurses to figure out how much and what type of contact is best.

A mother who can hold her baby might be able to breastfeed or pump milk and bottle-feed. Most NICUs have screens to allow mothers to breastfeed their babies at the bedside.

Kangaroo care (or skin-to-skin contact) is another option to help you forge a bond with your new baby. Here's how it works:

- Place your baby (who's usually dressed in just a diaper and a hat) on your chest underneath your shirt, so your little one is resting directly on your skin.

- Loosely close your shirt over your baby to help keep him or her warm.

Doctors and researchers have suggested that skin-to-skin contact can improve babies' recovery time and help them leave the NICU sooner.

But the best way for parents to help their babies in the NICU is to be there for them and learn to read their behaviors. This will help you to figure out:

- when your baby is stressed and needs to rest;

- when your baby is ready to bond with you;

- what type of interaction your baby likes (stroking, singing, etc.);

- what time of day your baby is the most alert;

- how long your baby can respond to you before getting tired.

Although you want to interact with your infant, you also want to allow periods of undisturbed sleep. Let your baby set the pace for your time together and you'll both get more out of it.

Other NICU Basics

Here are some basics to help make the NICU a little less mysterious. Everyone who comes into the NICU must wash their hands when they enter. (There will be a sink and antibacterial soap in the room and near the entrance of the NICU.) This is a crucial part of keeping the NICU environment as clean as possible so the babies won't be exposed to infections. Some units require visitors to wear hospital gowns, particularly if a child is in isolation. You may also need to wear gloves and a mask.

Ask the nurses what you're allowed to bring into the unit: The risk of infection limits what you can leave with your baby. Some parents tape pictures to the isolette or decorate the incubator. If you want to give your child a stuffed toy, the staff may wrap it in plastic first.

When you're in the NICU, keep noise and bright lights to a minimum: Try not to bang things on the isolette or infant warmer, talk in a loud voice, or slam doors. If you're concerned about light, ask a nurse if you can drape a blanket partially over the isolette. Most important, let your baby sleep when he or she needs to.

Making the NICU Stay More Manageable

The time when your baby is in the NICU can be stressful—you may be away from your friends and family, including any other children you may have. Your life may seem like it's been turned upside down as you wait for the day when your baby may be able to leave with you.

You may feel like you eat, sleep, and breathe the NICU twenty-four hours a day, seven days a week. And you might feel especially confused and overwhelmed if your baby was unexpectedly born prematurely and/or if the NICU is located far away from your home and your usual support system.

As hard as it may be sometimes, it's important to pay attention to your own needs and those of the rest of the family, particularly other kids. Make plans for a weekly family activity, and sit down together and talk about how this experience makes you feel. Doing something for yourself can be as simple as taking a relaxing bath, going for a walk, or reading a favorite book for an hour.

You also can turn to other parents in the NICU for comfort. They'll likely know better than anyone what you're feeling. Also be sure to talk to the NICU's social worker about parents' support groups, where you can share your feelings, worries, and triumphs together. The hospital's chaplain also might be able to provide you with support and even a shoulder to cry on.

When you take care of yourself, you'll be more rested and better prepared to take care of your baby. But that care doesn't have to center on your infant's illness. Enjoy your new baby, spend time together, and get to know your little one.

Your baby's NICU stay can be difficult, but also rewarding as you watch your little one grow and progress day after day.

Part Three

Structural Abnormalities and Functional Impairments

Chapter 22

Arteriovenous
Malformations

What are arteriovenous malformations?

Arteriovenous malformations (AVMs) are defects of the circulatory system that are generally believed to arise during embryonic or fetal development or soon after birth. They are comprised of snarled tangles of arteries and veins. Arteries carry oxygen-rich blood away from the heart to the body's cells; veins return oxygen-depleted blood to the lungs and heart. The absence of capillaries—small blood vessels that connect arteries to veins—creates a shortcut for blood to pass directly from arteries to veins. The presence of an AVM disrupts this vital cyclical process. Although AVMs can develop in many different sites, those located in the brain or spinal cord—the two parts of the central nervous system—can have especially widespread effects on the body.

What are the symptoms?

Most people with neurological AVMs experience few, if any, significant symptoms, and the malformations tend to be discovered only incidentally, usually either at autopsy or during treatment for an unrelated disorder. But for about 12 percent of the affected population

Excerpted from "Arteriovenous Malformations and Other Vascular Lesions of the Central Nervous System Fact Sheet," National Institute of Neurological Disorders and Stroke, National Institutes of Health, February 2011.

(about thirty-six thousand of the estimated three hundred thousand Americans with AVMs), these abnormalities cause symptoms that vary greatly in severity. For a small fraction of the individuals within this group, such symptoms are severe enough to become debilitating or even life threatening. Each year about 1 percent of those with AVMs will die as a direct result of the AVM.

Seizures and headaches are the most generalized symptoms of AVMs, but no particular type of seizure or headache pattern has been identified.

How do AVMs damage the brain and spinal cord?

AVMs become symptomatic only when the damage they cause to the brain or spinal cord reaches a critical level. This is one of the reasons why a relatively small fraction of people with these lesions experiences significant health problems related to the condition. AVMs damage the brain or spinal cord through three basic mechanisms: by reducing the amount of oxygen reaching neurological tissues; by causing bleeding (hemorrhage) into surrounding tissues; and by compressing or displacing parts of the brain or spinal cord.

Where do neurological AVMs tend to form?

AVMs can form virtually anywhere in the brain or spinal cord—wherever arteries and veins exist. Some are formed from blood vessels located in the dura mater or in the pia mater, the outermost and innermost, respectively, of the three membranes surrounding the brain and spinal cord. (The third membrane, called the arachnoid, lacks blood vessels.) AVMs affecting the spinal cord are of two types: AVMs of the dura mater, which affect the function of the spinal cord by transmitting excess pressure to the venous system of the spinal cord, and AVMs of the spinal cord itself, which affect the function of the spinal cord by hemorrhage, by reducing blood flow to the spinal cord, or by causing excess venous pressure. Spinal AVMs frequently cause attacks of sudden, severe back pain, often concentrated at the roots of nerve fibers where they exit the vertebrae; the pain is similar to that caused by a slipped disk. These lesions also can cause sensory disturbances, muscle weakness, or paralysis in the parts of the body served by the spinal cord or the damaged nerve fibers. Spinal cord injury by the AVM by either of the mechanisms described above can lead to degeneration of the nerve fibers within the spinal cord below the level of the lesion, causing widespread paralysis in parts of the body controlled by those nerve fibers.

What are the health consequences of AVMs?

The greatest potential danger posed by AVMs is hemorrhage. Researchers believe that each year between 2 and 4 percent of all AVMs hemorrhage. Most episodes of bleeding remain undetected at the time they occur because they are not severe enough to cause significant neurological damage. But massive, even fatal, bleeding episodes do occur. The present state of knowledge does not permit doctors to predict whether or not any particular person with an AVM will suffer an extensive hemorrhage. The lesions can remain stable or can suddenly begin to grow. In a few cases, they have been observed to regress spontaneously. Whenever an AVM is detected, the individual should be carefully and consistently monitored for any signs of instability that may indicate an increased risk of hemorrhage.

What other types of vascular lesions affect the central nervous system?

Besides AVMs, three other main types of vascular lesion can arise in the brain or spinal cord: cavernous malformations, capillary telangiectases, and venous malformations. These lesions may form virtually anywhere within the central nervous system, but unlike AVMs, they are not caused by high-velocity blood flow from arteries into veins. In contrast, cavernous malformations, telangiectases, and venous malformations are all low-flow lesions. Instead of a combination of arteries and veins, each one involves only one type of blood vessel. These lesions are less unstable than AVMs and do not pose the same relatively high risk of significant hemorrhage.

Cavernous malformations: These lesions are formed from groups of tightly packed, abnormally thin-walled, small blood vessels that displace normal neurological tissue in the brain or spinal cord. After AVMs, cavernous malformations are the type of vascular lesion most likely to require treatment.

Capillary telangiectases: These lesions consist of groups of abnormally swollen capillaries and usually measure less than an inch in diameter. Capillaries are the smallest of all blood vessels, with diameters smaller than that of a human hair; they have the capacity to transport only small quantities of blood, and blood flows through these vessels very slowly. Because of these factors, telangiectases rarely cause extensive damage to surrounding brain or spinal cord tissues. Any isolated hemorrhages that occur are microscopic in size. Thus, the lesions are usually benign.

Venous malformations: These lesions consist of abnormally enlarged veins. The structural defect usually does not interfere with the function of the blood vessels, which is to drain oxygen-depleted blood away from the body's tissues and return it to the lungs and heart. Venous malformations rarely hemorrhage. As with telangiectases, most venous malformations do not produce symptoms, remain undetected, and follow a benign course.

What causes vascular lesions?

Although the cause of these vascular anomalies of the central nervous system is not yet well understood, scientists believe that they most often result from mistakes that occur during embryonic or fetal development. These mistakes may be linked to genetic mutations in some cases. A few types of vascular malformations are known to be hereditary and thus are known to have a genetic basis. Some evidence also suggests that at least some of these lesions are acquired later in life as a result of injury to the central nervous system.

How are AVMs and other vascular lesions detected?

Angiography provides the most accurate pictures of blood vessel structure in AVMs. The technique requires injecting a special water-soluble dye, called a contrast agent, into an artery. The dye highlights the structure of blood vessels so that it can be recorded on conventional x-rays. Although angiography can record fine details of vascular lesions, the procedure is somewhat invasive and carries a slight risk of causing a stroke. Its safety, however, has recently been improved through the development of more precise techniques for delivering dye to the site of an AVM. Superselective angiography involves inserting a thin, flexible tube called a catheter into an artery; a physician guides the tip of the catheter to the site of the lesion and then releases a small amount of contrast agent directly into the lesion.

Two of the most frequently employed noninvasive imaging technologies used to detect AVMs are computed axial tomography (CT) and magnetic resonance imaging (MRI) scans. CT scans use x-rays to create a series of cross-sectional images of the head, brain, or spinal cord and are especially useful in revealing the presence of hemorrhage. MRI imaging, however, offers superior diagnostic information by using magnetic fields to detect subtle changes in neurological tissues. A recently developed application of MRI technology—magnetic resonance angiography (MRA)—can record the pattern and velocity of blood flow through vascular lesions as well as the flow of cerebrospinal fluid throughout the brain and spinal cord.

How can AVMs and other vascular lesions be treated?

Medication can often alleviate general symptoms such as headache, back pain, and seizures caused by AVMs and other vascular lesions. However, the definitive treatment for AVMs is either surgery or focused irradiation therapy. Venous malformations and capillary telangiectases rarely require surgery; moreover, their structures are diffuse and usually not suitable for surgical correction, and they usually do not require treatment anyway. Cavernous malformations are usually well defined enough for surgical removal, but surgery on these lesions is less common than for AVMs because they do not pose the same risk of hemorrhage.

Today, three surgical options exist for the treatment of AVMs: conventional surgery, endovascular embolization, and radiosurgery. The choice of treatment depends largely on the size and location of an AVM.

Conventional surgery involves entering the brain or spinal cord and removing the central portion of the AVM, including the fistula, while causing as little damage as possible to surrounding neurological structures. This surgery is most appropriate when an AVM is located in a superficial portion of the brain or spinal cord and is relatively small in size. AVMs located deep inside the brain generally cannot be approached through conventional surgical techniques because there is too great a possibility that functionally important brain tissue will be damaged or destroyed.

Endovascular embolization and radiosurgery are less invasive than conventional surgery and offer safer treatment options for some AVMs located deep inside the brain. In endovascular embolization the surgeon guides a catheter though the arterial network until the tip reaches the site of the AVM. The surgeon then introduces a substance that will plug the fistula, correcting the abnormal pattern of blood flow. This process is known as embolization because it causes an embolus (an object or substance) to travel through blood vessels, eventually becoming lodged in a vessel and obstructing blood flow. The embolic materials used to create an artificial blood clot in the center of an AVM include fast-drying biologically inert glues, fibered titanium coils, and tiny balloons. Since embolization usually does not permanently obliterate the AVM, it is usually used as an adjunct to surgery or to radiosurgery to reduce the blood flow through the AVM and make the surgery safer.

Radiosurgery is an even less invasive therapeutic approach. It involves aiming a beam of highly focused radiation directly on the AVM. The high dose of radiation damages the walls of the blood vessels making up the lesion. Over the course of the next several months, the irradiated vessels gradually degenerate and eventually close, leading to the resolution of the AVM.

Embolization frequently proves incomplete or temporary, although in recent years new embolization materials have led to improved results. Radiosurgery often has incomplete results as well, particularly when an AVM is large, and it poses the additional risk of radiation damage to surrounding normal tissues. Moreover, even when successful, complete closure of an AVM takes place over the course of many months following radiosurgery. During that period, the risk of hemorrhage is still present. However, both techniques now offer the possibility of treating deeply situated AVMs that had previously been inaccessible. And in many individuals, staged embolization followed by conventional surgical removal or by radiosurgery is now performed, resulting in further reductions in mortality and complication rates.

Chapter 23

Birthmarks

Newborns often have temporary pimples or blotches that soon disappear as they adapt to life outside the womb. It's also quite common to see birthmarks on their skin at birth or shortly after. Birthmarks range from hardly noticeable to disfiguring, but no matter how large or small they are, they can be upsetting.

Birthmarks can be flat or raised, have regular or irregular borders, and have different shades of coloring from brown, tan, black, or pale blue to pink, red, or purple. The two main types of birthmarks are red, vascular birthmarks (for example, "strawberry" hemangiomas, port-wine stains, and "stork bites") and pigmented birthmarks (such as moles, café au lait spots, and Mongolian spots).

They're mostly harmless and many even go away on their own or shrink over time. Sometimes birthmarks are associated with other health problems, though, so talk to your doctor about whether this might be the case for your child.

What Causes Birthmarks

Birthmarks can't be prevented and they're not caused by anything done or not done during pregnancy. There's no truth to old wives' tales

"Birthmarks," October 2009, reprinted with permission from www.kidshealth .org. This information was provided by KidsHealth®, one of the largest resources online for medically reviewed health information written for parents, kids, and teens. For more articles like this, visit www.KidsHealth.org, or www.TeensHealth .org. Copyright © 1995–2012 The Nemours Foundation. All rights reserved.

about "stains" being caused by something the mother did or ate. The cause of most birthmarks is unknown. They can be inherited, but usually are not, and typically are unrelated to trauma to the skin during childbirth.

Types of Birthmarks

The two main types of birthmarks are differentiated by their causes. Vascular (blood vessel) birthmarks happen when blood vessels don't form correctly—either there are too many of them or they're wider than usual. Pigmented birthmarks are caused by an overgrowth of the cells that create pigment in skin.

Vascular Birthmarks

The most common vascular birthmarks are macular stains, hemangiomas, and port-wine stains.

Macular stains: Also called salmon patches, angel kisses, or stork bites, these faint red marks are the most common type of vascular birthmark. They're often on the forehead or eyelids, the back of the neck, or on the nose, upper lip, or on the back of the head. They may be more noticeable when the baby cries. Most often they fade on their own by the time a child is one to two years old, although some last into adulthood.

Hemangiomas: Hemangiomas are classified as superficial when they appear on the surface of the skin ("strawberry marks") and deep when found deeper below the skin's surface. They can be slightly raised and bright red and sometimes aren't visible until a few days or weeks after a baby is born. Deep hemangiomas may be bluish because they involve blood vessels in deeper layers of the skin. Hemangiomas grow rapidly during the first six months or so of life, but usually shrink back and disappear by the time a child is five to nine years old. Some, particularly larger ones, may leave a scar as they regress that can be corrected by minor plastic surgery. Most are on the head or neck, although they can be anywhere on the body, and can cause complications if their location interferes with sight, feeding, breathing, or other body functions.

Port-wine stains: These are discolorations that look like wine was spilled on an area of the body, most often on the face, neck, arms, or legs. Port-wine stains can be any size, but grow only as the child grows. They tend to darken over time and can thicken and feel like pebbles in midlife adulthood unless treated. They never go away on their own. Ones near the eye must be assessed for possible complications involving the eye.

Pigmented Birthmarks

The most common pigmented birthmarks are café au lait spots, Mongolian spots, and moles.

Café au lait spots: These very common spots are the color of coffee with milk, hence their name. They can be anywhere on the body and sometimes increase in number as a child gets older. One alone is not a problem, but it's wise to have your child evaluated if there are several larger than a quarter, which can be a sign of neurofibromatosis (a genetic disorder that causes abnormal cell growth of nerve tissues).

Mongolian spots: These flat, bluish-gray patches are often found on the lower back or buttocks. They are most common on darker skin, such as on children of Asian, American Indian, African, Hispanic, and Southern European descent. They usually fade—often completely—by school age without treatment.

Moles (congenital nevi, hairy nevus): Mole is a general term for brown nevi (one is called a "nevus"). Most people get moles at some point in life. One present at birth is called a congenital nevus and will last a lifetime. Large or giant congenital nevi are more likely to develop into skin cancer (melanoma) later in life. Smaller moles may have a slight increase in risk. Moles can be tan, brown, or black; flat or raised; and may have hair growing out of them.

When to Call the Doctor

A doctor should evaluate a birthmark when it first appears to determine its type and what kind of monitoring and treatment it needs, if any. Call the doctor if a birthmark ever bleeds, hurts, itches, or becomes infected. Like any injury where there is bleeding, you should clean the wound with soap and water and, using a gauze bandage, place firm pressure on the area until the bleeding stops. If the bleeding doesn't stop, call the doctor.

Open sores sometimes form with hemangiomas and can get infected. Pigmented birthmarks rarely cause other problems, although moles should be checked throughout life for changes in size, color, or texture, which may be normal or could be a sign of skin cancer.

Treating Birthmarks

Pigmented birthmarks are usually left alone, with the exception of moles and, occasionally, café au lait spots. Moles—particularly large or giant congenital nevi—sometimes are surgically removed, though larger ones may be more difficult to remove. Café au lait spots can be removed with lasers (highly concentrated light energy) but often return.

Vascular birthmarks, on the other hand, can be treated. The exception is macular stains, which usually fade away on their own; ones at the back of the neck may be more persistent but are not very noticeable.

Port-wine stains and certain hemangiomas can be disfiguring and embarrassing for children. Hemangiomas are usually left alone, as they typically shrink back into themselves by age nine. Larger or more serious hemangiomas often are treated with steroids.

Lasers are the treatment of choice for port-wine stains. Most lighten significantly after several treatments with a "pulsed-dye" laser, although some return and need retreatment. Laser treatment is often started in infancy when the stain and the blood vessels are smaller. Marks on the head and neck are the most responsive to laser treatment. Special opaque makeup also can camouflage a port-wine stain.

Helping Kids Deal with Birthmarks

It can be a shock at first to see a birthmark on your newborn. Nobody is perfect, yet many people have an image of a perfect baby in their heads. If the birthmark is clearly visible, people might ask questions or stare, which can feel rude. It helps to have a simple explanation ready to handle intrusions like this. Most people mean no harm, but it's also ok to let them know if they've gone too far.

Even at a young age, kids watch how their parents respond to situations like this. This is how they lean how to cope with others' reactions. Talking simply and openly about a birthmark with kids makes them more likely to accept one as just another part of themselves, like hair color. And practice simple answers they can use when asked about it: "It's just a birthmark. I was born with it." It's also important emotionally for kids to be around supportive family and friends who treat them normally.

Chapter 24

Brain Defects

Chapter Contents

Section 24.1

Agenesis of the Corpus Callosum

"Agenesis of the Corpus Callosum Information Page,"
National Institute of Neurological Disorders and Stroke,
National Institutes of Health, February 7, 2011.

What is Agenesis of the Corpus Callosum?

Agenesis of the corpus callosum (ACC) is a birth defect in which the structure that connects the two hemispheres of the brain (the corpus callosum) is partially or completely absent. ACC can occur as an isolated condition or in combination with other cerebral abnormalities, including Arnold-Chiari malformation, Dandy-Walker syndrome, Andermann syndrome, schizencephaly (clefts or deep divisions in brain tissue), and holoprosencephaly (failure of the forebrain to divide into lobes.) Girls may have a gender-specific condition called Aicardi syndrome, which causes severe mental retardation, seizures, abnormalities in the vertebra of the spine, and lesions on the retina of the eye. ACC can also be associated with malformations in other parts of the body, such as midline facial defects. The effects of the disorder range from subtle or mild to severe, depending on associated brain abnormalities. Intelligence may be normal with mild compromise of skills requiring matching of visual patterns. But children with the most severe brain malformations may have intellectual retardation, seizures, hydrocephalus, and spasticity.

Is there any treatment?

There is no standard course of treatment for ACC. Treatment usually involves management of symptoms and seizures if they occur.

What is the prognosis?

Prognosis depends on the extent and severity of malformations. ACC does not cause death in the majority of children. Mental retardation does not worsen. Although many children with the disorder have average intelligence and lead normal lives, neuropsychological testing reveals subtle differences in higher cortical function compared to individuals of the same age and education without ACC.

What research is being done?

The National Institute of Neurological Disorders and Stroke (NINDS) conducts and supports a wide range of studies that explore the complex mechanisms of normal brain development. The knowledge gained from these fundamental studies helps researchers understand how the process can go awry and provides opportunities for more effectively treating, and perhaps even preventing, developmental brain disorders such as ACC.

Section 24.2

Cerebral Palsy

Excerpted from "Cerebral Palsy," National Dissemination Center for Children with Disabilities, June 2010.

What Is Cerebral Palsy?

Cerebral palsy—also known as CP—is a condition caused by injury to the parts of the brain that control our ability to use our muscles and bodies. Cerebral means having to do with the brain. Palsy means weakness or problems with using the muscles. Often the injury happens before birth, sometimes during delivery, or soon after being born.

CP can be mild, moderate, or severe. Mild CP may mean a child is clumsy. Moderate CP may mean the child walks with a limp. He or she may need a special leg brace or a cane. More severe CP can affect all parts of a child's physical abilities. A child with moderate or severe CP may have to use a wheelchair and other special equipment.

Sometimes children with CP can also have learning problems, problems with hearing or seeing (called sensory problems), or intellectual disabilities. Usually, the greater the injury to the brain, the more severe the CP. However, CP doesn't get worse over time, and most children with CP have a normal life span.

What Are the Signs of CP?

There are four main types of CP:

- Spastic CP is where there is too much muscle tone or tightness. Movements are stiff, especially in the legs, arms, and/or back. Children with this form of CP move their legs awkwardly, turning in or scissoring their legs as they try to walk. This form of CP occurs in 50 to 75 percent of all cases.

- Athetoid CP (also called dyskinetic CP) can affect movements of the entire body. Typically, this form of CP involves slow, uncontrolled body movements and low muscle tone that makes it hard for the person to sit straight and walk. This form occurs in 10 to 20 percent of all cases.

- Ataxic CP involves poor coordination, balance, and depth perception and occurs in approximately 5 to 10 percent of all cases.

- Mixed CP is a combination of the symptoms listed above. A child with mixed CP has both high- and low-tone muscle. Some muscles are too tight, and others are too loose, creating a mix of stiffness and involuntary movements. (March of Dimes, 2007)

More words used to describe the different types of CP include:

- **Diplegia:** This means only the legs are affected.

- **Hemiplegia:** This means one half of the body (such as the right arm and leg) is affected.

- **Quadriplegia:** This means both arms and legs are affected, sometimes including the facial muscles and torso.

Is There Help Available?

Yes, there's a lot of help available, beginning with the free evaluation of the child. The nation's special education law, the Individuals with Disabilities Education Act (IDEA), requires that all children suspected of having a disability be evaluated without cost to their parents to determine if they do have a disability and, because of the disability, need special services under IDEA. Those special services are:

- **Early intervention:** A system of services to support infants and toddlers with disabilities (before their third birthday) and their families.

- **Special education and related services:** Services available through the public school system for school-aged children, including preschoolers (ages three to twenty-one).

Under IDEA, children with CP are usually found eligible for services under the category of "Orthopedic Impairment." IDEA's definition of orthopedic impairment reads as follows:

... a severe orthopedic impairment that adversely affects a child's educational performance. The term includes impairments caused by a congenital anomaly, impairments caused by disease (e.g., poliomyelitis, bone tuberculosis), and impairments from other causes (e.g., cerebral palsy, amputations, and fractures or burns that cause contractures). [34 CFR §300.8(c)(9)]

To access special education services for a school-aged child, get in touch with your local public school system. Calling the elementary school in your neighborhood is an excellent place to start.

What about Treatment?

With early and ongoing treatment the effects of CP can be reduced. Many children learn how to get their bodies to work for them in other ways. For example, one infant whose CP keeps him from crawling may be able to get around by rolling from place to place.

Typically, children with CP may need different kinds of therapy, including:

- Physical therapy (PT), which helps the child develop stronger muscles such as those in the legs and trunk. Through PT, the child works on skills such as walking, sitting, and keeping his or her balance.

- Occupational therapy (OT), which helps the child develop fine motor skills such as dressing, feeding, writing, and other daily living tasks.

- Speech-language pathology (S/L), which helps the child develop his or her communication skills. The child may work in particular on speaking, which may be difficult due to problems with muscle tone of the tongue and throat.

All of these are available as related services in both early intervention programs (for very young children) and special education (for school-aged children).

Children with CP may also find a variety of special equipment helpful. For example, braces (also called ankle-foot orthoses [AFOs]) may be used to hold the foot in place when the child stands or walks. Custom splints can provide support to help a child use his or her hands. A variety of therapy equipment and adapted toys are available to help children play and have fun while they are working their bodies. Activities such as swimming or horseback riding can help strengthen weaker muscles and relax the tighter ones.

New medical treatments are being developed all the time. Sometimes surgery, Botox injections, or other medications can help lessen the effects of CP, but there is no cure for the condition. It's also important to understand that cerebral palsy is not contagious, not inherited, and not progressive. The symptoms will differ from person to person and change as children and their nervous systems mature. (Healthcommunities.com, 2007)

Tips for Parents

Learn about CP. The more you know, the more you can help yourself and your child.

Love and play with your child. Treat your son or daughter as you would a child without disabilities. Take your child places, read together, have fun.

Learn from professionals and other parents how to meet your child's special needs, but try not to turn your lives into one round of therapy after another.

Ask for help from family and friends. Caring for a child with CP is hard work. Teach others what to do and give them plenty of opportunities to practice while you take a break.

Keep informed about new treatments and technologies that may help. New approaches are constantly being worked on and can make a huge difference to the quality of your child's life. However, be careful about unproven new "fads."

Learn about assistive technology that can help your child. This may include a simple communication board to help your child express needs and desires, or may be as sophisticated as a computer with special software.

Be patient, and keep up your hope for improvement. Your child, like every child, has a whole lifetime to learn and grow.

Work with professionals in early intervention or in your school to develop an IFSP or an IEP that reflects your child's needs and abilities. Be sure to include related services such as speech-language pathology, physical therapy, and occupational therapy if your child needs these. Don't forget about assistive technology either!

Tips for Teachers

Learn more about CP.

This may seem obvious, but sometimes the "look" of CP can give the mistaken impression that a child who has CP cannot learn as much as others. Focus on the individual child and learn firsthand what needs and capabilities he or she has.

Tap into the strategies that teachers of students with learning disabilities use for their students. Become knowledgeable about different learning styles. Then you can use the approach best suited for a particular child, based upon that child's learning abilities as well as physical abilities.

Be inventive. Ask yourself (and others), "How can I adapt this lesson for this child to maximize active, hands-on learning?"

Learn to love assistive technology. Find experts within and outside your school to help you. Assistive technology can mean the difference between independence for your student or not.

Always remember, parents are experts, too. Talk candidly with your student's parents. They can tell you a great deal about their daughter or son's special needs and abilities.

Effective teamwork for the child with CP needs to bring together professionals with diverse backgrounds and expertise. The team must combine the knowledge of its members to plan, implement, and coordinate the child's services.

Section 24.3

Chiari Malformation

"Chiari Malformation Fact Sheet," National Institute of Neurological Disorders and Stroke, National Institutes of Health, February 1, 2012.

What are Chiari malformations?

Chiari malformations (CMs) are structural defects in the cerebellum, the part of the brain that controls balance. Normally the cerebellum and parts of the brain stem sit in an indented space at the lower rear of the skull, above the foramen magnum (a funnel-like opening to the spinal canal). When part of the cerebellum is located below the foramen magnum, it is called a Chiari malformation.

CMs may develop when the bony space is smaller than normal, causing the cerebellum and brain stem to be pushed downward into the foramen magnum and into the upper spinal canal. The resulting pressure on the cerebellum and brain stem may affect functions controlled by these areas and block the flow of cerebrospinal fluid (CSF)—the clear liquid that surrounds and cushions the brain and spinal cord—to and from the brain.

What causes these malformations?

CM has several different causes. It can be caused by structural defects in the brain and spinal cord that occur during fetal development, whether caused by genetic mutations or lack of proper vitamins or nutrients in the maternal diet. This is called primary or congenital CM. It can also be caused later in life if spinal fluid is drained excessively from the lumbar or thoracic areas of the spine either due to injury, exposure to harmful substances, or infection. This is called acquired or secondary CM. Primary CM is much more common than secondary CM.

How are they classified?

CMs are classified by the severity of the disorder and the parts of the brain that protrude into the spinal canal.

Type I involves the extension of the cerebellar tonsils (the lower part of the cerebellum) into the foramen magnum, without involving the brain stem. Normally, only the spinal cord passes through this opening. Type I—which may not cause symptoms—is the most common form of CM and is usually first noticed in adolescence or adulthood, often by accident during an examination for another condition. Type I is the only type of CM that can be acquired.

Type II, also called classic CM, involves the extension of both cerebellar and brain stem tissue into the foramen magnum. Also, the cerebellar vermis (the nerve tissue that connects the two halves of the cerebellum) may be only partially complete or absent. Type II is usually accompanied by a myelomeningocele—a form of spina bifida that occurs when the spinal canal and backbone do not close before birth, causing the spinal cord and its protective membrane to protrude through a sac-like opening in the back. A myelomeningocele usually results in partial or complete paralysis of the area below the spinal opening. The term Arnold-Chiari malformation (named after two pioneering researchers) is specific to Type II malformations.

Type III is the most serious form of CM. The cerebellum and brain stem protrude, or herniate, through the foramen magnum and into the spinal cord. Part of the brain's fourth ventricle, a cavity that connects with the upper parts of the brain and circulates CSF, may also protrude through the hole and into the spinal cord. In rare instances, the herniated cerebellar tissue can enter an occipital encephalocele, a pouch-like structure that protrudes out of the back of the head or the neck and contains brain matter. The covering of the brain or spinal cord can also protrude through an abnormal opening in the back or skull. Type III causes severe neurological defects.

Type IV involves an incomplete or underdeveloped cerebellum—a condition known as cerebellar hypoplasia. In this rare form of CM, the cerebellar tonsils are located in a normal position, but parts of the cerebellum are missing, and portions of the skull and spinal cord may be visible.

Another form of the disorder, under debate by some scientists, is Type 0, in which there is no protrusion of the cerebellum through the foramen magnum but headache and other symptoms of CM are present.

What are the symptoms of a Chiari malformation?

Individuals with CM may complain of neck pain, balance problems, muscle weakness, numbness or other abnormal feelings in the arms or legs, dizziness, vision problems, difficulty swallowing, ringing or buzzing in the ears, hearing loss, vomiting, insomnia, depression, or headache made worse by coughing or straining. Hand coordination and fine motor skills may be affected. Symptoms may change for some individuals, depending on the buildup of CSF and resulting pressure on the tissues and nerves. Persons with a Type 1 CM may not have symptoms. Adolescents and adults who have CM but no symptoms initially may, later in life, develop signs of the disorder. Infants may have symptoms from any type of CM and may have difficulty swallowing, irritability when being fed, excessive drooling, a weak cry, gagging or vomiting, arm weakness, a stiff neck, breathing problems, developmental delays, and an inability to gain weight.

Are other conditions associated with Chiari malformations?

Individuals who have a CM often have these related conditions:

- Hydrocephalus is an excessive buildup of CSF in the brain. A CM can block the normal flow of this fluid, resulting in pressure within the head that can cause mental defects and/or an enlarged or misshapen skull. Severe hydrocephalus, if left untreated, can be fatal. The disorder can occur with any type of CM, but is most commonly associated with Type II.

- Spina bifida is the incomplete development of the spinal cord and/or its protective covering. The bones around the spinal cord don't form properly, leaving part of the cord exposed and resulting in partial or complete paralysis. Individuals with Type II CM usually have a myelomeningocele, a form of spina bifida in which the bones in the back and lower spine don't form properly and extend out of the back in a sac-like opening.

- Syringomyelia, or hydromyelia, is a disorder in which a CSF-filled tubular cyst, or syrinx, forms within the spinal cord's central canal. The growing syrinx destroys the center of the spinal cord, resulting in pain, weakness, and stiffness in the back, shoulders, arms, or legs. Other symptoms may include headaches and a loss of the ability to feel extremes of hot or cold, especially in the hands. Some individuals also have severe arm and neck pain.

- Tethered cord syndrome occurs when the spinal cord attaches itself to the bony spine. This progressive disorder causes abnormal stretching of the spinal cord and can result in permanent damage to the muscles and nerves in the lower body and legs. Children who have a myelomeningocele have an increased risk of developing a tethered cord later in life.

- Spinal curvature is common among individuals with syringomyelia or CM Type I. Two types of spinal curvature can occur
in conjunction with CMs: scoliosis, a bending of the spine to the
left or right; and kyphosis, a forward bending of the spine. Spinal
curvature is seen most often in children with CM, whose skeleton has not fully matured.

CMs may also be associated with certain hereditary syndromes that
affect neurological and skeletal abnormalities, other disorders that
affect bone formation and growth, fusion of segments of the bones in
the neck, and extra folds in the brain.

How common are Chiari malformations?

In the past, it was estimated that the condition occurs in about one
in every one thousand births. However, the increased use of diagnostic
imaging has shown that CM may be much more common. Complicating
this estimation is the fact that some children who are born with the
condition may not show symptoms until adolescence or adulthood, if
at all. CMs occur more often in women than in men and Type II malformations are more prevalent in certain groups, including people of
Celtic descent.

How are Chiari malformations diagnosed?

Many people with CMs have no symptoms and their malformations
are discovered only during the course of diagnosis or treatment for
another disorder. The doctor will perform a physical exam and check
the person's memory, cognition, balance (a function controlled by the
cerebellum), touch, reflexes, sensation, and motor skills (functions
controlled by the spinal cord). The physician may also order one of the
following diagnostic tests:

- An x-ray uses electromagnetic energy to produce images of bones
and certain tissues on film. An x-ray of the head and neck cannot
reveal a CM but can identify bone abnormalities that are often
associated with CM. This safe and painless procedure can be
done in a doctor's office and takes only a few minutes.

- Computed tomography (also called a CT scan) uses x-rays and a
computer to produce two-dimensional pictures of bone and vascular irregularities, certain brain tumors and cysts, brain damage from head injury, and other disorders. Scanning takes about
three to five minutes. This painless, noninvasive procedure is

335

done at an imaging center or hospital on an outpatient basis and can identify hydrocephalus and bone abnormalities associated with CM.

- Magnetic resonance imaging (MRI) is the imaging procedure most often used to diagnose a CM. Like CT, it is painless and noninvasive and is performed at an imaging center or hospital. MRI uses radio waves and a powerful magnetic field to produce either a detailed three-dimensional picture or a two-dimensional "slice" of body structures, including tissues, organs, bones, and nerves. Depending on the part(s) of the body to be scanned, MRI can take up to an hour to complete.

How are they treated?

Some CMs are asymptomatic and do not interfere with a person's activities of daily living. In other cases, medications may ease certain symptoms, such as pain.

Surgery is the only treatment available to correct functional disturbances or halt the progression of damage to the central nervous system. Most individuals who have surgery see a reduction in their symptoms and/or prolonged periods of relative stability. More than one surgery may be needed to treat the condition.

Posterior fossa decompression surgery is performed on adults with CM to create more space for the cerebellum and to relieve pressure on the spinal column. Surgery involves making an incision at the back of the head and removing a small portion of the bottom of the skull (and sometimes part of the spinal column) to correct the irregular bony structure. The neurosurgeon may use a procedure called electrocautery to shrink the cerebellar tonsils. This surgical technique involves destroying tissue with high-frequency electrical currents.

A related procedure, called a spinal laminectomy, involves the surgical removal of part of the arched, bony roof of the spinal canal (the lamina) to increase the size of the spinal canal and relieve pressure on the spinal cord and nerve roots.

The surgeon may also make an incision in the dura (the covering of the brain) to examine the brain and spinal cord. Additional tissue may be added to the dura to create more space for the flow of CSF.

Infants and children with myelomeningocele may require surgery to reposition the spinal cord and close the opening in the back.

Hydrocephalus may be treated with a shunt system that drains excess fluid and relieves pressure inside the head. A sturdy tube that is surgically inserted into the head is connected to a flexible tube that is placed under the skin, where it can drain the excess fluid into either the chest wall or the abdomen so it can be absorbed by the body. An alternative surgical treatment to relieve hydrocephalus is third ventriculostomy, a procedure that improves the flow of CSF. A small perforation is made in the floor of the third ventricle and the CSF is diverted into the subarachnoid space to relieve pressure.

Similarly, surgeons may open the spinal cord and insert a shunt to drain a syringomyelia or hydromyelia. A small tube or catheter may be inserted into the syrinx for continued drainage.

What research is being done?

Within the federal government, the National Institute of Neurological Disorders and Stroke (NINDS), a component of the National Institutes of Health (NIH), supports and conducts research on brain and nervous system disorders, including Chiari malformations. The NINDS conducts research in its laboratories at the NIH, in Bethesda, Maryland, and supports research through grants to major medical institutions across the country.

In one study, NINDS scientists are trying to locate the genes responsible for the malformation by examining individuals with CM who have a family member with either a CM or syringomyelia.

Another NINDS study is reviewing an alternative surgical treatment for syringomyelia. By examining people with syringomyelia, in which there is an obstruction in CSF flow, NINDS scientists hope to learn whether a surgical procedure that relieves the obstruction in CSF flow can correct the problem without having to cut into the spinal cord itself.

The NIH's Management of Myelomeningocele Study is comparing prenatal surgery to the conventional post-birth approach of closing the opening in the spine and back that is common to some forms of CM. The study will enroll two hundred women whose fetuses have spina bifida and will compare the safety and efficacy of the different surgeries. Preliminary clinical evidence of intrauterine closure of the myelomeningocele suggests the procedure reduces the incidence of shunt-dependent hydrocephalus and restores the cerebellum and brain stem to more normal configuration. At one year and two and a half years after surgery the children will be tested for motor function, developmental progress, and bladder, kidney, and brain development.

Section 24.4

Dandy-Walker Syndrome

"Dandy-Walker Syndrome Information Page,"
National Institute of Neurological Disorders and Stroke,
National Institutes of Health, December 16, 2011.

What is Dandy-Walker syndrome?

Dandy-Walker syndrome is a congenital brain malformation involving the cerebellum (an area at the back of the brain that controls movement) and the fluid-filled spaces around it. The key features of this syndrome are an enlargement of the fourth ventricle (a small channel that allows fluid to flow freely between the upper and lower areas of the brain and spinal cord), a partial or complete absence of the area of the brain between the two cerebellar hemispheres (cerebellar vermis), and cyst formation near the lowest part of the skull. An increase in the size of the fluid spaces surrounding the brain as well as an increase in pressure may also be present.

The syndrome can appear dramatically or develop unnoticed. Symptoms, which often occur in early infancy, include slow motor development and progressive enlargement of the skull. In older children, symptoms of increased intracranial pressure such as irritability and vomiting, and signs of cerebellar dysfunction such as unsteadiness, lack of muscle coordination, or jerky movements of the eyes may occur. Other symptoms include increased head circumference, bulging at the back of the skull, problems with the nerves that control the eyes, face and neck, and abnormal breathing patterns.

Dandy-Walker syndrome is frequently associated with disorders of other areas of the central nervous system, including absence of the area made up of nerve fibers connecting the two cerebral hemispheres (corpus callosum) and malformations of the heart, face, limbs, fingers, and toes.

Is there any treatment?

Treatment for individuals with Dandy-Walker syndrome generally consists of treating the associated problems, if needed. A surgical procedure called a shunt may be required to drain off excess fluid within the brain. This will reduce intracranial pressure and help control swelling. Parents of children with Dandy-Walker syndrome may benefit from genetic counseling if they intend to have more children.

What is the prognosis?

The effect of Dandy-Walker syndrome on intellectual development is variable, with some children having normal cognition and others never achieving normal intellectual development even when the excess fluid buildup is treated early and correctly. Longevity depends on the severity of the syndrome and associated malformations. The presence of multiple congenital defects may shorten life span.

What research is being done?

The NINDS conducts and supports a wide range of studies that explore the complex mechanisms of normal brain development. The knowledge gained from these fundamental studies provides the foundation for understanding abnormal brain development and offers hope for new ways to treat and prevent developmental brain disorders such as Dandy-Walker syndrome.

Section 24.5

Encephalocele

"Facts about Encephalocele," Centers for Disease
Control and Prevention, March 25, 2011.

Encephalocele is a rare type of neural tube defect (NTD) present
at birth that affects the brain. The neural tube is a narrow channel
that folds and closes during the third and fourth weeks of pregnancy
to form the brain and spinal cord. Encephalocele is described as a
sac-like protrusion or projection of the brain and the membranes
that cover it through an opening in the skull. Encephalocele happens
when the neural tube does not close completely during pregnancy. The
result is an opening in the midline of the upper part of the skull, the
area between the forehead and nose, or the back of the skull.

Usually encephaloceles are found right after birth, but sometimes
a small encephalocele in the nose and forehead region can go undetected.

What We Know about Encephalocele

How Often Does Encephalocele Occur?

The Centers for Disease Control and Prevention (CDC) estimates
that each year about 375 babies in the United States are born with
encephalocele.[1] In other words, about one out of every ten thousand
babies born in the United States each year will have encephalocele.

What Problems Do Children with Encephalocele Have?

When located in the back of the skull, encephalocele often is linked
to nervous system problems. Encephalocele usually is seen with other
brain and face defects.

Signs of encephalocele can include the following:

• Buildup of too much fluid in the brain

• Complete loss of strength in the arms and legs

- An unusually small head
- Uncoordinated movement of the voluntary muscles, such as those involved in walking and reaching
- Developmental delay
- Vision problems
- Mental and growth retardation
- Seizures

What We Still Do Not Know about Encephalocele

What Causes Encephalocele?

Although the exact cause of encephalocele is unknown, scientists believe that many factors are involved.

There is a genetic component to the condition, meaning it often occurs among families with a history of spina bifida and anencephaly. Some researchers also believe that certain environmental exposures before or during pregnancy might be causes, but more research is needed. We at CDC work with many other researchers to study risk factors that can increase the chance of having a baby with encephalocele, as well as outcomes of babies with encephalocele. Following is an example of what our research has found:

- Several factors appear to lead to lower survival rates for infants with encephalocele, including preterm birth, low birth weight, having multiple birth defects, and being black or African American.[2]

Can Encephalocele Be Prevented?

Currently, there is no known way to prevent encephalocele, although steps can be taken to lower the risk. Recent studies have shown that the addition of a B vitamin called folic acid to the diet of women who might become pregnant can greatly reduce the number of babies born with NTDs. CDC has recommended that all women of childbearing age consume 400 micrograms of folic acid daily. A single daily serving of most multivitamins and fortified cereals contains 400 micrograms of folic acid.

In addition, mothers can take steps before and during pregnancy to be healthy, including not smoking and not drinking alcohol during pregnancy.

References

1. Canfield MA, Honein MA, Yuskiv N, Xing J, Mai CT, Collins JS, et al. National estimates and race/ethnic-specific variation of selected birth defects in the United States, 1999–2001. *Birth Defects Res Part A Clin Mol Teratol*. 2006;76(11):747–56.

2. Siffel C, Wong LC, Olney RS, Correa A. Survival of infants diagnosed with encephalocele in Atlanta, 1978–98. *Paediatr Perinat Epidemiol*. 2003; 17:40–48.

Section 24.6

Hydrocephalus

"Hydrocephalus Fact Sheet,"
National Institute of Neurological Disorders and Stroke,
National Institutes of Health, December 16, 2011.

What is hydrocephalus?

The term hydrocephalus is derived from the Greek words "hydro" meaning water and "cephalus" meaning head. As the name implies, it is a condition in which the primary characteristic is excessive accumulation of fluid in the brain. Although hydrocephalus was once known as "water on the brain," the "water" is actually cerebrospinal fluid (CSF)—a clear fluid that surrounds the brain and spinal cord. The excessive accumulation of CSF results in an abnormal widening of spaces in the brain called ventricles. This widening creates potentially harmful pressure on the tissues of the brain.

The ventricular system is made up of four ventricles connected by narrow passages. Normally, CSF flows through the ventricles, exits into cisterns (closed spaces that serve as reservoirs) at the base of the brain, bathes the surfaces of the brain and spinal cord, and then reabsorbs into the bloodstream.

CSF has three important life-sustaining functions: to keep the brain tissue buoyant, acting as a cushion or "shock absorber"; to act as the vehicle for delivering nutrients to the brain and removing waste; and to flow between the cranium and spine and compensate for changes in intracranial blood volume (the amount of blood within the brain).

The balance between production and absorption of CSF is critically important. Because CSF is made continuously, medical conditions that block its normal flow or absorption will result in an over-accumulation of CSF. The resulting pressure of the fluid against brain tissue is what causes hydrocephalus.

What are the different types of hydrocephalus?

Hydrocephalus may be congenital or acquired. Congenital hydrocephalus is present at birth and may be caused by either events or influences that occur during fetal development, or genetic abnormalities. Acquired hydrocephalus develops at the time of birth or at some point afterward. This type of hydrocephalus can affect individuals of all ages and may be caused by injury or disease.

Hydrocephalus may also be communicating or noncommunicating. Communicating hydrocephalus occurs when the flow of CSF is blocked after it exits the ventricles. This form is called communicating because the CSF can still flow between the ventricles, which remain open. Noncommunicating hydrocephalus—also called "obstructive" hydrocephalus—occurs when the flow of CSF is blocked along one or more of the narrow passages connecting the ventricles. One of the most common causes of hydrocephalus is "aqueductal stenosis." In this case, hydrocephalus results from a narrowing of the aqueduct of Sylvius, a small passage between the third and fourth ventricles in the middle of the brain.

There are two other forms of hydrocephalus that do not fit exactly into the categories mentioned above and primarily affect adults: hydrocephalus ex-vacuo and normal pressure hydrocephalus.

Hydrocephalus ex-vacuo occurs when stroke or traumatic injury cause damage to the brain. In these cases, brain tissue may actually shrink. Normal pressure hydrocephalus can happen to people at any age, but it is most common among the elderly. It may result from a subarachnoid hemorrhage, head trauma, infection, tumor, or complications of surgery. However, many people develop normal pressure hydrocephalus even when none of these factors are present for reasons that are unknown.

Who gets this disorder?

The number of people who develop hydrocephalus or who are currently living with it is difficult to establish since there is no national registry or database of people with the condition. However, experts estimate that hydrocephalus affects approximately one in every five hundred children.

What causes hydrocephalus?

The causes of hydrocephalus are still not well understood. Hydrocephalus may result from inherited genetic abnormalities (such as the genetic defect that causes aqueductal stenosis) or developmental disorders (such as those associated with neural tube defects including spina bifida and encephalocele). Other possible causes include complications of premature birth such as intraventricular hemorrhage, diseases such as meningitis, tumors, traumatic head injury, or subarachnoid hemorrhage, which block the exit of CSF from the ventricles to the cisterns or eliminate the passageway for CSF into the cisterns.

What are the symptoms?

Symptoms of hydrocephalus vary with age, disease progression, and individual differences in tolerance to the condition. For example, an infant's ability to compensate for increased CSF pressure and enlargement of the ventricles differs from an adult's. The infant skull can expand to accommodate the buildup of CSF because the sutures (the fibrous joints that connect the bones of the skull) have not yet closed.

In infancy, the most obvious indication of hydrocephalus is often a rapid increase in head circumference or an unusually large head size. Other symptoms may include vomiting, sleepiness, irritability, downward deviation of the eyes (also called "sunsetting"), and seizures.

Older children and adults may experience different symptoms because their skulls cannot expand to accommodate the buildup of CSF. Symptoms may include headache followed by vomiting, nausea, papilledema (swelling of the optic disk which is part of the optic nerve), blurred or double vision, sunsetting of the eyes, problems with balance, poor coordination, gait disturbance, urinary incontinence, slowing or loss of developmental progress, lethargy, drowsiness, irritability, or other changes in personality or cognition including memory loss.

Symptoms of normal pressure hydrocephalus include problems with walking, impaired bladder control leading to urinary frequency and/or incontinence, and progressive mental impairment and dementia. An individual with this type of hydrocephalus may have a general slowing of movements or may complain that his or her feet feel "stuck." Because some of these symptoms may also be experienced in other disorders such as Alzheimer disease, Parkinson disease, and Creutzfeldt-Jakob disease, normal pressure hydrocephalus is often incorrectly diagnosed and never properly treated. Doctors may use a variety of tests, including brain scans (computed tomography [CT] and/or magnetic resonance imaging [MRI]), a spinal tap or lumbar catheter, intracranial pressure monitoring, and neuropsychological tests, to help them accurately diagnose normal pressure hydrocephalus and rule out any other conditions.

The symptoms described in this section account for the most typical ways in which progressive hydrocephalus manifests itself, but it is important to remember that symptoms vary significantly from one person to the next.

How is hydrocephalus diagnosed?

Hydrocephalus is diagnosed through clinical neurological evaluation and by using cranial imaging techniques such as ultrasonography, computed tomography (CT), magnetic resonance imaging (MRI), or pressure-monitoring techniques. A physician selects the appropriate diagnostic tool based on an individual's age, clinical presentation, and the presence of known or suspected abnormalities of the brain or spinal cord.

What is the current treatment?

Hydrocephalus is most often treated by surgically inserting a shunt system. This system diverts the flow of CSF from the central nervous system (CNS) to another area of the body where it can be absorbed as part of the normal circulatory process.

A shunt is a flexible but sturdy plastic tube. A shunt system consists of the shunt, a catheter, and a valve. One end of the catheter is placed within a ventricle inside the brain or in the CSF outside the spinal cord. The other end of the catheter is commonly placed within the abdominal cavity, but may also be placed at other sites in the body such as a chamber of the heart or areas around the lung where the CSF can drain and be absorbed. A valve located along the catheter maintains one-way flow and regulates the rate of CSF flow.

A limited number of individuals can be treated with an alternative procedure called third ventriculostomy. In this procedure, a neuroendoscope—a small camera that uses fiber-optic technology to visualize small and difficult to reach surgical areas—allows a doctor to view the ventricular surface. Once the scope is guided into position, a small tool makes a tiny hole in the floor of the third ventricle, which allows the CSF to bypass the obstruction and flow toward the site of resorption around the surface of the brain.

What are the possible complications of a shunt system?

Shunt systems are not perfect devices. Complications may include mechanical failure, infections, obstructions, and the need to lengthen or replace the catheter. Generally, shunt systems require monitoring and regular medical follow-up. When complications occur, the shunt system usually requires some type of revision.

Some complications can lead to other problems, such as overdraining or underdraining. Overdraining occurs when the shunt allows CSF to drain from the ventricles more quickly than it is produced. Overdraining can cause the ventricles to collapse, tearing blood vessels and causing headache, hemorrhage (subdural hematoma), or slit-like ventricles (slit ventricle syndrome). Underdraining occurs when CSF is not removed quickly enough and the symptoms of hydrocephalus recur. In addition to the common symptoms of hydrocephalus, infections from a shunt may also produce symptoms such as a low-grade fever, soreness of the neck or shoulder muscles, and redness or tenderness along the shunt tract. When there is reason to suspect that a shunt system is not functioning properly (for example, if the symptoms of hydrocephalus return), medical attention should be sought immediately.

What is the prognosis?

The prognosis for individuals diagnosed with hydrocephalus is difficult to predict, although there is some correlation between the specific cause of the hydrocephalus and the outcome. Prognosis is further complicated by the presence of associated disorders, the timeliness of diagnosis, and the success of treatment. The degree to which relief of CSF pressure following shunt surgery can minimize or reverse damage to the brain is not well understood.

Affected individuals and their families should be aware that hydrocephalus poses risks to both cognitive and physical development. However, many children diagnosed with the disorder benefit from rehabilitation therapies and educational interventions and go on to lead normal lives with few limitations. Treatment by an interdisciplinary team of medical professionals, rehabilitation specialists, and educational experts is critical to a positive outcome. Left untreated, progressive hydrocephalus may be fatal.

The symptoms of normal pressure hydrocephalus usually get worse over time if the condition is not treated, although some people may experience temporary improvements. While the success of treatment with shunts varies from person to person, some people recover almost completely after treatment and have a good quality of life. Early diagnosis and treatment improves the chance of a good recovery.

What research is being done?

The National Institute of Neurological Disorders and Stroke (NINDS) and other institutes of the National Institutes of Health (NIH) conduct research related to hydrocephalus in laboratories and clinics at the NIH and support additional research through grants to major medical institutions across the country. Much of this research focuses on finding better ways to prevent, treat, and ultimately cure disorders such as hydrocephalus. The NINDS also conducts and supports a wide range of fundamental studies that explore the complex mechanisms of normal and abnormal brain development.

Section 24.7

Other Cephalic Disorders

"Cephalic Disorders Fact Sheet," National Institute of Neurological Disorders and Stroke, National Institutes of Health, March 16, 2012.

What are cephalic disorders?

Cephalic disorders are congenital conditions that stem from damage to, or abnormal development of, the budding nervous system. Cephalic is a term that means "head" or "head end of the body." Congenital means the disorder is present at, and usually before, birth. Although there are many congenital developmental disorders, this section briefly describes only cephalic conditions.

Cephalic disorders are not necessarily caused by a single factor but may be influenced by hereditary or genetic conditions or by environmental exposures during pregnancy such as medication taken by the mother, maternal infection, or exposure to radiation. Some cephalic disorders occur when the cranial sutures (the fibrous joints that connect the bones of the skull) join prematurely. Most cephalic disorders are caused by a disturbance that occurs very early in the development of the fetal nervous system.

The human nervous system develops from a small, specialized plate of cells on the surface of the embryo. Early in development, this plate of cells forms the neural tube, a narrow sheath that closes between the third and fourth weeks of pregnancy to form the brain and spinal cord of the embryo. Four main processes are responsible for the development of the nervous system: cell proliferation, the process in which nerve cells divide to form new generations of cells; cell migration, the process in which nerve cells move from their place of origin to the place where they will remain for life; cell differentiation, the process during which cells acquire individual characteristics; and cell death, a natural process in which cells die. Understanding the normal development of the human nervous system, one of the research priorities of the National Institute of Neurological Disorders and Stroke, may lead to a better understanding of cephalic disorders.

Damage to the developing nervous system is a major cause of chronic, disabling disorders and, sometimes, death in infants, children, and even adults. The degree to which damage to the developing nervous system harms the mind and body varies enormously. Many disabilities are mild enough to allow those afflicted to eventually function independently in society. Others are not. Some infants, children, and adults die, others remain totally disabled, and an even larger population is partially disabled, functioning well below normal capacity throughout life.

What are the different kinds of cephalic disorders?

Anencephaly: This is a neural tube defect that occurs when the cephalic (head) end of the neural tube fails to close, usually between the twenty-third and twenty-sixth days of pregnancy, resulting in the absence of a major portion of the brain, skull, and scalp. Infants with this disorder are born without a forebrain—the largest part of the brain consisting mainly of the cerebrum, which is responsible for thinking and coordination. The remaining brain tissue is often exposed—not covered by bone or skin.

Infants born with anencephaly are usually blind, deaf, unconscious, and unable to feel pain. Although some individuals with anencephaly may be born with a rudimentary brainstem, the lack of a functioning cerebrum permanently rules out the possibility of ever gaining consciousness. Reflex actions such as breathing and responses to sound or touch may occur. The disorder is one of the most common disorders of the fetal central nervous system. Approximately one thousand to two thousand American babies are born with anencephaly each year. The disorder affects females more often than males.

The cause of anencephaly is unknown. Although it is believed that the mother's diet and vitamin intake may play a role, scientists agree that many other factors are also involved.

There is no cure or standard treatment for anencephaly and the prognosis for affected individuals is poor. Most infants do not survive infancy. If the infant is not stillborn, then he or she will usually die within a few hours or days after birth. Anencephaly can often be diagnosed before birth through an ultrasound examination.

Recent studies have shown that the addition of folic acid to the diet of women of childbearing age may significantly reduce the incidence of neural tube defects. Therefore it is recommended that all women of childbearing age consume 0.4 mg of folic acid daily.

Colpocephaly: This is a disorder in which there is an abnormal enlargement of the occipital horns—the posterior or rear portion of the lateral ventricles (cavities or chambers) of the brain. This enlargement occurs when there is an underdevelopment or lack of thickening of the white matter in the posterior cerebrum. Colpocephaly is characterized by microcephaly (abnormally small head) and mental retardation. Other features may include motor abnormalities, muscle spasms, and seizures.

Although the cause is unknown, researchers believe that the disorder results from an intrauterine disturbance that occurs between the second and sixth months of pregnancy. Colpocephaly may be diagnosed late in pregnancy, although it is often misdiagnosed as hydrocephalus (excessive accumulation of cerebrospinal fluid in the brain). It may be more accurately diagnosed after birth when signs of mental retardation, microcephaly, and seizures are present.

There is no definitive treatment for colpocephaly. Anticonvulsant medications can be given to prevent seizures, and doctors try to prevent contractures (shrinkage or shortening of muscles). The prognosis for individuals with colpocephaly depends on the severity of the associated conditions and the degree of abnormal brain development. Some children benefit from special education.

Holoprosencephaly: This is a disorder characterized by the failure of the prosencephalon (the forebrain of the embryo) to develop. During normal development the forebrain is formed and the face begins to develop in the fifth and sixth weeks of pregnancy. Holoprosencephaly is caused by a failure of the embryo's forebrain to divide to form bilateral cerebral hemispheres (the left and right halves of the brain), causing defects in the development of the face and in brain structure and function.

There are three classifications of holoprosencephaly. Alobar holoprosencephaly, the most serious form in which the brain fails to separate, is usually associated with severe facial anomalies. Semilobar holoprosencephaly, in which the brain's hemispheres have a slight tendency to separate, is an intermediate form of the disease. Lobar holoprosencephaly, in which there is considerable evidence of separate brain hemispheres, is the least severe form. In some cases of lobar holoprosencephaly, the patient's brain may be nearly normal.

Holoprosencephaly, once called arhinencephaly, consists of a spectrum of defects or malformations of the brain and face. At the most severe end of this spectrum are cases involving serious malformations of the brain, malformations so severe that they are incompatible with life and often cause spontaneous intrauterine death. At the other end of the spectrum are individuals with facial defects—which may affect the eyes, nose, and upper lip—and normal or near-normal brain development. Seizures and mental retardation may occur.

The most severe of the facial defects (or anomalies) is cyclopia, an abnormality characterized by the development of a single eye, located in the area normally occupied by the root of the nose, and a missing nose or a nose in the form of a proboscis (a tubular appendage) located above the eye.

Ethmocephaly is the least common facial anomaly. It consists of a proboscis separating narrow-set eyes with an absent nose and microphthalmia (abnormal smallness of one or both eyes). Cebocephaly, another facial anomaly, is characterized by a small, flattened nose with a single nostril situated below incomplete or underdeveloped closely set eyes.

The least severe in the spectrum of facial anomalies is the median cleft lip, also called premaxillary agenesis.

Although the causes of most cases of holoprosencephaly remain unknown, researchers know that approximately one-half of all cases have a chromosomal cause. Such chromosomal anomalies as Patau syndrome (trisomy 13) and Edwards syndrome (trisomy 18) have been found in association with holoprosencephaly. There is an increased risk for the disorder in infants of diabetic mothers.

There is no treatment for holoprosencephaly and the prognosis for individuals with the disorder is poor. Most of those who survive show no significant developmental gains. For children who survive, treatment is symptomatic. Although it is possible that improved management of diabetic pregnancies may help prevent holoprosencephaly, there is no means of primary prevention.

Hydranencephaly: This is a rare condition in which the cerebral hemispheres are absent and replaced by sacs filled with cerebrospinal fluid. Usually the cerebellum and brainstem are formed normally. An infant with hydranencephaly may appear normal at birth. The infant's head size and spontaneous reflexes such as sucking, swallowing, crying, and moving the arms and legs may all seem normal. However, after a few weeks the infant usually becomes irritable and has increased muscle tone (hypertonia). After several months of life, seizures and hydrocephalus may develop. Other symptoms may include visual impairment, lack of growth, deafness, blindness, spastic quadriparesis (paralysis), and intellectual deficits.

Hydranencephaly is an extreme form of porencephaly (a rare disorder, discussed later in this section, characterized by a cyst or cavity in the cerebral hemispheres) and may be caused by vascular insult (such as stroke) or injuries, infections, or traumatic disorders after the twelfth week of pregnancy.

Diagnosis may be delayed for several months because the infant's early behavior appears to be relatively normal. Transillumination, an examination in which light is passed through body tissues, usually confirms the diagnosis. Some infants may have additional abnormalities at birth, including seizures, myoclonus (involuntary sudden, rapid jerks), and respiratory problems.

There is no standard treatment for hydranencephaly. Treatment is symptomatic and supportive. Hydrocephalus may be treated with a shunt.

The outlook for children with hydranencephaly is generally poor, and many children with this disorder die before age one. However, in rare cases, children with hydranencephaly may survive for several years or more.

Iniencephaly: This is a rare neural tube defect that combines extreme retroflexion (backward bending) of the head with severe defects of the spine. The affected infant tends to be short, with a disproportionately large head. Diagnosis can be made immediately after birth because the head is so severely retroflexed that the face looks upward. The skin of the face is connected directly to the skin of the chest and the scalp is directly connected to the skin of the back. Generally, the neck is absent.

Most individuals with iniencephaly have other associated anomalies such as anencephaly, cephalocele (a disorder in which part of the cranial contents protrudes from the skull), hydrocephalus, cyclopia, absence of the mandible (lower jaw bone), cleft lip and palate, cardiovascular disorders, diaphragmatic hernia, and gastrointestinal malformation. The disorder is more common among females.

The prognosis for those with iniencephaly is extremely poor. Newborns with iniencephaly seldom live more than a few hours. The distortion of the fetal body may also pose a danger to the mother's life.

Lissencephaly: Lissencephaly, which literally means "smooth brain," is a rare brain malformation characterized by microcephaly and the lack of normal convolutions (folds) in the brain. It is caused by defective neuronal migration, the process in which nerve cells move from their place of origin to their permanent location.

The surface of a normal brain is formed by a complex series of folds and grooves. The folds are called gyri or convolutions, and the grooves are called sulci. In children with lissencephaly, the normal convolutions are absent or only partly formed, making the surface of the brain smooth.

Symptoms of the disorder may include unusual facial appearance, difficulty swallowing, failure to thrive, and severe psychomotor retardation. Anomalies of the hands, fingers, or toes, muscle spasms, and seizures may also occur.

Lissencephaly may be diagnosed at or soon after birth. Diagnosis may be confirmed by ultrasound, computed tomography (CT), or magnetic resonance imaging (MRI).

Lissencephaly may be caused by intrauterine viral infections or viral infections in the fetus during the first trimester, insufficient blood supply to the baby's brain early in pregnancy, or a genetic disorder. There are two distinct genetic causes of lissencephaly—X-linked and chromosome 17-linked.

The spectrum of lissencephaly is only now becoming more defined as neuroimaging and genetics has provided more insights into migration disorders. Other causes that have not yet been identified are likely as well.

Lissencephaly may be associated with other diseases, including isolated lissencephaly sequence, Miller-Dieker syndrome, and Walker-Warburg syndrome.

Treatment for those with lissencephaly is symptomatic and depends on the severity and locations of the brain malformations. Supportive care may be needed to help with comfort and nursing needs. Seizures may be controlled with medication, and hydrocephalus may require shunting. If feeding becomes difficult, a gastrostomy tube may be considered.

The prognosis for children with lissencephaly varies depending on the degree of brain malformation. Many individuals show no significant development beyond a three- to five-month-old level. Some may have near-normal development and intelligence. Many will die before the age of two. Respiratory problems are the most common causes of death.

Megalencephaly: Megalencephaly, also called macrencephaly, is a condition in which there is an abnormally large, heavy, and usually malfunctioning brain. By definition, the brain weight is greater than average for the age and gender of the infant or child. Head enlargement may be evident at birth or the head may become abnormally large in the early years of life.

Megalencephaly is thought to be related to a disturbance in the regulation of cell reproduction or proliferation. In normal development, neuron proliferation—the process in which nerve cells divide to form new generations of cells—is regulated so that the correct number of cells is formed in the proper place at the appropriate time.

Symptoms of megalencephaly may include delayed development, convulsive disorders, corticospinal (brain cortex and spinal cord) dysfunction, and seizures. Megalencephaly affects males more often than females.

The prognosis for individuals with megalencephaly largely depends on the underlying cause and the associated neurological disorders. Treatment is symptomatic. Megalencephaly may lead to a condition called macrocephaly (defined later in this section). Unilateral megalencephaly or hemimegalencephaly is a rare condition characterized by the enlargement of one-half of the brain. Children with this disorder may have a large, sometimes asymmetrical head. Often they suffer from intractable seizures and mental retardation. The prognosis for those with hemimegalencephaly is poor.

Microcephaly: Microcephaly is a neurological disorder in which the circumference of the head is smaller than average for the age and gender of the infant or child. Microcephaly may be congenital or it may develop in the first few years of life. The disorder may stem from a wide variety of conditions that cause abnormal growth of the brain, or from syndromes associated with chromosomal abnormalities.

Infants with microcephaly are born with either a normal or a reduced head size. Subsequently the head fails to grow while the face continues to develop at a normal rate, producing a child with a small head, a large face, a receding forehead, and a loose, often wrinkled scalp. As the child grows older, the smallness of the skull becomes more obvious, although the entire body also is often underweight and dwarfed. Development of motor functions and speech may be delayed. Hyperactivity and mental retardation are common occurrences, although the degree of each varies. Convulsions may also occur. Motor ability varies, ranging from clumsiness in some to spastic quadriplegia in others.

Generally there is no specific treatment for microcephaly. Treatment is symptomatic and supportive.

In general, life expectancy for individuals with microcephaly is reduced and the prognosis for normal brain function is poor. The prognosis varies depending on the presence of associated abnormalities.

Porencephaly: Porencephaly is an extremely rare disorder of the central nervous system involving a cyst or cavity in a cerebral hemisphere. The cysts or cavities are usually the remnants of destructive lesions, but are sometimes the result of abnormal development. The disorder can occur before or after birth.

Porencephaly most likely has a number of different, often unknown causes, including absence of brain development and destruction of brain tissue. The presence of porencephalic cysts can sometimes be detected by transillumination of the skull in infancy. The diagnosis may be confirmed by CT, MRI, or ultrasonography.

More severely affected infants show symptoms of the disorder shortly after birth, and the diagnosis is usually made before age one. Signs may include delayed growth and development, spastic paresis (slight or incomplete paralysis), hypotonia (decreased muscle tone), seizures (often infantile spasms), and macrocephaly or microcephaly.

Individuals with porencephaly may have poor or absent speech development, epilepsy, hydrocephalus, spastic contractures (shrinkage or shortening of muscles), and mental retardation. Treatment may include physical therapy, medication for seizure disorders, and a shunt for hydrocephalus. The prognosis for individuals with porencephaly varies according to the location and extent of the lesion. Some patients with this disorder may develop only minor neurological problems and have normal intelligence, while others may be severely disabled. Others may die before the second decade of life.

Schizencephaly: Schizencephaly is a rare developmental disorder characterized by abnormal slits, or clefts, in the cerebral hemispheres. Schizencephaly is a form of porencephaly. Individuals with clefts in both hemispheres, or bilateral clefts, are often developmentally delayed and have delayed speech and language skills and corticospinal dysfunction. Individuals with smaller, unilateral clefts (clefts in one hemisphere) may be weak on one side of the body and may have average or near-average intelligence. Patients with schizencephaly may also have varying degrees of microcephaly, mental retardation, hemiparesis (weakness or paralysis affecting one side of the body), or quadriparesis (weakness or paralysis affecting all four extremities), and may have reduced muscle tone (hypotonia). Most patients have seizures and some may have hydrocephalus.

In schizencephaly, the neurons border the edge of the cleft implying a very early disruption in development. There is now a genetic origin for one type of schizencephaly. Causes of this type may include environmental exposures during pregnancy such as medication taken by the mother, exposure to toxins, or a vascular insult. Often there are associated heterotopias (isolated islands of neurons), which indicate a failure of migration of the neurons to their final position in the brain.

Treatment for individuals with schizencephaly generally consists of physical therapy, treatment for seizures, and, in cases that are complicated by hydrocephalus, a shunt.

The prognosis for individuals with schizencephaly varies depending on the size of the clefts and the degree of neurological deficit.

What are other less common cephalies?

Acephaly: Acephaly literally means absence of the head. It is a much rarer condition than anencephaly. The acephalic fetus is a parasitic twin attached to an otherwise intact fetus. The acephalic fetus has a body but lacks a head and a heart; the fetus's neck is attached to the normal twin. The blood circulation of the acephalic fetus is provided by the heart of the twin. The acephalic fetus cannot exist independently of the fetus to which it is attached.

Exencephaly: Exencephaly is a condition in which the brain is located outside of the skull. This condition is usually found in embryos as an early stage of anencephaly. As an exencephalic pregnancy progresses, the neural tissue gradually degenerates. It is unusual to find an infant carried to term with this condition because the defect is incompatible with survival.

Macrocephaly: Macrocephaly is a condition in which the head circumference is larger than average for the age and gender of the infant or child. It is a descriptive rather than a diagnostic term and is a characteristic of a variety of disorders. Macrocephaly also may be inherited. Although one form of macrocephaly may be associated with mental retardation, in approximately one-half of cases mental development is normal. Macrocephaly may be caused by an enlarged brain or hydrocephalus. It may be associated with other disorders such as dwarfism, neurofibromatosis, and tuberous sclerosis.

Micrencephaly: Micrencephaly is a disorder characterized by a small brain and may be caused by a disturbance in the proliferation of nerve cells. Micrencephaly may also be associated with maternal problems such as alcoholism, diabetes, or rubella (German measles). A genetic factor may play a role in causing some cases of micrencephaly. Affected newborns generally have striking neurological defects and seizures. Severely impaired intellectual development is common, but disturbances in motor functions may not appear until later in life.

Otocephaly: Otocephaly is a lethal condition in which the primary feature is agnathia—a developmental anomaly characterized by total or virtual absence of the lower jaw. The condition is considered lethal because of a poorly functioning airway. In otocephaly, agnathia may occur alone or together with holoprosencephaly.

Another group of less common cephalic disorders are the craniostenoses. Craniostenoses are deformities of the skull caused by the premature fusion or joining together of the cranial sutures. Cranial sutures are fibrous joints that join the bones of the skull together. The nature of these deformities depends on which sutures are affected.

Brachycephaly: Brachycephaly occurs when the coronal suture fuses prematurely, causing a shortened front-to-back diameter of the skull. The coronal suture is the fibrous joint that unites the frontal bone with the two parietal bones of the skull. The parietal bones form the top and sides of the skull.

Oxycephaly: Oxycephaly is a term sometimes used to describe the premature closure of the coronal suture plus any other suture, or it may be used to describe the premature fusing of all sutures. Oxycephaly is the most severe of the craniostenoses.

Plagiocephaly: Plagiocephaly results from the premature unilateral fusion (joining of one side) of the coronal or lambdoid sutures. The lambdoid suture unites the occipital bone with the parietal bones of the skull. Plagiocephaly is a condition characterized by an asymmetrical distortion (flattening of one side) of the skull. It is a common finding at birth and may be the result of brain malformation, a restrictive intrauterine environment, or torticollis (a spasm or tightening of neck muscles).

Scaphocephaly: Scaphocephaly applies to premature fusion of the sagittal suture. The sagittal suture joins together the two parietal bones of the skull. Scaphocephaly is the most common of the craniostenoses and is characterized by a long, narrow head.

Trigonocephaly: Trigonocephaly is the premature fusion of the metopic suture (part of the frontal suture which joins the two halves of the frontal bone of the skull) in which a V-shaped abnormality occurs at the front of the skull. It is characterized by the triangular prominence of the forehead and closely set eyes.

What research is being done?

Within the federal government, the National Institute of Neurological Disorders and Stroke (NINDS), one of the National Institutes of Health (NIH), has primary responsibility for conducting and supporting research on normal and abnormal brain and nervous system development, including congenital anomalies. The National Institute of Child Health and Human Development, the National Institute of Mental Health, the National Institute of Environmental Health Sciences, the National Institute of Alcohol Abuse and Alcoholism, and the National Institute on Drug Abuse also support research related to disorders of the developing nervous system. Gaining basic knowledge about how the nervous system develops and understanding the role of genetics in fetal development are major goals of scientists studying congenital neurological disorders.

Scientists are rapidly learning how harmful insults at various stages of pregnancy can lead to developmental disorders. For example, a critical nutritional deficiency or exposure to an environmental insult during the first month of pregnancy (when the neural tube is formed) can produce neural tube defects such as anencephaly.

Scientists are also concentrating their efforts on understanding the complex processes responsible for normal early development of the brain and nervous system and how the disruption of any of these processes results in congenital anomalies such as cephalic disorders. Understanding how genes control brain cell migration, proliferation, differentiation, and death, and how radiation, drugs, toxins, infections, and other factors disrupt these processes will aid in preventing many congenital neurological disorders.

Currently, researchers are examining the mechanisms involved in neurulation—the process of forming the neural tube. These studies will improve our understanding of this process and give insight into how the process can go awry and cause devastating congenital disorders. Investigators are also analyzing genes and gene products necessary for human brain development to achieve a better understanding of normal brain development in humans.

Section 24.8

Ventriculomegaly

This condition is an enlargement of the lateral ventricles (the fluid-filled spaces normally found in each side of the brain).

Ventriculomegaly is found via ultrasound in approximately one to two per one thousand babies.

A normal lateral ventricle is usually less than 10 millimeters wide until thirty-five weeks of pregnancy.

Mild ventriculomegaly is generally in the range of 10–15 mm.

Severe ventriculomegaly (hydrocephalus) is defined as a width greater than 15 mm.

Most babies with mild ventriculomegaly are normal. However, it can sometimes indicate a chromosome problem, bleeding, infection, or a genetic syndrome.

Causes of Ventriculomegaly

- Lateral ventricles are normally filled with cerebrospinal fluid (CSF). If the amount of fluid increases enough, the ventricles will also grow. CSF may increase because it isn't circulating well, too much CSF is being produced, or there is a problem with the brain.

- If we can determine the cause, we can more effectively determine its effects on the baby.

- Some cases of ventriculomegaly improve, some stay the same, and some get worse. Because it is difficult to predict the outcome, it is a good idea to have repeat ultrasounds.

Further Testing

- You can have a more detailed ultrasound to look for other abnormalities.

- The maternal serum screening can assess your risk of having a baby with Down syndrome, through twenty-one weeks' gestation.

- A blood test may be suggested to look for some infections or bleeding conditions.

- An amniocentesis can diagnose a chromosome abnormality or infection. Amniocentesis involves obtaining a sample of the fluid surrounding the baby, which is then used to study the fetal chromosomes. There is a small risk of miscarriage from amniocentesis.

Chapter 25

Craniofacial Defects

Chapter Contents

Section 25.1

Anophthalmia and Microphthalmia

"Facts about Anophthalmia and Microphthalmia,"
National Eye Institute, National Institutes of Health, August 2009.

Anophthalmia and Microphthalmia Defined

Anophthalmia and microphthalmia are often used interchangeably. Microphthalmia is a disorder in which one or both eyes are abnormally small, while anophthalmia is the absence of one or both eyes. These rare disorders develop during pregnancy and can be associated with other birth defects.

Causes and Risk Factors

Causes of these conditions may include genetic mutations and abnormal chromosomes. Researchers also believe that environmental factors, such as exposure to x-rays, chemicals, drugs, pesticides, toxins, radiation, or viruses, increase the risk of anophthalmia and microphthalmia, but research is not conclusive. Sometimes the cause in an individual patient cannot be determined.

Treatment

Can Anophthalmia and Microphthalmia Be Treated?

There is no treatment for severe anophthalmia or microphthalmia that will create a new eye or restore vision. However, some less severe forms of microphthalmia may benefit from medical or surgical treatments. In almost all cases improvements to a child's appearance are possible. Children can be fitted for a prosthetic (artificial) eye for cosmetic purposes and to promote socket growth. A newborn with anophthalmia or microphthalmia will need to visit several eye care professionals, including those who specialize in pediatrics, vitreoretinal disease, orbital and oculoplastic surgery, ophthalmic genetics, and prosthetic devices for the eye. Each specialist can provide information and possible treatments resulting in the best care for the child and family.

The specialist in prosthetic diseases for the eye will make conformers, plastic structures that help support the face and encourage the eye socket to grow. As the face develops, new conformers will need to be made. A child with anophthalmia may also need to use expanders in addition to conformers to further enlarge the eye socket. Once the face is fully developed, prosthetic eyes can be made and placed. Prosthetic eyes will not restore vision.

How Do Conformers and Prosthetic Eyes Look?

A painted prosthesis that looks like a normal eye is usually fitted between ages one and two. Until then, clear conformers are used. When the conformers are in place the eye socket will look black. These conformers are not painted to look like a normal eye because they are changed too frequently. Every few weeks a child will progress to a larger size conformer until about two years of age. If a child needs to wear conformers after age two, the conformers will be painted like a regular prosthesis, giving the appearance of a normal but smaller eye. The average child will need three to four new painted prostheses before the age of ten.

How Is Microphthalmia Managed If There Is Residual Vision in the Eye?

Children with microphthalmia may have some residual vision (limited sight). In these cases, the good eye can be patched to strengthen vision in the microphthalmic eye. A prosthesis can be made to cap the microphthalmic eye to help with cosmetic appearance, while preserving the remaining sight.

Section 25.2

Cleft Lip and Palate

What Is a Cleft Lip and Palate?

A cleft lip and palate is a gap that occurs when the lip or roof of
the mouth does not completely fuse during the first trimester of fetal
development. The lip and palate develop separately, so it is possible
for a child to have a cleft lip, a cleft palate, or both. The size of the
cleft lip may range from a small notch in the upper lip to an opening
that extends into the base of the nostril (see Figure 25.1). The cleft
may be single sided (unilateral, see Figure 25.2) or occur on both sides
(bilateral, see Figure 25.3). A cleft palate may involve only the hard
palate or soft palate or a combination of both (see Figures 25.4–25.6).

How Often Does Clefting Occur?

The incidence of cleft lip with or without cleft palate is estimated to
be between 1 in 300 and 1 in 2,500 births, depending on the patient's
ethnic origin. It is most common in Native Americans and Asians and
least common in African Americans. Cleft palate alone occurs in 1 in
1,000 births. Cleft lip occurs more frequently in males and cleft palate
occurs more frequently in females. The majority of children born with
cleft lip and palate are otherwise normal with no associated syndromes.

What Are the Chances of My Baby Having a Cleft Lip and/or Palate?

If two unaffected parents have a child with a cleft lip/palate or
isolated cleft palate, their chance of having another child with a cleft
is 3 to 5 percent. If either parent has a cleft lip/palate, but no affected
children, the risk of having any other children with a cleft is 5 percent.
If more than one of the parents and/or children have a cleft, the risk
for future offspring is greater.

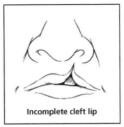

Incomplete cleft lip

Figure 25.1. *Incomplete cleft lip.*

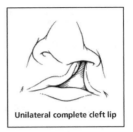

Unilateral complete cleft lip

Figure 25.2. *Unilateral complete cleft lip.*

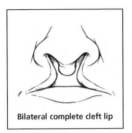

Bilateral complete cleft lip

Figure 25.3. *Bilateral complete cleft lip.*

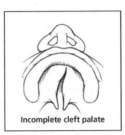

Incomplete cleft palate

Figure 25.4. *Incomplete cleft palate.*

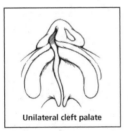

Unilateral cleft palate

Figure 25.5. *Unilateral cleft palate.*

Bilateral cleft palate

Figure 25.6. *Bilateral cleft palate.*

Parents who have had a baby with a cleft lip/palate or who have a family history of clefts can consult a genetic counselor to discuss the risk of having futu`re children with a cleft.

What Causes Clefting?

The cause of clefting is multifactorial and probably involves a combination of genetic and environmental factors, however, the cause of clefting is usually unknown. Environmental factors that may increase the risk of clefting are smoking and alcohol use during pregnancy, poor maternal nutrition, and certain medications. Many mothers who have a baby born with a cleft have a normal pregnancy.

How Is a Cleft Lip and/or Palate Diagnosed?

A cleft lip can sometimes be diagnosed on prenatal ultrasound. An examination of the nose, lip, and mouth confirm the presence of a cleft lip or palate.

What Other Problems Might We Expect and How Will They Be Treated?

Children with only a cleft lip and no cleft of the gum line or palate frequently have no other problems. Children with a cleft palate may have ear infections and hearing loss, dental problems, and difficulty with feeding and speech. An experienced cleft lip and palate team has specialists to help with each of these potential problems.

Feeding Difficulties

A child with a cleft palate can have difficulty sucking through a regular nipple due to the gap in the roof of the mouth. Most babies require a modified or special nipple to properly feed. It may take a couple of days for the baby and parents to adjust to using the nipple before going home. Most babies learn to feed normally with a cleft palate nipple. The pediatrician and cleft team will keep close track of the child's weight.

Most babies with a cleft palate cannot generate enough suck to breast-feed. To take advantage of the health benefits of breast milk, many mothers elect to feed their baby breast milk in a bottle with a cleft palate nipple. The hospital nursery and cleft team have feeding specialists available to evaluate the baby and meet with the parents before going home.

Speech Issues

Children with an unrepaired cleft palate have a nasal quality to their speech because air escapes through the gap in the roof of the mouth and out the nose. These children may also have difficulty generating enough pressure to produce certain sounds. After cleft palate repair, most children develop near normal speech. Some children will require speech therapy or another surgery when they are older to improve persistent nasal speech.

Hearing and Ear Infections

Any child with a cleft palate is at risk of developing frequent ear infections. The Eustachian tube, which drains the middle ear, malfunctions, causing persistent fluid buildup in the middle ear. A combination of fluid and repeat ear infections can cause scarring of the tympanic membrane (ear drum) and hearing loss. Pressure equalizing eardrum tubes can be inserted at the time of lip or palate repair to drain the middle ear and reduce the risk of ear infection and hearing loss.

Dental Concerns

A child with a cleft palate or a cleft through the gum line may have missing or abnormally shaped baby and permanent teeth. In addition, the upper jaw may not grow as far forward as the lower jaw, necessitating corrective surgery later in life. Your cleft team will refer you and your child to a dental and orthodontic expert who can successfully treat these problems.

Treatment

The care of an infant with cleft lip and/or palate begins at birth with accurate diagnosis, identification of the child's needs, and the location of a proper treatment center. All children with cleft lip and palate should be followed by a cleft team. The cleft team consists of multiple specialists, including a plastic surgeon, speech therapist, dentist, orthodontist, otolaryngologist, audiologist, geneticist, pediatrician, and feeding specialist. Team members will work closely with you and your child to determine the best treatment plan.

The cleft lip is usually repaired between the ages of three to six months. The cleft palate is repaired between the ages of nine to twelve months. Some children may require a two-stage lip repair or molding device if the cleft is wide. Ear tubes are often placed at the time of palate surgery, if needed.

Your child's speech, hearing, and dental development will be followed closely by the cleft team. Secondary surgeries such as pharyngeal flap, alveolar bone graft, rhinoplasty, and upper jaw surgery may be recommended.

Section 25.3

Craniosynostosis

Excerpted from "Craniosynostosis," reproduced with permission from
FACES: The National Craniofacial Association (www.faces-cranio.org),
© 2011. All rights reserved.

What is craniosynostosis?

Craniosynostosis is caused by the premature closing of one or more
of the sutures of the bones that make up the skull. Usually, computed
tomography (CT) scans are taken to determine if the abnormal skull
shape is craniosynostosis, rather that just a result of fetal head position
or birth trauma. There are four types of craniosynostosis.

Scaphocephaly is caused by the fusion of the sagittal suture, which
runs from front to back down the middle of the top of the skull. This
is the most common type of craniosynostosis. Characteristics include:

- a long narrow-shaped head from front to back;

- narrow from ear to ear;

- the head appears boat-shaped.

Trigonocephaly is the fusion of the metopic suture, which runs from
the top of the head, down the middle of the forehead, towards the nose.
Characteristics include:

- triangular-shaped forehead;

- eyes are closer together than usual.

Plagiocephaly is the premature fusion of one of the coronal sutures,
which extend from ear to ear over the top of the head. Characteristics
include:

- fusion of either the right or left side;

- the forehead and brow look like they are pushed backwards;

- the eye on the affected side has a different shape than the one
on the unaffected side.

Brachycephaly results when both sides of the coronal sutures fuse prematurely. Characteristics include:

- wide-shaped head, with short skull;
- fusion prevents the entire forehead from growing in a forward direction, causing a tall, flattened forehead.

Why did this happen?

At this time, doctors are unsure why craniosynostosis happens. In some families, it does appear to be an inherited trait. It is most likely that some mutation occurred in the early development to one of the baby's genes; however, research cannot yet give us definitive answers on this. There is no indication that there is anything the mother did or did not do to cause this.

Will this happen to children I have in the future?

The chances that other children will have this problem are very slim ... 0 to 4 percent. These are also the chances of your child's children being born with craniosynostosis. The only exception is when the craniosynostosis is a part of Crouzon or Apert syndromes, in which there is a 50 percent chance of being passed on from parent to child.

What kinds of problems could my child have?

Depending on the severity of the craniosynostosis, your child may have some or all of these problems:

- Abnormal skull shape
- Abnormal forehead
- Asymmetrical eyes and or ears
- Intracranial pressure (pressure inside the skull) which can cause delays in development or permanent brain damage if not corrected

Will my child need surgery?

Babies born with craniosynostosis usually will need surgery, unless it is a very mild case. It is important that the proper x-rays and CT scans are made in order for your physician to make a correct diagnosis, as well as show you the fused sutures and how they will be reconstructed. Usually, only one surgery is required to separate the sutures, reshape the bones, and place them in the proper position. Only 10 percent of children will need a second surgery. Surgery to correct craniosynostosis is usually performed between four and eight months of age.

New advances in procedures to correct craniosynostosis are being developed all the time. Be an advocate for your child!

How do I get help for my child?

Your child should be treated by a qualified craniofacial medical team at a craniofacial center.

Section 25.4

Facial Palsy

Excerpted from "A Guide to Understanding Facial Palsy," © 2005 Children's Craniofacial Association. All rights reserved. Reprinted with permission. For additional information, visit www.ccakids.com. Reviewed by David A. Cooke, M.D., FACP, December 2012.

What is facial palsy?

Facial palsy is a congenital deformity, which dates from birth, or an acquired deformity, which causes complete or partial paralysis of the facial motion. The act of facial motion starts in the brain and travels through the facial nerves to the muscles in the face. These muscles then contract in response to a stimulus. Inside the skull, the facial nerve is a single nerve. Once the nerve is traced outside the skull, it branches into many smaller limbs that go to many different facial muscles. These muscles control facial expression. The coordinated activity of this nerve and these muscles causes motions such as smiling, blinking, frowning, and a full range of normal facial motions. Diseases or injuries affecting the brain, the facial nerve, or the muscles of the face can cause facial palsy.

Are there other names for this condition?

Facial palsy is also called paresis. Paresis suggests a weakness in facial motion. Moebius syndrome is a subtype of facial palsy. This syndrome involves a weakness of the muscles responsible for facial expression and side-to-side eye movement. Moebius syndrome may also involve abnormalities of the limbs.

What causes facial palsy?

A variety of things can cause facial palsy. Congenital facial palsy is a condition present at birth. Moebius syndrome is a congenital condition. In most cases the exact cause of congenital palsy is uncertain. A lack of proper nerve and/or muscle development causes some cases of congenital palsy. The reason for this is unknown. Other palsies may result from stretching of the muscles or nerves during the birthing process. Most congenital palsies involve one side of the face with the exception of Moebius, which is typically bilateral. This means that it affects both sides of the face. A large number of cases of facial palsy develop when a weakness or complete palsy occurs later in life despite a normal facial movement at birth. This group is called the acquired group. Causes of acquired palsy include trauma to the facial nerve and muscle, certain inflammatory or infectious disease such as Lyme disease, and tumors in and around the regions of the head and neck.

What are the chances of producing a child with this condition?

The incidence of facial palsy is rare. The chance of producing a child with Moebius syndrome is very rare. The incidence of other forms of congenital facial palsy is approximately two in every one thousand births. Most congenital facial palsies have no apparent cause but can be associated with syndromes of the head and neck.

Does facial palsy ever improve?

In most cases, other than Moebius syndrome, the condition does improve. However, the return of function is usually only a partial one. In most cases of congenital palsy, the weakness in incomplete, and some motion is present. Moebius syndrome is usually an incomplete palsy, and some patients have movement of the lower face and the lip region. It does not improve with time. However, 90 percent of the other congenital palsy patients can expect an improvement. With acquired facial palsy, patients may experience improvement if the cause of the palsy is trauma to the nerve or muscle, or if the pressure from a tumor on the nerve can be treated.

What are problems caused by facial palsy?

With children there are no immediate effects. This is due to the normal elastic skin tone. Therefore, the structures of the face do not sag. With adults, however, the sudden onset of facial palsy generally results in a significant loss of tone in the tissues and considerable facial sagging. One of the most important functions of the facial nerves and muscles is helping the eyelid to close. If the eyelid does not close, the eye is more prone to injury such as scratches. Injury can then result in scarring and visual loss. It is critical for young children with this condition to be evaluated by an ophthalmologist so that appropriate eye protection and lubrication can be started.

Facial palsy can cause problems with normal sucking and chewing. Drooling may also be a problem. Appearance is a major concern. Asymmetry of the face can cause the face to be significantly distorted. Occasionally a child discovers that smiling frequently causes facial imbalance. For that reason, he may avoid smiling altogether.

What can be done surgically to correct this condition?

For infants with newly diagnosed facial palsy, eye protection is the primary concern. Lubricants are usually sufficient to prevent injury to the eye. When lubrication is not adequate, then the eyelids are partially sewn shut. This procedure, called tarsorrhaphy, does not block the child's vision.

A watchful, conservative approach is usually best for a child with congenital facial palsy. Since many children improve, treatment should not start before the age of five or six except in the case of the eye as mentioned above. Once the child has reached the age of five or six, there are several treatment options available.

Two methods of treatment are static slings and dynamic muscle transfers. Static slings involve procedures in which a patient's own tissue is used to elevate the sagging portions of the face that produces a smile, as well as the eyelid region. These static slings improve facial balance and eyelid closure. Dynamic procedures include muscle transfers and man-made devices to improve lid closure. Muscle transfers involve moving locally available muscles, such as those for chewing, to substitute for nonfunctioning or absent facial muscles. Once the transfer is made, the patient relies on the act of biting to contract and bring on a smile or to cause the eyelid to close.

Very sophisticated methods of muscle transfers have been developed. The "gold standard" at the present is a two-staged procedure. Nerves are first transferred from "the good side of the face" to the paralyzed side of the face. After this, a muscle transfer is done to reproduce a smile effect. Using a microscope, this muscle is transferred and hooked up to the nerve grafts. If this is successful, nerve activity from the "good side of the face" travels instantly through the nerve grafts to the new muscle on the opposite side. This can then cause a motion. However, this motion is, at best, unrefined because a few nerves and one muscle are being asked to take the place of many muscles that work together during normal facial expression.

When there is not a side of the face with normal motion, as in the case of Moebius syndrome or bilateral facial palsy, muscles can be transferred using a microscopic technique. They are then connected to nerves that activate biting muscles if done in a sequence on both sides. Facial motion can be restored, but the patient must bite in order to activate the muscles. Procedures have also been developed to improve eyelid closure. One method involves placing gold weights in the upper eyelid to help it close when the lid is relaxed. The use of surgical springs can accomplish the same thing.

How successful are the surgeries?

The success of the operations varies from patient to patient. The success is dictated by the severity of the facial weakness. Normal facial motion depends on multiple facial muscles and nerves working together to produce a full spectrum of motion. Presently, procedures result in a replacement of a portion of this facial activity. Complete normalization of the facial motion is rarely possible. Due to the many microscopic techniques, there is a chance that nerve growth may not be complete or that circulation to the transferred muscle may fail. This can result in no marked improvement. This occurs in 5 to 10 percent of patients.

If my child needs surgery, when is the best time?

Generally, early surgery is not necessary unless eye exposure is a problem. In this case, surgery can be done at any age. The most complicated muscle transfers and static slings require a high degree of patient cooperation. This is true during the surgery and the rehabilitation process. For that reason, these procedures are best accomplished after the age of five or six.

Where should my child go for treatment?

Surgeons who are familiar with facial nerve paralysis are frequently a part of a craniofacial team. There are a number of microsurgeons in the United States who have a great deal of experience with facial paralysis. A craniofacial team can guide you to the appropriate physician. Facial reanimation procedures are extremely complex. It is important to seek care from a team of surgeons specialized and experienced in the area of facial palsy.

Section 25.5

Goldenhar Syndrome

Excerpted from "Goldenhar Syndrome," reproduced
with permission from FACES: The National Craniofacial Association
(www.faces-cranio.org), © 2011. All rights reserved.

What is Goldenhar syndrome?

Goldenhar syndrome is a congenital birth defect which involves deformities of the face. It usually affects one side of the face only. Characteristics include:

* a partially formed or totally absent ear (microtia);

* the chin may be closer to the affected ear;

* one corner of the mouth may be higher than the other;

* benign growths of the eye;

* a missing eye.

Goldenhar is also known as oculoauricular dysplasia or OAV.

Why did this happen?

Doctors are uncertain why Goldenhar occurs. However, they do not believe it is the result of anything the mother did while she was pregnant. Environmental factors may play a part and there does seem to be an increased incidence of Goldenhar among the children of Gulf War veterans.

Will this happen to children I have in the future?

The chance of having another child with Goldenhar is 1 percent or less. Your child has about a 3 percent chance of passing it on to his or her children.

What kinds of problems could my child have?

In addition to the physical characteristics common to Goldenhar, your child may have the following problems:

- hearing problems;

- weakness in moving the side of the face that is smaller;

- dental problems: the soft palate may move to the unaffected side of the face;

- the tongue may be smaller on the affected side of the face;

- fusion of the bones of the neck.

Will my child need surgery?

Depending on the severity of Goldenhar syndrome, your child may have some or all of the following surgeries:

- lowering of the jaw on the affected side;

- lengthening of the lower jaw;

- three to four operations to rebuild the outer ear;

- addition of bone to build up the cheeks;

- soft tissue may need to be added to the face.

New advances in procedures to correct the symptoms of Goldenhar syndrome are constantly being developed. Be an advocate for your child!

How do I get help for my child?

Your child should be treated by a qualified craniofacial medical team at a craniofacial center.

Section 25.6

Hemifacial Microsomia

Excerpted from "Hemifacial Microsomia," reproduced with permission from FACES: The National Craniofacial Association (www.faces-cranio.org), © 2011. All rights reserved.

What is hemifacial microsomia?

Hemifacial microsomia is a condition in which the lower half of one side of the face is underdeveloped and does not grow normally. It is sometimes also referred to as first and second branchial arch syndrome, oral-mandibular-auricular syndrome, lateral facial dysplasia, or otomandibular dysostosis. The syndrome varies in severity, but always includes the maldevelopment of the ear and the mandible. This is the second most common facial birth defect after clefts.

Why did this happen?

Researchers are still not sure why this happens, however, most agree that something occurred in the early stages of development such as a disturbance of the blood supply to the first and second branchial arches in the first six to eight weeks of pregnancy. Studies do *not* link this condition with the mother's activities or actions during her pregnancy.

Will this happen to children I have in the future?

For parents with one child with hemifacial microsomia, the chances are between 0 and 1 percent. Adults with this condition have a 3 percent chance of passing it to their children.

Will my child need surgery?

The surgeries recommended for children with hemifacial microsomia have a goal to improve facial symmetry by reconstructing the bony and soft tissue and establishing normal occlusion and joint junction. The timing for such surgeries varies among the surgeons and the severity of the problems. Common surgeries include:

- Lowering the upper jaw to match the opposite side and lengthening the lower jaw. Sometimes a bone graft is used to lengthen the jaw and sometimes a distraction device is used.

- Ear reconstruction at about five to six years of age, which involves three to four surgeries.

- Occasionally, it may be necessary to add bone to build up the cheekbone.

- Some children benefit from the addition of soft tissues to further balance the face.

What kinds of problems could my child have?

- Your child may have skin tags in front of the ear or on different parts of the face.

- Hearing problems depend on the structures that are involved.

- Some children have some weakness in movement on the affected side of the face.

New advances in procedures to correct the symptoms of hemifacial microsomia are constantly being developed. Be an advocate for your child!

How do I get help for my child?

Your child should be treated by a qualified craniofacial medical team at a craniofacial center.

Section 25.7

Klippel-Feil Syndrome

"Klippel-Feil Syndrome Information Page,"
National Institute of Neurological Disorders and Stroke,
National Institutes of Health, September 16, 2011.

What is Klippel-Feil syndrome?

Klippel-Feil syndrome is a rare disorder characterized by the congenital fusion of any two of the seven cervical (neck) vertebrae. It is caused by a failure in the normal segmentation or division of the cervical vertebrae during the early weeks of fetal development. The most common signs of the disorder are short neck, low hairline at the back of the head, and restricted mobility of the upper spine. Associated abnormalities may include scoliosis (curvature of the spine), spina bifida (a birth defect of the spine), anomalies of the kidneys and the ribs, cleft palate, respiratory problems, and heart malformations. The disorder also may be associated with abnormalities of the head and face, skeleton, sex organs, muscles, brain and spinal cord, arms, legs, and fingers.

Is there any treatment?

Treatment for Klippel-Feil syndrome is symptomatic and may include surgery to relieve cervical or craniocervical instability and constriction of the spinal cord, and to correct scoliosis. Physical therapy may also be useful.

What is the prognosis?

The prognosis for most individuals with Klippel-Feil syndrome is good if the disorder is treated early and appropriately. Activities that can injure the neck should be avoided.

What research is being done?

Research supported by the National Institute of Neurological Disorders and Stroke (NINDS) includes studies to understand how the brain and nervous system normally develop and function and how they are affected by disease and trauma. These studies contribute to a greater understanding of birth defects such as Klippel-Feil syndrome and open promising new avenues for treatment.

Section 25.8

Microtia

What is microtia?

Microtia is an incompletely formed ear. It ranges in severity from a bump of tissue to a partially formed ear. In most cases, only one ear is affected. In that case, it is called unilateral microtia. If both ears are affected, it is called bilateral microtia. Unilateral microtia occurs in one out of eight thousand births and bilateral microtia occurs in one out of twenty-five thousand births.

Why did this happen?

At this time, no one knows why microtia occurs; however, there is nothing to suggest that the mother's actions during pregnancy caused the microtia. Further research is necessary to determine the exact cause.

Will this happen to other children I have in the future?

The possibility of passing microtia on to another child is believed to be less than 6 percent.

What kinds of problems could my child have?

In addition to the physical characteristics, your child may have some or all of these problems:

- about a 40 percent reduction of hearing in the affected ear;
- problems locating the direction from which a sound comes;
- ear infections.

Will my child need surgery?

Your child will either require reconstructive surgery to rebuild the outer ear or he/she may wish to wear a prosthesis. There are several types of prostheses and ear implants that are currently available. We suggest gathering information about all the options and visiting with others who have chosen different options. The choices are increasing every year, so try to keep up with all of the current research. If you choose reconstructive surgery, it is a three- to four-step process, usually done two to three months apart. Surgical procedures usually begin around six years of age, because the ear is 90 percent of its adult size, so it is easier to determine the size of the ear that must be made:

- Portions of ribs 5, 6, 7, and 8 are carved into the shape of the external ear.
- The ear is then grafted into place and the overlying skin is draped onto the graft.
- Other operations may be needed to rotate the lobule and possibly to reposition the cartilage framework into its final position.

New advances in procedures to treat microtia are constantly being made. Be an advocate for your child!

How do I get help for my child?

Your child should be treated by a qualified craniofacial medical team at a craniofacial center.

Section 25.9

Pierre Robin Sequence

What is Pierre Robin?

Pierre Robin is not a syndrome or a disease. It is usually referred to as Pierre Robin sequence, although it is also known as "Pierre Robin malformation sequence," "Robin anomalad," and "cleft palate, micrognathia and glossoptosis." It is the name given to the following birth defects if they appear together:

- Small lower jaw (micrognathia)

- A tongue which tends to ball up at the back of the mouth and fall back towards the throat (glossoptosis)

- Breathing problems

- Horseshoe-shaped cleft palate may or may not be present

Why did this happen?

Doctors do not know exactly why Pierre Robin occurs. They do not believe it is the result of anything the mother did or did not do during pregnancy. If the child only has Pierre Robin, many experts believe that it is the result of the positioning of the fetus in the early weeks of pregnancy.

Will this happen to children I have in the future?

Pierre Robin does not tend to run in families. The chances of you having another child with Pierre Robin are very small, unless the Pierre Robin sequence is a part of a syndrome.

What kinds of problems could my child have?

In addition to the physical characteristics common to Pierre Robin, your child may have the following problems:

- Feeding problems in infancy

- Ear infections

- Reduced hearing

About 40 percent of infants with Pierre Robin have Stickler syndrome and about 15 percent have velocardiofacial syndrome. FACES recommends genetic testing be done to determine if your infant has either of these associated syndromes. The Pierre Robin Network has excellent information concerning genetic testing for babies born with Pierre Robin sequence.

Will my child need surgery?

Depending on the severity of Pierre Robin, your child may have some or all of the following surgeries:

- Surgery to repair the cleft palate

- Special devices to protect the airway and aid in feeding

- Surgery to improve breathing

The small jaw associated with Pierre Robin usually grows out on its own during the first two years, and usually no surgery is necessary on the jaw.

New advances in procedures to correct the problems associated with Pierre Robin are constantly being made. Be an advocate for your child!

How do I get help for my child?

Your child should be treated by a qualified craniofacial medical team at a craniofacial center.

Chapter 26

Digestive Tract Defects

Chapter Contents

Section 26.1

Congenital Diaphragmatic Hernia

"Congenital Diaphragmatic Hernia (CDH)," reprinted with permission from the Junior League Fetal Center at Vanderbilt, Monroe Carell Jr. Children's Hospital at Vanderbilt (http://childrenshospital.vanderbilt.org), © 2012. All rights reserved.

What is a congenital diaphragmatic hernia (CDH)?

The diaphragm is a large dome-shaped muscle that separates the chest from the abdomen. The diaphragm normally develops between the seventh and tenth weeks of pregnancy.

An abnormal opening or hole in the diaphragm is called a diaphragmatic hernia. This opening allows some of the baby's abdominal organs to move into the chest. The stomach, small intestine, spleen, part of the liver, and the kidney can enter the chest cavity. The intestine takes up some of the space where the lung should develop, so that the lung cannot develop normally. When this happens, we say that the lung is "hypoplastic." The more space the abdominal organs take up in the chest, the more severe the effects on the lung.

What causes a diaphragmatic hernia?

The abnormal opening ("hernia") is caused when the diaphragm muscles do not grow together normally during the baby's development. We do not yet know why this occurs, or how to prevent this from happening. The two types of diaphragmatic hernia are based on which side of the chest is affected:

- Left-sided hernias are called Bochdalek hernias. Ninety percent of hernias are on this side and they are slightly more common in boys. This type of hernia can be due to the diaphragm not forming properly or the intestine becoming trapped in the chest cavity as the diaphragm forms.

- Right-sided hernias are known as Morgagni hernias. Two percent of hernias are on this side and they are more common in girls. This type of hernia is caused when the tendon in the middle of the diaphragm does not develop properly.

Could my baby have any other abnormalities?

About one in three infants with diaphragmatic hernia will also have another birth defect. In these cases, it is most often a heart defect. Rarely the baby may have a chromosomal abnormality such as trisomy 21 or Down syndrome.

What are the chances this will happen with my next baby?

There is a 2 percent chance of your having another baby with congenital diaphragmatic hernia (CDH). This means there is a 98 percent chance that the condition would not be seen in a future pregnancy.

How is CDH detected?

There are usually no signs or symptoms in the pregnancy. The pregnant mother may have an increased amount of amniotic fluid surrounding the baby. This excess of fluid is called "polyhydramnios." The fetal ultrasound may show abdominal organs in the chest cavity, but the defect is not always seen on routine ultrasound. Because of this, some infants are not diagnosed until after they are born.

How will this condition affect my baby's health?

A diaphragmatic hernia is a life-threatening condition. The diaphragm muscle is not properly formed and allows the lung to be crowded by other organs. Because of this crowding, these babies have serious difficulty breathing. Your baby will need efforts to help his or her breathing and heart function immediately after birth and during and after surgery. Even with excellent care, about 25 percent of babies with diaphragmatic hernia live for only a short time.

Treatment during pregnancy: On rare occasions would a baby with CDH be considered eligible for surgery before birth. Any surgery before birth is called "fetal intervention." Whether your baby is eligible or not depends on three things:

1. The side of the chest most affected by the diaphragmatic hernia

2. The time of diagnosis

3. The severity of the problem for the lung

How will CDH affect my baby's birth?

Many babies born with this condition will experience common signs, but babies may have different symptoms. Babies often are unable to get enough air or the oxygen it contains shortly after birth. This is called "respiratory distress," and occurs because the diaphragm does not move properly and because the lung is crowded by the organs. The baby's doctor will examine him or her for the following signs:

- Abnormal chest development with one side larger than the other

- Breath sounds absent on the affected side

- Bowel sounds heard in the chest

- Abdomen that appears to be caved in (concave) and feels less full to the touch

- Severe breathing difficulty

- Bluish coloration of the skin due to lack of oxygen

- Fast breathing (tachypnea)

- Fast heart rate (tachycardia)

If the baby is in enough distress they will be "intubated" with a breathing tube in order to help them breathe and a "replogle" will be placed to get rid of extra air in the stomach.

What will happen after my baby is born?

Several studies may need to be performed to evaluate the baby:

- Chest x-ray may show abdominal organs in the chest cavity.

- A blood test will be performed to evaluate the baby's breathing ability.

- Echocardiogram (to evaluate the heart).

Will my baby need surgery later?

Babies born with this condition will need treatment in a neonatal intensive care unit (NICU). After birth, surgery is needed to place the abdominal organs into the abdominal cavity and to repair the opening in the diaphragm. Most centers wait until the baby is stable before doing surgery. Some babies are good candidates for placement on a modified heart/lung bypass machine called ECMO (extracorporeal membrane oxygenation). The medical team and family together discuss whether this machine will improve the baby's outcome. ECMO gives the lungs more time to recover and function normally. Babies who require ECMO due to the severity of CDH have a 50 percent survival rate.

Expected progress: The infant's lung tissue on the affected side may be underdeveloped, and the infant's progress depends upon the development of the lung tissue. Generally, the prognosis is good for infants who have adequate lung tissue. With advances in neonatal and surgical care, overall survival is now greater than 80 percent. The infant may require several weeks of hospitalization after surgery, depending on how long breathing needs to be supported by a ventilator. Feeding begins after the first bowel movement is passed. Feeding is usually done through a tube into the stomach or small intestine until the breathing tube is removed. Due to the abnormal position of the stomach and esophagus, feeding difficulty is very common and can delay discharge.

What are the long-term complications my baby may face?

Your baby may have long-term complications of CDH. These include:

- breathing problems;
- recurrent lung infections;
- gastrointestinal problems;
- difficulty growing;
- developmental problems.

Section 26.2

Esophageal Atresia

Excerpted from "Esophageal Atresia,"
© 2012 A.D.A.M., Inc. Reprinted with permission.

Esophageal atresia is a disorder of the digestive system in which the esophagus does not develop properly. The esophagus is the tube that normally carries food from the mouth to the stomach.

Causes

Esophageal atresia is a congenital defect, which means it occurs before birth. There are several types. In most cases, the upper esophagus ends and does not connect with the lower esophagus and stomach. The top end of the lower esophagus connects to the windpipe. This connection is called a tracheoesophageal fistula (TEF). Some babies with TEF will also have other problems, such as heart or other digestive tract disorders.

Other types of esophageal atresia involve narrowing of the esophagus, and may also be associated with other birth defects.

Esophageal atresia occurs in about one out of four thousand births. Symptoms

- Bluish coloration to the skin (cyanosis) with attempted feedings
- Coughing, gagging, and choking with attempted feeding
- Drooling
- Poor feeding

Exams and Tests

Before birth, an ultrasound performed on the pregnant mother may show too much amniotic fluid, which can be a sign of esophageal atresia or other blockage of the digestive tract.

The disorder is usually detected shortly after birth when feeding is attempted and the infant coughs, chokes, and turns blue. As soon as the diagnosis is suspected, an attempt to pass a small feeding tube through the mouth or nose into the stomach should be made. The feeding tube will not be able to pass all the way to the stomach in a baby with esophageal atresia.

An x-ray of the esophagus shows an air-filled pouch and air in the stomach and intestine. If a feeding tube has been inserted, it will appear coiled up in the upper esophagus.

Treatment

Esophageal atresia is considered a surgical emergency. Surgery to repair the esophagus should be done quickly after the baby is stabilized so that the lungs are not damaged and the baby can be fed.

Before the surgery, the baby is not fed by mouth. Care is taken to prevent the baby from breathing secretions into the lungs.

Outlook (Prognosis)

An early diagnosis gives a better chance of a good outcome.

Possible Complications

The infant may breathe saliva and other fluids into the lungs, causing aspiration pneumonia, choking, and possibly death.

Other complications may include:

- feeding problems;

- reflux (the repeated bringing up of food from the stomach) after surgery;

- narrowing (stricture) of the esophagus due to scarring from surgery.

Prematurity may complicate the condition.

Section 26.3

Gastroschisis

Excerpted from "Facts about Gastroschisis,"
Centers for Disease Control and Prevention, February 24, 2011.

Gastroschisis is a birth defect of the abdominal (belly) wall. The baby's intestines stick outside of the baby's body, through a hole beside the belly button. The hole can be small or large and sometimes other organs, such as the stomach and liver, can also stick outside of the baby's body.

Gastroschisis occurs early during pregnancy when the muscles that make up the baby's abdominal wall do not form correctly. A hole occurs, which allows the intestines and other organs to extend outside of the body, usually to the right side of belly button. Because the intestines are not covered in a protective sac and are exposed to the amniotic fluid, the bowel can become irritated, causing it to shorten, twist, or swell.

Soon after the baby is born, surgery will be needed to place the abdominal organs inside the baby's body and repair the defect. After the repair, infants with gastroschisis can have problems with feeding, digestion of food, and absorption of nutrients.

The Centers for Disease Control and Prevention (CDC) estimates that about 1,871 babies are born each year in the United States with gastroschisis.[1]

Causes and Risk Factors

Recently, CDC researchers have reported important findings about some factors that affect the risk of having a baby with gastroschisis:

- **Younger age:** Teenage mothers were more likely to have a baby with gastroschisis than older mothers, and white teenagers had higher rates than black or African American teenagers.[2]

- **Alcohol and tobacco:** Women who consumed alcohol or were smokers were more likely to have a baby with gastroschisis.[3]

- **Certain medications:** Use of ibuprofen during pregnancy increased the risk for gastroschisis.[4]

- **Infections:** Women who reported a genitourinary tract infection just before or during early pregnancy were shown to have an increased risk of having a baby with gastroschisis.[4]

Diagnosis

Gastroschisis can be diagnosed during pregnancy or after the baby is born.

During Pregnancy

During pregnancy, there are screening tests (prenatal tests) to check for birth defects and other conditions. Gastroschisis might result in an abnormal result on a blood or serum screening test or it might be seen during an ultrasound (which creates pictures of the body).

After the Baby Is Born

Gastroschisis is immediately seen at birth.

Treatments

Soon after the baby is born, surgery will be needed to place the abdominal organs inside the baby's body and repair the defect.

If the gastroschisis defect is small (only some of the intestine is outside of the belly), it is usually treated with surgery soon after birth to put the organs back into the belly and close the opening. If the gastroschisis defect is large (many organs outside of the belly), the repair might done slowly, in stages. The exposed organs might be covered with a special material and slowly moved back into the belly. After all of the organs have been put back in the belly, the opening is closed.

Babies with gastroschisis often need other treatments as well, including receiving nutrients through an intravenous (IV) line, antibiotics to prevent infection, and careful attention to control their body temperature.

References

1. Parker SE, Mai CT, Canfield MA, Rickard R, Wang Y, Meyer RE, et al; for the National Birth Defects Prevention Network. Updated national birth prevalence estimates for selected birth

defects in the United States, 2004–2006. *Birth Defects Res A Clin Mol Teratol*. 2010 Sept 28. [Epub ahead of print]

2. Williams LJ, Kucik JE, Alverson CJ, Olney RS, Correa A. Epidemiology of gastroschisis in metropolitan Atlanta, 1968 through 2000. *Birth Defects Res A*. 2005; 73:177–83.

3. Bird TM, Robbins JM, Druschel C, Cleves MA, Yang S, Hobbs CA, & the National Birth Defects Prevention Study (2009). Demographic and environmental risk factors for gastroschisis and omphalocele in the National Birth Defects Prevention Study. *J Pediatr Surg*, 44:1546–51.

4. Feldkamp ML, Reefhuis J, Kucik J, Krikov S, Wilson A, Moore CA, Carey JC, Botto LD and the National Birth Defects Prevention Study. Case-control study of self reported genitourinary infections and risk of gastroschisis: findings from the national birth defects prevention study, 1997–2003. *BMJ*. 2008 Jun 21; 336(7658): 1420–23.

Section 26.4

Hirschsprung Disease

Excerpted from "What I Need to Know about Hirschsprung Disease," National Institute of Diabetes and Digestive and Kidney Diseases, National Institutes of Health, May 10, 2012.

What is Hirschsprung disease (HD)?

Hirschsprung disease (HD) is a disease of the large intestine that causes severe constipation or intestinal obstruction. Constipation means stool moves through the intestines slower than usual. Bowel movements occur less often than normal and stools are difficult to pass. Some children with HD can't pass stool at all, which can result in the complete blockage of the intestines, a condition called intestinal obstruction. People with HD are born with it and are usually diagnosed when they are infants. Less severe cases are sometimes diagnosed when a child is older. An HD diagnosis in an adult is rare.

Why does HD cause constipation?

People with HD have constipation because they lack nerve cells in a part or all of the large intestine. The nerve cells signal muscles in the large intestine to push stool toward the anus. Without a signal to push stool along, stool will remain in the large intestine.

How severe HD is depends on how much of the large intestine is affected. Short-segment HD means only the last part of the large intestine lacks nerve cells. Long-segment HD means most or all of the large intestine, and sometimes the last part of the small intestine, lacks nerve cells.

In a person with HD, stool moves through the large intestine until it reaches the part lacking nerve cells. At that point, the stool moves slowly or stops, causing an intestinal obstruction.

What causes HD?

Before birth, a child's nerve cells normally grow along the intestines in the direction of the anus. With HD, the nerve cells stop growing too soon. Why the nerve cells stop growing is unclear. Some HD is inherited, meaning it is passed from parent to child through genes. HD is not caused by anything a mother did while pregnant.

What are the symptoms of HD?

The main symptoms of HD are constipation or intestinal obstruction, usually appearing shortly after birth. Constipation in infants and children is common and usually comes and goes, but if your child has had ongoing constipation since birth, HD may be the problem.

Symptoms in newborns: Newborns with HD almost always fail to have their first bowel movement within forty-eight hours after birth. Other symptoms include the following:

- Green or brown vomit

- Explosive stools after a doctor inserts a finger into the rectum

- Swelling of the belly, also known as the abdomen

- Lots of gas

- Bloody diarrhea

Symptoms in toddlers and older children: Symptoms of HD in toddlers and older children include the following:

- Not being able to pass stools without laxatives or enemas. A laxative is medicine that loosens stool and increases bowel movements. An enema is performed by flushing water, or sometimes a mild soap solution, into the anus using a special wash bottle.

- Swelling of the abdomen.

- Lots of gas.

- Bloody diarrhea.

- Slow growth or development.

- Lack of energy because of a shortage of red blood cells, called anemia.

How is HD diagnosed?

HD is diagnosed based on symptoms and test results.

A doctor will perform a physical exam and ask questions about your child's bowel movements. HD is much less likely if parents can identify a time when their child's bowel habits were normal.

If HD is suspected, the doctor will do one or more tests.

X-rays: An x-ray is a black-and-white picture of the inside of the body. To make the large intestine show up better, the doctor may fill it with barium liquid. Barium liquid is inserted into the large intestine through the anus.

If HD is the problem, the last segment of the large intestine will look narrower than normal. Just before this narrow segment, the intestine will look bulged. The bulging is caused by blocked stool stretching the intestine.

Manometry: During manometry, the doctor inflates a small balloon inside the rectum. Normally, the rectal muscles will relax. If the muscles don't relax, HD may be the problem. This test is most often done in older children and adults.

Biopsy: Biopsy is the most accurate test for HD. The doctor removes a tiny piece of the large intestine and looks at it with a microscope. If nerve cells are missing, HD is the problem.

How is HD treated?

Pull-through procedure: HD is treated with surgery called a pull-through procedure. A surgeon removes the segment of the large intestine lacking nerve cells and connects the healthy segment to the anus. The pull-through procedure is usually done soon after diagnosis.

Ostomy surgery: An ostomy allows stool to leave the body through an opening in the abdomen. Although most children with HD do not need an ostomy, a child who has been very sick from HD may need an ostomy to get better before the pull-through procedure.

For ostomy surgery, the surgeon first takes out the diseased segment of the large intestine. The end of the healthy intestine is moved to an opening in the abdomen where a stoma is created. A stoma is created by rolling the intestine's end back on itself, like a shirt cuff, and stitching it to the abdominal wall. An ostomy pouch is attached to the stoma and worn outside the body to collect stool. The pouch will need to be emptied several times each day.

If the surgeon removes the entire large intestine and connects the small intestine to the stoma, the surgery is called an ileostomy. If the surgeon leaves part of the large intestine and connects it to the stoma, the surgery is called a colostomy.

Later, during the pull-through procedure, the surgeon removes the stoma and closes the abdomen with stitches.

What will my child's life be like after surgery?

After ostomy surgery: Infants will feel better after ostomy surgery because they will be able to easily pass gas and stool.

Older children will feel better, too, but they must adjust to living with an ostomy. They will need to learn how to take care of the stoma and how to change the ostomy pouch. With a few changes, children with ostomies can lead normal lives. However, they may worry about being different from their friends. A special nurse called an ostomy nurse can answer questions and show how to care for an ostomy.

After the pull-through procedure: Most children pass stool normally after the pull-through procedure. Children may have diarrhea for a while, and infants and toddlers may develop diaper rash, which is treatable with diaper creams. Over time, stool will become more solid and the child will go to the bathroom less often. Toilet training may take longer. Children often must learn how to use the muscles of the anus after surgery. Some children may leak stool for a while, but most will learn to have better bowel control as they get older.

Diet and nutrition: After the pull-through procedure, children with long-segment HD need to drink more fluids. Now that the large intestine is shorter, or entirely gone, it is less able to absorb fluids the body needs. Drinking more helps make up for the loss.

Some infants may need tube feedings for a while. A feeding tube allows infant formula or milk to be pumped directly into the stomach or small intestine. The feeding tube is passed through the nose or through an incision in the abdomen.

Eating high-fiber foods can help reduce constipation and diarrhea. Fiber helps form stool, making bowel movements easier. High-fiber foods include whole-grain breads, vegetables, and fruits. Some children may need laxatives to treat ongoing constipation. Consult a doctor before giving a laxative to your child.

Infection: People with HD can suffer from an infection of the intestines, called enterocolitis, before or after surgery. Symptoms include the following:

- Fever

- Swollen abdomen

- Vomiting

- Diarrhea

- Bleeding from the rectum

- Lack of energy

Call the doctor right away if your child shows any of these signs.

Children with enterocolitis need to go to the hospital. An intravenous (IV) tube is inserted into a vein to give fluids and antibiotics. The large intestine is rinsed regularly with a mild saltwater solution until all stool has been removed. The solution may also contain antibiotics to kill bacteria. A temporary ostomy may be needed to help the intestine heal.

Sometimes infection is a sign of a problem with the pull-through procedure. More surgery may be needed to correct the problem and prevent future infections.

If I have more children, will they also have HD?

If you have a child with HD, your chance of having more children with HD is greater. Talk with your doctor about the risk.

Section 26.5

Imperforate Anus

What is imperforate anus?

Imperforate anus occurs when the anal opening is absent or not in a normal position. It is a birth defect caused by the failure of normal development of the anal area. Sometimes a fistula (abnormal passage) is present between the bowel and the vagina in girls, or between the bowel and the urinary tract in boys.

There are three types of imperforate anus:

- **High type:** No anal opening is present and the rectum ends above the muscles at the bottom of the pelvis (hip bones). These children may have a fistula.

- **Intermediate type:** The end of the rectum and anal canal extend through the muscle at the bottom of the pelvis. These children may have a fistula.

- **Low type:** The rectum ends below the muscles at the bottom of the pelvis. There is often an anal opening present, but it is in an abnormal position or is covered by a membrane.

What causes an imperforate anus?

There is no known cause for the condition, which occurs in one out of every five thousand infants.

What are the symptoms?

- No anal opening

- Misplaced anal opening

- Anal opening very near the vaginal opening in a female

- No bowel movement within twenty-four to forty-eight hours after birth
- Stool passed through the vagina or urethra
- Abdominal distension (bloating)

How is it diagnosed?

Diagnosis is made at birth when the anal opening is checked during the newborn's physical examination.

What is the treatment?

The low type may be corrected by one or more of the following:

- Opening the membrane in surgery
- Repeated dilating (stretching) of the opening
- Surgical reconstruction

The high type is corrected with surgeries over a period of time. A temporary colostomy (re-routing the bowel out through the abdominal wall) is created. The baby then has bowel movements into a pouch (ostomy bag).

At about three to nine months of age, surgical reconstruction of an anal opening is performed, and any possible fistula is closed.

The colostomy is reconnected six to eight weeks later.

If your child needs a colostomy, a WOCN (wound ostomy continence nurse) will teach you how to take care of the colostomy and how to apply the pouch. You will be able to practice taking care of the stoma before your baby goes home from the hospital.

What else do I need to know?

The outcome is good with treatment. Children with imperforate anus are often constipated, even after surgical repair. In these children, a bowel management program may be needed to treat constipation.

Section 26.6

Intestinal Atresia

Intestinal atresia refers to a part of the fetal bowel that is not developed, and the intestinal tract becomes partially or completely blocked (bowel obstruction). This condition can occur anywhere in the intestinal tract. Intestinal atresia generally refers to blockages of the small intestine—the most common. Blockages of the large intestine are called colonic atresias.

Blockages that occur in the first portion of the intestine, immediately after the stomach, are called duodenal atresias and present differently.

Atresias can also occur in other hollow organs, such as the esophagus. Esophageal atresia is a common defect in fetuses, but it's not often diagnosed before birth.

How common is it?

Intestinal atresia occurs between one in one thousand and five thousand live births. The only treatment is surgery, no matter where the atresia is located. Your baby will remain in the hospital for several weeks while the bowel heals and function is restored.

How is it diagnosed?

The effects of intestinal atresia, such as a dilated bowel or an excess of amniotic fluid, are visible through routine prenatal ultrasound, alerting your doctor to the condition. Usually, however, your doctor cannot determine the reason for the blockage through ultrasound alone. Other prenatal tests may be necessary. Your doctor may recommend amniocentesis to look for chromosomal abnormalities or other genetic conditions that can be related to bowel obstructions, as well as serial level II ultrasound to closely monitor the level of amniotic fluid and the growth of your baby.

What can happen before birth?

When the blockage occurs high in the intestines, the fetus can't absorb all of the amniotic fluid that is swallowed. This excess of amniotic fluid is called "polyhydramnios." Severe polyhydramnios may increase the risk of premature delivery.

When the blockage is farther down the intestinal tract, the preceding loops of bowel dilate and fill with fluid. Usually, dilated bowel loops are not a threat to the fetus. In rare cases, the bowel can twist and cut off its own blood supply.

What can be done before birth?

It is difficult to predict whether a bowel will twist, and if diagnosed, it may be too late to repair. Because of this and the risk to the fetus, it is generally not recommended to intervene before birth.

What are my delivery options?

Unless there are signs that the fetus is in trouble, pre-term delivery or Cesarean section is not necessary. Cesarean section may be necessary for obstetrical reasons, however. It is recommended that mothers deliver in a hospital that has immediate access to a specialized neonatal intensive care unit (NICU), with a pediatric surgical specialist present.

What will happen at birth?

Most babies with intestinal atresia do not have immediate problems at birth. You will most likely be able to hold your baby after delivery. Neonatologists will be present to assess your baby and start treatment if necessary, or bring him or her to the NICU.

Once your doctor has fully assessed your baby (and has determined where the blockage is), a pediatric surgeon will perform an operation to correct the intestinal atresia. The goal of this surgery is to remove the bowel obstruction and allow the digestive tract to function. The type and number of operations depend on the location of the obstruction and the condition of the intestine, and can only be determined during the initial operation.

While your baby recovers, he or she will receive nutrition and calories intravenously. This allows for normal growth until you can attempt feeding by mouth, which happens when there are signs of good bowel function. This may take days or weeks, depending on the type of intestinal atresia and the operation. The intestinal tract usually takes about two to three weeks to fully function.

After bowel function is restored, it will take some time before your baby can handle enough breast milk or formula for proper nourishment. He or she may be in the hospital for several weeks or longer, depending on the degree of prematurity and the condition of the bowel.

What is the long-term outcome?

The long-term outcome for most intestinal atresias is excellent. Infants typically experience minor intestinal problems in the first few weeks after birth, but recover fully. If your baby is missing a large amount of small intestine—either because too little developed during pregnancy or because it had to be removed during surgery—he or she may have trouble absorbing enough nutrients and may continue to receive nutrients intravenously for a longer period of time.

The long-term outcome may depend on associated conditions. Some conditions, such as cystic fibrosis, can be the underlying cause of intestinal atresia. Geneticists and other pediatric specialists will work together to help treat your baby.

Section 26.7

Intestinal Malrotation and Volvulus

What is malrotation?

Malrotation is an abnormality in which the intestine does not form in the correct way in the abdomen. It occurs early in the pregnancy (around the tenth week) and develops when the intestine fails to coil into the proper position in the abdomen. Malrotation is often not evident until the baby experiences a twisting of the intestine known as a volvulus. A volvulus is a disorder that causes an obstruction in the intestine, preventing food from being digested normally. The blood supply to the twisted part of the intestine can also be cut off, leading to the death of that segment of the intestine. This situation can become fatal if not treated as soon as possible.

Malrotation occurs in one out of every five hundred births in the United States. Among those children who have malrotation and develop symptoms, most symptoms will occur in the first year of life. Nearly 60 percent of cases are diagnosed during the first week of life. Malrotation occurs equally in boys and girls. However, more boys show symptoms within the first month of life than girls.

What causes malrotation?

The exact cause of malrotation is unknown.

What are the symptoms of malrotation?

One of the earliest signs of malrotation is abdominal pain and cramping caused by the inability of the bowel to push food past the obstruction. A baby with cramps and pain due to malrotation frequently follows a typical pattern where he or she will begin crying while pulling his or her legs up, stop crying suddenly, act normal for ten or fifteen minutes, then begin crying suddenly again, starting the pattern all over.

Other symptoms of malrotation may include:

- frequent vomiting, often green or yellow-green in color;

- a swollen, firm abdomen;

- pale color;

- poor appetite;

- little or no urine (due to fluid loss);

- infrequent bowel movements;

- blood in the stools;

- fever;

- lethargy (showing little energy).

How is malrotation diagnosed?

After performing a thorough physical exam, the doctor will order tests that evaluate the position of the intestine, and show whether it is twisted or blocked. These tests may include:

- **Abdominal x-ray:** An x-ray that may show intestinal obstructions.

- **Barium enema x-ray:** Barium is a liquid that makes the intestine show up better on the x-ray. For this test, barium is inserted into the intestine through the anus and then x-rays are taken.

- **CT scan:** CAT or CT is an abbreviation for computerized axial tomography. This test uses computers and x-rays to produce many pictures from multiple angles to give doctors an accurate picture of the body. In the case of possible malrotation, the doctor will use a CT scan to look for a blockage in one of the intestines. To assist in doing this, a harmless dye may be injected so that the blockage is more easily seen.

How is malrotation treated?

Malrotation is considered an emergency situation and the development of volvulus is considered a life-threatening condition. Surgery is required to fix the problem.

Often, the baby will be started on IV (intravenous) fluids to prevent dehydration. Antibiotics will be given to prevent infection.

A volvulus is surgically repaired as soon as possible. First, the intestine is untwisted and checked for damage. If the intestine is healthy, it is then replaced in the abdomen. If the blood supply to the intestine is in question, the intestine may be untwisted and placed back into the abdomen. Another operation is performed within twenty-four to forty-eight hours to check the health of the intestine. If it appears that the intestine has been damaged, the injured section may be removed.

For cases in which there is a large section of intestine that is damaged, a significant amount of intestine may be removed. When this occurs, the remaining parts of the intestine may not be able to be attached to each other surgically. To correct this, a colostomy may be done to enable the digestive process to continue. With a colostomy, the two remaining healthy ends of intestine are brought through openings in the abdomen. Stool will pass through the opening (called a stoma) and then into a collection bag. The colostomy may be temporary or permanent, depending on the amount of intestine that needed to be removed.

What is the prognosis for malrotation?

Although surgery is required to repair malrotation, most children experience normal growth and development once the condition is treated and corrected. The majority of children with malrotation who experienced a volvulus do not have long-term problems if the volvulus was repaired promptly and there was no intestinal damage. Consult your baby's physician regarding the specific prognosis for your baby.

Section 26.8

Meckel Diverticulum

Excerpted from "Meckel's Diverticulum,"
© 2012 A.D.A.M., Inc. Reprinted with permission.

A Meckel diverticulum is a pouch on the wall of the lower part of the intestine that is present at birth (congenital). The diverticulum may contain tissue that is the same as tissue of the stomach or pancreas.

Causes

A Meckel diverticulum is tissue left over from when the baby's digestive tract was forming before birth. A small number of people have a Meckel diverticulum, but only a few develop symptoms.

Symptoms

- Pain in the abdomen that can be mild or severe

- Blood in the stool

Symptoms often occur during the first few years of life, but they may not start until adulthood.

Exams and Tests

You may have the following tests:
- Hematocrit
- Hemoglobin
- Stool smear for invisible blood (stool occult blood test)
- Technetium scan

Treatment

You may need surgery to remove the diverticulum if bleeding develops. The segment of small intestine that contains the diverticulum is surgically removed. The ends of the intestine are sewn back together.

You may need iron replacement to correct anemia. If you have a lot of bleeding, you may need a blood transfusion.

Outlook (Prognosis)

You can expect a full recovery with surgery.

Possible Complications

- Excess bleeding (hemorrhage) from the diverticulum
- Folding of the intestines (intussusception), a type of blockage
- Peritonitis
- Tear (perforation) of the bowel at the diverticulum

When to Contact a Medical Professional

See your health care provider right away if your child passes blood or bloody stool or has ongoing complaints of abdominal pain.

Section 26.9

Omphalocele

"Facts about Omphalocele," Centers for
Disease Control and Prevention, February 24, 2011.

Omphalocele, also known as exomphalos, is a birth defect of the abdominal (belly) wall. The infant's intestines, liver, or other organs stick outside of the belly through the belly button. The organs are covered in a thin, nearly transparent sac that hardly ever is open or broken.

As the baby develops during weeks six through ten of pregnancy, the intestines get longer and push out from the belly into the umbilical cord. By the eleventh week of pregnancy, the intestines normally go back into the belly. If this does not happen, an omphalocele occurs.

The omphalocele can be small, with only some of the intestines outside of the belly, or it can be large, with many organs outside of the belly. Because some or all of the abdominal (belly) organs are outside of the body, babies born with an omphalocele can have other problems as well. The abdominal cavity, the space in the body that holds these organs, might not grow to its normal size. Also, infection is a concern, especially if the sac around the organs is broken. Sometimes, an organ might become pinched or twisted, and loss of blood flow might damage the organ.

The Centers for Disease Control and Prevention (CDC) estimates that each year about 775 babies in the United States are born with an omphalocele.[1] In other words, about 1 out of every 5,386 babies born in the United States each year is born with an omphalocele. Many babies born with an omphalocele also have other birth defects, such as heart defects, neural tube defects, and chromosomal abnormalities.[2]

Causes and Risk Factors

Like many families affected by birth defects, we at CDC want to find out what causes them. Understanding factors that can increase the chance of having a baby with a birth defect will help us learn more about the causes. Currently, we are working on one of the largest U.S. studies the National Birth Defects Prevention Study to understand the causes of and risk factors for birth defects. This study is looking at many possible risk factors for birth defects, such as omphalocele.

Recently, CDC researchers have reported important findings about some factors that can affect the risk of having a baby with an omphalocele:

- **Alcohol and tobacco:** Women who consumed alcohol or were heavy smokers (more than 1 pack a day) were more likely to have a baby with omphalocele.[3]

- **Certain medications:** Women who used selective serotonin reuptake inhibitors (SSRIs) during pregnancy were more likely to have a baby with an omphalocele.[4]

- **Obesity:** Women who were obese or overweight before pregnancy were more likely to have a baby with an omphalocele.[5]

CDC continues to study birth defects such as omphaloceles and how to prevent them. If you consume alcohol or smoke cigarettes, take medications, or are obese, and you are pregnant or thinking about getting pregnant, talk with your doctor about ways to increase your chances of having a healthy baby.

Diagnosis

An omphalocele can be diagnosed during pregnancy or after a baby is born.

During Pregnancy

During pregnancy, there are screening tests (prenatal tests) to check for birth defects and other conditions. An omphalocele might result in an abnormal result on a blood or serum screening test or it might be seen during an ultrasound (which creates pictures of the baby).

After a Baby Is Born

In some cases, an omphalocele might not be diagnosed until after a baby is born. An omphalocele is seen immediately at birth.

Treatments

Treatment for infants with an omphalocele depends on a number of factors, including:

- the size of the omphalocele;

- the presence of other birth defects or chromosomal abnormalities; and

- the baby's gestational age.

If the omphalocele is small (only some of the intestine is outside of the belly), it usually is treated with surgery soon after birth to put the intestine back into the belly and close the opening. If the omphalocele is large (many organs outside of the belly), the repair might be done in stages. The exposed organs might be covered with a special material, and slowly, over time, the organs will be moved back into the belly. When all the organs have been put back in the belly, the opening is closed.

References

1. Parker SE, Mai CT, Canfield MA, Rickard R, Wang Y, Meyer RE, et al; for the National Birth Defects Prevention Network. Updated national birth prevalence estimates for selected birth defects in the United States, 2004–2006. *Birth Defects Res A Clin Mol Teratol.* 2010 Sept 28.

2. Stoll C, Alembik Y, Dott B, Roth MP. Omphalocele and gastroschisis and associated malformations. *Am J Med Genet A.* 2008 May 15;146A(10):1280–85.

3. Bird TM, Robbins JM, Druschel C, Cleves MA, Yang S, Hobbs CA, & the National Birth Defects Prevention Study. Demographic and environmental risk factors for gastroschisis and omphalocele in the National Birth Defects Prevention Study. *J Pediatr Surg*, 2009;44:1546–51.

4. Alwan S, Reefhuis J, Rasmussen SA, Olney RS, Friedman JM, & the National Birth Defects Prevention Study. Use of Selective Serotonin-Reuptake Inhibitors in Pregnancy and the Risk of Birth Defects. *N Engl J Med*, 2007;356:2684–92.

5. Waller DK, Shaw GM, Rasmussen SA, Hobbs CA, Canfield MA, Siega-Riz AM, Gallaway MS, Correa A, & the National Birth Defects Prevention Study. Prepregnancy obesity as a risk factor for structural birth defects. *Arch Pediatr Adolesc Med*, 2007;161(8):745–50.

Section 26.10

Pyloric Stenosis

While you were anticipating your new baby, you probably mentally
prepared yourself for the messier aspects of child rearing: poopy diapers, food stains, and of course, spit up. But what's normal and what's
not when it comes to spitting up or vomiting in infants?

About Pyloric Stenosis

Pyloric stenosis, a condition that may affect the gastrointestinal
tract during infancy, isn't normal — it can cause your baby to vomit
forcefully and often and may cause other problems such as dehydration and salt and fluid imbalances. Immediate treatment for pyloric
stenosis is extremely important.

Pyloric stenosis is a narrowing of the pylorus, the lower part of the
stomach through which food and other stomach contents pass to enter
the small intestine. When an infant has pyloric stenosis, the muscles
in the pylorus have become enlarged and cause narrowing within the
pyloric channel to the point where food is prevented from emptying
out of the stomach.

Also called infantile hypertrophic pyloric stenosis, pyloric stenosis is
a form of gastric outlet obstruction, which means a blockage from the
stomach to the intestines. Pyloric stenosis is fairly common—it affects
about three out of one thousand babies in the United States. It's about
four times more likely to occur in firstborn male infants and also has
been shown to run in families—if a parent had pyloric stenosis, then
an infant has up to a 20 percent risk of developing it. Pyloric stenosis
occurs more commonly in Caucasian infants than in babies of other
ethnic backgrounds.

Most infants who develop symptoms of pyloric stenosis are usually between three to five weeks. It is one of the more common causes of intestinal obstruction during infancy that requires surgery.

Causes

It is believed that babies who develop pyloric stenosis are not born with it, but that the progressive thickening of the pylorus occurs after birth. A baby will start to show symptoms when the pylorus is so thickened that the stomach can no longer empty properly.

It is not known exactly what causes the thickening of the muscles of the pylorus. It may be a combination of several factors; for example, the use of erythromycin in the first two weeks of life has been associated with pyloric stenosis, and there is also a connection in babies whose mothers took this antibiotic at the end of pregnancy or during breastfeeding.

Signs and Symptoms

Symptoms of pyloric stenosis generally begin around three weeks of age. They include:

- **Vomiting:** The first symptom of pyloric stenosis is usually vomiting. At first it may seem that the baby is simply spitting up frequently, but then it tends to progress to projectile vomiting, in which the breast milk or formula is ejected forcefully from the mouth, in an arc, sometimes over a distance of several feet. Projectile vomiting usually takes place soon after the end of a feeding, although in some cases it may be delayed for hours. In some cases, the vomited milk may smell curdled because it has mixed with stomach acid. The vomit will not contain bile, a greenish fluid from the liver that mixes with digested food after it leaves the stomach. Despite vomiting, a baby with pyloric stenosis is usually hungry again soon after vomiting and will want to eat. The symptoms of pyloric stenosis can be deceptive because even though a baby may seem uncomfortable, he may not appear to be in great pain or at first look very ill.

- **Changes in stools:** Babies with pyloric stenosis usually have fewer, smaller stools because little or no food is reaching the intestines. Constipation or stools that have mucus in them may also be symptoms.

- **Failure to gain weight and lethargy:** Most babies with pyloric stenosis will fail to gain weight or will lose weight. As the condition worsens, they are at risk for developing fluid and salt abnormalities and becoming dehydrated. Dehydrated infants are less active than usual, and they may develop a sunken "soft spot" on their heads, sunken eyes, and their skin may appear wrinkled. Because less urine is made it may be more than four to six hours between wet diapers. After feeds, increased stomach contractions may make noticeable ripples, or waves of peristalsis, which move from left to right over the baby's belly as the stomach tries to empty itself against the thickened pylorus.

It's important to contact your doctor if your baby experiences any of these symptoms.

Other conditions can have similar symptoms. For instance, gastroesophageal reflux disease (GERD) usually begins before eight weeks of age, with excess spitting up, or reflux—which may resemble vomiting—taking place after feedings. However, the majority of infants with GERD do not experience projectile vomiting, and although they may have poor weight gain, they tend to have normal stools.

In infants, symptoms of gastroenteritis—inflammation in the digestive tract that can be caused by viral or bacterial infection—may also somewhat resemble pyloric stenosis. Vomiting and dehydration are seen with both conditions; however, infants with gastroenteritis usually also have diarrhea with loose, watery, or sometimes bloody stools. Diarrhea usually isn't seen with pyloric stenosis.

Diagnosis and Treatment

Your doctor will ask detailed questions about the baby's feeding and vomiting patterns, including the appearance of the vomit. The most important part of diagnosing pyloric stenosis is a reliable and consistent history and description of the vomiting.

The baby will be examined, and any weight loss or failure to maintain growth since birth will be noted. During the exam, the doctor will check for a lump in the abdomen—which is usually firm and movable and feels like an olive. Doctors sometimes feel this lump and if they do, it's a strong indication that a baby has pyloric stenosis.

If the baby's feeding history and physical examination suggest pyloric stenosis, an ultrasound of the baby's abdomen will usually be performed. The enlarged, thickened pylorus can be seen on ultrasound images.

Sometimes instead of an ultrasound, a barium swallow is performed. The baby swallows a small amount of a chalky liquid (barium), and then special x-rays are taken to view the pyloric region of the stomach to see if there is any narrowing or blockage.

Infants suspected of having pyloric stenosis usually undergo blood tests because the continuous vomiting of stomach acid, as well as the resulting dehydration from fluid losses, can cause salt and other imbalances in the blood that need to be corrected.

When an infant is diagnosed with pyloric stenosis, either by ultrasound or barium swallow, the baby will be admitted to the hospital and prepared for surgery. Any dehydration or electrolyte problems in the blood will be corrected with intravenous (IV) fluids, usually within twenty-four hours.

A surgical procedure called pyloromyotomy, which involves cutting through the thickened muscles of the pylorus, is performed to relieve the blockage that results from pyloric stenosis. The pylorus is examined through a very small incision, and the muscles that are overgrown and thickened are spread and relaxed.

The surgery can also be performed through laparoscopy. This is a technique that uses a tiny scope placed in an incision in the belly button allowing the doctor to see the area of the pylorus. With the help of other small instruments placed in nearby incisions, the surgery is completed.

Most babies are able to return to normal feedings fairly quickly, usually three to four hours after the surgery. Because of swelling at the surgery site, the baby may still vomit small amounts for a day or so after surgery. As long as there are no complications, most babies who have undergone pyloromyotomy can return to a normal feeding schedule and be sent home within twenty-four to forty-eight hours of the surgery.

If you are breastfeeding, you may be concerned about being able to continue feeding while your baby is hospitalized. The hospital should be able to provide you with a breast pump and assist you in its use so that you can continue to express milk until your baby can once again feed regularly.

After a successful pyloromyotomy, your infant will not need to follow any special feeding schedules. Your doctor will probably want to examine your child at a follow-up appointment to make sure the surgical site is healing properly and that your baby is feeding well and maintaining or gaining weight.

Pyloric stenosis should not recur after a complete pyloromyotomy. If your baby continues to display symptoms weeks after the surgery, it may suggest another medical problem, such as inflammation of the stomach (gastritis) or GERD—or it could indicate that the initial pyloromyotomy was incomplete.

When to Call the Doctor

Pyloric stenosis is an urgent condition that requires immediate evaluation. Call your doctor if your baby has vomiting and any of the following symptoms:

- Persistent or projectile vomiting after feeding

- Poor weight gain or weight loss

- Decreased activity or lethargy

- Few or no stools over a period of one or two days

- Signs of dehydration such as decreased urination (more than four to six hours between wet diapers)

- Sunken "soft spot" on the head; sunken eyes

Chapter 27

Fetal Alcohol
Spectrum Disorders

Fetal alcohol spectrum disorders (FASDs) are a group of conditions that can occur in a person whose mother drank alcohol during pregnancy. These effects can include physical problems and problems with behavior and learning. Often, a person with an FASD has a mix of these problems.

Cause and Prevention

FASDs are caused by a woman drinking alcohol during pregnancy. There is no known amount of alcohol that is safe to drink while pregnant. There is also no safe time to drink during pregnancy and no safe kind of alcohol to drink while pregnant.

To prevent FASDs, a woman should not drink alcohol while she is pregnant, or even when she might get pregnant. This is because a woman could get pregnant and not know for several weeks or more. In the United States, half of pregnancies are unplanned.

Signs and Symptoms

FASDs refer to the whole range of effects that can happen to a person whose mother drank alcohol during pregnancy. These conditions can affect each person in different ways, and can range from mild to severe.

Excerpted from "Facts about FASDs," Centers for Disease Control and Prevention, September 26, 2011.

A person with an FASD might have:

- abnormal facial features, such as a smooth ridge between the nose and upper lip (this ridge is called the philtrum);

- small head size;

- shorter-than-average height;

- low body weight;

- poor coordination;

- hyperactive behavior;

- difficulty paying attention;

- poor memory;

- difficulty in school (especially with math);

- learning disabilities;

- speech and language delays;

- intellectual disability or low intelligence quotient (IQ);

- poor reasoning and judgment skills;

- sleep and sucking problems as a baby;

- vision or hearing problems;

- problems with the heart, kidneys, or bones.

Types of FASDs

Different terms are used to describe FASDs, depending on the type of symptoms:

- **Fetal alcohol syndrome (FAS):** FAS represents the severe end of the FASD spectrum. Fetal death is the most extreme outcome from drinking alcohol during pregnancy. People with FAS might have abnormal facial features, growth problems, and central nervous system (CNS) problems. People with FAS can have problems with learning, memory, attention span, communication, vision, or hearing. They might have a mix of these problems. People with FAS often have a hard time in school and trouble getting along with others.

- **Alcohol-related neurodevelopmental disorder (ARND):** People with ARND might have intellectual disabilities and problems with behavior and learning. They might do poorly in school and have difficulties with math, memory, attention, judgment, and poor impulse control.

- **Alcohol-related birth defects (ARBD):** People with ARBD might have problems with the heart, kidneys, or bones or with hearing. They might have a mix of these.

The term fetal alcohol effects (FAE) was previously used to describe intellectual disabilities and problems with behavior and learning in a person whose mother drank alcohol during pregnancy. In 1996, the Institute of Medicine (IOM) replaced FAE with the terms alcohol-related neurodevelopmental disorder (ARND) and alcohol-related birth defects (ARBD).

Diagnosis

Diagnosing FAS can be hard because there is no medical test, like a blood test, for it. And other disorders, such as ADHD (attention-deficit/hyperactivity disorder) and Williams syndrome, have some symptoms like FAS.

To diagnose FAS, doctors look for:

- abnormal facial features (e.g., smooth ridge between nose and upper lip);

- lower-than-average height, weight, or both;

- central nervous system problems (e.g., small head size, problems with attention and hyperactivity, poor coordination);

- prenatal alcohol exposure; although confirmation is not required to make a diagnosis.

Treatment

FASDs last a lifetime. There is no cure for FASDs, but research shows that early intervention treatment services can improve a child's development.

There are many types of treatment options, including medication to help with some symptoms, behavior and education therapy, parent training, and other alternative approaches. No one treatment is right for every child. Good treatment plans will include close monitoring, follow-ups, and changes as needed along the way.

Also, "protective factors" can help reduce the effects of FASDs and help people with these conditions reach their full potential.[1,2] Protective factors include:

- diagnosis before six years of age;
- loving, nurturing, and stable home environment during the school years;
- absence of violence;
- involvement in special education and social services.

Get Help!

If you think your child might have an FASD, talk to your child's doctor and share your concerns. Don't wait!

If you or the doctor thinks there could be a problem, ask the doctor for a referral to a specialist (someone who knows about FASDs), such as a developmental pediatrician, child psychologist, or clinical geneticist. In some cities, there are clinics whose staffs have special training in diagnosing and treating children with FASDs.

At the same time, call your state's public early childhood system to ask for a free evaluation to find out if your child qualifies for treatment services. This is sometimes called a Child Find evaluation. You do not need to wait for a doctor's referral or a medical diagnosis to make this call.

Where to call for a free evaluation from the state depends on your child's age:

- If your child is younger than three years old, contact your local early intervention system.
- If your child is three years old or older, contact your local public school system.

Even if your child is not old enough for kindergarten or is not enrolled in a public school, call your local elementary school or board of education and ask to speak with someone who can help you have your child evaluated.

References

1. Streissguth, A.P., Bookstein, F.L., Barr, H.M., Sampson, P.D., O'Malley, K., & Young, J.K. (2004). Risk factors for adverse life outcomes in fetal alcohol syndrome and fetal alcohol effects. *Developmental and Behavioral Pediatrics*, 5(4), 228–38.

2. Streissguth, A.P., Barr, H.M., Kogan, J. & Bookstein, F. L., Understanding the occurrence of secondary disabilities in clients with fetal alcohol syndrome (FAS) and fetal alcohol effects (FAE). Final report to the Centers for Disease Control and Prevention (CDC). Seattle: University of Washington, Fetal Alcohol & Drug Unit; August 1996. Tech. Rep. No. 96-06.

Chapter 28

Fetal Tumors

Chapter Contents

Section 28.1

Fetal Neck Masses

What is a fetal neck mass?

A fetal neck mass is a condition where there is an abnormal growth
in the neck of the fetus. Most neck masses are harmless and can be
managed after a normal pregnancy and delivery.

They become a problem when the growth starts to distort the anatomy of the neck. The mass can become so large that the esophagus and
airway may be blocked. If the esophagus, which connects the mouth to
the stomach, is blocked then the baby cannot swallow amniotic fluid.
This can lead to polyhydramnios (too much amniotic fluid), which can
cause pre-term labor. Blockage of the airway can prevent the baby from
breathing at birth, which is a life-threatening problem.

What causes a fetal neck mass?

Fetal neck masses are rare and usually there is not a genetic cause.
The most common type of fetal neck mass is a cystic hygroma, also
known as a cervical lymphatic malformation or lymphangioma. This is
caused by an abnormality in the development of the lymphatic channels in the neck. When one of the main channels becomes blocked, other
channels become dilated and distorted and a cystic mass filled with
lymphatic fluid develops. This type of fluid-filled cyst can distort the
neck anatomy, causing the esophagus or airway to be blocked.

A cervical teratoma is another, more rare, kind of neck mass. This
is usually a noncancerous tumor caused when reproductive cells become abnormally located in the neck and begin to grow irregularly.
Teratomas form a solid tumor created by a variety of different cells.
Although the neck masses form differently, the prenatal treatment
is similar.

How is a fetal neck mass diagnosed and evaluated?

Typically around twenty weeks of pregnancy, a routine ultrasound will show if the baby has a neck mass. Following the initial diagnosis, a series of medical tests will be done to determine the size and impact of the mass on the baby:

- Frequent ultrasounds will allow your doctor to see the mass, and learn more about how it is impacting the baby.

- A fetal echocardiogram (ultrasound of the heart performed by a pediatric cardiologist) will rule out structural heart defects and assess heart function.

- A fetal magnetic resonance imaging (MRI) will determine the nature and size of the mass, as well as how it is impacting the airway, esophagus, and other surrounding organs.

With all of this information, your doctor can help you and your family make the best possible decision about treatment.

How are fetal neck masses managed and treated during pregnancy?

The primary goal of an evaluation is to determine the severity of the neck mass. This may take several evaluations during which it is determined if the mass is growing rapidly, and how it is impacting the fetus. If the mass is compromising the airway or esophagus, or is causing an increase in amniotic fluid, then fetal intervention may be considered.

What fetal interventions are done for fetal neck masses?

Currently, there is not a fetal surgery option for fetal neck masses. However, if there is too much amniotic fluid (polyhydramnios), amnioreduction may be performed to remove the excess fluid, and lower the risk of preterm labor. During an amnioreduction, a local anesthetic is used to numb the skin of the mother's abdomen, then a needle is inserted into the womb to remove the excess amniotic fluid. The baby is monitored via ultrasound throughout the procedure to ensure it is not touched by the needle.

The mother may also be placed on bed rest, or given special medications to reduce the amniotic fluid.

How will a fetal neck mass impact delivery?

Most babies with a small neck mass can be delivered vaginally without any apparent complications. These babies typically go home and are followed as an outpatient two to four weeks after birth. The baby will be referred to a pediatric surgeon, who will help determine if, when, and how the mass should be removed. Sometimes, a giant neck mass can prevent the baby from breathing at birth. In these cases, your doctor may recommend that an "EXIT" procedure be performed for delivery.

During an "EXIT" procedure, the mother has a cesarean section delivery while asleep under general anesthesia. The baby's upper body is removed from the womb, but the placenta and umbilical cord remain attached to the mother and baby to give fetal surgeons time to evaluate the baby's lung function and the neck mass, secure an airway, and determine the best course of treatment.

Depending on the severity of the neck mass, the surgeon may need to drain or remove the mass, or perform a tracheotomy to secure an airway while the baby is still attached to the placenta. Once an airway is secured, a breathing tube is inserted and breathing is assisted using a ventilator machine.

If the baby is having difficulty breathing because the lungs are not fully developed, extracorporeal membrane oxygenation (ECMO) is used to give the baby's lungs more time to grow. Once the baby is breathing well, the umbilical cord is cut and the baby is fully delivered.

Following the EXIT procedure, the mother's cesarean incision is repaired and her recovery will be similar to those of a standard cesarean section.

What can I expect after my baby is born with a fetal neck mass?

Babies who are born with a fetal neck mass often have difficulty breathing and eating at birth. Neck masses can compress the baby's airway, making it soft and prone to collapse. If this is the case the baby may need a tracheostomy (a surgical opening in the trachea, often called a breathing tube) to make breathing easier. A temporary feeding tube to help provide nutrition may be necessary if the baby is unable to swallow at birth.

The impact on your baby will vary depending on the type of neck mass. For example, lymphangioma may cause challenges with feeding, speaking, and swallowing, while some cervical teratomas can require thyroid supplements after birth. Some babies may also require plastic surgery later in life.

The long-term outcomes for fetal neck masses after surgery are excellent. In nearly all cases, your baby will develop normally without any problems. But ongoing follow-up care is encouraged since these babies have a higher chance of a mass regrowth.

Section 28.2

Sacrococcygeal Teratoma

What is a sacrococcygeal teratoma?

A sacrococcygeal teratoma (SCT) is a tumor that grows at the base of the baby's spine near the coccyx (tailbone). Sacrococcygeal teratomas may grow to become very large and may cause problems for your baby before birth. This is the most common tumor found in newborns, and is more common in boys than in girls. Most are not cancerous but may become so if not removed. SCTs are removed surgically after the baby is born and most babies recover completely with no further problems. In rare situations, the tumor needs to be addressed before birth because of its effect on the baby's heart or other organs.

How is a sacrococcygeal teratoma diagnosed?

If your baby has an SCT, a mass may be detected on a prenatal ultrasound. The mass may look like a fluid-filled sac called a "cyst," or appear to be solid, or may be both cystic and solid. There are other symptoms that indicate that your baby may have an SCT. These include raised levels of alpha-fetoprotein (AFP) in your own blood.

How does a sacrococcygeal teratoma affect my baby's health?

SCTs may grow outside the baby's abdomen, inside the abdomen, or both. A mass growing internally may put pressure on the baby's organs such as the bladder, causing more health problems. Before birth your obstetrician will measure the tumor to follow growth and determine how it affects the baby's other organs. A solid tumor can cause more of a problem than a cystic one, as solid tumors contain more blood vessels. This increase in blood flow may stress the baby's heart and result in heart failure. This causes extra fluid to develop in the baby and is called hydrops. This a life-threatening condition.

Babies with large SCTs that are mostly cystic rarely develop hydrops. It is rare for SCTs to be cancerous. Most newborns with SCT survive and recover well. Babies that have solid SCT's that grow quite large are at highest risk for hydrops. Babies with SCT are at risk for bleeding from the SCT and into the SCT around the time of delivery and shortly thereafter.

How will a sacrococcygeal teratoma affect my baby's birth?

Your doctor will recommend delivery of your baby by a Cesarean section if the tumor is too large, or at risk for rupture. All babies with SCT should be delivered at a hospital called a "tertiary center," meaning that it has the staff and equipment ready to support a baby needing surgery or intensive care. The neonatologist will provide special care for your baby in the intensive care nursery until the baby is stable enough for surgery.

What will happen after birth?

While most babies with sacrococcygeal tumors do well with surgery after birth, several factors are involved in the health of your baby after delivery:

- **Small external tumors:** The pediatric surgeon removes the tumor with the coccyx bone (tailbone) after birth. These babies can be expected to live normal lives.

- **Large external tumors:** Surgery is more complex but the tumor and a portion of the tailbone are removed.

- **Large internal tumors and combined internal and external (dumbbell) tumors:** Surgery may require both an abdominal and a pelvic procedure but most babies recover well with no long-term problems.

- **Very large tumors:** Fetuses with very large tumors, in some cases as large as the fetus itself, pose a difficult problem both before and after birth.

Chapter 29

Heart Defects

Chapter Contents

Section 29.1

Aortic Stenosis

Excerpted from "Aortic Valve Stenosis (AVS)," reprinted with permission
from www.heart.org. © 2012 American Heart Association, Inc.

Stenosis (narrowing or obstruction) of the aortic valve makes the
left ventricle pump harder to get blood past the blockage.

Insufficiency (also called regurgitation) is when blood that's just
been pumped through the valve leaks backwards into the pumping
chamber between heartbeats.

Some children can have mostly obstruction; others mostly insufficiency. Some children have a valve with both problems.

Aortic stenosis (AS) occurs when the aortic valve didn't form properly. A normal valve has three parts (leaflets or cusps), but a stenotic
valve may have only one cusp (unicuspid) or two cusps (bicuspid),
which are thick and stiff, rather than thin and flexible.

What causes it?

In most children, the cause isn't known. It's a common type of heart
defect. Some children can have other heart defects along with AS.

How does it affect the heart?

In a child with AS, the pressure is much higher than normal in
the left pumping chamber (left ventricle) and the heart must work
harder to pump blood out into the body arteries. Over time this can
cause thickening (hypertrophy) and damage to the overworked heart
muscle. In a child with AS, the heart also works harder to pump the
normal amount of blood required by the body, and also all the blood that
has leaked back into the left ventricle through the valve in between
heartbeats. This can cause the left ventricle to be enlarged (dilated)
and also may cause damage to the heart muscle.

How does the abnormal aortic valve affect my child?

If the obstruction and leak are mild, the heart won't be overworked
and symptoms don't occur. Sometimes stenosis is severe and symptoms

occur in infancy. In some children chest pain, unusual tiring, dizziness, or fainting may occur. Otherwise, most children with aortic stenosis have no symptoms, and special tests may be needed to determine the severity of the problem.

What can be done about the aortic valve?

The valve can be treated to improve the obstruction and leak, but the valve can't be made normal.

Children with aortic stenosis will need treatment when the pressure in the left ventricle is high (even though there may be no symptoms). In most children the obstruction can be relieved during cardiac catheterization by balloon valvotomy. In this procedure, a special tool, a catheter containing a balloon, is placed across the aortic valve. The balloon is inflated for a short time to stretch open the valve (called a valvotomy).

Some children with stenosis may need surgery. The surgeon may be able to enlarge the valve opening if it's too small. Some valve leakage is likely to develop or increase after a balloon or surgical treatment for obstruction.

If your child's aortic valve no longer responds to valvotomy or has become severely insufficient (leaky), it will probably need to be replaced. The aortic valve can be surgically replaced in three ways:

1. The Ross procedure, a surgery in which the abnormal aortic valve is removed and replaced by the child's own pulmonary valve. Then the pulmonary valve is replaced with a preserved donor pulmonary valve.

2. Aortic valve replacement with a preserved donor valve.

3. Aortic valve replacement with a mechanical valve.

Each option has advantages and disadvantages. Discuss them with your child's pediatric cardiologist, cardiac surgeon, or both.

What activities can my child do?

If the aortic valve is abnormally formed but has no important obstruction or leak, your child may not need any special precautions regarding physical activities and may be able to participate in normal activities without increased risk. Some children with obstruction, leak, or heart muscle abnormalities may have to limit how much they do some kinds of exercise. Check with your child's pediatric cardiologist about this.

What will my child need in the future?

Children with aortic stenosis need lifelong medical follow-up. Your child's pediatric cardiologist will examine periodically to look for problems such as worsening of the obstruction or leak. Even mild stenosis may worsen over time. Also, balloon or surgical relief of a blockage is sometimes incomplete. After treatment the valve keeps working in a mildly abnormal way.

What about preventing endocarditis?

Children with AS and aortic insufficiency (AI) risk developing endocarditis. Children who have had their aortic valve replaced will need to take antibiotics before certain dental procedures.

Section 29.2

Atrial Septal Defect

Excerpted from "Facts about Atrial Septal Defect,"
Centers for Disease Control and Prevention, February 24, 2011.

An atrial septal defect is a birth defect of the heart in which there is a hole in the wall (septum) that divides the upper chambers of the heart (atria). A hole can vary in size and may close on its own or may require surgery. An atrial septal defect is one type of congenital heart defect. Congenital means present at birth.

As a baby develops during pregnancy, there are normally several openings in the wall dividing the upper chambers of the heart (atria). These usually close during pregnancy or shortly after birth.

If one of these openings does not close, a hole is left, and it is called an atrial septal defect. The hole increases the amount of blood that flows through the lungs and over time, it may cause damage to the blood vessels in the lungs. Damage to the blood vessels in the lungs may cause problems in adulthood, such as high blood pressure in the lungs and heart failure. Other problems may include abnormal heartbeat, and increased risk of stroke.

Causes and Risk Factors

The causes of heart defects such as atrial septal defect among most babies are unknown. Some babies have heart defects because of changes in their genes or chromosomes. These types of heart defects also are thought to be caused by a combination of genes and other risk factors, such as things the mother comes in contact with in the environment or what the mother eats or drinks or the medicines the mother uses.

Diagnosis

An atrial septal defect may be diagnosed during pregnancy or after the baby is born. In many cases, it may not be diagnosed until adulthood.

During Pregnancy

During pregnancy, there are screening tests (prenatal tests) to check for birth defects and other conditions. An atrial septal defect might be seen during an ultrasound (which creates pictures of the body), but it depends on the size of the hole and its location. If an atrial septal defect is suspected, a specialist will need to confirm the diagnosis.

After the Baby Is Born

An atrial septal defect is present at birth, but many babies do not have any signs or symptoms. Signs and symptoms of a large or un-treated atrial septal defect may include the following:

- Frequent respiratory or lung infections
- Difficulty breathing
- Tiring when feeding (infants)
- Shortness of breath when being active or exercising
- Skipped heartbeats or a sense of feeling the heartbeat
- A heart murmur, or a whooshing sound that can be heard with a stethoscope
- Swelling of legs, feet, or stomach area
- Stroke

It is possible that an atrial septal defect might not be diagnosed until adulthood. One of the most common ways an atrial septal defect is found is by detecting a murmur when listening to a person's heart with a stethoscope. If a murmur is heard or other signs or symptoms are present, the health care provider might request one or more tests to confirm the diagnosis. The most common test is an echocardiogram, which is an ultrasound of the heart.

Treatments

Treatment for an atrial septal defect depends on the age of diagnosis, the number of or seriousness of symptoms, size of the hole, and presence of other conditions. Sometimes surgery is needed to repair the hole. Sometimes medications are prescribed to help treat symptoms. There are no known medications that can repair the hole.

If a child is diagnosed with an atrial septal defect, the health care provider may want to monitor it for a while to see if the hole closes on its own. During this period of time, the health care provider might treat symptoms with medicine. A health care provider may recommend surgery for a child with a large atrial septal defect, even if there are few symptoms, to prevent problems later in life. Surgery may also be recommended for an adult who has many or severe symptoms. Surgery involves fixing the hole and may be done through cardiac catheterization or open-heart surgery. After surgery, follow-up care will depend on the size of the defect, the person's age, and whether the person has other birth defects.

Section 29.3

Coarctation of the Aorta

What is it?

A narrowing of the major artery (the aorta) that carries blood to the body.

This narrowing affects blood flow where the arteries branch out to carry blood along separate vessels to the upper and lower parts of the body. Coarctation of the aorta (CoA) can cause high blood pressure or heart damage.

If the obstruction is mild, the heart won't be very overworked and symptoms may not occur. In some children and adolescents, coarctation is discovered only after high blood pressure is found.

What causes it?

In most children, the cause isn't known. Some children can have other heart defects along with coarctation.

How does it affect the heart?

Coarctation obstructs blood flow from the heart to the lower part of the body. Blood pressure increases above the constriction. The blood pressure is much higher than normal in the left pumping chamber (left ventricle) and the heart must work harder to pump blood through the constriction in the aorta. This can cause thickening (hypertrophy) and damage to the overworked heart muscle.

How does the coarctation affect my child?

Usually no symptoms exist at birth, but they can develop as early as the first week after birth. A baby may develop congestive heart failure or high blood pressure.

What can be done about the coarctation?

The coarctation obstruction can be relieved using surgery or catheterization.

During cardiac catheterization a special catheter containing a balloon is placed in the constricted area. Then the balloon is inflated for a short time, stretching the constricted area open. The balloon and catheter are then removed.

Surgery is often used to repair coarctation. A surgeon doesn't have to open the heart to repair the coarctation. It can be fixed in several ways. One way is for the surgeon to remove the narrowed segment of aorta. Another option is to sew a patch over the narrowed section using part of the blood vessel to the arm or a graft of synthetic material.

An infant with a severe coarctation should have a procedure to relieve the obstruction. This may relieve heart failure in infancy and prevent problems later, such as developing high blood pressure as an adult because of the coarctation.

What activities can my child do?

If the coarctation has been repaired and there is no important left-over obstruction or high blood pressure, your child may not need any special precautions regarding physical activity, and may be able to participate in normal activities without increased risk.

Some children with obstruction, hypertension, heart muscle abnormalities, or other heart defects may have to limit their physical activity. Check with your child's pediatric cardiologist about this.

What will my child need in the future?

The outlook after surgery is favorable, but long-term follow-up by a pediatric cardiologist is needed. Rarely, coarctation of the aorta may recur. Then another procedure to relieve the obstruction may be needed. Also, blood pressure may stay high even when the aorta's narrowing has been repaired.

What about preventing endocarditis?

Children with coarctation of the aorta may risk developing endocarditis. Your child's cardiologist may recommend that your child receive antibiotics before certain dental procedures for a period of time after coarctation repair.

Section 29.4

Ebstein Anomaly

What is it?

A malformed heart valve that does not properly close to keep the blood flow moving in the right direction. Blood may leak back from the lower to upper chambers on the right side of the heart. This syndrome also is commonly seen with an atrial septal defect, or ASD (or a hole in the wall dividing the two upper chambers of the heart).

Can it be repaired?

Ebstein anomaly is mild in many children that they don't need surgery. But sometimes the tricuspid valve leaks severely enough to result in heart failure or cyanosis. Then surgery may be required.

Several different operations have been used in patients with Ebstein anomaly. The most common involves a repair of the tricuspid valve. The valve can't be made normal, but often surgery significantly reduces the amount of leaking. If there's an ASD, it's usually closed at the same time. In some cases the tricuspid valve can't be adequately repaired. Then it's replaced with an artificial valve.

What ongoing care will my child need?

Children with Ebstein anomaly should receive continued care from a pediatric cardiologist. Besides getting information from routine exams, the cardiologist may use tests such as electrocardiograms, Holter monitor, and echocardiograms.

What activities will my child be able to do?

If valve leakage is mild and tests show no abnormal heart rhythms, your child can usually participate in most sports. Your cardiologist may recommend avoiding certain intense competitive sports. Ask your child's cardiologist which activities are appropriate.

What problems might my child have?

Children with Ebstein anomaly may have a rapid heart rhythm called supraventricular tachycardia (SVT) often as a result of a condition called Wolf-Parkinson-White syndrome (WPW). An episode of SVT may cause palpitations (older children may feel their heart racing). Sometimes this is associated with fainting, dizziness, lightheadedness, or chest discomfort. Infants may be unusually fussy or have other symptoms that can't easily be connected with rapid heart rhythm. If your child has had these symptoms, contact your doctor. If your symptoms persist, seek immediate attention. Recurrent SVT may be prevented with medicines. In many cases, the source of the abnormal heart rhythm may be removed by a catheter procedure called radiofrequency ablation.

If the valve abnormality is especially severe, you may have decreased stamina, fatigue, cyanosis, and sometimes fluid retention. Infants may not feed or grow normally. The symptoms may respond to medicines such as diuretics. In some instances surgery (described above) may be recommended.

What about preventing endocarditis?

People with unrepaired or incompletely repaired Ebstein anomaly are at risk for endocarditis. Ask your pediatric cardiologist about your child's need to take antibiotics before certain dental procedures to help prevent endocarditis.

Section 29.5

Hypoplastic
Left Heart Syndrome

"Facts about Hypoplastic Left Heart Syndrome," Centers for Disease Control and Prevention, September 6, 2011.

Hypoplastic left heart syndrome (HLHS) is a birth defect that affects normal blood flow through the heart. As the baby develops during pregnancy, the left side of the heart does not form correctly. Hypoplastic left heart syndrome is one type of congenital heart defect. Congenital means present at birth.

Hypoplastic left heart syndrome affects a number of structures on the left side of the heart that do not fully develop, for example:

- The left ventricle is underdeveloped and too small.

- The mitral valve is not formed or is very small.

- The aortic valve is not formed or is very small.

- The ascending portion of the aorta is underdeveloped or is too small.

- Often, babies with hypoplastic left heart syndrome also have an atrial septal defect, which is a hole between the left and right upper chambers (atria) of the heart.

In a baby without a congenital heart defect, the right side of the heart pumps oxygen-poor blood from the heart to the lungs. The left side of the heart pumps oxygen-rich blood to the rest of the body. When a baby is growing in a mother's womb during pregnancy, there are two small openings between the left and right sides of the heart: the patent ductus arteriosus and the patent foramen ovale. Normally, these openings will close a few days after birth.

In babies with hypoplastic left heart syndrome, the left side of the heart cannot pump oxygen-rich blood to the body properly. During the first few days of life for a baby with hypoplastic left heart syndrome, the oxygen-rich blood bypasses the poorly functioning left side of the heart through the patent ductus arteriosus and the patent foramen ovale. The right side of the heart then pumps blood to both the lungs and the rest of the body. However, among babies with hypoplastic left heart syndrome, when these openings close, it becomes hard for oxygen-rich blood to get to the rest of the body.

Causes and Risk Factors

The causes of heart defects such as hypoplastic left heart syndrome among most babies are unknown. Some babies have heart defects because of changes in their genes or chromosomes. These types of heart defects also are thought to be caused by a combination of genes and other risk factors, such as things the mother comes in contact with in the environment or what the mother eats or drinks or the medicines the mother uses.

Diagnosis

Hypoplastic left heart syndrome may be diagnosed during pregnancy or soon after the baby is born.

During Pregnancy

During pregnancy, there are screening tests (also called prenatal tests) to check for birth defects and other conditions. Hypoplastic left heart syndrome may be diagnosed during pregnancy with an ultrasound (which creates pictures of the body). Some findings from the ultrasound may make the health care provider suspect a baby may have hypoplastic left heart syndrome. If so, the health care provider can request a fetal echocardiogram to confirm the diagnosis. A fetal echocardiogram is an ultrasound of the heart of the fetus. This test can show problems with the structure of the heart and how the heart is working with this defect.

After the Baby Is Born

Babies with hypoplastic left heart syndrome might not have trouble for the first few days of life while the patent ductus arteriosus and the patent foramen ovale (the normal openings in the heart) are open, but quickly develop signs after these openings are closed, including the following:

- Problems breathing

- Pounding heart

- Weak pulse

- Ashen or bluish skin color

During a physical examination, a doctor can see these signs or might hear a heart murmur (an abnormal whooshing sound caused by blood not flowing properly). If a murmur is heard or other signs are present, the health care provider might request one or more tests to make a diagnosis, the most common being an echocardiogram. Echocardiography also is useful for helping the health care provider follow the child's health over time.

Treatments

Treatments for some health problems associated with hypoplastic left heart syndrome might include medicines, nutrition, or surgery.

Medicines

Some babies and children will need medicines to help strengthen the heart muscle, lower their blood pressure, and help the body get rid of extra fluid.

Nutrition

Some babies with hypoplastic left heart syndrome become tired while feeding and do not eat enough to gain weight. To make sure babies have a healthy weight gain, a special high-calorie formula might be prescribed. Some babies become extremely tired while feeding and might need to be fed through a feeding tube.

Surgery

Soon after a baby with hypoplastic left heart syndrome is born, multiple surgeries done in a particular order are needed to increase blood flow to the body and bypass the poorly functioning left side of the heart. The right ventricle becomes the main pumping chamber to the body. These surgeries do not cure hypoplastic left heart syndrome, but help restore heart function. Sometimes medicines are given to help treat symptoms of the defect before or after surgery. Surgery for hypoplastic left heart syndrome usually is done in three separate stages.

Norwood procedure: This surgery usually is done within the first two weeks of a baby's life. Surgeons create a "new" aorta and connect it to the right ventricle. They also place a tube from either the aorta or the right ventricle to the vessels supplying the lungs (pulmonary arteries). Thus, the right ventricle can pump blood to both the lungs and the rest of the body. This can be a very challenging surgery. After this procedure, an infant's skin still might look bluish because oxygen-rich and oxygen-poor blood still mix in the heart.

Bi-directional Glenn shunt procedure: This usually is performed when an infant is four to six months of age. This procedure creates a direct connection between the pulmonary artery and the vessel (the superior vena cava) returning oxygen-poor blood from the upper part of the body to the heart. This reduces the work the right ventricle has to do by allowing blood returning from the body to flow directly to the lungs.

Fontan procedure: This procedure usually is done sometime during the period when an infant is eighteen months to three years of age. Doctors connect the pulmonary artery and the vessel (the inferior vena cava) returning oxygen-poor blood from the lower part of the body to the heart, allowing the rest of the blood coming back from the body to go to the lungs. Once this procedure is complete, oxygen-rich and oxygen-poor blood no longer mix in the heart and an infant's skin will no longer look bluish.

Infants who have these surgeries are not cured; they may have lifelong complications.

Infants with hypoplastic left heart syndrome will need regular follow-up visits with a cardiologist (a heart doctor) to monitor their progress. If the hypoplastic left heart syndrome defect is very complex, or the heart becomes weak after the surgeries, a heart transplant may be needed. Infants who receive a heart transplant will need to take medicines for the rest of their lives to prevent their body from rejecting the new heart.

Section 29. 6

Patent Ductus Arteriosus

What is it?

An unclosed hole in the aorta.

Before a baby is born, the fetus's blood does not need to go to the lungs to get oxygenated. The ductus arteriosus is a hole that allows the blood to skip the circulation to the lungs. However, when the baby is born, the blood must receive oxygen in the lungs and this hole is supposed to close. If the ductus arteriosus is still open (or patent) the blood may skip this necessary step of circulation. The open hole is called the patent ductus arteriosus (PDA).

What causes it?

The ductus arteriosus is a normal fetal artery connecting the main body artery (aorta) and the main lung artery (pulmonary artery). The ductus allows blood to detour away from the lungs before birth.

Every baby is born with a ductus arteriosus. After birth, the opening is no longer needed and it usually narrows and closes within the first few days.

Sometimes, the ductus doesn't close after birth. Failure of the ductus to close is common in premature infants but rare in full-term babies. In most children, the cause of PDA isn't known. Some children can have other heart defects along with the PDA.

How does it affect the heart?

Normally the heart's left side only pumps blood to the body, and the right side only pumps blood to the lungs. In a child with PDA, extra blood gets pumped from the body artery (aorta) into the lung (pulmonary) arteries. If the PDA is large, the extra blood being pumped into the lung arteries makes the heart and lungs work harder and the lungs can become congested.

How does the PDA affect my child?

If the PDA is small, it won't cause symptoms because the heart and lungs don't have to work harder. The only abnormal finding may be a distinctive type of murmur (noise heard with a stethoscope).

If the PDA is large, the child may breathe faster and harder than normal. Infants may have trouble feeding and growing at a normal rate. Symptoms may not occur until several weeks after birth. High pressure may occur in the blood vessels in the lungs because more blood than normal is being pumped there. Over time this may cause permanent damage to the lung blood vessels.

What can be done about the PDA?

If the PDA (ductus) is small, it doesn't make the heart and lungs work harder. Surgery and other treatments may not be needed. Small PDAs often close on their own within the first few months of life.

Most children can have the PDA closed by inserting catheters (long thin tubes) into the blood vessels in the leg to reach the heart and the PDA, and a coil or other device can be inserted through the catheters into the PDA like a plug. If surgery is needed, an incision is made in the left side of the chest, between the ribs. The ductus is closed by tying it with suture (thread-like material) or by permanently placing a small metal clip around the ductus to squeeze it closed. If there's no other heart defect, this restores the child's circulation to normal. In premature newborn babies, medicine can often help the ductus close. After the first few weeks of life, medicine won't work as well to close the ductus and surgery may be required.

What activities can my child do?

If the PDA is small, or if it has been closed with catheterization or surgery, your child may not need any special precautions regarding physical activity and may be able to participate in normal activities without increased risk.

As far as follow-up in the future, depending on the type of PDA closure, your child's pediatric cardiologist may examine it periodically to look for uncommon problems. The long-term outlook is excellent, and usually no medicines and no additional surgery or catheterization are needed.

Section 29.7

Pulmonary Atresia

Pulmonary atresia is a heart defect in which a valve on the right side of the heart, called the pulmonary valve, does not form. Without this valve, blood can't flow from the right side of the heart to the pulmonary artery and on to the lungs to become oxygenated. This isn't a problem before birth because the fetus relies on oxygenated blood from the mother to live, rather than the lungs.

The heart consists of four chambers: the two upper chambers, called atria, where blood enters the heart, and the two lower chambers, called ventricles, where blood is pumped out of the heart. The flow between the chambers is controlled by a set of valves that act as one-way doors.

Normally blood is pumped from the right ventricle through the pulmonary valve and the pulmonary artery to the lungs, where the blood is filled with oxygen. From the lungs, the blood travels back down to the left atrium and left ventricle. The newly oxygenated blood is then pumped through another big blood vessel, called the aorta, to the rest of the body.

While a baby is in the womb, a temporary blood vessel called the patent ductus arteriosus (PDA) is open and connects the pulmonary artery and the aorta.

In pulmonary atresia, because there is no way for blood to leave the right ventricle; blood that enters the right atrium passes across an opening into the left side of the heart, which pumps it into the aorta. The only way that blood can reach the lungs is through the PDA.

Babies with pulmonary atresia have reduced oxygen in their blood, a condition called hypoxia. They often have a small right ventricle as well.

Signs and Symptoms

Babies with pulmonary atresia may turn blue, a condition called cyanosis; pulmonary atresia may also be called "blue baby syndrome." Other symptoms include:

- difficult or rapid breathing;
- lethargy;
- cool sweat.

Diagnosis

Blueness is always a sign of a problem. Your baby's doctor may also notice a heart murmur, an extra noise that occurs during the heartbeat. Tests used to diagnose pulmonary atresia include:

- chest x-ray;
- electrocardiogram (ECG or EKG);
- echocardiogram;
- catheter procedures to determine pressure and oxygen in the heart

Treatment

Initial treatment is a medication, given intravenously, called prostaglandin E-1 to keep the patent ductus arteriosus (PDA) from closing. This allows blood to flow between the pulmonary artery and aorta, thereby bypassing the valve and heart. But this only works temporarily. Your child may also be placed on a ventilator or oxygen to improve respiration.

Immediate surgery usually is necessary to increase blood flow to the lungs. Surgeons create a passageway by inserting a tiny piece of tubing called a shunt between the pulmonary artery and the aorta to increase flow to the lungs. Later, after the first year of life when the baby's lungs have developed more, a second operation called a Fontan procedure may be performed. It connects the right atrium, where deoxygenated blood collects from the body, directly to the pulmonary artery by creating a channel through or just outside the heart to bypass the undeveloped pulmonary valve.

Long-term treatment may include drugs to control heart rhythm disturbances and antibiotics to prevent infection during other surgery or dental procedures.

Section 29.8

Pulmonary Valve Stenosis

"Pulmonary Valve Stenosis," reprinted with permission from
www.heart.org. Copyright 2012 American Heart Association, Inc.

What is it?

A thickened or fused heart valve that does not fully open. The pulmonary valve allows blood to flow out of the heart, into the pulmonary artery and then to the lungs.

What causes it?

In most children, the cause isn't known. It's a common type of heart defect. Some children can have other heart defects along with pulmonary stenosis (PS).

How does it affect the heart?

Normally the right side of the heart pumps blood to the lungs. In a child with PS, the pressure is much higher than normal in the right pumping chamber (right ventricle) and the heart must work harder to pump blood out into the lung arteries. Over time this can cause damage to the overworked heart muscle.

How does the PS affect my child?

If the stenosis is severe, especially in babies, some cyanosis (blueness) may occur. Older children usually have no symptoms.

What can be done about the pulmonary valve?

The pulmonary valve can be treated to improve the obstruction and leak, but the valve can't be made normal.

Treatment is needed when the pressure in the right ventricle is high (even though there may be no symptoms). In most children the obstruction can be relieved during cardiac catheterization by balloon valvuloplasty. In this procedure, a special tool, a catheter containing a balloon, is placed across the pulmonary valve. The balloon is inflated for a short time to stretch open the valve. Some children may need surgery.

What activities can my child do?

If the obstruction is mild, or if the PS obstruction has mostly been relieved with a balloon or surgery, your child may not need any special precautions regarding physical activities, and can participate in normal activities without increased risk.

What will my child need in the future?

The long-term outlook after balloon valvuloplasty or surgery is excellent, and usually no medicines and no additional surgery are needed. Your child's pediatric cardiologist will examine your child periodically to look for uncommon problems such as worsening of the obstruction again.

What about preventing endocarditis?

Ask about your child's risk of developing endocarditis. Children who have had pulmonary valve replacement will need to receive antibiotics before certain dental procedures.

Section 29.9

Tetralogy of Fallot

Excerpted from "Facts about Tetralogy of Fallot,"
Centers for Disease Control and Prevention, March 29, 2012.

Tetralogy of Fallot is a birth defect that affects normal blood flow through the heart. It happens when a baby's heart does not form correctly as the baby grows and develops in the mother's womb during pregnancy. It is a congenital defect, meaning the baby is born with it. Tetralogy of Fallot is made up of the following four defects of the heart and its blood vessels:

1. A hole in the wall between the two lower chambers—or ventricles—of the heart. This condition also is called a ventricular septal defect.

2. A narrowing of the pulmonary valve and main pulmonary artery. This condition also is called pulmonary stenosis.

3. The aortic valve, which opens to the aorta, is enlarged and seems to open from both ventricles, rather than from the left ventricle only, as in a normal heart. In this defect, the aortic valve sits directly on top of the ventricular septal defect.

4. The muscular wall of the lower right chamber of the heart (right ventricle) is thicker than normal. This also is called ventricular hypertrophy.

This heart defect can cause oxygen in the blood that flows to the rest of the body to be reduced. Infants with tetralogy of Fallot can have a bluish-looking skin color called cyanosis because their blood doesn't carry enough oxygen. At birth, infants might not have blue-looking skin, but later might develop sudden episodes of bluish skin during crying or feeding. These episodes are called tet spells. Infants with tetralogy of Fallot or other conditions causing cyanosis can have problems including the following:

- A higher risk of getting an infection of the layers of the heart, called endocarditis

- A higher risk of having irregular heart rhythms, called arrhythmia

- Dizziness, fainting, or seizures, because of the low oxygen levels in their blood

- Delayed growth and development

Causes and Risk Factors

The causes of heart defects (such as tetralogy of Fallot) among most babies are unknown. Some babies have heart defects because of changes in their genes or chromosomes. Heart defects such as tetralogy of Fallot also are thought to be caused by a combination of genes and other risk factors, such as the things the mother or fetus come in contact with in the environment or what the mother eats or drinks or the medicines she uses.

Diagnosis

Tetralogy of Fallot may be diagnosed during pregnancy or soon after a baby is born.

During Pregnancy

During pregnancy, there are screening tests (also called prenatal tests) to check for birth defects and other conditions. Tetralogy of Fallot might be seen during an ultrasound (which creates pictures of the body). Some findings from the ultrasound may make the health care provider suspect a baby may have tetralogy of Fallot. If so, the health care provider can request a fetal echocardiogram to confirm the diagnosis. A fetal echocardiogram is an ultrasound of the heart of the fetus. This test can show problems with the structure of the heart and how the heart is working with this defect.

After a Baby Is Born

Tetralogy of Fallot usually is diagnosed after a baby is born, often after the infant has an episode of turning blue during crying or feeding (a tet spell). Some findings on a physical exam may make the health care provider think a baby may have tetralogy of Fallot, including bluish-looking skin or a heart murmur (a "whooshing" sound caused by blood not flowing properly through the heart). The health care provider can request one or more tests to confirm the diagnosis. The most common test is an echocardiogram. An echocardiogram is an ultrasound of the heart that can show problems with the structure of the heart and how the heart is working (or not) with this defect. Echocardiography also is useful for helping the doctor follow the child's health over time.

Treatments

Tetralogy of Fallot can be treated by surgery soon after the baby is born. During surgery, doctors widen or replace the pulmonary valve and enlarge the passage to the pulmonary artery. They also will place a patch over the ventricular septal defect to close the hole between the two lower chambers of the heart. These actions will improve blood flow to the lungs and the rest of the body. Most infants will live active, healthy lives after surgery. However, they will need regular follow-up visits with a cardiologist (a heart doctor) to monitor their progress and check for other health conditions that might develop as they get older. As adults, they may need more surgery or medical care for other possible problems.

Section 29.10

Transposition of the Great Arteries

Excerpted from "Facts about Transposition of the Great Arteries,"
Centers for Disease Control and Prevention, September 6, 2011.

Transposition of the great arteries (TGA) is a heart condition that is present at birth, and often is called a congenital heart defect. TGA occurs when the two main arteries going out of the heart—the pulmonary artery and the aorta—are switched in position, or "transposed."

Normally, blood returning to the heart from the body is pumped from the right side of the heart through the pulmonary artery to the lungs. There, it receives oxygen and returns to the left side of the heart. Then, the oxygen-rich blood is pumped from the left side of the heart through the aorta to the body. In TGA, blood returning from the body bypasses the lungs and is pumped back out to the body. This occurs because the main connections are reversed. The pulmonary artery, which normally carries oxygen-poor blood from the right side of the heart to the lungs, now arises from the left side and carries oxygen-rich blood returning from the lungs back to the lungs. The aorta, which normally carries blood from the left side of the heart to the body, now arises from the right side and carries oxygen-poor blood back out to the body. The result of transposition of these two vessels is that too little oxygen is in the blood that is pumped from the heart to the rest of the body.

What We Know about Transposition of the Great Arteries

What Problems Do Children with Transposition of the Great Arteries Have?

Because the main arteries are switched, there are two separate blood circulations instead of a single connected one. Thus, blood with oxygen from the lungs does not get to the rest of the body. This means that TGA is a cyanotic (lacking oxygen) heart defect that leads to a bluish-purple coloring of the skin and shortness of breath.

Symptoms appear at birth or very soon afterwards. How bad the symptoms are depends on whether there is a way for the two separate blood circuits to mix, allowing some oxygen-rich blood to get out to the body. This mixing can occur through other defects, such as a hole between the bottom chambers of the heart (a ventricular septal defect), or through a shunt that normally is present at birth. Symptoms also can depend on whether other defects are present as well. Common symptoms of TGA include the following:

- Blueness of the skin

- Shortness of breath

- Poor feeding

Surgery might be needed shortly after birth. In most hospitals, a type of surgery called an arterial switch procedure can be used to permanently correct the problem within the first week of life.

Without corrective surgery, severe cases of TGA can be fatal during the first six months of life. Babies who have surgery to correct TGA sometimes have the following associated conditions later in life:

- Leaky heart valves

- Problems with the arteries that supply the heart muscle with blood (coronary arteries)

- Abnormal heart rhythm (arrhythmias)

- A decline in function of the heart muscle or heart valves

- Heart failure

- Damage to the lungs and difficulty breathing

Babies with TGA will require lifelong follow-up with a cardiologist. Even so, with proper treatment, most babies with TGA grow up to lead healthy, productive lives.

What We Still Do Not Know about Transposition of the Great Arteries

What Causes Transposition of the Great Arteries?

The cause of TGA is unknown at this time. Scientific researchers have found that some diseases and behaviors might be associated with a higher risk for TGA. These include the following:

451

- The mother having a viral illness during pregnancy

- The mother having poor nutrition during pregnancy

- The mother using an excessive amount of alcohol during pregnancy

- The mother being older than forty years of age

- The mother having diabetes during pregnancy

- The baby having Down syndrome

Can Transposition of the Great Arteries Be Prevented?

There is no known way to prevent this defect, but some of the problems experienced later in life by babies born with TGA can be prevented or lessened if the defect is found early.

Even so, mothers can take steps before and during pregnancy to have a healthy pregnancy. Steps include taking a daily multivitamin with folic acid (400 micrograms), not smoking, and not drinking alcohol during pregnancy.

Section 29.11

Vascular Ring

Vascular ring is an abnormal formation of the aorta, the large artery that carries blood from the heart to the rest of the body. It is a congenital problem, which means it is present at birth.

Causes

Vascular ring is rare. It accounts for less than 1 percent of all congenital heart problems. The condition occurs as often in males as females. Some infants with vascular ring also have another congenital heart problem.

Vascular ring occurs very early in the baby's development in the womb. Normally, the aorta develops from one of several curved pieces of tissue (arches). The body breaks down some of the remaining arches, while others form into arteries. Some arteries that should break down do not; this forms vascular rings.

With vascular ring, some of the arches and vessels that should have changed into arteries or disappeared are still present when the baby is born. These arches form a ring of blood vessels, which encircles and presses down on the windpipe (trachea) and esophagus.

Several different types of vascular ring exist. In some types, the vascular ring only partially encircles the trachea and esophagus, but it still can cause symptoms.

Symptoms

Some children with a vascular ring never develop symptoms. However, in most cases, symptoms are seen during infancy. Pressure on the windpipe (trachea) and esophagus can lead to breathing and digestive problems. The more the ring presses down, the more severe the symptoms will be.

Breathing problems may include:

- high-pitched cough;
- loud breathing (stridor);
- repeated pneumonias or respiratory infections;
- respiratory distress;
- wheezing.

Eating may make breathing symptoms worse. Digestive symptoms are rare, but may include:

- choking;
- difficulty eating solid foods;
- difficulty swallowing (dysphagia);
- gastroesophageal reflux (GERD);
- slow breast or bottle feeding;
- vomiting.

Exams and Tests

The doctor will listen to the baby's breathing to rule out other breathing disorders such as asthma. Listening to the child's heart through a stethoscope can help identify murmurs and other heart problems.

The following tests can help diagnose vascular ring:

- Chest x-ray
- Computed tomography (CT) scan of the heart
- Camera down the throat to examine the airways (bronchoscopy)
- Magnetic resonance imaging (MRI) of the heart
- Ultrasound examination (echocardiogram) of heart
- X-ray of blood vessels (angiography)
- X-ray of the esophagus using a special dye to better highlight the area (esophagram or barium swallow)

Treatment

Surgery is usually performed as soon as possible on children with symptoms. The goal of surgery is to split the vascular ring and relieve pressure on the surrounding structures. The surgery is not very invasive. The procedure is usually done through a small surgical cut in the left side of the chest between the ribs.

Changing the child's diet may help relieve the digestive symptoms of vascular ring. The doctor will prescribe medications (such as antibiotics) to treat any respiratory tract infections, if they occur.

Children who don't have symptoms may not need treatment, but should be carefully watched to make sure the condition doesn't become worse.

Outlook (Prognosis)

How well the infant does depends on how much pressure the vascular ring is putting on the esophagus and trachea and how quickly the infant is diagnosed and treated.

Surgery works well in most cases and often relieves symptoms right away. Severe breathing problems may take months to go away. Some children may continue to have loud breathing, especially when they are very active or have respiratory infections.

Possible Complications

Delaying surgery can lead to serious complications such as damage to the trachea and even death.

Section 29.12

Ventricular Septal Defect

Excerpted from "Facts about Ventricular Septal Defect,"
Centers for Disease Control and Prevention, March 17, 2011.

A ventricular septal defect (VSD) is a birth defect of the heart in which there is a hole in the wall (septum) that separates the two lower chambers (ventricles) of the heart. This wall also is called the ventricular septum. A ventricular septal defect happens during pregnancy if the wall that forms between the two ventricles does not fully develop, leaving a hole.

An infant with a ventricular septal defect can have one or more holes in different places of the septum. There are several names for these holes. Some common locations and names are as follows:

- **Conoventricular ventricular septal defect:** In general, this is a hole where portions of the ventricular septum should meet just below the pulmonary and aortic valves.

- **Perimembranous ventricular septal defect:** This is a hole in the upper section of the ventricular septum.

- **Inlet ventricular septal defect:** This is a hole in the septum near to where the blood enters the ventricles through the tricuspid and mitral valves. This type of ventricular septal defect also might be part of another heart defect called an atrioventricular septal defect (AVSD).

- **Muscular ventricular septal defect:** This is a hole in the lower, muscular part of the ventricular septum and is the most common type of ventricular septal defect.

In a baby without a congenital heart defect, the right side of the heart pumps oxygen-poor blood from the heart to the lungs, and the left side of the heart pumps oxygen-rich blood to the rest of the body.

In babies with a ventricular septal defect, blood often flows from the left ventricle through the ventricular septal defect to the right ventricle and into the lungs. This extra blood being pumped into the lungs forces the heart and lungs to work harder. Over time, if not repaired, this defect can increase the risk for other complications, including heart failure, high blood pressure in the lungs (called pulmonary hypertension), irregular heart rhythms (called arrhythmia), or stroke.

Causes and Risk Factors

The causes of heart defects (such as a ventricular septal defect) among most babies are unknown. Some babies have heart defects because of changes in their genes or chromosomes. Heart defects also are thought to be caused by a combination of genes and other risk factors, such as the things the mother comes in contact with in the environment or what the mother eats or drinks or the medicines the mother uses.

Diagnosis

A ventricular septal defect usually is diagnosed after a baby is born. The size of the ventricular septal defect will influence what symptoms, if any, are present, and whether a doctor hears a heart murmur during a physical examination. Signs of a ventricular septal defect might be present at birth or might not appear until well after birth. If the hole is small, it usually will close on its own and the baby might not show any signs of the defect. However, if the hole is large, the baby might have symptoms, including the following:

- Shortness of breath
- Fast or heavy breathing
- Sweating
- Tiredness while feeding
- Poor weight gain

During a physical examination the doctor might hear a distinct whooshing sound, called a heart murmur. If the doctor hears a heart murmur or other signs are present, the doctor can request one or more tests to confirm the diagnosis. The most common test is an echocardiogram, which is an ultrasound of the heart that can show problems with the structure of the heart, show how large the hole is, and show how much blood is flowing through the hole.

Treatments

Treatments for symptoms associated with ventricular septal defect can include the following.

Medicines

Some children will need medicines to help strengthen the heart muscle, lower their blood pressure, and help the body get rid of extra fluid.

Nutrition

Some babies with a ventricular septal defect become tired while feeding and do not eat enough to gain weight. To make sure babies have a healthy weight gain, a special high-calorie formula might be prescribed. Some babies become extremely tired while feeding and might need to be fed through a feeding tube.

Treatments for this type of defect depend on the size of the hole and the problems it might cause. Many ventricular septal defects are small and close on their own; if the hole is small and not causing any symptoms, the doctor will check the infant regularly to ensure there are no signs of heart failure and that the hole closes on its own. If the hole does not close on its own or if it is large, further actions might need to be taken. Depending on the size of the hole, symptoms, and general health of the child, the doctor might recommend either cardiac catheterization or open-heart surgery to close the hole and restore normal blood flow. After surgery, the doctor will set up regular follow-up visits to make sure that the ventricular septal defect remains closed. Most children who have a ventricular septal defect that closes (either on its own or with surgery) live healthy lives.

Chapter 30

Kidney Defects

Chapter Contents

Section 30.1

Ectopic Kidneys

Most people are born with two kidneys, which are located in the
back of the abdominal cavity on either side of the body, covered by the
ribs. But factors can occasionally interfere with the development of the
kidneys, as is the case for people with ectopic kidneys. The following
information will help you talk to your urologist when your condition,
or that of your child, belongs to this family of diseases.

What happens under normal conditions?

The kidney is the organ whose principal function is to filter toxins
from the blood and maintain an appropriate chemical environment
so that the body's other organ systems can function properly. Other
functions that the kidneys serve include maintaining appropriate blood
pressure and ensuring that enough red blood cells are produced by the
bone marrow. As a child develops in its mother's uterus, the kidneys
are formed lower in the abdomen and gradually ascend to their final
position as they develop.

What is an ectopic kidney?

Renal ectopia or ectopic kidney describes a kidney that is not located in its usual position. Ectopic kidneys are thought to occur in
approximately one in one thousand births, but only about one in ten
of these are ever diagnosed. Some of these are discovered incidentally, such as when a child or adult is having surgery or an x-ray for a
medical condition unrelated to the renal ectopia. Ectopic kidneys can
be located anywhere along the path of their usual ascent from where
they initially form to where normal kidneys lie in the upper abdomen.
Simple renal ectopia refers to a kidney that is located on the proper
side but is in an abnormal position. Crossed renal ectopia refers to a
kidney that has crossed from the left to the right side (or vice versa)
so that both kidneys are located on the same side of the body. These

kidneys may or may not be fused. It is important to note that renal ectopia is frequently associated with congenital abnormalities of other organ systems.

What are the symptoms of an ectopic kidney?

The function of the kidney itself is generally not abnormal to begin with, but because of the change in the usual anatomic relationships, the kidney may have difficulty draining. Up to 50 percent of ectopic kidneys are at least partially blocked. Over time, obstruction can lead to serious complications, including urinary tract infections, kidney stones, and kidney failure. Ectopic kidneys are also associated with vesicoureteral reflux (VUR), a condition where urine backs up from the bladder through the ureters into the kidneys. Over time, VUR can lead to infections that also can destroy the kidney. Interestingly, the non-ectopic kidney can also have functional abnormalities such as obstruction or VUR.

The most common symptoms related to the ectopic kidney that lead to diagnosis include urinary tract infections, abdominal pain, or a lump that can be felt in the abdomen.

What are some treatment options for ectopic kidney?

Treatment for the ectopic kidney is only necessary if obstruction or vesicoureteral reflux (VUR) is present. If the kidney is not severely damaged by the time the abnormality is discovered, the obstruction can be relieved or the VUR corrected with an operation. However, if the kidney is badly scarred and not working well, removing it may be the best choice.

What can I expect after treatment for ectopic kidney?

It is possible to live a normal life after removal of a kidney, provided that the remaining kidney functions well.

Section 30.2

Horseshoe Kidney (Renal Fusion)

What is horseshoe kidney?

Horseshoe kidney occurs in about one in five hundred children. It occurs during fetal development as the kidneys move into their normal position. With horseshoe kidney, however, as the kidneys of the fetus rise from the pelvic area, they fuse together at the lower end or base. By fusing, they form a "U" shape, which gives it the name "horseshoe." It is believed that this condition exists more frequently in males.

What are the symptoms of a horseshoe kidney?

Horseshoe kidneys are much more frequently symptomatic than other varieties of fused and ectopic kidneys. Up to 70 percent of children and adults with this abnormality will have symptoms, which can include abdominal pain, nausea, kidney stones, and urinary tract infections. Although still rare, cancerous tumors are somewhat more likely to occur in horseshoe kidneys than in normal kidneys. Blood in the urine, a mass in the abdomen, and flank pain can be symptoms of a kidney tumor.

How is horseshoe kidney treated?

In a child without symptoms, treatment may not be necessary. If your child has complications, they may require supportive treatment, which means their symptoms will be treated, but there is no cure for the condition. As with ectopic kidneys, obstruction and vesicoureteral reflux are very common in these patients and may require surgical correction.

What can be expected after treatment for horseshoe kidney?

It is important to note that if the patient's only complaint from the horseshoe kidney is pain, surgery frequently will not relieve the pain.

Section 30.3

Hydronephrosis

What is hydronephrosis?

Hydronephrosis is the dilation or stretching of the kidneys that occurs when there is an obstruction to the flow of urine at some point along the urinary tract. Normally, urine flows from the kidneys through the ureters and into the bladder. If there is a blockage that prevents the urine from draining properly, urine can back up in the kidneys and hydronephrosis occurs.

What are the signs and symptoms?

Children with mild hydronephrosis may have no symptoms at all, or the condition may improve or disappear within the first year of life. In more severe cases, when the kidneys are affected, symptoms may include pain with urination, hematuria (blood in the urine), and infection. Symptoms may not occur until months or years after the hydronephrosis has been detected.

How do you diagnose it?

Hydronephrosis can be detected prebirth through a routine prenatal ultrasound. Hydronephrosis is not a diagnosis; it is a finding that indicates an obstruction. Once the cause of the obstruction is decided, the appropriate treatment will be determined.

If hydronephrosis is discovered after birth, or if a child develops hydronephrosis, the underlying cause of the obstruction will need to be determined by utilizing one or more of the following tests, depending on the severity of the condition:

- Voiding cystourethrogram (VCUG)

- Renal ultrasound (RUS)

- Renal Scan (mercaptoacetyltriglycine [MAG 3] with Lasix)

- Intravenous pyelogram (IVP)

At some point, your child's hydronephrosis will be classified as mild, moderate, or severe, unilateral (occurring in one kidney) or bilateral (occurring in both kidneys). Based on these classifications, a mode of treatment will be determined.

How is it treated?

Treatment of hydronephrosis varies depending on the cause and the severity of the condition. In mild cases caused by mild obstruction, the child may only need to be monitored with regular ultrasound scans, as the condition may improve or resolve on its own. In moderate to severe cases of hydronephrosis, treatment of severe unilateral hydronephrosis or severe bilateral hydronephrosis may include antibiotics with serial radiologic testing (scans).

Imaging studies are used to decide if surgical treatment is necessary. Surgery is usually necessary to correct the cause in severe unilateral or severe bilateral cases, but may be beneficial in some moderate cases as well.

Who gets it, and can it be prevented?

Most children with hydronephrosis are born with the condition, but occasionally it can occur during childhood. For example, it may develop because of a stone or injury to the urinary tract. Hydronephrosis is more common in males than in females.

There are many different kinds of urinary tract obstructions that can lead to hydronephrosis. The most common type is at the junction where the ureter joins the kidney, called the ureteropelvic junction. This blockage is caused by an abnormal narrowing of the ureter at this location. The next most common site of narrowing is where the ureter meets the bladder, called the ureterovesical junction.

Below are some conditions commonly associated with blockage of the kidneys:

- Ureteropelvic junction obstruction

- Vesicoureteral reflux

- Posterior urethral valves

- Ectopic ureter

- Ureterocele

Hydronephrosis cannot be prevented, but it may be prevented from worsening, depending on the degree of the condition.

When should I seek medical attention?

If your child experiences any of the symptoms described above, seek medical attention. If your child has already been diagnosed with hydronephrosis, it is important to continue regular follow-up appointments to evaluate if the condition is worsening or improving.

Section 30.4

Multicystic Dysplastic Kidney

What is multicystic dysplastic kidney (MCDK)?

Multicystic dysplastic kidney (MCDK) is the abnormal development of a kidney while in utero. Multiple cysts (sac-like structures) form in place of the healthy kidney and are said to resemble a "bunch of grapes." There is no function in the affected kidney. About 50 percent of the patients with MCDK have other urologic conditions affecting the other kidney (e.g., obstruction or reflux). MCDK more commonly occurs on the left side.

What are the symptoms and/or complications of MCDK?

Most children with a MCDK have no symptoms. If a child does have symptoms they might include:

- enlarged kidney;

- high blood pressure (rare and resolved after nephrectomy);

- renal disease and renal failure (only if opposite side has urinary problems).

How is MCDK diagnosed?

With the current use of prenatal ultrasound, MCDK is most often found prior to birth. Less often, the MCDK is found as an abdominal mass during physical exam.

With the diagnosis of MCDK, other possible causes of the abnormal kidney must be ruled out with other testing. Your physician will discuss the possibility of further testing with you.

What is the treatment for MCDK?

The affected kidney may need no treatment. If the child has one healthy kidney and has no symptoms, the child will be monitored periodically with a renal ultrasound, until the cystic kidney regresses or becomes undetectable with ultrasound. Removal of the cystic kidney may be considered if it causes pain, high blood pressure, shows abnormal and atypical changes on ultrasound, is quite large, or does not regress after a period of observation.

Oftentimes, the healthy kidney is screened for any defects such as a blockage or reflux. If there is something wrong, this allows the physician time to intervene quickly to in order to save the functioning kidney before it worsens.

What to expect for the future?

Most children that have MCDK and one normal functioning kidney lead normal healthy lives. The affected kidney frequently shrinks as the child matures and may be undetectable by imaging studies by the age of five. The important thing is to maintain the kidney function in the remaining kidney.

Children and adults with only one working kidney should have regular checkups for high blood pressure and evaluate kidney function.

Section 30.5

Renal Agenesis

What is renal agenesis?

Renal agenesis is the absence of one or both kidneys. It can be unilateral (one kidney absent) or bilateral (both kidneys absent). Normally, the kidneys filter and remove waste from the blood, form urine, and maintain blood pressure.

Approximately 1 out of every 550 babies born each year has unilateral renal agenesis. Babies with unilateral renal agenesis may have other associated birth defects (most commonly, involving the urinary system or genitals). If your child has unilateral renal agenesis, his or her doctor(s) will perform a thorough examination to identify any other birth defects which may be present. Most babies with unilateral renal agenesis lead normal lives; however, these individuals have an increased risk of kidney infections, kidney stones, hypertension (high blood pressure), and/or kidney failure.

Approximately 1 out of every 4,000 babies born each year have bilateral renal agenesis.

Babies with bilateral renal agenesis often have additional birth defects, including abnormalities of the urinary system, genitals, limbs (arms and legs), heart, and/or lungs. If both kidneys are absent, the baby cannot produce urine, which is necessary to form amniotic fluid (the fluid surrounding the baby in the womb). Amniotic fluid is needed for proper development of the baby's lungs; if amniotic fluid is not present, the baby's lungs cannot grow and mature properly. Since babies with bilateral renal agenesis have immature lungs, they have a higher risk of stillbirth and early death. Most babies with bilateral renal agenesis have a poor prognosis.

What causes renal agenesis?

Currently, the exact cause of renal agenesis is not known. Renal agenesis is thought to be a "multifactorial" condition, meaning that

467

multiple factors (including genetics and the environment) are necessary for renal agenesis to occur. There have also been reports of families with hereditary renal agenesis (multiple family members have renal agenesis).

How is renal agenesis treated?

For babies with bilateral renal agenesis, there is no treatment that can help produce amniotic fluid or help the lungs develop. Most babies with unilateral renal agenesis lead normal lives; any necessary treatment will depend on other birth defects that may be present. Your child's doctor(s) will discuss appropriate treatment options with you.

Chapter 31

Liver and Pancreatic Defects

Chapter Contents

Section 31.1

Biliary Atresia

Excerpted from "Biliary Atresia," National Institute of
Diabetes and Digestive and Kidney Diseases, August 1, 2012.

What is biliary atresia?

Biliary atresia is a life-threatening condition in infants in which
the bile ducts inside or outside the liver do not have normal openings.

Bile ducts in the liver, also called hepatic ducts, are tubes that
carry bile from the liver to the gallbladder for storage and to the small
intestine for use in digestion. Bile is a fluid made by the liver that
serves two main functions: carrying toxins and waste products out of
the body and helping the body digest fats and absorb the fat-soluble
vitamins A, D, E, and K.

With biliary atresia, bile becomes trapped, builds up, and damages
the liver. The damage leads to scarring, loss of liver tissue, and cirrhosis. Cirrhosis is a chronic, or long lasting, liver condition caused by
scar tissue and cell damage that makes it hard for the liver to remove
toxins from the blood. These toxins build up in the blood and the liver
slowly deteriorates and malfunctions. Without treatment, the liver
eventually fails and the infant needs a liver transplant to stay alive.

The two types of biliary atresia are fetal and perinatal. Fetal biliary atresia appears while the baby is in the womb. Perinatal biliary
atresia is much more common and does not become evident until two
to four weeks after birth. Some infants, particularly those with the
fetal form, also have birth defects in the heart, spleen, or intestines.

What are the symptoms of biliary atresia?

The first symptom of biliary atresia is jaundice—when the skin and
whites of the eyes turn yellow. Jaundice occurs when the liver does not
remove bilirubin, a reddish-yellow substance formed when hemoglobin
breaks down. Hemoglobin is an iron-rich protein that gives blood its
red color. Bilirubin is absorbed by the liver, processed, and released into
bile. Blockage of the bile ducts forces bilirubin to build up in the blood.

Other common symptoms of biliary atresia include the following:

- Dark urine, from the high levels of bilirubin in the blood spilling over into the urine

- Gray or white stools, from a lack of bilirubin reaching the intestines

- Slow weight gain and growth

What causes biliary atresia?

Biliary atresia likely has multiple causes, though none are yet proven. Biliary atresia is not an inherited disease, meaning it does not pass from parent to child.

Biliary atresia is most likely caused by an event in the womb or around the time of birth. Possible triggers of the event may include one or more of the following:

- A viral or bacterial infection after birth, such as cytomegalovirus, reovirus, or rotavirus

- An immune system problem, such as when the immune system attacks the liver or bile ducts for unknown reasons

- A genetic mutation, which is a permanent change in a gene's structure

- A problem during liver and bile duct development in the womb

- Exposure to toxic substances

How is biliary atresia diagnosed?

No single test can definitively diagnose biliary atresia, so a series of tests is needed. All infants who still have jaundice two to three weeks after birth, or who have gray or white stools two weeks after birth, should be checked for liver damage.

The health care provider may order some or all of the following tests to diagnose biliary atresia and rule out other causes of liver problems. If biliary atresia is still suspected after testing, the next step is diagnostic surgery for confirmation.

Blood test: A blood test involves drawing blood at a health care provider's office or commercial facility and sending the sample to a lab for analysis. High levels of bilirubin in the blood can indicate blocked bile ducts.

471

Abdominal x-rays: An x-ray is a picture created by using radiation and recorded on film or on a computer. The amount of radiation used is small. An x-ray is performed at a hospital or outpatient center by an x-ray technician, and the images are interpreted by a radiologist—a doctor who specializes in medical imaging. Anesthesia is not needed, but sedation may be used to keep infants still. The infant will lie on a table during the x-ray. The x-ray machine is positioned over the abdominal area. Abdominal x-rays are used to check for an enlarged liver and spleen.

Ultrasound: Ultrasound uses a device, called a transducer, that bounces safe, painless sound waves off organs to create an image of their structure. The procedure is performed in a health care provider's office, outpatient center, or hospital by a specially trained technician, and the images are interpreted by a radiologist. Anesthesia is not needed, but sedation may be used to keep the infant still. The images can show whether the liver or bile ducts are enlarged and whether tumors or cysts are blocking the flow of bile. An ultrasound cannot be used to diagnose biliary atresia, but it does help rule out other common causes of jaundice.

Liver scans: Liver scans are special x-rays that use chemicals to create an image of the liver and bile ducts. Liver scans are performed at a hospital or outpatient facility, usually by a nuclear medicine technician. The infant will usually receive general anesthesia or be sedated before the procedure. Hepatobiliary iminodiacetic acid scanning, a type of liver scan, uses injected radioactive dye to trace the path of bile in the body. The test can show if and where bile flow is blocked. Blockage is likely to be caused by biliary atresia.

Liver biopsy: A biopsy is a procedure that involves taking a piece of liver tissue for examination with a microscope. The biopsy is performed by a health care provider in a hospital with light sedation and local anesthetic. The health care provider uses imaging techniques such as ultrasound or a computerized tomography scan to guide the biopsy needle into the liver. The liver tissue is examined in a lab by a pathologist—a doctor who specializes in diagnosing diseases. A liver biopsy can show whether biliary atresia is likely. A biopsy can also help rule out other liver problems, such as hepatitis—an irritation of the liver that sometimes causes permanent damage.

Diagnostic surgery: During diagnostic surgery, a pediatric surgeon makes an incision, or cut, in the abdomen to directly examine the liver and bile ducts. If the surgeon confirms that biliary atresia is the problem, a Kasai procedure will usually be performed immediately. Diagnostic surgery and the Kasai procedure are performed at a hospital or outpatient facility; the infant will be under general anesthesia during surgery.

How is biliary atresia treated?

Biliary atresia is treated with surgery, called the Kasai procedure, or a liver transplant.

Kasai procedure: The Kasai procedure, named after the surgeon who invented the operation, is usually the first treatment for biliary atresia. During a Kasai procedure, the pediatric surgeon removes the infant's damaged bile ducts and brings up a loop of intestine to replace them. As a result, bile flows straight to the small intestine.

While this operation doesn't cure biliary atresia, it can restore bile flow and correct many problems caused by biliary atresia. Without surgery, infants with biliary atresia are unlikely to live past age two. This procedure is most effective in infants younger than three months old, because they usually haven't yet developed permanent liver damage. Some infants with biliary atresia who undergo a successful Kasai procedure regain good health and no longer have jaundice or major liver problems.

If the Kasai procedure is not successful, infants usually need a liver transplant within one to two years. Even after a successful surgery, most infants with biliary atresia slowly develop cirrhosis over the years and require a liver transplant by adulthood.

Liver transplant: Liver transplantation is the definitive treatment for biliary atresia, and the survival rate after surgery has increased dramatically in recent years. As a result, most infants with biliary atresia now survive. Progress in transplant surgery has also increased the availability and efficient use of livers for transplantation in children, so almost all infants requiring a transplant can receive one.

In years past, the size of the transplanted liver had to match the size of the infant's liver. Thus, only livers from recently deceased small children could be transplanted into infants with biliary atresia. New methods now make it possible to transplant a portion of a deceased adult's liver into an infant. This type of surgery is called a reduced-size or split-liver transplant.

Part of a living adult donor's liver can also be used for transplantation. Healthy liver tissue grows quickly; therefore, if an infant receives part of a liver from a living donor, both the donor and the infant can grow complete livers over time.

Infants with fetal biliary atresia are more likely to need a liver transplant—and usually sooner—than infants with the more common perinatal form. The extent of damage can also influence how soon an infant will need a liver transplant.

What are possible complications after the Kasai procedure?

After the Kasai procedure, some infants continue to have liver problems and, even with the return of bile flow, some infants develop cirrhosis. Possible complications after the Kasai procedure include ascites, bacterial cholangitis, portal hypertension, and pruritus.

Ascites: Problems with liver function can cause fluid to build up in the abdomen, called ascites. Ascites can lead to spontaneous bacterial peritonitis, a serious infection that requires immediate medical attention. Ascites usually only lasts a few weeks. If ascites lasts more than six weeks, cirrhosis is likely present and the infant will probably need a liver transplant.

Bacterial cholangitis: Bacterial cholangitis is an infection of the bile ducts that is treated with bacteria-fighting medications called antibiotics.

Portal hypertension: The portal vein carries blood from the stomach, intestines, spleen, gallbladder, and pancreas to the liver. In cirrhosis, scar tissue partially blocks and slows the normal flow of blood, which increases the pressure in the portal vein. This condition is called portal hypertension. Portal hypertension can cause gastrointestinal bleeding that may require surgery and an eventual liver transplant.

Pruritus: Pruritus is caused by bile buildup in the blood and irritation of nerve endings in the skin. Prescription medication may be recommended for pruritus, including resins that bind bile in the intestines and antihistamines that decrease the skin's sensation of itching.

What medical care is needed after a liver transplant?

After a liver transplant, a regimen of medications is used to prevent the immune system from rejecting the new liver. Health care providers may also prescribe blood pressure medications and antibiotics, along with special diets and vitamin supplements.

Eating, diet, and nutrition: Infants with biliary atresia often have nutritional deficiencies and require special diets as they grow up. They may need a higher-calorie diet, because biliary atresia leads to a faster metabolism. The disease also prevents them from digesting fats and can lead to protein and vitamin deficiencies. Vitamin supplements may be recommended, along with adding medium-chain triglyceride oil to foods, liquids, and infant formula. The oil adds calories and is easier to digest without bile than other types of fats. If an infant or child is too sick to eat, a feeding tube may be recommended to provide high-calorie liquid meals.

After a liver transplant, most infants and children can go back to their usual diet. Vitamin supplements may still be needed because the medications used to keep the body from rejecting the new liver can affect calcium and magnesium levels.

Section 31.2

Annular Pancreas

Excerpted from "Annular Pancreas,"
© 2012 A.D.A.M., Inc. Reprinted with permission.

An annular pancreas is a ring of pancreatic tissue that encircles the duodenum (the first part of the small intestine). Normally, the pancreas sits next to, but does not surround, the duodenum.

Causes

Annular pancreas is a congenital defect, which means it is present at birth. Symptoms occur when the ring of pancreas squeezes and narrows the small intestine so that food cannot pass easily or at all.

Newborns may have symptoms of complete blockage of the intestine. However, up to half of people with this condition do not have symptoms until adulthood. There are also cases that are not detected because the symptoms are mild.

Conditions that may be associated with annular pancreas include:

- Down syndrome;

- excess amniotic fluid during pregnancy (polyhydramnios);

- other congenital gastrointestinal problems;

- pancreatitis.

Symptoms

Newborns may not tolerate feedings. They may spit up more than normal, not drink enough breast milk or formula, and cry.

Adult symptoms may include:

- fullness after eating;
- nausea or vomiting.

Exams and Tests

Tests include:

- abdominal ultrasound;
- abdominal x-ray;
- computed tomography (CT) scan;
- upper gastrointestinal (GI) and small bowel series.

Treatment

Surgical bypass of the blocked part of the duodenum is the usual treatment for this disorder.

Outlook (Prognosis)

The outcome is usually good with surgery. Adults with an annular pancreas are at increased risk for pancreatic or biliary tract cancer.

Possible Complications

- Obstructive jaundice
- Pancreatic cancer
- Pancreatitis (inflammation of the pancreas)
- Peptic ulcer
- Perforation (tearing a hole) of the intestine due to obstruction
- Peritonitis

Section 31.3

Pancreas Divisum

Pancreas divisum is a birth defect in which parts of the pancreas fail to join together. The pancreas is a long flat organ located between the stomach and spine that is involved in food digestion.

Causes

Pancreas divisum is the most common birth defect of the pancreas. In many cases this defect goes undetected and causes no problems. The cause of the defect is unknown.

As a baby develops in the womb, two separate pieces of tissue join together to form the pancreas. Each part has a tube, called a duct. When the parts join together, a final duct called the pancreatic duct is formed. Fluid and digestive chemicals (enzymes) produced by the pancreas normally flow through this duct.

If the ducts fail to join together while the baby is developing in the womb, pancreas divisum results. Fluid from the two parts of the pancreas drains into separate areas of the upper portion of the small intestine (duodenum). This occurs in 5 to 15 percent of people.

If a pancreatic duct becomes blocked, swelling and tissue damage (pancreatitis) may develop.

Symptoms

- Abdominal pain, usually in the mid-abdomen, that may be felt in the back

- Abdominal swelling (distention)

- Nausea or vomiting

Note: Unless you have pancreatitis, you will not have symptoms.

477

Exams and Tests

- Abdominal ultrasound
- Abdominal computed tomography (CT) scan
- Amylase and lipase blood test
- Endoscopic retrograde cholangiopancreatography (ERCP)
- Magnetic resonance cholangiopancreatography (MRCP)

Treatment

If you have this condition and have symptoms or pancreatitis that keeps returning, your doctor may recommend surgery.

Outlook (Prognosis)

The outcome is usually good.

Possible Complications

The main complication of pancreas divisum is pancreatitis.

When to Contact a Medical Professional

Call for an appointment with your health care provider if you develop symptoms of this disorder.

Prevention

Because this condition is present at birth, there is no known way to prevent it.

References

Forsmark CE. Pancreatitis. In: Goldman L, Schafer AI, eds. *Cecil Medicine. 24th ed.* Philadelphia, Pa: Saunders Elsevier; 2011: chap 146.

Chapter 32

Musculoskeletal Defects

Chapter Contents

Section 32.1

Arthrogryposis

"Arthrogryposis Multiplex Congenita: What It Is and How It Is Treated," reprinted from www.avenuesforamc.com. © Avenues: A National Support Group for Arthrogryposis Multiplex Congenita. This document is available online at http://www.avenuesforamc.com/publications/pamphlet.htm; accessed April 16, 2012.

What Is arthrogryposis?

"Arthrogryposis" (arthrogryposis multiplex congenita) is a term describing the presence of multiple joint contractures at birth. A contracture is a limitation in the range of motion of a joint.

In some cases, few joints maybe affected and the range of motion may be nearly normal. In the "classic" case of arthrogryposis, hands, wrists, elbows, shoulders, hips, feet, and knees are affected. In the most severe cases, nearly every body joint may be involved, including the jaw and back. Frequently, the joint contractures are accompanied by muscle weakness, which further limits movement.

Arthrogryposis is relatively rare, occurring in perhaps one in three thousand births.

Can arthrogryposis occur again in the same family?

In most cases, Arthrogryposis is not a genetic condition and does not occur more than once in a family. In about 30 percent of the cases, a genetic cause can be identified. The risk of recurrence for these cases varies with the type of genetic disorder.

What causes it?

Research on animals has shown that anything which prevents normal joint movement before birth can result in joint contractures. The joint itself may be normal. However, when a joint is not moved for a period of time, extra connective tissue tends to grow around it, fixing it in position. Lack of joint movement also means that tendons connecting to the joint are not stretched to their normal length; short tendons, in turn, make normal joint movement difficult. (This same kind of problem can develop after birth in joints which are immobilized for long periods of time in casts.)

In general, there are four causes for limitation of joint movement before birth:

- Muscles do not develop properly (atrophy). In most cases, the specific cause for muscular atrophy cannot be identified. Suspected causes include muscle diseases (for example, congenital muscular dystrophies), maternal fever during pregnancy, and viruses which may damage cells which transmit nerve impulses to the muscles.

- There is not sufficient room in the uterus for normal movement. For example, the mother may lack normal amount of amniotic fluid, or have an abnormally shaped uterus.

- Central nervous system and spinal cord are malformed. In these cases, arthrogryposis is usually accompanied by a wide range of other conditions.

- Tendons, bones, joints, or joint linings may develop abnormally. For example, tendons may not be connected to the proper place in a joint.

What is the treatment?

For most types of arthrogryposis, physical and occupational therapy has proven very beneficial in improving muscle strength and function and increasing the range of motion of affected joints. Parents are encouraged to become active participants in a therapy program and to continue therapy at home on a daily basis.

Splints can be made to augment the stretching exercises to increase range of motion. Casting is often used to improve foot position. However, emphasis should be placed on achieving as much joint mobility as possible. Some type of removable splint (perhaps a bi-valve cast) maybe used on knees and feet so that the joints can be moved and muscles exercised periodically. In some cases, merely wearing a splint at night may be sufficient.

Surgery should be viewed as a supportive measure to other forms of treatment when they have achieved their maximum result. Surgeries are commonly performed on ankles to put feet in position for weight bearing and walking. Less frequently, surgery is required on knees, hips, elbows, and wrists to achieve better position or greater range of motion. In some cases, tendon transfers have been done to improve muscle function.

In the past, surgeries were often repeated since the deformities reoccurred. With newer surgical techniques and careful follow-up treatment with physical therapy and splints, surgical success appears to be much improved. However, before any surgery is performed, it is important to be aware of the risks and the amount of improvement which can be expected. It is wise to seek a second or even a third opinion before proceeding with surgery. If possible, talk to someone whose child has had a similar surgery.

Since the term "arthrogryposis" refers to a group of relatively rare conditions, few therapists or doctors have dealt with very many cases. Therefore, it is advisable to contact doctors and therapists in treatment centers where a large number of patients with arthrogryposis are seen.

What is the outlook?

There is a wide variation in the degree to which muscles and joints are affected in those with arthrogryposis. In some cases, arthrogryposis may be accompanied by other conditions, such as central nervous system disorders, which complicate the picture. However, in most cases, the outlook for those with arthrogryposis is a positive one. Unlike many other conditions, arthrogryposis is nonprogressive. That is, it does not worsen with age. Furthermore, with physical therapy and other available treatments, substantial improvement in function is normally possible. Most people with arthrogryposis are of normal intelligence and are able to lead productive, independent lives as adults.

Section 32.2

Clubfoot

Parents know immediately if their newborn has a clubfoot. Some will even know before the child is born, if an ultrasound was done during the pregnancy. A clubfoot occurs in approximately one in every one thousand births, with boys slightly outnumbering girls. One or both feet may be affected.

Cause

Doctors still aren't certain why it happens, though it can occur in some families with previous clubfeet. In fact, your baby's chance of having a clubfoot is twice as likely if you, your spouse, or your other children also have it. Less severe infant foot problems are common and are often incorrectly called clubfoot.

Symptoms

The appearance is unmistakable: the foot is turned to the side and it may even appear that the top of the foot is where the bottom should be.

The involved foot, calf, and leg are smaller and shorter than the normal side.

It is not a painful condition. But if it is not treated, clubfoot will lead to significant discomfort and disability by the teenage years.

Treatment

Nonsurgical Treatment

Treatment should begin right away to have the best chance for a successful outcome without the need for surgery. Over the past ten to fifteen years, more and more success has been achieved in correcting clubfeet without the need for surgery. A particular method of stretching and casting, known as the Ponseti method, has been responsible for this. With this method, the doctor changes the cast every week for several weeks, always stretching the foot toward the correct position. The heel cord is then released followed by one more cast for three weeks.

Once the foot has been corrected, the infant must wear a brace at night for two years to maintain the correction. This has been extremely effective but requires the parents to actively participate in the daily care by applying the braces. Without the parents' participation, the clubfoot will almost certainly recur. That's because the muscles around the foot can pull it back into the abnormal position.

The goal of this, and any treatment program, is to make your newborn's clubfoot (or feet) functional, painless, and stable by the time he or she is ready to walk. (Note: Any time your baby wears a cast, watch for changes in skin color or temperature that may indicate problems with circulation.)

Surgical Treatment

On occasion, stretching, casting, and bracing are not enough to correct your baby's clubfoot. Surgery may be needed to adjust the tendons, ligaments, and joints in the foot/ankle. Usually done at nine to twelve months of age, surgery corrects all of your baby's clubfoot deformities at the same time. After surgery, a cast holds the clubfoot still while it heals. It's still possible for the muscles in your child's foot to try to return to the clubfoot position, and special shoes or braces will likely be used for up to a year or more after surgery. Surgery will likely result in a stiffer foot than nonsurgical treatment, particularly as the years pass by.

Without any treatment, your child's clubfoot will result in severe functional disability. With treatment, your child should have a nearly normal foot. He or she can run and play without pain and wear normal shoes. The corrected clubfoot will still not be perfect, however. You should expect it to stay 1 to 1 1/2 sizes smaller and somewhat less mobile than the normal foot. The calf muscles in your child's clubfoot leg will also stay smaller.

Section 32.3

Congenital Amputation

What is a congenital amputation?

A congenital amputation is the loss of the arm and/or hand due to incomplete development before birth.

What are the different types of congenital amputation?

Congenital amputations of the upper limb are classified by where the child's arm stopped growing. The most common amputations are at the level of the mid-forearm, wrist, partial-hand, and humerus bone. Forearm and wrist amputations usually affect only one side and are more common on the left.

How common is this?

One in twenty thousand children are born with a congenital forearm amputation. One in twenty-seven thousand children are born with a congenital arm amputation.

Why does this occur?

This condition is not usually related to any other medical problems. It is thought that this condition is not genetically inherited. It is thought that congenital amputations are a result of bleeding or blood clots in the hand as it is developing before birth.

What are the treatment options?

Children with congenital arm amputations generally demonstrate excellent functional abilities. These children adapt well to daily living activities, schoolwork, and sports. Artificial limbs that replace the absent portion of the limb are sometimes appropriate for these children.

Other devices can be made to help the child perform daily activities with greater independence.

Surgery is rarely recommended for these children. Some children may require minor surgery to improve the fitting of the prosthetic.

Section 32.4

Fibrous Dysplasia

Excerpted from "A Guide to Understanding Fibrous Dysplasia," © 2005 Children's Craniofacial Association. All rights reserved. Reprinted with permission. For additional information, visit www.ccakids.com. Revised by David A. Cooke, M.D., FACP, December 2012.

What is fibrous dysplasia?

Fibrous dysplasia is a condition of the skeleton (bones). It is a birth defect that is a noncancerous disease. It has been linked to a mutation in a gene called GNAS, which causes abnormal bone growth. It is believed that the gene mutation occurs during early embryotic development, and only involves some of the cells in the affected person's body.

Despite having a genetic cause, fibrous dysplasia is *not* hereditary. Your child did not get it from you, because the mutation appeared after conception, not before. Your child will not pass it along to his or her children, because the mutation is generally not present in the reproductive organs.

How do I recognize this condition in my child?

Fibrous dysplasia is usually detected in early childhood as a result of swelling of the jaw. Also, in some cases it may cause the teeth to separate. When it occurs outside the jaw and skull, it can lead to localized pain, deformities of the arms or legs, scoliosis, or differences in limb length, depending upon the location involved.

How does the disease progress?

Fibrous dysplasia gets progressively worse from birth until the bones finish growing. As it progresses, normal bone is replaced by

486

various amounts of structurally weak fibrous and osseous (bone-like) tissue. In normal bone formation, woven bone appears first and later matures into lamellar bone. In fibrous dysplasia, bone does not mature and development stops in the woven bone stage.

Fibrous dysplasia causes misshapen bones. It can occur in the bones in the front of the head and/or sphenoid bones that are situated at the base of the skull. If this happens, it can eventually lead to deformation of facial features and affect the shape of the skull.

How many types of fibrous dysplasia are there?

There are three types of fibrous dysplasia.

Monostotic disease is the most common type of fibrous dysplasia, occurring in 70 percent of cases. Monostotic simply means involving one bone. It most often occurs on the long bones such as the femur (thigh bone), ribs, and skull.

Polyostotic disease affects 30 percent of patients. Polyostotic means occurring in more than one bone. The head and neck are involved in half of these patients.

The third type is McCune-Albright syndrome. It occurs in only 3 percent of cases. It is characterized by polyostotic fibrous dysplasia (fibrous dysplasia occurring in more than one bone); skin pigmentation; and, in females, early puberty.

How often does fibrous dysplasia affect the face and head?

Skull involvement occurs in 27 percent of monostotic and up to 50 percent of polyostotic patients. Fibrous dysplasia involving the face and skull is called "Leontiasis ossea." Without treatment, one or more bones progressively increase in size, and move into the cavities of the eye, mouth, and/or the nose and its sinuses. Also, abnormal protrusion of the eyeball (exophthalmos) may develop and eventually cause complete loss of sight because it presses on the optic nerve. In addition, there may be interference of the nasal passage and with eating.

What are the effects of fibrous dysplasia of the skull base?

When fibrous dysplasia of the frontal (forehead bone) and/or sphenoid (bone at the base of the skull) bones progresses, these bones become thick and dense. This increase in size eventually causes the facial features and skull to become misshapen. In these cases more than one bone is usually involved. It can also result in cranial nerve problems. If the temporal bone is affected, the patient may suffer as much as 80 percent hearing loss when the inner ear canal narrows. It may also cause facial nerve paralysis or dizziness. However, any of our twelve cranial nerves can be involved with fibrous dysplasia. The more common results could include cranial nerve problems, and sight and hearing loss.

Are there any other effects of fibrous dysplasia?

It is estimated that patients with fibrous dysplasia are four hundred times more likely than the general population to develop a malignant bone tumor.

What is the treatment for fibrous dysplasia?

Physicians decide on treatment options after assessing a patient's symptoms. First the doctor observes the patient. Mild disease that does not cause serious deformities or risk of fracture may not require any treatment. Conservative treatment such as surgically shaving or removing the fibrous tissue is sometimes performed, although more recent data suggests it should be reserved for very specific situations. In more severe cases the doctor may recommend complete removal of the bone. Because fibrous dysplasia located in the arm or leg can lead to fracture, surgical fixation with internal rods and similar hardware is sometimes performed.

Surgery is used to return the face to its normal structure and/or to relieve effects when a cranial nerve is being pinched. In these cases the abnormal bone must be completely removed. It is best to wait until adolescence for surgery. However, if the progression of the disease affects nerve function, a decompressive procedure should be considered early in childhood to keep normal function.

There is limited data that suggest that bisphosphonate drugs may be helpful in treatment of fibrous dysplasia. Bisphosphonates are most commonly used in treatment of osteoporosis or cancer that has spread to bone, but they may also slow abnormal bone turnover in fibrous dysplasia. Initial reports are promising, but there is insufficient evidence at this point to say whether this should become part of standard treatment.

If surgery is recommended, how many will be necessary?

Sometimes the fibrous tissue can be completely removed successfully by a single procedure. However, most fibrous tissue can be managed through staged procedures with overall very favorable results and good long-term prognosis.

Section 32.5

Macrodactyly

Macrodactyly is an uncommon condition in which a baby's toes or fingers are abnormally large due to the overgrowth of the underlying bone and soft tissue. The condition is congenital, meaning babies are born with it.

Macrodactyly happens more often to hands than feet.

Most of the time, only one hand or one foot is affected, but usually more than one digit on that hand or foot is involved.

Macrodactyly may coexist with syndactyly, a condition in which two fingers or toes are fused together.

Although it is a benign condition, macrodactyly is deforming and can look cosmetically displeasing to you and your child.

Surgery, usually involving multiple procedures, can help the problem.

What causes macrodactyly?

Researchers do not know why macrodactyly occurs, but they believe that it doesn't result from anything the mother did (or didn't do) during her pregnancy. Although babies are born with the condition, macrodactyly is not inherited.

It can occur in association with other conditions and syndromes, including:

- neurofibromatosis;

- vascular malformations;

- multiple enchondromatosis;

- Maffucci syndrome;

- tuberous sclerosis.

What are the symptoms of macrodactyly?

One or more of your child's fingers or toes will be much larger than his other fingers or toes. Macrodactyly is more commonly considered static, which means that the enlarged finger or toe grows at the same rate as the normal finger or toe on your child's hand.

However, it can also be progressive, with the affected digits growing faster than the rest of the hand.

In the static type, your child's involved digits will generally be about one-and-a-half times the length and width of the normal digits.

If the condition is progressive, the involved digit or digits can become enormous.

How is macrodactyly diagnosed?

Most of the time, a child's macrodactyly is obvious soon after birth.

Occasionally, however, the progressive type may not be detected until later in infancy, when continued enlargement occurs.

Your child's doctor will perform the following diagnostic tests to determine which underlying layers of tissue are enlarged:

- **X-rays:** A diagnostic test that uses invisible electromagnetic energy beams to produce images of internal tissues, bones, and organs on film.

- **Magnetic resonance imaging (MRI):** A diagnostic procedure that uses a combination of large magnets, radiofrequencies and a computer to produce detailed images of organs and structures within the body.

How is macrodactyly treated?

Your child's physician will discuss specific treatment options with you, and treatment depends on whether the condition occurs in the hand or the foot.

Your doctor's goal will be to give your child optimal function of the affected area:

- A hand can still be quite functional with a finger or two larger than the rest.

- Even a slightly enlarged toe may make wearing shoes impossible.

In mild cases, treatment for macrodactyly may involve observation or, in the case of an enlarged foot, shoe modification alone.

Surgery: Most of the time, however, surgery is required to correct macrodactyly. The surgery is complex because it involves multiple layers of tissue. It may take several surgical procedures to achieve the desired result.

Size-altering surgery will involve extensive observation and planning, because doctors will want to plot the rate of growth of your child's normal digits versus the enlarged digits.

Your child's doctor may recommend some combination of the following surgical procedures:

- **Soft tissue debulking:** To help correct width, this procedure involves the surgical removal of the thickened layers of skin and fat and the replacement of skin with skin grafts harvested from healthy skin in a nearby area. This procedure is usually performed in several stages around three months apart. It's more often used to treat the milder forms of macrodactyly or as a part of the treatment of the more progressive forms.

- **Shortening procedures:** To help correct length, shortening procedures usually involve either surgical removal of one of the phalanges of the finger or toe, or removal of a metacarpal (hand bone) or metatarsal (foot bone).

- **Ray resection:** Surgical removal of the entire digit or digits is sometimes necessary, particularly when the condition is progressive. It is also an option if there is excessive widening of the forefoot, where the digital shortening and debulking procedures may not be effective.

What is the long-term outlook for my child?

The long-term outlook for a child treated for macrodactyly varies from child to child, depending on how severe his problem is.

You and your child can expect an overall improvement in appearance and function. However, it's rare that a child's affected digits look and move perfectly.

Section 32.6

Polydactyly

Polydactyly literally means "extra digits." There may be an extra thumb, small finger, or, less commonly, an extra digit in the central part of the hand. Polydactyly is one of the most common congenital hand anomalies.

Does polydactyly cause my baby any pain?

No, typically there is no pain associated with polydactyly.

What are the different types of polydactyly?

Radial, or preaxial polydactyly means that there is an extra thumb; there are several different types of radial polydactyly. Ulnar, or postaxial polydactyly means that there is an extra small finger; there may be a well-formed extra small finger, or just a poorly formed extra digit attached by a thin stalk of soft tissue. Central polydactyly means that the extra digit is in the central part of the hand, between the thumb and small finger.

Who gets polydactyly?

Polydactyly can occur in any newborn infant. Most types of radial polydactyly are not inherited. Postaxial polydactyly with a small, poorly formed extra digit is ten times more common in African Americans than in Caucasians and is inherited as an autosomal dominant trait (that is, there is a 50 percent chance of polydactyly in the children of an affected individual). However, postaxial polydactyly with a well-formed extra digit is equally common in all ethnicities. Central polydactyly is inherited as an autosomal dominant condition with variable expression, meaning that it may be more or less severe from one generation to the next.

What causes polydactyly?

When the hands and feet are developing in the womb, they start out as flat "paddles" that then normally separate into five digits. Polydactyly occurs when this separation process is excessive, and an extra "segment" is created. This may be caused by a genetic abnormality or by environmental influences.

What are the main issues related to polydactyly?

The primary issue in most types of polydactyly is function of the hand and digits; appearance of the hand is also an issue, but is secondary to function.

Are there other problems that occur commonly with polydactyly?

Certain rare types of preaxial polydactyly are associated with other problems, such as blood disorders, heart abnormalities, or craniofacial abnormalities. Postaxial polydactyly in which the extra digit is well formed is associated with polydactyly of the feet, also.

What is the treatment for babies with polydactyly?

Polydactyly is treated surgically. In preaxial polydactyly, a single thumb must be reconstructed from the two duplicated, or split, thumbs. This procedure involves reconstructing the skin and soft tissues, the tendons, joints, and ligaments to create a single thumb. In postaxial polydactyly, when the extra digit is attached only by a narrow stalk of soft tissue, this may be removed either with a minor operation or, if the stalk is narrow enough, by ligating the stalk in the nursery. When the extra digit is well formed, the surgery is more involved and may involve reconstruction of soft tissues, tendons, joints, and ligaments as in preaxial polydactyly. Finally, central polydactyly requires a complex surgical procedure to reconstruct the hand. Again, the soft tissues, tendons, ligaments, and joints must be reconstructed. In some of these cases, more than one operation is required.

What is done between the time my baby is born and the first surgery?

You will meet with your surgeon soon after your baby is born. In some cases, the diagnosis is made prenatally by ultrasound exam, and you may have the opportunity to meet your surgeon before your baby is born. Your surgeon will examine your baby and take x-rays of the affected hand. Your baby will be examined in the clinic periodically during the months before surgery. The treatment plan and the details of the surgical procedures will be carefully explained to you by your surgeon. Usually, no special treatment or therapy is required before surgery.

What sorts of specialists will be involved in my baby's care?

At the very least, your child will be treated by the hand surgeon and a certified hand therapist. In addition, a geneticist and developmental pediatrician are sometimes involved in the care of babies with polydactyly.

Will we get to know our surgeon?

Ideally, you will meet your surgeon either prenatally or soon after your baby is born. You will meet with your surgeon several times before surgery, and will get to know him quite well.

Section 32.7

Syndactyly

Syndactyly, the most common congenital hand anomaly, is an abnormal connection of fingers or toes to one another—the digits are "webbed," and have failed to separate normally during development. It most commonly involves the middle and ring fingers. In about 50 percent of cases, both hands are involved. Syndactyly may occur alone, or with other anomalies as part of a syndrome.

Does syndactyly cause my baby any pain?

Typically, syndactyly is not painful. However, in some very severe cases, in which the nails might dig into the joined fingertips, minor infections and wounds can cause some discomfort.

What are the different types of syndactyly?

Syndactyly may occur in different forms. Complete syndactyly occurs when the digits are joined all the way to their tips, while in incomplete syndactyly, the digits are joined only for part of their length. Simple syndactyly means that the digits are joined by the skin and soft tissue only, while complex syndactyly means that the bones of the digits are fused together.

Who gets syndactyly?

Syndactyly can occur in any newborn infant. Overall, syndactyly occurs in approximately one out of 2,500 newborns. In up to approximately 40 percent of cases, there is a family history of syndactyly. If syndactyly occurs alone, it is inherited as an autosomal dominant condition; that is, the children of an affected individual will have a 50 percent chance of having syndactyly. However, syndactyly is not the same from one generation to the next, and can be more or less severe than in the affected parents. Syndactyly is more common in Caucasians than in other ethnicities, and affects boys twice as often as girls.

What causes syndactyly?

When the hands and feet are developing in the womb, they start out as flat "paddles" that then normally separate into five digits. Syndactyly occurs when there is a failure of this separation process. This may be caused by a genetic abnormality or by environmental influences.

What are the main issues related to syndactyly?

The primary issue in syndactyly is function of the hand and digits. Syndactyly causes limitation of function, because the involved digits cannot move completely independently. In very severe cases, with multiple digits involved in complex syndactyly, there can be problems with infections and skin breakdown.

Are there other problems that occur commonly with syndactyly?

Some children with syndactyly will have other congenital abnormalities or syndromes. Syndactyly may occur as part of several different syndromes. For example, in the craniofacial dysostosis syndromes, such as Apert syndrome, in addition to very severe, symmetric syndactyly of the hands and feet, there are also significant head and face abnormalities.

What is the treatment for babies with syndactyly?

While every patient is treated individually, with treatment plans made specifically for him or her, some generalizations are possible. Syndactyly is treated surgically, with an operation that separates the digits using skin from the digits and, usually, skin grafts from the lower abdomen to cover the separated fingers. When the small finger or thumb is involved, this operation is done at about six months of age, to avoid distortion of the adjacent ring or index finger with growth, since the thumb and small finger are shorter than their neighboring digits. Otherwise, syndactyly release is usually done at about eighteen months of age. Before this age, the incidence of wound healing complications and skin graft failures is significantly higher. In special cases with very complex syndactyly—or complicated syndactyly—such as in Apert syndrome, surgery may begin earlier, and multiple procedures may be required in a staged sequence to achieve separation of all the digits.

What is done between the time my baby is born and the first surgery?

You will meet with your surgeon soon after your baby is born. In some cases, diagnosis is made prenatally by ultrasound exam, and you may have the opportunity to meet your surgeon before your baby is born. Your surgeon will examine your baby and take x-rays of the affected hand. Your baby will be examined in the clinic periodically during the months before surgery. The treatment plan and the details of the surgical procedures will be carefully explained to you by your surgeon. Usually, no special treatment or therapy is required before surgery.

What sorts of specialists will be involved in my baby's care?

At the very least, your child will be treated by a hand surgeon and a certified hand therapist. In addition, a geneticist and developmental pediatrician are usually involved in the care of babies with syndactyly.

Will we get to know our surgeon?

Ideally, you will meet your surgeon either prenatally or soon after your baby is born. You will meet with your surgeon several times before surgery, and will get to know him quite well.

Section 32.8

Torticollis

"Congenital Torticollis (Twisted Neck)," reproduced with permission from *Your Orthopaedic Connection*, © American Academy of Orthopaedic Surgeons (www.aaos.org), Rosemont, IL, 2007. Reviewed by David A. Cooke, M.D., FACP, December 2012.

Congenital muscular torticollis, also called wryneck, is usually discovered in the first six to eight weeks of life. The infant keeps his or her head tilted to one side and has difficulty turning the head to the opposite side.

If the infant is examined in the first month, a mass, or "tumor," may be felt in the neck. This is nontender and soft. It is attached to the muscle in the neck on the side to which the head is tilting. The mass gradually regresses so that by four to six months of age the "tumor" is gone.

Congenital muscular torticollis can be associated with hip dysplasia (10 to 20 percent), so the hips should be examined in children with torticollis.

If you notice that your child holds the head tilted to one side, consult your physician. Other conditions can cause torticollis, and the physician will check for those during the physical examination. X-rays and/or an ultrasound of the neck and/or hips may be taken.

Ninety percent of children can be treated successfully with a stretching exercise program.

Cause

Firstborn children are more likely to have torticollis (and hip dislocation). This is likely from intrauterine "packing," resulting in injury to the muscle. The "tumor" is seen with response to the injury. As this resolves, the amount of scar in the muscle determines how tight the muscle is. There is no known prevention.

Symptoms

The head tilts to one side and the chin points to the opposite shoulder. The right side is involved 75 percent of the time. The lump is found in the muscle and it gradually goes away. There is limited range of motion of the neck. One side of the face and head may flatten as the child always sleeps on one side.

Treatment

The usual treatment consists of stretching exercises to turn the head so that the chin touches each shoulder and also so that the ear touches the shoulder.

There are other options that can help. Position toys where the infant has to turn his head to see them. Carry the child so that they have to look to the involved side. Place the child in bed with the involved side toward the wall so that they have to look the opposite way to see you outside the crib.

In 10 percent of children, surgery may be needed to correct the torticollis. This is an outpatient surgery to lengthen the short muscle.

Chapter 33

Reproductive Organ Defects

Chapter Contents

Section 33.1

Ambiguous Genitalia

Ambiguous genitalia is a condition usually discovered at birth, in which an infant's genitals may not appear to be clearly male or female. In ambiguous genitalia, a baby's genitals may not be well formed, or the baby may have characteristics of both sexes. Ambiguous genitalia can be very difficult for families.

Oftentimes, pediatric urologists are first to evaluate newborns whose outside genitals are abnormal. Sometimes the baby's sex cannot be determined from the appearance of the organs. Testing and/ or surgery may be needed to help a family decide which gender to raise the baby. This can be a very emotional time for families. Other specialists such as geneticists and endocrinologists are frequently needed to make recommendations to families when determining the child's sex.

What Causes Ambiguous Genitalia?

Many different genes influence fetal sex development. Mutations (defects) in these genes can lead to disorders of sex development. Chromosomal abnormalities, such as a missing sex chromosome or an extra one, can also cause ambiguous genitalia. In some cases, disorders of sex development seem to happen by chance.

Causes of ambiguous genitalia in a genetic female may include:

- **Congenital adrenal hyperplasia (CAH):** Certain forms of this genetic condition cause the adrenal glands to make excess male hormones (androgens). This is the most common cause of disorders of sex development.

- **Prenatal exposure to substances with male hormone activity:** Certain drugs, including progesterone (taken in the early stages of pregnancy to stop bleeding) and anabolic steroids, can cause developing female genitals to become more masculine.

502

- **Tumors:** Rarely, a tumor in the fetus or the mother can produce male hormones.

Causes of ambiguous genitalia in a genetic male may include:

- **Impaired testicle development:** This may be due to genetic abnormalities or unknown causes.

- **Congenital adrenal hyperplasia (CAH):** Certain forms of this genetic condition can impair production of male hormones.

- **Androgen insensitivity syndrome:** In this condition, developing genital tissues don't respond normally to male hormones.

- **Abnormalities with testes or testosterone:** Various abnormalities can interfere with the testes' activity. This may include structural problems with the testes, problems with production of the male hormone testosterone, or problems with cellular receptors that respond to testosterone.

- **5-alpha-reductase deficiency:** This is an enzyme defect that impairs normal male hormone production.

- **Prenatal exposure to substances with female hormone activity:** If a woman continues taking birth control pills during pregnancy, the fetus may be exposed to the female hormone estrogen.

There are a number of different causes of ambiguous genitalia, with the most common described above. The cause, in many cases, is not known and the disorder appears to occur by chance.

How Is the Gender Determined in a Child with Ambiguous Genitalia?

When a child's genitalia appear ambiguous at birth, your child's doctor will conduct both a medical history of the family and a physical examination of your child's genitalia. To determine the sex, your child's doctor and medical team will consider the following:

- A pelvic ultrasound to check for the presence of female reproductive organs

- A genitourethrogram to look at the urethra and vagina if present

- A chromosomal analysis (to help determine genetic sex: XX or XY)

- Size and potential for growth of a penis present in a male pseudohermaphrodite

- Ability of an internal reproductive organ to produce appropriate sex hormones for the gender "assigned" to the child

- Risk of future health conditions (i.e., cancer) that may develop in the original reproductive organs later in life

Treatment for Ambiguous Genitalia

Treatment for ambiguous genitalia depends of the type of the disorder, but normally includes surgery to remove or create reproductive organs appropriate for the gender of the child. Hormone replacement therapy (HRT) may also be included in treatment for ambiguous genitalia.

In some conditions causing ambiguous genitalia, there is an increased risk for tumors in the gonads. In these cases the gonads may need to be removed.

Families of babies born with ambiguous genitalia may need long-term support to help with ongoing issues regarding gender and sexuality. Making a correct determination of gender is both important for treatment purposes, as well as the emotional well-being of the child.

Some children born with ambiguous genitalia may have normal internal reproductive organs that allow them to live normal, fertile lives. However, others may experience reduced or absent fertility (difficulty or inability to conceive a child).

Section 33.2

Cloacal Exstrophy

Sometimes factors can occasionally interfere with bladder development, as is the case for children with cloacal exstrophy. If your newborn has been diagnosed with this condition, what can you expect? The following information should help you talk to your child's doctor if he or she has been diagnosed with cloacal exstrophy.

What is cloacal exstrophy?

This is the most severe birth defect in the exstrophy-epispadias complex. A child with this condition will have the bladder and a portion of the intestines exposed outside the abdomen, with the bony pelvis open like a book. In males the penis is either flat and short or sometimes split. In females the clitoris is split and there may be two vaginal openings. Also, frequently the intestine is short and the anus is not open. There is a high association with other birth defects, especially spina bifida, which occurs in up to 75 percent of cases. Omphalocele, a defect of the abdominal wall in the region of the umbilicus, is also common, as are kidney abnormalities.

How often does it occur?

It is rare, occurring in approximately one in every 250,000 births and is slightly more common in males than females.

What causes this condition?

There is no known cause but it is also very unlikely that anything could have been done to prevent it.

How is it diagnosed?

Frequently it can be detected before birth during a routine sonogram. Nonetheless, this condition will be obvious at birth.

What is the treatment?

Surgical reconstruction is undertaken when the child is medically stable. The surgery is staged, but the schedule of surgery is very dependent on the individual child. The first surgical consideration is repair of any coexistent spinal abnormality, and perhaps repair of a large omphalocele. Once the child has recovered sufficiently from this, the gastrointestinal tract is then treated. A significant number of cases require a stoma because the colon is not normal and the anus is not formed. Closure of the bladder and reconstruction of the genitalia are similar to that for classic exstrophy, although the procedure is sometimes staged because the pelvic bones are widely separated. In select cases the abdominal wall and genitourinary system can be repaired at the same time as the bowel. For a successful closure, a pelvic osteotomy (cutting the bones to allow the pelvis to close more easily) is mandatory. Achieving eventual continence almost always involves bladder reconstruction and using a catheter.

What can be expected after treatment?

The management of cloacal exstrophy has advanced to provide great improvement in the quality of life of affected children. With advances in pediatric anesthesia and infant nutrition the survival rate in the newborn is high and the incidence of life-threatening complications from surgery has reduced significantly. The child born with cloacal exstrophy can usually, with reconstructive surgery, achieve the ability to manage urine and stool in a socially acceptable way over time. The neurological deficit associated with spina bifida, if present, is manageable but requires ongoing medical services.

Will my child be able to have children when they reach adulthood?

In many cases, the answer to this question is yes. However, this will almost certainly require assisted fertility treatment.

Section 33.3

Hypospadias

Excerpted from "Facts about Hypospadias,"
Centers for Disease Control and Prevention, February 24, 2011.

Hypospadias is a birth defect in boys in which the opening of the urethra (the tube that carries urine from the bladder to the outside of the body) is not located at the tip of the penis.

In boys with hypospadias, the urethra forms abnormally during weeks eight to fourteen of pregnancy. The abnormal opening can form anywhere from just below the end of the penis to the scrotum. There are different degrees of hypospadias; some can be minor and some more severe.

The type of hypospadias a boy has depends on the location of the opening of the urethra:

- **Subcoronal:** The opening of the urethra is located somewhere near the head of the penis.

- **Midshaft:** The opening of the urethra is located along the shaft of the penis.

- **Penoscrotal:** The opening of the urethra is located on the scrotum.

Boys with hypospadias can sometimes have a curved penis. They could have problems with abnormal spraying of urine and might have to sit to urinate. In some cases boys with hypospadias can also have a testicle that has not fully descended into the scrotum. If hypospadias is not treated it can lead to problems later in life, such as difficulty performing sexual intercourse or difficulty urinating while standing.

It is estimated that each year about five baby boys out of every one thousand born in the United States are born with hypospadias.[1]

Causes and Risk Factors

Recently, CDC researchers have reported important findings about some factors that affect the risk of having a baby boy with hypospadias:

- **Age and weight:** Mothers who were age thirty-five years or older and who were considered obese had a higher risk of having a baby with hypospadias.[2]

- **Fertility treatments:** Women who used assisted reproductive technology to help with pregnancy had a higher risk of having a baby with hypospadias.[3]

- **Certain hormones:** Women who took certain hormones just before or during pregnancy were shown to have a higher risk of having baby with hypospadias.[4]

The CDC continues to study birth defects like hypospadias and how to prevent them. If you are pregnant or thinking about becoming pregnant, talk with your doctor about ways to increase your chance of having a healthy baby.

Diagnosis

Hypospadias is usually diagnosed during a physical examination after the baby is born.

Treatments

Treatment for hypospadias depends on the type of defect the boy has. Most cases of hypospadias will need surgery to correct the defect.

If surgery is needed, it is usually done when the boy is between the ages of three and eighteen months old. In some cases the surgery is done in stages. Some of the repairs done during the surgery might include placing the opening of the urethra in the right place, correcting the curve in the penis, and repairing the skin around the opening of the urethra. Because the doctor might need to use the foreskin to make some of the repairs, a baby boy with hypospadias should not be circumcised.

References

1. Paulozzi LJ, Erickson JD, Jackson RJ. Hypospadias trends in two US surveillance systems. *Pediatrics* 1997; 100:831–34.

2. Carmichael SL, Shaw GM, Laurent C, Olney RS, Lammer EJ, and the National Birth Defects Prevention Study. Maternal reproductive and demographic characteristics as risk factors for hypospadias. *Paediatr Perinat Epidemiol.* 2007; 21: 210–18.

3. Reefhuis J, Honein MA, Schieve LA, Correa A, Hobbs CA, Rasmussen SA, and the National Birth Defects Prevention Study. Assisted reproductive technology and major structural birth defects in the United States. *Human Rep.* 2009; 24:360–66.

4. Carmichael SL, Shaw GM, Laurent C, Croughan MS, Olney RS, Lammer EJ. Maternal progestin intake and risk of hypospadias. *Arch Pediatr Adolesc Med.* 2005;159: 957–62.

Section 33.4

Inguinal Hernia and Hydrocele

What is an inguinal hernia and hydrocele?

During normal pre-birth development, the testis descends though the groin into the scrotum, bringing with it part of the lining of the abdomen. This tube-like communication between the abdomen and the scrotum usually closes off by the time a child is born. If the communication does not close off, fluid is free to move back and forth from the abdomen into the scrotum—this is called a communicating hydrocele or an inguinal hernia. This is typically characterized by intermittent swelling of the scrotum that may extend into the groin.

If the communication is small only fluid can pass and this is a hydrocele; however, if the communication is large enough, bowel can move into the hernia sac and is called a hernia.

What are the signs and symptoms?

A noncommunicating hydrocele usually causes scrotal swelling that gradually decreases in size.

A communicating hydrocele, or inguinal hernia, usually causes intermittent swelling of the scrotum that may extend into the groin.

This is usually best appreciated when the child is crying or having a bowel movement, or at the end of the day.

A hydrocele does not typically cause any pain or problems. These conditions are usually identified shortly after birth. However, a communicating hydrocele, or inguinal hernia, may present later in life following periods of increased straining.

An incarcerated inguinal hernia usually presents with a firm mass within the groin that may extend into the scrotum; it occurs when bowel gets stuck in the hernia sac. It is usually tender to the touch, and may be associated with nausea and vomiting or a change in bowel habits. This is an emergency, and should be addressed immediately.

How do you diagnose it?

A medical history will be taken and a physical examination will be performed to diagnose these conditions. Usually, this is all that is needed to make the diagnosis. Occasionally, a scrotal ultrasound is obtained to confirm the diagnosis.

How is it treated?

A hydrocele is usually observed during the first year or two of life, as it will often go away on its own. If it persists, surgical correction may be necessary.

An inguinal hernia is treated surgically. A small incision is made in the groin, through which the urologist ties off the hernia sac with a suture. If the fluid around the testis does not decompress, the testis is delivered through the incision and the fluid-filled sac around the testis—a noncommunicating hydrocele—is opened. The testis is then returned to the scrotum and the incision is closed.

Who gets it, and can it be prevented?

Approximately 1 to 3 percent of children are diagnosed with a communicating hydrocele, or inguinal hernia, with a higher incidence in premature and low birth weight infants.

When should I seek medical attention?

Signs or symptoms of a communicating hydrocele, or inguinal hernia, should prompt further evaluation by a pediatric urologist. Signs or symptoms of an incarcerated inguinal hernia should be evaluated immediately.

Section 33.5

Undescended Testicle

What is an undescended testicle?

When the testicle is formed it is located in the abdomen. In most boys it comes down into the scrotum by birth. Even after birth some testicles will still come down to the normal position in the scrotum (most of these come down by four months of age). If a testicle is not in the scrotum by six months of age, it is unlikely that it will come down. This testicle is called an undescended testicle. If the testicle can't be felt at all, it is called a "cryptorchid testicle." An undescended testicle requires surgery, called "orchidopexy," to place it in the scrotum.

Why is surgery necessary?

There are several reasons for placing an undescended testicle in the scrotum:

1. **Fertility:** The temperature in the scrotum is less than up in the abdomen. We know that the sperm-producing cells in the testicle do better if they are in the cooler scrotal environment. Bringing the testicle down into the scrotum at an early age may improve the semen quality and chances of fertility later in life.

2. **Cancer:** Undescended testicles have an increased chance of developing cancer later in life. It is unclear if early placement of the testicle in the scrotum decreases this chance of cancer. Placement of the testicle in the scrotum does permit self-examination of the testicle and earlier detection of testicular cancer should it occur.

3. **Hernia:** A hernia sac is almost always associated with an undescended testicle. During the operation to bring the testicle down, this hernia is routinely identified and fixed.

4. **Protection:** A testicle left in the abdomen may be at increased risk for injury or torsion (twisting and cutting of its blood supply).

5. **Cosmesis:** Placement of the testicle in the scrotum makes the scrotum look normal.

When should surgery be performed?

Since some testicles that are not descended at birth will come down, it is best to wait until around six months of age. By this age if a testicle cannot be felt or is very high, it is unlikely that it will come down.

What is the surgery like?

In most cases the child will go home on the same day the surgery is performed. A small incision is made in the groin and on the scrotum. No stitches will need to be removed. In some boys when the testicle can't be felt (known as "cryptorchidism"), laparoscopy may be used. Laparoscopy involves making an incision in the abdomen and placing a lighted telescope through this incision to look for the missing testicle. If it is found (some testicles are absent), laparoscopy is used for bringing it down into the scrotum.

What are some of the specific complications with orchidopexy?

Wound infection or bleeding may occur with any operation. Injury to the testicular blood vessels or vas deferens (the tube that carries sperm) may occur when performing an orchidopexy. These structures are delicate and avoidance of injury requires delicacy and precision while performing the surgery. Rarely, there are some testicles that don't reach the scrotum after the first surgery and require a second surgery (about a year later) to bring them into their normal scrotal position.

Section 33.6

Urogenital Sinus

The urethra and vagina are separate anatomical entities in normal females. But in rare instances, they are joined in what urologists call a urogenital sinus anomaly. The following information can help you talk to your child's urologist about correcting this rare birth defect.

What are urogenital sinus anomalies?

A urogenital sinus anomaly is a defect present at birth in which the vagina and urethra open into a common channel, rather than separately. There are two general types of urogenital sinus anomalies. In a low confluence urogenital sinus anomaly, the common channel is short, the urethral opening is close to its normal location, and the vagina is almost normal in length. In a high confluence urogenital sinus anomaly, the common channel is long, the urethral opening is internal, and the vagina is quite short. This type is sometimes associated with an anus that is located too far forward.

How are urogenital sinus anomalies diagnosed?

Urogenital sinus malformations are usually diagnosed during infancy by physical examination. If a urogenital sinus defect is suspected in an infant, an examination called a genitogram will be performed. To do a retrograde genitogram, contrast dye will be injected into the common opening. An x-ray will then be taken which will permit the doctors to determine the length of the common channel and the spatial relationship between the urethra and the vagina. This information will allow the urologist to determine the type of urogenital sinus anomaly and implement the appropriate treatment.

If a retrograde genitogram is inadequate, endoscopy may be done. In endoscopy, a fiber-optic camera is inserted into the common channel, which will allow the anatomy to be seen and identified. Other tests used under special situations include an ultrasound and magnetic resonance imaging (MRI).

How are urogenital sinus anomalies treated?

Surgery to separate the vagina and urethra is the only treatment for urogenital sinus anomalies. Since there are many procedures for this operation, you and your child's doctor will decide the best approach, depending on the type of anomaly. If your child is diagnosed with a low confluence urogenital sinus anomaly, the surgeon will perform what is known as a flap vaginoplasty—a procedure to open the sinus so that the vagina and urethra have separate exterior openings. If she has a high confluence urogenital sinus anomaly, the surgeon will perform a pull-through vaginoplasty. In this procedure the vagina is brought to its normal location on the surface of the skin while the urethra continues to drain through what was once the common channel. Sometimes, a piece of skin or a section of bowel may be needed for this procedure.

Will my daughter have control over urination?

If the problem is corrected, urination should be normal.

Will my daughter have a normal sex life?

Yes, once the disorder has been corrected, she will be able to have a normal, enjoyable sex life.

Will she be able to have children?

Yes, once corrected, she should have no problem conceiving or bearing children.

Will she have a normal vaginal delivery?

Yes, she should be able to deliver children normally.

Section 33.7

Vaginal Agenesis, Obstruction, Fusion, and Duplication

Vaginal Agenesis

Vaginal agenesis is a birth defect that affects few women. But unless corrected, it can make a sexual life, not to mention childbearing, impossible. The following information should explain this condition and how it can be fixed.

What Is Vaginal Agenesis?

Vaginal agenesis is a congenital disorder of the reproductive system affecting one in five thousand females. It occurs when the vagina, the muscular canal connecting the cervix of the uterus to the vulva, stops developing because the vaginal plate fails to form the channel.

Some patients may have a shorter vagina, a remnant of one, or lack of one altogether (Mayer-von Rokitansky-Kuster-Hauser syndrome). With vaginal agenesis, it is not uncommon to have other malformations in the reproductive tract, such as an absent or small uterus.

In addition, 30 percent of patients with vaginal agenesis will have kidney abnormalities, the most common of which is the absence of one kidney or the dislocation of one or both organs. The two kidneys may also be fused together, forming a horseshoe-like shape. Approximately 12 percent of patients also have skeletal abnormalities, with two-thirds of this group experiencing problems affecting the spine, ribs, or limbs.

How Is Vaginal Agenesis Diagnosed?

Because external genitalia appear normal, vaginal agenesis is typically not diagnosed until puberty (around age fifteen), when a young girl notices that she has not had her menstrual period and seeks medical attention. The diagnosis is made by physical examination and diagnostic imaging. They may include an ultrasound to check if the uterus and ovaries are both present and entirely intact. The patient may even be asked to undergo a magnetic resonance imaging (MRI) that will show a more detailed picture of her reproductive tract.

While most vaginal agenesis sufferers are not aware of their condition until their teen years, a subgroup of these patients will be diagnosed during infancy. In this case, the abnormality is usually detected during an examination or test for unrelated problems.

How Is Vaginal Agenesis Treated?

Self-dilation: Some women can have their vagina reconstructed without having an operation. Pressure is applied over the area where the vagina should be with a very small tube, called a dilator. The dilator is held against the skin and pressure is applied for about fifteen to twenty minutes a day. Usually, this is more comfortable after the patient has taken a bath because the skin is soft and stretches more easily.

Vaginoplasty: Most young women, however, will require surgical reconstruction. Techniques vary widely, but the vagina can be constructed using a graft either of skin or a buccal mucosa (inner lining of the cheek) or using a segment of large bowel. In the first procedure, the surgeon creates a vagina by harvesting a thin piece of skin from the patient's buttocks (artificial skin has been recently recommended to reduce the morbidity from the skin donor site) and placing it over a mold to create a vagina. He or she then makes a small incision where a normal vagina would be located and inserts the mold so the graft will attach naturally to make the inside of a vagina. After the surgery, the patient is usually on bed rest for a week, during which time a catheter is placed into the bladder for drainage. The mold is removed after seven days. With a bowel vaginoplasty, a portion of the lower colon is removed through an abdominal incision. One end of the bowel is then closed, while the other remains open, functioning as a vaginal opening. The colon is sewn into the vaginal remnant. The night before surgery, patients undergoing this vaginoplasty must empty their bowels to remove stool and bacteria. Following the surgery, a mold will be inserted into the new vagina for three days. During this period a catheter is placed into the bladder through the urethra so that urine can drain.

What Can Be Expected After Treatment for Vaginal Agenesis?

Patients undergoing a skin graft usually wear a vaginal dilator for three months after surgery. It is removed for urination, bowel movements, showering, and sexual intercourse. After three months, the patient usually wears the dilator only at night for approximately six months. Vaginal stenosis, or a tightening of the vagina, is the major complication of this procedure.

Only one operation is needed with bowel vaginoplasty. The patient will be seen three weeks after the surgery and again in three months. Some women will experience a tightening of the vagina. If this occurs, dilation will be performed under anesthesia. Home dilation is not necessary.

At what age should my daughter consider having a vagina created?

When she starts is up to her. Most girls begin the process in their teens, but she may want to wait until sometime in the future when she is ready to become sexually active.

After surgery, when can she begin to have sexual intercourse?

Although patients should consult their physician before having sexual intercourse, it is usually acceptable to begin four to six weeks after the procedure. The patient will probably need lubrication since the skin will not produce the same substances as normal vaginal tissue. Lubrication after a bowel vaginoplasty is less of a problem.

Will she be able to lead a normal sex life?

Since much of sexual pleasure comes from stimulation of the clitoris, the female erectile structure, and not the vagina, she should enjoy normal sensations and a good sex life. Since reconstruction is internal, no one will be able to tell that a patient has undergone the procedure.

Will my daughter be able to have children?

Your daughter's individual anatomy will be the biggest factor in whether or not she will be able to have children. It is very likely she will be able to become pregnant if her uterus, ovaries, and fallopian tubes are normal. It is unlikely that she will be capable of going through pregnancy by herself if her uterus is tiny or absent. However, since the ovaries usually remain normal, fertility specialists will be able to harvest an egg, fertilize it with her partner's sperm, and implant it into a surrogate mother who would carry it to term. Adoption is another option.

Do doctors know the cause of vaginal agenesis?

There are no known risk factors for vaginal agenesis.

Congenital Vaginal Obstruction

Vaginal blockages at birth are rare but must be surgically corrected. Here is what you need to know if your daughter is diagnosed with this condition.

What Are Congenital Vaginal Obstructions?

Female infants are normally born with a thin membrane (hymen) that surrounds the vaginal opening. In rare instances, a congenital vaginal blockage occurs that results in the absence of an external vaginal opening. The most common reason for this medical abnormality is an imperforate hymen—a layer of connective tissue that forms the hymen has no opening and thus the vaginal opening remains covered. Less commonly, obstruction is due to a high transverse septum. A high transverse septum is usually due to incomplete canalization of the vagina during development.

Either of these can result in hydrocolpos, an abnormal swelling of the vagina, or hydrometrocolpos, abnormal swelling of both the vagina and uterus.

How Are Congenital Vaginal Obstructions Diagnosed?

Congenital vaginal obstructions are typically diagnosed in a newborn. Usually the physician finds an abdominal swelling, which is the vagina filled by secretions from the cervical glands in response to the mother's hormones. Typically, an ultrasound will confirm the lump. Additionally, a needle may be inserted into the mass to inject dye for an x-ray examination or to withdraw fluids for analysis.

If no abdominal lump or urinary symptoms are present, this condition may not be identified until puberty. At that time, the girl will fail to pass blood during her period, despite regular ovulation. She may also experience cyclical abdominal pain as well as a lump created by a buildup of menstrual blood behind the blockage.

How Are Congenital Vaginal Obstructions Treated?

Treatment depends on the cause of the vaginal blockage. If the patient has an imperforate hymen, her urologist will make a simple incision that does not require anesthesia. Once drainage occurs, the anatomy should be examined for other abnormalities.

If the patient has a high transverse septum, treatment will depend on its thickness and location. If this partition is in the lower third of the vagina, the surgeon can cut upwards to remove it, reconnecting the upper and lower vagina. If it is located more to the interior, the patient may require an approach in which either skin or part of the intestine is used to bridge the gap between the upper and lower vagina.

Will our daughter be able to have children?

Fertility should not be affected if the reproductive tract is otherwise normal. A cesarean section may be recommended if the abnormality is a high transverse septum, which requires extensive surgical repair.

When she's older, will her sex life be affected?

No. Once corrected, she should have a normal, enjoyable sex life.

Fusion and Duplication

Having two of everything may be normal when you are talking about eyes, ears, hands, and feet, but in the female reproductive system, a doubling of certain organs—such as the uterus, cervix, and vagina—is not a welcome turn of events. What happens to cause these rare abnormalities? The following information should help you understand the whys and wherefores if your child's doctor diagnoses an "anomaly of fusion and duplication."

What Causes Vaginal Fusion and Duplication?

Much of the female reproductive system is derived from two structures, known as mullerian ducts—a pair of embryonic ducts that evolve into the fallopian tubes, uterus, and vagina in females. They come together during the ninth week of pregnancy. If this process is prevented or interrupted, "fusion" or "duplication" anomalies occur. In uterus didelphys, for instance, the patient has two each of a uterus, cervix, and vagina. While one vagina is obstructed, the other remains unblocked and the external sex organs appear normal. In uterus duplex bicollis, the patient again has two each of a uterus and cervix, but only one vagina. In bicornate uterus, the patient has two uteruses fused with one cervix and one vagina.

How Are Vaginal Fusion and Duplication Diagnosed?

The diagnosis of fusion abnormalities at times occurs in newborns with obvious abdominal lumps on external examination. An ultrasound will usually reveal a lump that pushes the bladder forward and the vagina backwards.

It is also common for women with complete vaginal duplication and blockage to be diagnosed at the time of puberty. Despite having their periods, a girl will experience discomfort accompanied by an abdominal lump. This lump is due to the buildup of menstrual fluid in the blocked vagina.

When a fusion anomaly is suspected, an examination called a vaginoscopy will be done—a scope is inserted into the vagina to enable the surgeon to see the anatomy.

How Is Vaginal Fusion and Duplication Treated?

Treatment for fusion abnormalities depends on a patient's anatomy. If there is complete vaginal duplication with blockage, the urologist will perform a simple incision of the obstructing septum, allowing the fluid to drain. In some cases, the procedure is technically difficult so more extensive surgery is required.

How will this affect our child's fertility in the future?

Your child's fertility will not be affected.

Will our daughter have normal menses?

Yes. Menstruation should not be affected.

Chapter 34

Respiratory System Defects

Chapter Contents

Section 34.1

Bronchopulmonary Sequestration

What is a bronchopulmonary sequestration?

A bronchopulmonary sequestration (also known as pulmonary sequestration or BPS) is a piece of lung tissue that develops without being connected to the airways, sometimes inside the lung and sometimes
outside of it. The blood vessels going to the BPS also form abnormally.
The BPS does not get blood flow like the rest of the lung. Rather it
steals blood flow away from the body via a separate artery.

These lung masses can cause breathing problems, infection, or
other complications if untreated. Most of the time a BPS does not
cause problems for the fetus. In these cases, the baby can be monitored
throughout the pregnancy and the BPS can be removed after the baby
is delivered. If the BPS is more severe, however, prenatal surgery may
be needed. Bronchopulmonary sequestrations are a very rare birth
defect. Nothing the mother does or has done during pregnancy causes
this problem.

How is a bronchopulmonary sequestration diagnosed dur-
ing pregnancy?

Typically around twenty weeks of gestation, a routine ultrasound
will show if the baby has a lung mass. A series of follow-up ultrasounds
can give the physicians more information about whether it is a bronchopulmonary sequestration and its level of severity.

Another test that may be recommended is a fetal echocardiogram.
This is an ultrasound of the heart performed by a pediatric cardiologist. This test is recommended to rule out structural heart defects and
assess heart function. Your doctor will also perform a fetal magnetic

resonance imaging (MRI) to determine the nature and size of the mass, as well as how well the rest of the lung has developed. With all of this information, your doctor can help patients and their families make the best possible decision about treatment.

How will a bronchopulmonary sequestration affect my baby?

Bronchopulmonary sequestrations usually cause problems by compressing the adjacent lung and heart. They usually continue to grow throughout the pregnancy, so your doctor will watch the growth very carefully by ultrasound examination. Very small sequestrations may not cause any complications, and can be removed within the first year of the baby's life. However, larger sequestrations can be life threatening both before birth and immediately at birth.

Before birth, the BPS can grow rapidly in the confined space of the chest. This can push the heart and lungs to the opposite side of the chest and cause heart failure. A sign of heart failure is the accumulation of fluid in multiple areas of the developing fetus. If this process continues, the baby can die before birth. If no heart failure develops, the BPS can still be life threatening at birth, by making the lungs too small to survive or preventing the lungs from expanding within the chest.

How are bronchopulmonary sequestrations managed and treated during pregnancy?

The primary goal of an evaluation is to determine the severity of the BPS. This may take several evaluations in which your doctor determines if the BPS is growing rapidly and how it is impacting the fetus.

Depending on the size and severity of the BPS, different types of surgery may be needed to treat it—in some cases before birth, and in some cases after birth:

- Laser ablation:

  - During this minimally invasive fetal intervention, a small needle is inserted into the BPS and a laser fiber is targeted at the abnormal blood vessel going to the BPS. The laser blocks the blood flow, causing it to stop growing. The goal of the operation is to reverse the process by which the BPS is causing heart failure in the fetus. After the surgery, the BPS steals less blood flow from the fetus, and the heart and lungs start growing more normally as the BPS shrinks in size.

- Open fetal surgery:

- If the laser ablation operation is not possible, or is not successful, then open fetal surgery may be needed.

- In this operation, the fetal surgeon opens the mother's uterus, exposing the baby's chest. The chest is opened and the BPS is removed. The uterus is closed and the pregnancy continues. After open fetal surgery, the baby must be delivered by cesarean section since the uterine wound from fetal surgery cannot tolerate labor.

How is BPS treated during and after delivery?

If fetal intervention is not necessary the infant will be evaluated and treated at delivery. Most babies with a small BPS can be delivered vaginally without any apparent complications. These babies typically go home and are followed as an outpatient in two to four weeks after birth. The baby will be referred to a pediatric surgeon, who will help determine if, when, and how the BPS should be removed.

Babies with a moderately large BPS may have some difficulty breathing after birth. Usually, these babies breathe very quickly and sometimes they require oxygen. This quick breathing can make eating difficult for the baby. These babies need to be in a neonatal intensive care unit (NICU) for stabilization until surgery is performed to remove the BPS, and to allow for the remaining normal lung to function optimally.

The baby will remain in the NICU until breathing and eating improve. Sometimes, a very large BPS can compress the lung so severely that it prevents the lungs from expanding and functioning immediately at birth. Your doctor will try to predict this problem based on the degree of shift of the lungs and heart to the opposite side of the chest. To avoid a crisis in the baby's breathing at birth, your doctor may recommend that an "EXIT" procedure be performed for delivery.

During an "EXIT" procedure, the mother has a cesarean section delivery while asleep under general anesthesia. The placenta and umbilical cord remain attached to the mother and support the baby while your doctor evaluates the baby's lung function. This gives the fetal surgeons time to evaluate the BPS and make sure that breathing will be adequate after birth. A breathing tube is inserted and breathing is assisted using a ventilator machine. If the baby breathes well, then the baby can be completely delivered and your doctor can plan for removal of the BPS later. If the baby's breathing is compromised, then the BPS needs to be removed immediately. The chest operation is performed while the mother's placenta supports the baby.

When the operation is finished, the umbilical cord is cut and the baby can breathe better without the compression of the BPS. Extracorporeal membrane oxygenation (ECMO) can also be used as a backup in case the lungs need more time to function optimally. The mother's cesarean incision is repaired and she is allowed to recover just like any cesarean delivery.

What happens after surgery?

The outcomes for bronchopulmonary sequestration after surgery are excellent. In nearly all cases, your baby will develop normally without breathing problems or heart problems.

Section 34.2

Congenital Cystic Adenomatoid Malformation (CCAM)

"CCAM/CPAM," by Dr. Mike (Emanuel) Vlastos, M.D., Director, St. Louis Fetal Care Institute. © 2013. All rights reserved. Reprinted with permission. To learn about the advanced diagnostic and treatment options available at St. Louis Fetal Care Institute for congenital cystic adenomatoid malformation and other fetal conditions and abnormalities, visit www.cardinalglennon .com/fetalcareinstitute.

What is congenital cystic adenomatoid malformation (CCAM)?

A CCAM is a cystic mass which forms in the lung tissue of a fetus. The mass is usually located in one lung, and it does not function as normal lung tissue. The cause of a CCAM is unknown, and it is not related to anything the mother did or did not do during the pregnancy. No cases of recurrence in a sibling have been reported. We suspect that a genetic problem causes a CCAM, as if a switch has made that part of the lung stay immature. As a result, it grows faster than normal and it forms abnormal air spaces which do not function like normal lung.

How is CCAM diagnosed?

CCAMs are detected during a routine prenatal ultrasound. The cyst appears as a bright mass in the area of the chest where only lung tissue should be seen. The size and location of the cystic mass may cause the heart to shift to the opposite side of the chest or push downward on the baby's diaphragm.

The diagnosis can be confirmed with a fetal magnetic resonance imaging (MRI) exam which will also document the size and location of the CCAM. Another test that may be recommended is a fetal echocardiogram. This is an ultrasound of the heart performed by a pediatric cardiologist. This test is recommended to rule out structural heart defects and assess heart function.

How does CCAM affect my baby?

The vast majority of babies do well and have normal development and lung function. During the pregnancy, the cyst often grows with the fetus and appears quite large, but usually the growth starts to slow down in the second trimester. Since the fetus and the remaining normal lung continue to grow rapidly, the CCAM appears to shrink over the pregnancy. Sometimes, the CCAM becomes very small and even undetectable before birth by ultrasound. It is always there, but studies will have to be done after birth to find the CCAM. In all these cases, the outlook for a normal life is excellent.

In a small number of fetuses, the CCAM may grow so rapidly as to become life threatening before birth. This usually happens between eighteen and twenty-six weeks' gestation. The large size of the CCAM causes compression of the heart and eventual heart failure. Compression of the lungs can also cause the lungs to be too small for survival. In these cases, either fetal surgery or early delivery needs to be performed, depending on how far the pregnancy has progressed.

How is CCAM managed during pregnancy?

During the initial ultrasound, your doctor will measure the volume of the CCAM relative to the size of the fetus. This ratio is called the CCAM volume ratio, or CVR. For every fetus with a CCAM, your doctor will start by measuring the CVR every week. By comparing the CVR measurements, your doctor can determine how fast the CCAM is growing and whether it will become life threatening. If the CVR remains small (less than 1.0) after twenty-eight weeks, then the ultrasound examinations can be performed every three to four weeks till delivery.

If the CCAM pushes the heart out of the normal position, then a second magnetic resonance imaging (MRI) may be performed at thirty-four weeks of pregnancy. The lung volume will be calculated and the information will be used to determine whether your baby should be delivered at a medical center where advanced breathing machines are available.

Babies with very large, rapidly growing CCAMs will have a high CVR, usually above 1.0. In this setting, your doctor will follow your baby very closely to determine if the heart function begins to decline. Usually, ultrasound exams need to be performed twice a week, and repeated echocardiograms may also be performed.

If signs of heart failure develop, or the CVR rises to 1.6 or higher, then fetal intervention may be required. Oftentimes, prenatal steroids are the first step in the intervention. If the steroids do not stop the growth of the CCAM, then open fetal surgery to remove the mass can be a life-saving option for the baby. If the CCAM has a dominant cyst of fluid then a needle can be used to drain the fluid and relieve the compression on the heart. When the CCAM is a solid mass, then open fetal surgery is necessary to remove the mass. If your baby has reached thirty-two weeks in pregnancy, then early delivery may be used instead of fetal surgery.

How is CCAM treated after delivery?

If fetal intervention is not necessary, the infant will be evaluated and treated after delivery. Babies with a relatively small CCAM can be born without any apparent complications. These babies typically go home and are followed as an outpatient in two to four weeks. The pediatric surgeons manage what to do with the CCAM. Often they recommend surgical removal to prevent future infection and possible malignancy. This is done though an operation in the chest and the part or lobe of the lung that contains the CCAM is removed.

Babies with moderately large CCAMs may have some difficulty breathing after birth. Usually, these babies breathe very quickly, and sometimes they require oxygen. Eating is difficult when breathing fast. These babies need to be in a neonatal intensive care unit (NICU) for stabilization, and surgery is performed to remove the CCAM and to allow for the remaining normal lung to function optimally. The baby will remain in the NICU until breathing and eating improve.

Rarely, a CCAM is so large that your doctor will anticipate the baby will have problems breathing right at birth. Your doctor will try to predict this based on the size of the CCAM and lungs by MRI, and the degree that heart has been pushed out of the way. To avoid a crisis in the baby's breathing at birth, your doctor may recommend that a special delivery method be used. When a baby is delivered using an ex utero intrapartum treatment (EXIT) procedure, the placenta and umbilical cord are maintained while your doctor evaluates the baby's lung function. If the baby breathes well, then the baby can be completely delivered and your doctor can plan for removal of the CCAM later. If the baby's breathing is compromised, then the CCAM will need to be removed immediately. The chest operation will be performed while the mother's placenta supports the baby. When the operation is finished, the cord will be cut and the baby will be able to breathe better without the compression of the CCAM.

What will happen after surgery?

The postoperative course varies depending on when the surgery is done, the size of the CCAM, and how much lung was removed. If the CCAM is removed during the neonatal period, then commonly a breathing tube and intravenous line is needed. The baby may also have a tube in the chest to drain any fluid and help expand the lung into the chest space. The baby will not be able to eat until his or her condition has stabilized but nourishment will be given through the intravenous fluids.

The baby will go home when he or she can breathe sufficiently and eat enough to maintain and gain weight. The average stay for the newborn can range from two to three days for small CCAMs to four to eight weeks for much larger ones. The long-term outcome for infants who have the cyst removed is excellent. These children usually have no limitations on their activities and have no increased risk for respiratory complications.

Section 34.3

Congenital High Airway Obstruction Syndrome (CHAOS)

Overview

Congenital high airway obstruction (CHAOS) is a complete or nearly complete obstruction of the fetal airway.

The obstruction can be due to a variety of causes including:

- a cyst in the larynx;

- a membrane that blocks the larynx or trachea;

- a malformation that closes off the trachea or larynx;

- a narrowing of the glottis (the middle part of the larynx).

This obstruction causes some serious problems in the fetus:

- swelling of the lungs;

- swelling of the trachea and bronchial tubes;

- heart failure.

Prenatally diagnosed CHAOS requires intervention sometime before your baby takes his first breath.

In-Depth

How Often Does Congenital High Airway Obstruction Occur?

CHAOS was once thought to be extremely rare. Yet, more than a dozen cases have been reported since 1989.

Researchers believe that CHAOS may be more common than they realized, since many fetuses affected with this condition either do not make it to term or are born without being diagnosed.

What Causes Congenital High Airway Obstruction?

No one knows. It occurs by chance. No hereditary basis has been identified.

Tests

How Is Congenital High Airway Obstruction Diagnosed?

CHAOS is first detected on prenatal ultrasound. If your doctor suspects a problem, you will be referred to a doctor who specializes in high-risk cases for a more detailed ultrasound.

What Signs Will My Doctors Look For in the Ultrasound?

The main signs are swollen and elongated trachea and bronchial tubes. This swelling happens as a result of a build-up of fluid normally expelled through the trachea with fetal breathing movements.

In more advanced cases, doctors may notice the following:

- signs of impending heart failure (hydrops);
- polyhydramnios (excess amniotic fluid);
- ascites (accumulation of fluid in the abdominal cavity).

The fetus may also appear to have abnormal breathing movements.

Will My Doctor Order Any Other Tests?

Your doctor may decide that you should have an MRI (magnetic resonance imaging) of your abdomen to get better pictures of the fetus and to determine what's causing the obstruction, whether it's a cyst in the larynx or atresia either of the larynx or trachea.

MRI may be necessary to rule out other conditions that resemble CHAOS, particularly congenital cystic adenomatoid malformation (CCAM).

Treatment and Care

How Is Congenital High Airway Obstruction Treated?

The first step in management may be further testing so that doctors can learn more about your baby's condition. There is a wide range of other congenital problems that seem to coincide with laryngeal atresia, such as abnormalities of the vertebrae, trachea, urinary tract, and heart.

These studies can include:

- **Fetal echocardiogram:** This test is an ultrasound test performed during pregnancy to evaluate the heart of the unborn baby. Echocardiography assesses the heart's structures and function.

- **Amniocentesis:** An amniocentesis is a procedure used to obtain a small sample of the amniotic fluid that surrounds the fetus to diagnose chromosomal disorders and open neural tube defects.

Will I Have to Have Surgery?

Probably. All fetuses with advanced CHAOS require surgery before birth since there is a significantly high risk of death at birth if no intervention takes place.

The operation is usually performed as the baby is delivered by a procedure called ex utero intrapartum treatment (EXIT). For this procedure, the baby must be delivered at a hospital that specializes in EXIT.

EXIT procedure: Doctors perform a cesarean section while the mother is under deep general anesthesia.

Doctors deliver only the fetus's head and neck so that the fetus is still sustained by the placenta.

The goal here is to stabilize the fetus's airway, so that when contractions begin the baby can breathe; the surgeons usually have about an hour.

This surgery may be performed as early as twenty-four weeks' gestation, depending on how severe the problem is. To secure the airway, surgeons will perform one or a combination of the following procedures, depending on what's causing the obstruction and how severe it is:

- **Laryngoscopy:** This allows doctors to examine the interior of the larynx with an instrument called a laryngoscope. They may try to bypass the obstruction with an endotracheal breathing tube.

- **Bronchoscopy:** This procedure uses a bronchoscope, which is designed to examine or treat the bronchi. Doctors may try to disrupt the obstruction if it's in the form of a cyst or a simple membrane.

- **Tracheostomy:** If other efforts have failed, doctors will create a surgical opening through the skin into the trachea below the obstruction to create a temporary airway.

If the airway cannot be secured in time, the baby may be placed onto extracorporeal membrane oxygenation (ECMO; a heart-lung bypass).

What Happens After the Airway Is Secured?

Your baby will be placed in critical care. There, a neonatologist will examine your baby for any possible problems associated with CHAOS discussed above. Your baby will probably have blood tests, x-rays, ultrasound, and an echocardiogram.

Once other conditions are ruled out, your baby will probably undergo surgery to either remove the obstruction, if necessary, and/or to repair the malformation in the larynx or trachea, such as atresia, that caused the problems.

What Treatment Will I Have?

After delivery, our surgeon will work closely with an anesthesiologist to make sure any risks of maternal bleeding are minimized.

For more information about maternal risks associated with fetal surgery, be sure to talk to your doctor so that you understand them fully.

What's the Outlook for My Child?

After treatment, your baby will require close follow-up care.

If the obstruction was caused by a simple cyst or web in the larynx, your child should have normal speech.

If there was a severe malformation in the larynx, normal speech is less certain.

Otherwise, your child should be very healthy.

Chapter 35

Spina Bifida

Chapter Contents

Section 35.1

Spina Bifida: Basic Facts

Excerpted from "Spina Bifida Fact Sheet,"
National Institute of Neurological Disorders and Stroke,
National Institutes of Health, July 20, 2012.

The human nervous system develops from a small, specialized plate of cells (the neural plate) along the back of an embryo. Early in fetal development, the edges of this plate begin to curl up toward each other, creating the neural tube—a narrow sheath that closes to form the brain and spinal cord of the embryo. As development progresses, the top of the tube becomes the brain and the remainder becomes the spinal cord. This process is usually complete by the twenty-eighth day of pregnancy. But if problems occur during this process, the result can be brain disorders called neural tube defects, including spina bifida.

What is spina bifida?

Spina bifida, which literally means "cleft spine," is characterized by the incomplete development of the brain, spinal cord, and/or meninges (the protective covering around the brain and spinal cord). It is the most common neural tube defect in the United States—affecting 1,500 to 2,000 of the more than 4 million babies born in the country each year. There are an estimated 166,000 individuals with spina bifida living in the United States.

What are the different types of spina bifida?

There are four types of spina bifida: occulta, closed neural tube defects, meningocele, and myelomeningocele.

Occulta is the mildest and most common form, in which one or more vertebrae are malformed. The name "occulta," which means "hidden," indicates that the malformation, or opening in the spine, is covered by a layer of skin. This form of spina bifida, present in 10 to 20 percent of the general population, rarely causes disability or symptoms.

Closed neural tube defects make up the second type of spina bifida. This form consists of a diverse group of spinal defects in which the spinal cord is marked by a malformation of fat, bone, or membranes. In some individuals there are few or no symptoms; in others the malformation causes partial paralysis with urinary and bowel dysfunction.

In the third type, meningocele, spinal fluid and the meninges protrude through an abnormal vertebral opening; the malformation contains no neural elements and may or may not be covered by a layer of skin. Some individuals with meningocele may have few or no symptoms while others may experience symptoms similar to closed neural tube defects.

Myelomeningocele, the fourth form, is the most severe and occurs when the spinal cord/neural elements are exposed through the opening in the spine, resulting in partial or complete motor paralysis and sensory deficits within the parts of the body below the spinal opening. The paralysis may be so severe that the affected individual is unable to walk and may have urinary and bowel dysfunction.

What causes spina bifida?

The exact cause of spina bifida remains a mystery. No one knows what disrupts complete closure of the neural tube, causing a malformation to develop. Scientists suspect that the cause is multifactorial: genetic, nutritional, and environmental factors play a role. Research studies indicate that insufficient intake of folic acid—a common B vitamin—in the mother's diet is a key factor in causing spina bifida and other neural tube defects. Prenatal vitamins that are prescribed for the pregnant mother typically contain folic acid as well as other vitamins.

What are the signs and symptoms of spina bifida?

The symptoms of spina bifida vary from person to person, depending on the type and level of involvement. Closed neural tube defects are often recognized or identified early in life due to an abnormal tuft or clump of hair or a small dimple or birthmark on the skin at the site of the spinal malformation.

Meningocele and myelomeningocele generally involve a fluid-filled sac—visible on the back—protruding from the spinal canal. In meningocele, the sac may be covered by a thin layer of skin. In most cases of myelomeningocele, there is no layer of skin covering the sac and an area of abnormally developed spinal cord tissue usually is exposed.

What are the complications of spina bifida?

Complications of spina bifida range from minor physical problems to severe physical and mental disabilities. It is important to note, however, that most people with spina bifida are of normal intelligence. Children with myelomeningocele and/or hydrocephalus (excess cerebrospinal fluid in and around the brain) may have learning disabilities, including difficulty paying attention, problems with language and reading comprehension, and trouble learning math.

Spina bifida's impact is determined by the size and location of the malformation, whether it is covered by skin, and which spinal nerves are involved. All nerves located below the malformation are affected to some degree. Therefore, the higher the malformation occurs on the back, the greater the amount of nerve damage and loss of muscle function and sensation.

In addition to abnormal sensation and paralysis, another neurological complication associated with spina bifida is Chiari II malformation—a condition common in children with myelomeningocele—in which the brain stem and the cerebellum (hindbrain) protrude downward into the spinal canal or neck area. This condition can lead to compression of the spinal cord and cause a variety of symptoms, including difficulties with feeding, swallowing, and breathing control; choking; and changes in upper extremity function (stiffness, swelling).

Chiari II malformation may also result in a blockage of cerebrospinal fluid, causing hydrocephalus. The buildup of fluid puts damaging pressure on the these structures. Hydrocephalus is commonly treated by surgically implanting a shunt—a hollow tube—in the brain to drain the excess fluid into the abdomen.

Some newborns with myelomeningocele may develop meningitis, an infection in the meninges. Meningitis may cause brain injury and can be life threatening.

Additional problems such as latex allergies, skin integrity breakdown, gastrointestinal conditions, disorders of sleep regulation, and depression may occur as children with spina bifida get older.

How is it diagnosed?

In most cases, spina bifida is diagnosed prenatally, or before birth. However, some mild cases may go unnoticed until after birth (postnatal). Very mild forms (such as spina bifida occulta), in which there are no symptoms, may never be detected.

Prenatal diagnosis: The most common screening methods used to look for spina bifida during pregnancy are second-trimester (sixteenth to eighteenth weeks of gestation) maternal serum alpha fetoprotein (MSAFP) screening and fetal ultrasound. The MSAFP screen measures the level of a protein called alpha-fetoprotein (AFP), which is made naturally by the fetus and placenta. During pregnancy, a small amount of AFP normally crosses the placenta and enters the mother's bloodstream. If abnormally high levels of this protein appear in the mother's bloodstream it may indicate that the fetus has an "open" (not skin-covered) neural tube defect.

Postnatal diagnosis: Mild cases of spina bifida (occulta; closed) not diagnosed during prenatal testing may be detected postnatally by x-ray during a routine examination. Doctors may use magnetic resonance imaging (MRI) or a computed tomography (CT) scan to get a clearer view of the spine and vertebrae. Individuals with the more severe forms of spina bifida often have muscle weakness in their feet, hips, and legs. If hydrocephalus is suspected, the doctor may request a CT scan and/or x-ray of the skull to look for extra cerebrospinal fluid inside the brain.

How is spina bifida treated?

There is no cure for spina bifida. The nerve tissue that is damaged or lost cannot be repaired or replaced, nor can function be restored to the damaged nerves. Treatment depends on the type and severity of the disorder. Generally, children with the mild form need no treatment, although some may require surgery as they grow.

The key early priorities for treating myelomeningocele are to prevent infection from developing through the exposed nerves and tissue through the spine defect, and to protect the exposed nerves and structures from additional trauma. Typically, a child born with spina bifida will have surgery to close the defect and minimize the risk of infection or further trauma within the first few days of life.

Selected medical centers continue to perform fetal surgery for treatment of myelomeningocele through a National Institute protocol (Management of Myelomeningocele Study, or MOMS). Fetal surgery is performed in utero (within the uterus) and involves opening the mother's abdomen and uterus and sewing shut the abnormal opening over the developing baby's spinal cord. Some doctors believe the earlier the defect is corrected, the better the baby's outcome. Although the procedure cannot restore lost neurological function, it may prevent additional losses from occurring.

Originally planned to enroll 200 expectant mothers carrying a child with myelomeningocele, the Management of Myelomeningocele Study was stopped after the enrollment of 183 women, because of the benefits demonstrated in the children who underwent prenatal surgery.

There are risks to the fetus as well as to the mother. The major risks to the fetus are those that might occur if the surgery stimulates premature delivery, such as organ immaturity, brain hemorrhage, and death. Risks to the mother include infection, blood loss leading to the need for transfusion, gestational diabetes, and weight gain due to bed rest.

Still, the benefits of fetal surgery are promising, and include less exposure of the vulnerable spinal nerve tissue and bones to the intrauterine environment, in particular the amniotic fluid, which is considered toxic. As an added benefit, doctors have discovered that the procedure affects the way the fetal hindbrain develops in the uterus, allowing certain complications such as Chiari II and hydrocephalus to correct themselves—thus, reducing or, in some cases, eliminating the need for surgery to implant a shunt.

Twenty to 50 percent of children with myelomeningocele develop a condition called progressive tethering, or tethered cord syndrome. A part of the spinal cord becomes fastened to an immovable structure—such as overlying membranes and vertebrae—causing the spinal cord to become abnormally stretched and the vertebrae elongated with growth and movement. This condition can cause change in the muscle function of the legs, as well as changes in bowel and bladder function. Early surgery on the spinal cord may allow the child to regain a normal level of functioning and prevent further neurological deterioration.

Some children will need subsequent surgeries to manage problems with the feet, hips, or spine. Individuals with hydrocephalus generally will require additional surgeries to replace the shunt, which can be outgrown or become clogged.

Some individuals with spina bifida require assistive mobility devices such as braces, crutches, or wheelchairs. The location of the malformation on the spine often indicates the type of assistive devices needed. Children with a defect high on the spine and more extensive paralysis will often require a wheelchair, while those with a defect lower on the spine may be able to use crutches, bladder catheterizations, leg braces, or walkers. Beginning special exercises for the legs and feet at an early age may help prepare the child for walking with braces or crutches when he or she is older.

Treatment of bladder and bowel problems typically begins soon after birth, and may include bladder catheterizations and bowel management regimens.

Can the disorder be prevented?

Folic acid, also called folate, is an important vitamin in the development of a healthy fetus. Although taking this vitamin cannot guarantee having a healthy baby, it can help. Recent studies have shown that by adding folic acid to their diets, women of childbearing age significantly reduce their risk of having a child with a neural tube defect, such as spina bifida. Therefore, it is recommended that all women of childbearing age consume 400 micrograms of folic acid daily. Foods high in folic acid include dark green vegetables, egg yolks, and some fruits. Many foods—such as some breakfast cereals, enriched breads, flours, pastas, rice, and other grain products—are now fortified with folic acid. Most multivitamins contain this recommended dosage of folic acid.

Women who have a child with spina bifida, have spina bifida themselves, or have already had a pregnancy affected by any neural tube defect are at greater risk (anywhere from 5 to 10 percent of the general population) of having a child with spina bifida or another neural tube defect. These women may benefit from taking a higher daily dose of folic acid before they become pregnant.

What is the prognosis?

Children with spina bifida can lead relatively active lives. Prognosis, activity, and participation depends on the number and severity of abnormalities and associated personal and environmental factors. Many children with the disorder have normal intelligence and can walk, usually with assistive devices. If learning problems develop, early educational intervention is helpful.

What research is being done?

Within the federal government, the National Institute of Neurological Disorders and Stroke (NINDS), a component of the National Institutes of Health (NIH), supports and conducts research on brain and nervous system disorders, including spina bifida.

In one study supported by NINDS, scientists are looking at the hereditary basis of neural tube defects. The goal of this research is to find the genetic factors that make some children more susceptible to neural tube defects than others. Lessons learned from this research may fill in gaps of knowledge about the causes of neural tube defects and may lead to ways to prevent these disorders. These researchers are also studying gene expression during the process of neural tube closure, which will provide information on the human nervous system during development.

In addition, NINDS-supported scientists are working to identify, characterize, and evaluate genes for neural tube defects. The goal is to understand the genetics of neural tube closure, and to develop information that will translate into improved clinical care, treatment, and genetic counseling.

Other scientists are studying genetic risk factors for spina bifida, especially those that diminish or lessen the function of folic acid in the mother during pregnancy, possibly leading to spina bifida in the fetus. This study will shed light on how folic acid prevents spina bifida and may lead to improved forms of folate supplements.

Another component of the NIH, the Eunice Kennedy Shriver National Institute of Child Health and Human Development (NICHD), is conducting a large five-year study to determine if fetal surgery to correct spina bifida in the womb is safer and more effective than the traditional surgery—which takes place a few days after birth. Researchers hope this study, called the Management of Myelomeningocele Study, or MOMS, will better establish which procedure, prenatal or postnatal, is best for the baby.

Section 35.2

Fetal Surgery for Spina Bifida

Excerpted from "Surgery on Fetus Reduces Complications of Spina Bifida," National Institutes of Health, February 9, 2011.

A surgical procedure to repair a common birth defect of the spine, if undertaken while a baby is still in the uterus, greatly reduces the need to divert, or shunt, fluid away from the brain, according to a study by the National Institutes of Health (NIH) and four research institutions.

The surgical procedure consists of closing an opening at the back of the fetal spine. The fetal surgery is a departure from the traditional approach, which involves repairing the defect in the spinal column after an infant has been born.

The fetal surgical procedure also increases the chances that a child will be able to walk without crutches or other devices.

However, infants who underwent this prenatal surgery were more likely to be born preterm than were the infants who had the surgery after birth, when it is typically performed. As with all infants born early, preterm infants in the study were at increased risk for breathing difficulties. Mothers who underwent the surgery during their pregnancies were at risk for uterine dehiscence, a thinning or tearing at the incision in the uterus.

Myelomeningocele is the most serious form of spina bifida, a condition in which the spinal column fails to close around the spinal cord. With myelomeningocele, the spinal cord protrudes through an opening in the spine.

Originally planned to enroll 200 expectant mothers carrying a child with myelomeningocele, the Management of Myelomeningocele Study (MOMS) was stopped after the enrollment of 183 women, because of the benefits demonstrated in the children who underwent prenatal surgery.

"In spite of an increased risk for preterm birth, children who underwent surgery while in the uterus did much better, on balance, than those who had surgery after birth," said Alan E. Guttmacher, M.D., director of NICHD, which funded the study. "However, caution is advised. Because the surgery is highly specialized, it is best undertaken in facilities with staff having experience in the procedure."

The study authors noted that myelomeningocele occurs in 3.4 of every 10,000 births, and 10 percent of affected infants die. Spina bifida is one of a class of birth defects known as neural tube defects, in which the brain or spine fails to develop normally in the early embryo. The condition often results in weakness or paralysis below the location of the defect on the spine. In addition to loss of bladder and bowel control, individuals with myelomeningocele often are unable to walk unassisted or may need a wheelchair. Also, the protrusion of the spinal cord creates a change in the flow of spinal fluid that may pull the brain stem into the base of the skull, which is known as hindbrain herniation. Children with myelomeningocele are subject to blockages that hinder or shut off the circulation of cerebrospinal fluid in the brain. The resultant fluid buildup can be life threatening, and so a tube, or shunt, is inserted into the brain to drain the excess fluid into the abdominal cavity. These shunts are susceptible to blockage and infection, and may require many replacements during the patient's lifetime.

Surgery for myelomeningocele has traditionally been undertaken after birth, explained co-author of the study Catherine Y. Spong, M.D., chief of NICHD's pregnancy and perinatology branch. It consists of inserting the cord back into the spinal cavity and sealing the opening with sutures. Study authors N. Scott Adzick M.D. of CHOP and Diana L. Farmer, M.D. of UCSF performed the initial animal studies suggesting that surgery in the womb might prevent many of the complications of myelomeningocele.

Women volunteering for the current study were assigned at random to one of two groups. The first group underwent prenatal surgery to close the spinal defect in the fetus before their twenty-sixth week of pregnancy. The second group had the surgery performed on the child after birth.

The children were examined at twelve months of age and again at thirty months. The study results were evaluated for two separate primary outcomes. The first primary outcome took into account whether, by twelve months, a child had died, or required a shunt. The second primary outcome, at thirty months, was a composite from a test of mental development and an assessment of motor function. The mental development score was taken from the Bayley Scales of Infant Development II Mental Development Index. The motor assessment score was calculated as the difference between the child's actual motor ability and the expected ability given the level of the defect on the spine.

The first primary outcome, death or the need for a shunt, was much less likely in those who had prenatal surgery, occurring in 67.9 percent of the infants in the prenatal surgery group and 97.5 percent of the traditional surgery group. For the second primary outcome, the infants who underwent prenatal surgery scored significantly higher (21 percent) than the infants who received traditional surgery.

In addition to evaluating the study results in terms of the two primary outcomes, the researchers also evaluated the results in terms of a number of secondary outcomes. Although the likelihood of being able to walk depends on the location of the spinal malformation, children in the prenatal surgery group were more likely to be able to walk without orthotics or crutches (41.9 percent) than were children in the postnatal surgery group (20.9 percent).

Hindbrain herniation, in which the base of the brain is pulled into the spinal canal, was present during pregnancy in all of the infants who participated in the trial. However, at twelve months of age, one-third of the children (35.7 percent) who had prenatal surgery no longer had any evidence of hindbrain herniation, compared to 4.3 percent in the postnatal surgery group.

"The findings suggest that the prenatal surgery allowed for more normal development of the nervous system and fewer complications," Dr. Spong said.

Children in the prenatal surgery group were more likely to be born preterm, at an average of 34.1 weeks of pregnancy, compared with the postnatal group, born at an average 37.3 weeks. In the prenatal surgery group, 20.8 percent of the infants had a breathing disorder associated with preterm birth (respiratory distress syndrome), which the study authors considered a consequence of being born preterm. For the postnatal surgery group, 6.3 percent had respiratory distress syndrome.

Mothers in the prenatal surgery group were also more likely to experience a thinning or tearing in the uterine incision used for the prenatal surgery procedure. In fact, one-third of all the women in the prenatal surgery group had some degree of thinning at the time of delivery. The study authors noted that prenatal incisions in the uterus increase the risk for dehiscence or outright rupture during a subsequent pregnancy. They recommended that all women who undergo such surgery should be informed that, in future pregnancies, they would require a cesarean delivery before labor begins, to avoid the risk of the scar tearing open with the force of the uterine contractions.

The researchers added that the surgery might pose greater risks for categories of women excluded from the study because of health concerns. For example, severely obese women (body mass index of 35 or higher) were not included in the study because of the increased risk for complications of surgery. They noted, however, that obesity is common in women carrying a child with myelomeningocele. Maternal obesity is estimated to increase the risk of spina bifida 1.5 to 3.5 times.

"Experimental outcomes from animal studies and the results from this MOMS clinical trial suggest that prenatal surgery for myelomeningocele stops exposure of the developing spinal cord to amniotic fluid and thereby averts further neurologic damage in-utero," Dr. Adzick said. "Prenatal surgery also stops cerebrospinal fluid leak from the myelomeningocele defect which serves to reverse hindbrain herniation in-utero, and we believe that this in turn mitigates the development of hydrocephalus and the need for shunting after birth."

The Centers for Disease Control and Prevention (CDC) recommends that all women of childbearing age consume 400 micrograms of folic acid, in a supplement or in a fortified grain product, to reduce the risk of having a child with a neural tube defect.

In 2009, an NIH study found that women with low levels of vitamin B12, found only in meat, eggs, and other foods of animal origin, were at increased risk for having a child with a neural tube defect.

Section 35.3

Spina Bifida: Urinary Tract Concerns

"Urological Care of Children with Spina Bifida," © 2004 Dartmouth-Hitchcock (www.dartmouth-hitchcock.org). All rights reserved. Reprinted with permission. Reviewed by David A. Cooke, M.D., FACP, December 2012.

The urologic care of children with spina bifida has changed in recent years. In the past, children with spina bifida often got urinary tract infections that caused serious kidney disease. Fortunately, this is no longer the case. We now try to prevent kidney disease. We also have made great progress in helping children with spina bifida become dry.

What Is the Urinary Tract System?

The urinary tract system consists of two kidneys, two ureters, the bladder, the sphincter muscle, which controls the flow of urine, and the urethra, which brings the urine from the bladder to the outside world.

The kidneys filter the blood and make urine. Urine goes from the kidneys to the bladder through tubes called the ureters. Where the ureters and the bladder join, there are one-way valves that stop the urine from going backwards into the kidneys. The bladder holds the urine, and then releases it through the urethra every few hours. Normally, as urine fills the bladder, it stretches to hold more and more urine at a low bladder pressure. When the bladder becomes full, a message is sent to the brain. Signals from the brain then tell the sphincter muscle to relax, and the bladder muscle to contract at the same time, so the bladder can empty. Normally, a person can wait until it is the right time to empty the bladder.

How Does Spina Bifida Affect the Kidneys and Bladder?

Most infants with spina bifida are born with kidneys that work well, although this can change. Most children with spina bifida have what is called a neurogenic bladder. In a neurogenic bladder, the nerves going from the spinal cord to the brain do not work properly. The child may not be aware that the bladder is full and often cannot empty the bladder well. Also, the sphincter muscle may not work. It may either stay relaxed or not relax when the bladder is contracting. If the bladder doesn't empty well, it can cause damage to the kidneys and/or lead to urinary tract infections. Only about 5 percent of children with spina bifida are able to empty their bladders without help.

Goals of Urological Management

- To make sure the kidneys are working well and prevent damage
- To help the child to empty the bladder
- To help the child stay dry

What Tests Will Be Done to Assess Your Child's Urinary Tract?

Ongoing assessment and monitoring of the urinary tract system will be an important part of your child's care. This may include any of the following tests:

- **Urinalysis and urine culture:** To check for infection.
- **Blood tests, including creatinine and BUN (blood urea nitrogen):** To check how well the kidneys are working.

- **Renal/bladder ultrasound:** This is a test done in the x-ray department and checks the size and shape of the kidneys and bladder, as well as checking for other abnormalities.

- **VCUG (voiding cystourethrogram):** This is a test done in the x-ray department to check for reflux, which is when the urine flows backwards from bladder to the kidneys. It also shows the shape of the bladder and urethra, and how well the bladder empties.

- **Urodynamic studies:** This is a special study that shows how the bladder works, including:

  - How much urine the bladder will hold.

  - At what pressures the bladder fills, stores, and empties urine.

  - How well the bladder empties.

  - How well the bladder and sphincter muscle work together.

  - If reflux is present, information from this test helps to show which children may be at risk for developing problems. It is also helpful in keeping track of how the child's bladder is responding to treatment.

- **Renal scans:** These scans provide information on:

  - how well the kidneys work;

  - if there is a problem with the drainage of urine from the kidneys to the bladder;

  - if there are scars on the kidneys (showing past infection) or other changes indicating current infection.

What Urological Problems Are Common in Children with Spina Bifida?

- **Urinary tract infections**.

- **Vesicoureteral reflux:** This is when the urine backs up from the bladder through the ureters to the kidneys. This can be caused by high pressures in the bladder. Reflux can cause kidney damage because infection can spread from the bladder to the kidneys.

- **Hydronephrosis:** Swelling of the kidney from the backup of urine. This can be caused by high bladder pressures.

- **Incontinence:** The child is unable to stay dry. This can cause both physical and social problems.

Why Do These Problems Occur?

Due to nerve damage, the bladder and sphincter muscle may not work properly. The bladder is supposed to fill and store urine at low pressure and empty every few hours. Both of these may be affected.

Problems with Filling and Storage

- The bladder is not able to keep pressures low as it fills with urine. High bladder pressures can hurt the kidney.
- The bladder is not able to hold as much urine as it should.

Problems with Bladder Emptying

- Leaking of urine can occur when bladder pressures are too high and the bladder overpowers the sphincter muscle. Leaking may also occur even with normal bladder pressures if the sphincter muscle is very relaxed and doesn't tighten when it should.

- The bladder may not empty all the way. This may happen because the bladder isn't strong enough, or because the sphincter muscle doesn't relax when the bladder contracts.

What Will Be Done to Keep Your Child's Urinary Tract Healthy?

Closely checking the child's urinary tract is necessary. At different ages, various suggestions may be made. These include:

- **Clean intermittent catheterization:** A procedure to empty the bladder by inserting a soft, flexible tube called a catheter into the bladder to drain the urine. This helps prevent infections, reduces bladder pressures, and helps the child to become dry.

- **Medication:** Medications are given to:
  - Prevent and treat infection. These are called antibiotics.
  - Relax the bladder so it may hold more urine at low pressures. These are called anticholinergics and include Ditropan, Levsin, or Levsinex/Levbid.
  - Help prevent leaking.

- **Surgery:** Sometimes surgery is needed when medicines and clean intermittent catheterization do not work well enough. There are several procedures used, depending on what type of problem needs to be treated. Some surgical procedures are temporary; some are permanent. Surgery may be done to treat reflux, to enlarge the bladder, to improve sphincter function, or to provide emptying of the bladder through other ways than the urethra.

Ongoing Assessment and Management by Age

Newborns

Several tests are done shortly after birth to learn about the baby's urinary tract system. Baseline studies include:

- Urinalysis or urine culture.

- BUN and creatinine.

- Post void residual. This is the amount of urine left in the bladder after the baby has wet a diaper. This is done by catheterizing the baby and measuring the amount of urine left in the bladder.

- Renal or bladder ultrasound to check for physical abnormalities that would put the baby at risk for problems.

- Urodynamic studies to check bladder pressures and emptying ability is usually done during the first month of life.

Your infant's urologist will make suggestions based on what is learned from the various tests. In general:

- If no reflux or swelling of the kidney is present, bladder pressures are low, and there is not a large amount of urine left in the bladder, nothing special may be needed and the baby may wet normally in the diapers.

- If reflux is present, the baby may be started on clean intermittent catheterization and a daily low dose of an antibiotic to prevent infections.

- If the bladder pressures are high, clean intermittent catheterization is started. Anticholinergic medications may also be started to help relax the bladder and lower pressures.

- If medicine and clean intermittent catheterization are not helping enough, or if it is too hard for the parents to catheterize their infant on a regular basis, surgery may be needed.

Infants

Close monitoring of the infant's urinary tract is done during the first year of life. Generally renal ultrasounds and/or urodynamic studies are done every three to six months. This is because there can be changes in how the bladder works as the baby grows and the nerves and spinal cord develop. The tests also show how the infant is responding to his current care plan. A catheterized urine culture should be done any time the baby may have a urinary tract infection. Symptoms of infection in a baby include fever, fussiness, and not eating well.

Toddlers

Continued close monitoring is important. Renal ultrasounds are obtained every three to six months and urodynamic studies every six months. A catheterized urine culture should be done if the child shows signs of infection.

Preschoolers

Renal ultrasounds and urodynamic studies are done every six to twelve months. Clean intermittent catheterization with or without medicine may be started to keep the child dry. A catheterized urine culture should be done if the child shows symptoms such as fever, back pain, foul-smelling urine, or increased wetting.

School-Age Children

Yearly renal ultrasound and urodynamic studies are done as indicated. Catheterized urine cultures should be done if the child shows symptoms of a urinary tract infection. The child may begin self clean intermittent catheterization if he feels ready.

Adolescents

Yearly renal ultrasound and other tests will be done as needed. Urine cultures should be done any time there are symptoms of infection. By this time, adolescents should know the signs and symptoms of urinary tract infection, how to take their medicines, and how to catheterize themselves. Sexual function and expectations should be discussed.

Section 35.4

Latex Allergy in Spina Bifida

People with spina bifida are at high risk for latex allergy.

What Is Natural Rubber Latex?

Natural rubber latex (NRL) is a milky substance tapped from the *Hevea brasiliensis* (a tropical rubber tree). It can be heated and molded into hard rubber products like tires; or it can be dipped to make softer products like balloons or medical examination gloves.

What Is Latex Allergy?

Latex allergy means that a person is allergic to proteins in the natural rubber latex. Although anyone can develop a latex allergy, it is thought to be caused by significant long-term exposure to latex proteins that are released during processing of the rubber. The amount of latex exposure needed to produce sensitization or an allergic reaction is unknown, but softer rubber products that have been processed longer (like gloves and balloons) are seen as more allergenic; and frequent exposure to latex products increases the risk of developing a sensitivity.

People who have spina bifida and catheterize, or have several surgeries from very early in life, such as bladder surgery or shunt revisions, are at very high risk for allergy because of a "cumulative" effect over time. Symptoms of latex sensitivity can be minor, but without warning, may become life threatening. Many people are unaware that they are sensitized to latex because the symptoms can be vague and nonspecific. Those people are at risk for a serious reaction.

What Are the Symptoms of Latex Allergy?

- Itching

- Skin redness, hives, or rash

- Sneezing

- Runny nose

- Itchy, watery eyes

- Scratchy throat

- Cough

- Wheezing

The most serious allergic reaction to latex is anaphylaxis, a type of shock. An anaphylactic response to latex is a medical emergency. Signs and symptoms include:

- Difficulty breathing caused by swelling of lips, tongue, or windpipe

- Severe wheezing

- Severe drop in blood pressure (hypotension)

- Dizziness

- Loss of consciousness

- Confusion

- Slurred speech

- Rapid or weak pulse

- Blue hue of the skin, including lips and nail beds

- Diarrhea

- Nausea and vomiting

Latex Items

Because of its low cost, durability, and versatility, natural latex has been widely used in the United States for over a century and is used in the production of many common items. Although most medical products are labeled, household or recreational items which contain latex may not be labeled. For that reason, the Latex Allergy Association and the Spina Bifida Association work diligently to keep a current list of products that contain latex and their "safe" (nonlatex) alternatives.

What Are Cross-Reactions to Latex Allergy?

People allergic to latex may also be allergic to the proteins in some fruits and vegetables. Some of them include: banana, avocado, chestnut, kiwi, apple, carrot, celery, papaya, potato, tomato, melon, and avocado. Due to nutritional risks, people should not avoid eating these foods unless they have had a reaction to them and are advised by a dietary or medical professional to avoid them.

What Steps Should I Take to Prevent Developing Latex Allergy?

The best way to prevent developing latex allergy is to avoid contact with latex or latex-contaminated powder. Contact occurs through contact with skin, inhaling latex spores, or internally through medical procedures or surgery, when latex touches the skin, mouth, eyes, genital areas, or bladder. Severe reactions can occur if latex enters the bloodstream. Powder from latex balloons or gloves gets into the air. Therefore, people with spina bifida are at high risk for latex allergy and should avoid exposure to natural latex products from birth. Products made of silicone, plastic, nitrile, or vinyl can be used instead.

Those who have had a serious reaction to latex should:

- wear a medic-alert bracelet or necklace;
- carry auto-injectable epinephrine; and
- carry sterile nonlatex gloves and other nonlatex medical items for emergencies.

Discuss latex allergy and avoidance with health care providers, schools, day care, camps, visitors, and anyone else who is involved with the person who has spina bifida.

Chapter 36

Urinary Tract Defects

Chapter Contents

Section 36.1

Bladder Exstrophy

Sometimes factors can occasionally interfere with bladder development, as is the case for children with bladder exstrophy. If your newborn has been diagnosed with this condition, what can you expect? The following information should help you talk to your child's doctor.

What is bladder exstrophy?

Bladder exstrophy is an abnormality present at birth in which the bladder and associated structures are improperly formed. Rather than being its normal round shape, the bladder is flattened. The skin, muscle, and pelvic bones joining the lower part of the abdomen do not form properly so the inside of the bladder is exposed outside the abdomen. There are associated deficiencies of the abdominal muscles and pelvic bones also.

How often does it occur?

It is a rare occurrence. The incidence of bladder exstrophy varies in different parts of the world, but is approximately one in thirty thousand live births and is slightly more common in males than females. The risk of a family having more than one child with this condition is approximately one in one hundred, and children born to a parent with exstrophy have a risk of approximately one in seventy of having the condition. Recent published evidence suggests that the risk of bladder exstrophy in children born as a result of assisted fertility techniques is seven times greater than in children conceived naturally without assistance.

Why does it happen?

There is no known cause for this condition but there are many theories. Some experts believe during the eleventh week of pregnancy the embryo undergoes structural changes including ingrowths of tissue in the lower abdominal wall, which stimulates development of muscles and pelvic bones. Up to this point the primitive bladder and rectum are contained within tissue called the cloacal membrane. The rectum then separates from the bladder, and if migration of tissue towards the midline over the primitive bladder fails the cloacal membrane may rupture, creating an exstrophied bladder. The exact timing of premature rupture of the membrane determines whether the child is born with isolated epispadias, classic bladder exstrophy, or cloacal exstrophy. Generally classic bladder exstrophy is an isolated birth defect but spinal cord abnormalities occur in about 13 percent of cases.

It is known, however, that it is not a result of anything that a parent did or did not do during pregnancy.

How is it diagnosed?

Frequently it can be detected before birth during a routine sonogram. Nonetheless, this condition will be obvious at birth.

What will happen when the child is born?

If this condition has been detected before birth, arrangements will usually be made for birth at a specialist unit where a pediatrician and surgeon can assess the baby immediately. Alternatively, if the condition is not detected until the time of birth, transfer to such a unit for assessment will need to be arranged for the first day of life. In either case, the bladder will be visible on the outside of the baby's abdomen and assessment of bladder size and quality, the shape of the pelvis, and also the condition of the genitals will be made.

What treatments are available?

Bladder exstrophy is treated surgically. Several surgical treatment options are available but they depend upon the severity of the condition. The primary treatment objectives are:

1. Securely closing the bladder, posterior urethra, and pelvis

2. Reconstruction of a cosmetically pleasing and functioning penis in the male and external genitalia in the female

3. Achieving urinary continence while ensuring preservation of kidney function

One form of treatment is modern staged reconstruction that involves closure of the bladder and pelvis in the newborn period, early reconstruction of the epispadiac urethra at approximately six months of age, and bladder neck surgery to achieve continence when the bladder has reached sufficient capacity and the child is psychologically ready to be dry (often around four to five years of age). Often further operations are needed to improve continence. Additional surgical procedures to improve the external genitalia are almost always required. In select cases where the bladder is of good quality and the penis is of good size, closure of the bladder and reconstruction of the penis and urethra can be combined in one operation. This is very technically demanding surgery and should only be performed by an experienced exstrophy surgeon.

The results of staged reconstruction have been well documented, and given the development of a bladder with sufficient capacity, continence can be achieved in up to 73 to 78 percent of cases. The most important factors in achieving continence are the quality of the bladder template and a successful initial bladder closure in the newborn. Of course, there are instances when the bladder at birth is of poor quality and unsuitable for closure in the way described, and a different management is adopted. Using techniques of modern reconstructive surgery, it is exceptionally rare for a patient to reach late adolescence without achieving continence and cosmetically acceptable external genitalia.

Other methods of treatment involve urinary diversion where the normal flow of urine is rerouted.

What is the outlook for a baby born with this condition?

There is no doubt that in modern times, children with exstrophy can and do grow up to be robust individuals with a normal life expectancy and no real restriction on their lifestyle.

Are there other disorders associated with bladder exstrophy?

Yes, some of these may include epispadias, vesicoureteral reflux, pubic diastasis, small bladder capacity, or missing bladder neck and sphincter.

Section 36.2

Ectopic Ureter

Most of us are born with two ureters, one to drain the urine from each kidney into the bladder. But nature has given some of us more than the normal allotment. In most cases, a bonus ureter causes no problems. Yet what if one of these ureters it is not connected correctly—and drains incorrectly? That is the case for children with an ectopic ureter, a bonus that is not a plus. Luckily, medicine has given urologists a bevy of diagnostic tests and surgical techniques to deal with this abnormality. So read below to see how your child's doctor might correct this condition.

What are the causes of ectopic ureter?

Normally, there is a single ureter draining the urine from each kidney to the bladder. The urine is then stored in the bladder until one voluntarily urinates. Occasionally, there may be two ureters draining a single kidney. One ureter drains the upper part of the kidney and the second ureter drains the lower portion. So long as they both enter the bladder normally, this "duplicated collecting system" is not a problem. Rarely a child may be born with an ectopic ureter. This is a ureter which fails to connect properly to the bladder and drains somewhere outside the bladder. In girls, the ectopic ureter usually drains into the urethra or even the vagina. In boys, it usually drains into the urethra near the prostate or into the genital duct system. An ectopic ureter can occur in a nonduplicated collecting system but is more common in a duplicated system.

What are the symptoms of ectopic ureter?

Blockage of the ureter or the inability to control urination (incontinence) can indicate an ectopic ureter. Poor drainage, accompanied by back pressure, can cause the ureter and portion of the kidney it services to become distended or swollen. This condition is called hydronephrosis and can be spotted easily on an ultrasound. For this reason, many babies with an ectopic ureter are detected when the pregnant mother undergoes a prenatal ultrasound. However, not all ectopic ureters are hydronephrotic, so they may not be detected by an ultrasound.

Poor drainage from an ectopic ureter may make children more likely to have urinary tract infections. In addition to hydronephrosis, ectopic ureters in girls may cause incontinence since the ureter drains urine directly into or near the vagina. This problem becomes evident after toilet-training. It is usually distinguished from other forms of incontinence in girls because the incontinence is a constant dripping moistness rather than episodes of loss of bladder control. Some girls will be treated with medication and other therapies for many years before the correct diagnosis of an ectopic ureter is made. Boys with ectopic ureters do not generally have incontinence since the ectopic ureter drains inside the body. However, they may still show symptoms of hydronephrosis or a urinary tract infection.

When an ectopic ureter is present, there may also be a slight flaw in the normal ureter's connection between the kidney and bladder. This flaw can result in vesicoureteral reflux, a disruption of the passage of urine from the kidney, through the ureter, to the bladder, and finally out the urethra. With reflux, as the bladder fills or empties some urine flows backward into the kidney. Vesicoureteral reflux places patients at a higher risk for kidney infections and is another reason some children with ectopic ureters show signs of a urinary tract infection.

How is ectopic ureter diagnosed?

The evaluation of an ectopic ureter depends on the problem shown by the patient (usually a child). For instance, if hydronephrosis is detected on a prenatal ultrasound, then the ultrasound is usually repeated after the child is born. A bladder x-ray, called a voiding cystourethrogram (VCUG) is then taken to rule out vesicoureteral reflux as the cause for swelling of the kidney and ureter. The VCUG is also used to determine if there is reflux in a second ureter associated with the ectopic ureter. Usually with the combination of an ultrasound and a VCUG the doctor can determine if there is hydronephrosis. Sometimes other diagnostic studies such as renal flow scan or a formal kidney x-ray, called an intravenous pyelogram (IVP), may help to clarify the anatomy. The kidney or portion of the kidney drained by the ectopic ureter often functions poorly. This can be assessed with a renal flow scan. Both tests involve an injection of contrast dye picked up by the kidney and then seen either by standard x-ray pictures (for an IVP) or with a special camera for detecting small amounts of radioactivity in the dye (for the renal flow scan). This functional information may be important in selecting the form of treatment. Finally, a cystoscopy may be performed (often at the time of definitive treatment). In this test, usually performed under a general anesthesia, a small telescope is placed into the urethra and vagina and the openings of the ureters from both kidneys are identified. Unfortunately, the ectopic ureter's opening cannot always be identified. However, by identifying the number and location of the other ureter openings, the diagnosis can usually be confirmed.

When a child shows symptoms of urinary incontinence, the same sequence of tests is usually undertaken. However, if the ureter is not swollen and there is no associated reflux, the ultrasound and VCUG may be normal. If the symptoms suggest an ectopic ureter, then sometimes this can be seen on a renal flow scan or IVP. Occasionally, a computed tomography (CT) scan is needed to see the ectopic ureter and the portion of the kidney it drains. The diagnosis is not always easy to make and since other causes of incontinence are very common in children, some children may be incontinent for years before the diagnosis is made.

How is an ectopic ureter treated?

The treatment for ectopic ureter is surgery. To control the risk of infection, the patient may be placed on a low dose of antibiotics prior to surgery.

While there are three surgical techniques—nephrectomy, ureteropyelostomy, and ureteral reimplantation—to correct this problem, each has advantages and disadvantages.

Nephrectomy (upper pole heminephrectomy): In this surgery, the kidney or the portion of it drained by the ectopic ureter is removed. This stops the flow of urine into the ectopic ureter, thus curing the incontinence and reducing the chance of infection. Technically the simplest operation, it also has the lowest complication risk. It is particularly attractive when the kidney or portion of the kidney draining through the ectopic ureter is functioning poorly. It may also be used when that kidney portion is functioning properly if the opposite kidney is normal. This operation has been traditionally performed through an incision under the ribs but can now be done laparoscopically in some patients. The main disadvantages are that the potentially functioning kidney tissue may be removed and the bottom end of the ectopic ureter is left in place. While usually not a problem, the remaining part of the ectopic ureter can be a future source for infection.

Ureteropyelostomy: In this procedure, the ectopic ureter is divided near the kidney and sewn into the normal collecting system of the lower part of the kidney. This allows the urine from the upper part of the kidney to drain normally. It has the advantage of protecting all the kidney tissue but still leaves the bottom half of the ectopic ureter in place. It also has a slightly higher complication rate than the other operations.

Ureteral reimplantation: In this operation, the ectopic ureter is divided near the bottom and sewn into the bladder in such a way that urine drains well and does not flow backwards. Usually performed through an incision above the pubic bone, this procedure has a slightly higher complication rate than the other two surgeries. It can also be technically difficult if performed in small infants. However, like ureteropyelostomy, this operation preserves all kidney tissue. Furthermore, it removes more of the abnormal ectopic ureter than the other two procedures and allows the surgeon to stop any vesicoureteral reflux.

What can be expected after treatment for ectopic ureter?

Recovery depends on the operation selected. However, infants and small children are usually hospitalized from one to five days after the surgery. A small catheter may be left at the time of surgery, which is removed painlessly and quickly before the child goes home or in the office at a follow-up visit. The small openings, where the catheter went in, heal on their own without the need for stitches.

Are boys or girls more likely to have an ectopic ureter?

This condition is more common in girls than boys, but can occur in either sex.

What is the optimal age for ectopic ureter surgery?

Nephrectomies and heminephrectomies can be performed any time after an infant reaches one month. Some surgeons prefer to wait until a child is older, usually after a first birthday, to perform a ureteral reimplantation.

What are the risk factors for an ectopic ureter?

There are no known risk factors for an ectopic ureter. It is a congenital problem that probably occurs because of a failure in the development of the connection between the ureter and bladder.

Was this caused by something that happened during pregnancy?

There is also no evidence that this abnormality is caused by anything a mother does or was exposed to during pregnancy.

Does an ectopic ureter have any impact on my child's future sexual function?

Although an ectopic ureter drains to the genital tract, it does not affect sexual function and rarely impairs fertility. In boys, the genital tract on the same side of the ectopic ureter may be abnormal but if the other side is unaffected (which is usually the case), then fertility should still be normal.

Are my other children at risk for an ectopic ureter?

The duplicated drainage system of the kidney is usually transmitted genetically as an autosomal dominant condition, meaning that each brother or sister has a one-half chance of having two ureters draining one or both kidneys. If both ureters drain into the bladder, however, they should not experience any urological problem or require surgery for the condition. The child with an ectopic ureter should be advised that each of their children have a one-half likelihood of having a duplicated drainage system, but that in most cases an ectopic ureter will not be present.

If part or all of a kidney is functioning poorly or removed, will my child have lifelong kidney problems?

No, not as long as the other kidney is normal. Most ectopic ureters affect just the upper part of one kidney, which provides only one-third of that kidney's function to the body. Even when an entire kidney is affected, long-term problems are unlikely. Children are frequently born with a single kidney and never know it, and patients who donate a kidney also do fine. The only implication is that the patient no longer has a "spare" kidney. Therefore, in the unlikely event that the person was to injure their only kidney in an accident, then they would develop kidney failure if a complete nephrectomy were performed. If only a portion of the kidney was removed during the nephrectomy, the patient will do very well in the long term.

Section 36.3

Epispadias

What is epispadias?

Epispadias occurs when the urethral opening, the tube that drains the urine from the bladder to the outside of the body, is not in the correct location. Epispadias can occur alone, but usually occurs in conjunction with bladder extrophy, which is a combination of disorders that occurs during fetal development.

When this condition occurs in boys, the urethra opens on the top side of the penis, instead of at the tip. In girls, the urethral opening is bigger and longer than normal, positioned further up the urethral tube, and can extend all the way to the bladder.

What are the signs and symptoms?

In boys the penis is typically short and broad and the urethral opening located on the top side of the penis. From the location of the abnormal opening to the tip, the penis may be split. There may also be an abnormal curvature of the penis toward the abdomen.

Girls will have a narrow vaginal opening, wide labia, a split clitoris, and a short urethra. Wide pubic bones, urinary tract infections, urinary incontinence, and reflux of urine into the kidneys are also symptoms of epispadias.

How do you diagnose it?

The diagnosis of epispadias typically happens at birth. If the malformation is not severe, it may be diagnosed when the child (usually female) continues to have wetting after potty training.

How is it treated?

The primary goal of treatment is to create typical-looking external genitalia that function well. In boys, surgical treatment is performed to maximize penile length and function by correcting the bend in the penis and moving the urethra so the boy pees from the end of the penis. In girls, this means fusing the clitoris, moving the urethra, and repairing the bladder's control mechanism to prevent urinary leaking.

Who gets it and can it be prevented?

Epispadias is a very rare congenital defect affecting 1 in 117,000 newborn boys and 1 in 484,000 newborn girls.

When should I seek medical attention?

A pediatric urologist should be consulted when you or the child's pediatrician have any concerns about the genitourinary tract appearance or function.

Section 36.4

Megaureter

The vast majority of children are born with urinary tracts that are normal in appearance and function normally efficiently. But in some infants, megaureters, an abnormal widening of the connecting tube between the kidneys and bladder, can cause infections and obstructions, and possibly serious kidney damage if the problem is not diagnosed and treated. But what are the symptoms? The information below should give you a head start about this potentially serious health hazard.

What are megaureters?

The ureters are tube-like structures in the body that carry or propel urine from the kidneys to the bladder. While the normal width of a child's ureter is three to five millimeters (mm.), a megaureter is a tube that is greater than 10 mm. (three-eighths of an inch) in diameter, hence the term "megaureter" ("large ureter"). Certain conditions produce this abnormal widening. The condition of megaureter can result from an abnormality of the ureter itself (primary) or from conditions related to the bladder obstruction (secondary).

What are the different types of megaureters?

Most megaureters are classified as the following:

- **Primary obstructed megaureter:** A distinct anatomical blockage where the ureter enters the bladder. This obstruction of the ureter then causes the abnormal widening of the ureter. The obstruction can produce damage to the kidney over time. This condition, when accurately diagnosed, is likely to require surgical repair for its correction and relief of obstruction. Even though the problem may improve with time, diligent follow-up is necessary.

- **Refluxing megaureters:** These ureters are wide because of abnormal backward flow of urine (vesicoureteral reflux) up the ureters from the bladder. Normally, once that urine is in the bladder, it should not go back up the ureters. Refluxing mega- ureters are an extreme presentation of vesicoureteral reflux, and can be seen more commonly in newborn males. In some of these patients, the degree of reflux, and widening of the ureters, can improve over the first year of life. Persistently refluxing megaureters require surgical correction by a procedure termed ureteral reimplantation, and by possibly tapering or surgically narrowing the caliber of the ureters. The condition of refluxing megaureters may be linked to the condition known as "mega- cystis megaureter syndrome," a condition where the bladder, instead of emptying completely, is enlarged due to cycling of urine between it and the ureters via reflux.

- **Nonobstructive, nonrefluxing megaureters:** These are wide ureters not caused by obstruction or urine backflow. Many of these improve with time. Accurate evaluation of these wide ureters is necessary to exclude both obstruction and reflux as the causes of the widening.

- **Obstructed, refluxing megaureters:** An obstructed ureter that also suffers from reflux. A dangerous combination since the ureters gets bigger and more blocked with time.

- **Secondary megaureters:** These enlarged ureters appear in as- sociation with other conditions such as posterior urethral valves, prune belly syndrome, and neurogenic bladder.

What are the symptoms of megaureter?

In the past, the majority of megaureters were found during the evaluation of a child with a urinary tract infection. These patients usually experience fever, back pain, and vomiting.

But today, because of the widespread use of prenatal fetal sonogra- phy, more megaureters are discovered as prenatal hydronephrosis or dilatation of the urinary tract in the fetus.

Because megaureters can cause a severe infection or obstruction that leads to kidney damage, this health issue is potentially serious. Dilatation of the urinary tract may imply a blockage or obstruction, but that is not always the case. In some situations, a dilated ureter may not affect the kidney at all. Also, most patients with prenatally detected megaureters do not experience symptoms related to this wide ureter, but evaluation is necessary to assure that there is no potential compromise of kidney function which may later produce symptoms.

How is a megaureter diagnosed?

If your child develops a urinary tract infection, or other symptoms that could signal this condition, check with your doctor. Further investigation is warranted. You can expect the urologist to conduct a series of tests to clarify the anatomy and function of the urinary tract. They include:

- **Ultrasound:** Also known as sonography, this simple and painless imaging test is usually done to evaluate the appearance of the kidney, ureter, and bladder. The study is highly sensitive in detecting widened ureters. In fact, while sonography rarely picks up normal ureters because of their narrowed size, this technology produces excellent images of dilated ones.

- **Voiding cystourethrogram (VCUG):** A VCUG is done to determine if vesicoureteral reflux is occurring. A small catheter is inserted through the urethra into the bladder and a contrast dye is injected into the bladder before x-rays are taken. If reflux is present, the image will show the contrast produced by the backflow into the ureter.

- **Diuretic renal scans:** Used to evaluate for a possible obstruction, this test is performed by injecting a radioactive substance into a vein, which is then carried to the kidneys. While the study yields data about a possible blockage, it also gives physicians information about the organ's function.

- **Intravenous pyelogram (IVP):** Also referred to as excretory program, IVP is performed by injecting dye into a vein and taking x-ray pictures of the abdomen as the dye is emptied from the kidneys. While renal scans have replaced IVP in evaluating dilated urinary tracts, this test can be extremely helpful in questionable cases.

- **Magnetic resonance of the urinary tract (MR-U):** This evolving technology produces excellent imaging of the urinary tract, much more accurately than IVPs, and may become the most anatomically sensitive imaging study of the urinary tract for conditions such as megaureters. It also involves injecting dye and imaging the urinary tract using magnetic resonance technology. Its use in small children is limited because of the need for sedation or possibly general anesthesia.

How is a megaureter treated?

If tests reveal an obstruction or impaired kidney function, your child may need surgery to correct the problem. The typical operation for megaureters is called ureteral reimplantation and ureteral tapering, the technical term urologists use for inserting the ureters back into the bladder and for trimming the widened ureter. Unless the child has a urinary tract infection or decrease in kidney function, the surgery can be delayed until twelve months of age. Surgery in infants is technically demanding and should be performed by individuals experienced with neonatal surgery. Many babies are kept on antibiotic prophylaxis during this period of observation to minimize the likelihood of infections.

During the procedure, the surgeon makes an incision in the lower abdomen and, depending on the child's anatomy, approaches the ureter through either the bladder (transvesical) or from outside the bladder (extravesical). The ureter is disconnected from the bladder, and if very wide, it may need to be trimmed (tapered) and then replaced in the bladder. If an obstruction exists, it is removed. Your child may have a catheter for a few days to improve healing. Hospitalization is usually between two and four days.

Currently, most symptomatic megaureters are best treated by this open type of surgery where the blockage is removed (for obstructed megaureters), the efflux is corrected (for refluxing megaureters), and possibly the ureters are trimmed (for very wide ureters). Minimally invasive technologies such as injection of substances to correct reflux or laparoscopy for ureteral reimplantation are not currently applicable for megaureters.

What can be expected after treatment for a megaureter?

Several weeks after surgery, some of the tests that were done before surgery may need to be repeated to determine the success of the surgery. The size of the ureter may not improve immediately after surgery, so evaluation over time will be necessary to ensure a good outcome. Potential complications of surgery are bleeding, obstruction of the ureter, and persistent or new vesicoureteral reflux. Obstruction may occur soon after the operation or after a longer period of time. Fortunately, this complication occurs in only 5 percent of cases and it may require additional surgery. Vesicoureteral reflux complication may occur after surgery in 5 percent of the cases and may improve with time. Most patients are followed for a number of years, using ultrasound, to ensure that the appearance of the kidney and ureter continues to improve. A renal scan is often done to assure that function is preserved or improved, and that obstruction is corrected, and a VCUG is often obtained a few months after surgery to assure that reflux is not present.

Is this condition genetic?

At this time scientists do not know if there are genetic links.

Is surgery always necessary to correct a megaureter?

No. Some megaureters may improve over time without the need for surgery. However, it is important to prevent infections during the time of observation, so antibiotics are usually prescribed.

Is minimally invasive surgery an option?

It may be possible to place a stent or catheter through the blocked portion of the megaureter as a temporary procedure to improve the drainage of the kidney. Laparoscopic techniques are not presently well developed to correct most megaureters but that may change in the future.

Are there long-term problems if we do not do anything?

Possibly yes. They include ureteral stones, urinary tract infection, deterioration of kidney function, and back pain.

Section 36.5

Urachal Anomalies

Before birth, there is a connection between the belly button and the bladder. This connection, called the urachus, normally disappears before birth. But what happens if part of the urachus remains after birth? Read on to learn more about what problems can arise.

What happens under normal conditions?

The bladder, located in the lower abdomen, is formed from structures located in the lower half of the developing fetus that are directly connected to the umbilical cord. After the first few weeks of gestation, this thick pathway to and from the placenta contains blood vessels, a merged channel to the future intestine, and a tubular structure called the allantois. The internal part of the allantois is connected to the top of the developing bladder, and in ordinary circumstances, collapses and becomes a cord-like structure called the urachus. The formation and regression of this connection from the top of the bladder to the bellybutton are completed by the middle of the second trimester of pregnancy (approximately twenty weeks).

Although the urachus is easily seen by a surgeon whenever an operation inside the abdomen or around the bladder is performed, it is a remnant of development that serves no further purpose but can be a source of specific health problems. Such problems are rare and usually seen in childhood, but occasionally can be seen for the first time in adults.

What are the symptoms of urachal abnormalities?

Because this remnant of early development is found between the belly button and the top of the bladder, diseases of the urachus can appear anywhere in that space. In newborns and infants, persistent drainage or "wetness" of the belly button can be a sign of a urachal problem. However, the most common detectable problem at the belly button is a granuloma, a reddened area that is present because the base of the umbilical cord stump did not heal properly.

Urachal abnormalities can also be seen without persistent umbilical drainage—35 percent of urachal problems are manifestations of an enclosed urachal cyst or infected urachal cyst (abscess). This type of problem is seen more often in older children and adults. Instead of visible belly button drainage, the symptoms of such a cyst consist of lower abdominal pain, fever, a lump that can be felt, pain with urination, urinary tract infection, or hematuria.

How are urachal abnormalities treated?

An umbilical granuloma is usually treated by chemical cauterization in the office of the primary care provider. The condition is a superficial abdominal wall problem that heals after treatment and has no long-term implications; it is not caused by an urachal problem.

In contrast to the simple granuloma, persistent umbilical wetness needs to be further evaluated. Approximately 65 percent of all urachal problems appear as a sinus or drainage opening at the belly button. Most of those are not connected all the way to the bladder, but a small percentage represents an open pathway from the bladder to belly button, called a patent urachus. The drainage can be analyzed for urea and creatinine levels, which would be high if the fluid was primarily made of urine from a bladder connection instead of inflammatory tissue fluid. There can be associated redness from the drainage itself. Skin infection—indicated by tenderness, fever, or spreading redness of the surrounding skin—can occur and requires prompt antibiotic treatment and possible hospitalization. This is called omphalitis and can be caused by bacteria that have become involved with a urachal sinus or the other embryologic structure in the belly button that was once connected to the intestinal system and might also be persistent. Once inflammation is controlled, the nature and extent of an opening at the belly button can be determined by a sinogram. This involves placing a small tube into the sinus opening and allowing contrast material to flow in while taking x-rays to determine the direction and extent of the channel. If the channel follows the expected pathway toward the top of the bladder, the diagnosis is urachal sinus. Treatment should be directed toward complete surgical removal of the urachus and all of its connections, including a small amount of the top of the bladder. Leaving any portion of the structure allows for the possible development of a future malignancy. Less than 1 percent of all bladder malignancies occur in the urachus, but once the urachus has become a potential problem, it should be removed.

When there is no draining sinus to investigate, an ultrasound of the lower abdomen will show the typical findings of a fluid-filled, enclosed lump in the location of the urachus. In an adult, where the rare possibility of malignancy could be present, an abdominal and pelvic computed tomography (CT) scan might be helpful. Again, complete removal of the urachus is important. Simple needle or other drainage of the cyst will result in recurrence in at least one-third of patients, since the linings and structures are still present. About 80 percent of infected cysts are populated by *Staphylococcus aureus*, and one-third contains multiple types of bacteria. Almost all the time, such an infected cyst stays confined to its predetermined anatomical location; rarely, an infected cyst can drain into the peritoneal cavity and present with additional signs of peritonitis and febrile illness.

Therefore, most urachal problems can be characterized by the physical examination and a sinogram or ultrasound. Sometimes a combination of these is needed, and occasionally it is useful to obtain a voiding cystourethrogram. This is done when the draining urachus is associated with outlet obstruction of the bladder, which would also need to be treated. This possibility is usually determined by the age, gender, and physical examination of the patient. There are also situations where a direct look inside the bladder (cystoscopy) can add a bit more information to the diagnostic picture, but most urologists recommend that the basic course of action be determined by the previously described approach.

What can be expected after treatment for urachal abnormalities?

After complete surgical removal of a troublesome urachus with no immediate postoperative problems, there should be no further issues and no need for follow-up or evaluation on a regular basis.

Besides the problems that have already been outlined, are there other diseases that appear at the belly button?

As you might expect, there have been rare reports of other inflammatory problems involving the structures that are contained in the umbilical cord. These include infections of the remnant blood vessels. In addition, the vitelline duct, which is supposed to regress in its course between the belly button and the small intestine, sometimes has its own remnant problems. The sinogram that is useful for identifying urachal problems will also serve to identify a likely vitelline duct problem.

Occasionally, an intra-abdominal process such as appendicitis or ovarian cyst can mimic some of the symptoms of a urachal problem.

Are urachal abnormalities hereditary?

No. There is no evidence that they are inherited.

After my baby's umbilical cord stump came off, his belly button was extremely red. Is this normal or does he need immediate evaluation?

Some redness is expected after the stump falls away. Dabbing a small amount of alcohol on the site with a Q-tip twice a day will usually allow complete healing in two to three days. If the redness fails to improve or worsens, contact your primary care provider.

Section 36.6

Ureterocele

Most of us are born with two ureters, one from each kidney to drain the urine into the bladder. Yet what if the portion of the ureter closest to the bladder becomes enlarged because the ureter opening is very tiny and obstructs urine outflow? That is the case for people with a ureterocele. Luckily, medicine has given urologists a range of diagnostic tests and surgical techniques to deal with this abnormality. So read below to see how your urologist might correct this condition.

What happens under normal conditions?

Within the urinary tract, the kidneys filter and remove waste and water from the blood to produce urine. The urine travels from the kidneys down narrow tubes called the ureters, where it is then stored in the bladder. Normally, the attachment between the ureters and the bladder is a one-way flap valve that allows unimpeded urinary flow into the bladder but prevents urine from flowing backward (when urine flows backwards from the bladder it is called vesicoureteral reflux) into the kidneys. Approximately 1 out of 125 people may have two ureters draining a single kidney. One ureter drains the upper part of the kidney and the second ureter drains the lower portion. This "duplicated collecting system" is not a problem as long as each ureter enters the bladder normally. When the bladder empties, urine flows out of the body through the urethra, a tube at the bottom of the bladder. The opening of the urethra is at the end of the penis in boys and in front of the vagina in girls.

What is a ureterocele?

A ureterocele is a birth defect that affects the kidney, ureter, and bladder. When a person has a ureterocele, the portion of the ureter closest to the bladder swells up like a balloon because the ureteral opening is very tiny and obstructs urine outflow. As the urine flow is obstructed, urine backs up in the ureter. Approximately one in two thousand persons is affected by this condition. In 90 percent of girls the ureterocele occurs in the upper half of a duplicated urinary tract (two ureters draining from one kidney). Approximately half of boys have a duplicated urinary tract and half have a single system. Ureteroceles may be "ectopic" when a portion protrudes through the bladder outlet into the urethra, or "orthotopic" when they remain entirely within the bladder. In 5 to 10 percent of cases there is a ureterocele on both sides (bilateral). The majority of ureteroceles are diagnosed in children less than two years of age, although occasionally older children or adults are found to have a ureterocele.

What are some complications of a ureterocele?

This condition often predisposes an individual to a kidney infection. Vesicoureteral reflux is also common, particularly in individuals with a duplication of the urinary tract, because the ureterocele distorts the normal one-way valve attachment between the ureter and bladder. In addition, reflux into the opposite kidney is common for similar reasons. In rare cases, a ureterocele may prevent the passage of kidney stones. Also, the ureterocele may be so large that it completely obstructs the flow of urine from the bladder into the urethra. Occasionally, in girls, the ureterocele may sink and protrude all the way out from the opening of the urethra.

What are some symptoms of a ureterocele?

Usually a ureterocele has no symptoms. However, patients can have flank or back pain, urinary tract infection, fever, painful urination, foul-smelling urine, abdominal pain, blood in the urine (hematuria), and/or excessive urination.

How is a ureterocele diagnosed?

Usually doctors detect ureteroceles during maternal ultrasounds performed before birth, but they may not be diagnosed until a patient is being evaluated for another medical condition like a urinary tract infection.

Ultrasonography is the first imaging test used in evaluation. Additional imaging studies may also be necessary to help delineate the anatomy. One such test is a voiding cystourethrogram (VCUG), which is an x-ray examination of the bladder and lower urinary tract. A catheter is inserted through the urethra, the bladder is filled with a water-soluble contrast, and then the catheter is withdrawn. Several x-ray images of the bladder and urethra are captured as the patient empties the bladder. These images allow radiologists to diagnose any abnormalities in the flow of urine through the body.

In individuals with a ureterocele, it is also important to evaluate the function of the kidneys, specifically to determine whether the affected portion of the kidney has any function. In most cases, this evaluation is performed with a renal scan.

Abdominal computed tomography (CT) scans and magnetic resonance imaging (MRI) tests are additional studies that may also be performed in the evaluation of a patient with a ureterocele. These tests are usually performed in situations where the urinary tract anatomy is extremely ambiguous, and will allow the surgeon to better identify anatomical variations.

What are some treatment options?

The timing and type of treatment are based on the age of the patient, whether the affected portion of the kidney is functioning, and whether vesicoureteral reflux is present. In some cases, more than one procedure is necessary. In rare cases, observation (no treatment) may be recommended.

Because a ureterocele predisposes an individual to a kidney infection, usually an antibiotic is prescribed until the ureterocele and its complicating features have been treated. The following are available treatment options:

- **Transurethral puncture:** A form of minimally invasive therapy is to puncture and decompress the ureterocele using a cystoscope that is inserted through the urethra. The procedure usually takes fifteen to thirty minutes, and often can be done on an outpatient basis. In some cases, this treatment is unsuccessful if the ureterocele wall is thick and difficult to recognize. The advantage of this treatment is that there is no surgical incision. Risks include failure to adequately decompress the ureterocele, possibly causing urine to flow into the ureterocele, which could necessitate an open operation. In addition, there is a slight risk of causing an obstructive flap valve with the ureterocele, which can make it difficult to urinate. This treatment is best suited for ureteroceles entirely within the bladder (orthotopic) than for those that extend beyond the bladder, in which case it can be helpful, but is rarely the only treatment needed.

- **Upper pole nephrectomy:** Often, if the upper half of the kidney does not function because of the ureterocele and there is no vesicoureteral reflux, removal of the affected portion of the kidney is recommended. In many cases, this operation is performed through a small incision under the rib cage. In more and more cases it may be performed laparoscopically.

- **Nephrectomy:** If the entire kidney does not function because of the ureterocele, removal of the kidney is recommended. Usually this can be done laparoscopically, although at some centers it is performed through a very small incision under the rib cage.

- **Removal of the ureterocele and ureteral reimplantation:** If it is deemed necessary to remove the ureterocele, then an operation is performed in which the bladder is opened, the ureterocele is removed, the floor of the bladder and bladder neck are reconstructed, and the ureters are reimplanted in such a way to create a nonrefluxing connection between the ureters and the bladder. The operation is performed through a small lower abdominal incision. The success rate with this procedure is 90 to 95 percent. Complications include vesicoureteral reflux or obstruction.

- **Ureteropyelostomy or upper-to-lower ureteroureterostomy:** If the upper portion of the ureter shows significant function, one option is to connect the obstructed upper portion to the nonobstructed lower portion of the ureter or pelvis of the kidney. The operation is done through a small lower abdominal incision. The success rate with this procedure is 95 percent.

Is there any way to prevent this condition?

There is no known prevention for this condition; it is present at birth but may not be discovered until later in life.

My baby was diagnosed with a ureterocele on a prenatal ultrasound. She seems very healthy. Is it absolutely necessary for her to undergo treatment?

In the past, most children with a ureterocele had their condition detected following a serious kidney infection, which often required hospitalization for intravenous antibiotics. Consequently, it would be unusual for her not to develop a urinary tract infection unless her ureterocele was treated.

My doctor has recommended that my daughter take antibiotic prophylaxis because she has a ureterocele and urinary reflux. Is it safe to take antibiotics every day?

Many children and adults take a low dose of an antibiotic every day to prevent urinary tract infections. This form of therapy has been used for over thirty-five years and has proven to be relatively safe, as long as the dose is maintained at one-fourth to one-half the full dose. Although we recognize that using antibiotics has some downsides, one needs to weigh the risk of taking the antibiotic against the risk of a serious kidney infection if the antibiotic were not taken.

My child was diagnosed with a ureterocele and it was punctured through a small scope. Now there is reflux into the ureterocele and the lower part of the kidney also. Will more surgery be necessary?

In most cases, if there is reflux up the ureter into the lower part of the kidney and/or the ureterocele, the reflux is unlikely to disappear with time, and removal of the ureterocele and ureteral reimplantation is often necessary.

Section 36.7

Urinary Tract Obstruction

The urinary tract consists of two kidneys, two ureters (the tube that connects the kidney to the bladder), the bladder, and the urethra. Urine flows from the kidneys through the ureters into the bladder. Passing through the urethra, urine empties into the amniotic cavity. Fetal urine is the main component of amniotic fluid.

Urinary tract obstructions are caused by a narrowing at some point in the urinary tract that slows or stops the flow of urine. If one ureter is blocked, the kidney will not be able to produce urine and may become enlarged (hydronephrosis) or even damaged. If both ureters are blocked, or if the blockage is in the urethra, the fetus is unable to discharge (or "void") urine and cannot produce amniotic fluid, which can lead to underdeveloped lungs.

How common is it?

Congenital urinary tract obstruction occurs in one in five thousand to seven thousand births, most commonly in males.

How is it diagnosed?

It's normally diagnosed through ultrasound in the middle of the second trimester. Ultrasound is a noninvasive test that allows us to assess overall fetal growth and development, the severity of the obstruction, and the condition of the kidneys.

If an obstruction is detected, it's essential to assess the kidneys for functionality and damage. This also helps to determine whether a fetus may benefit from fetal intervention.

An additional test to monitor kidney function involves extracting a sample of fetal urine and analyzing the electrolytes and protein levels. This procedure is performed exactly like amniocentesis—a fine needle is inserted into the fetal bladder under ultrasound guidance. For the most accurate assessment of kidney function, a urine sample is taken twice, since the first sample has been in the bladder for a long time and may not provide the most accurate information.

What can happen before birth?

When the obstruction occurs in both kidneys or low in the urinary tract, it can damage or hinder the development of the kidneys (renal dysplasia) and the lungs. Fetal lungs need sufficient amniotic fluid to grow. If there is little or no fluid (oligohydramnios), the lungs cannot expand and may not fully develop (pulmonary hypoplasia).

In males, severe lower urinary tract obstructions are usually due to posterior urethral valves. The male urethra (the tube that connects the bladder to the tip of the penis) has a few folds that can become large enough to block the passage of urine. However, most of these blockages are incomplete and can be treated after birth.

What can be done before birth?

Most urinary tract problems of the fetus are minor: either a partial blockage on one side or an enlarged ureter or renal pelvis (the part of the kidney where urine collects before flowing into the ureter). As long as there is sufficient amniotic fluid, fetal intervention is unnecessary in these cases. Serial ultrasound will be used to monitor fetal development and amniotic fluid levels, and to help plan the delivery and care after birth.

Fetal intervention may be considered only when the risk of progressive damage to the kidneys or, more importantly, to the lungs, is high—for example, in cases of oligohydramnios.

Using local anesthesia and ultrasound guidance, a small tube (catheter) will be inserted through the abdominal wall of the fetus, into the bladder. The catheter is called a "double pigtail" because of its shape: both ends of the tube are curled to make sure that it stays in place; one end in the bladder and the other in the amniotic cavity. This allows urine to bypass the blockage in the urinary tract and empty into the amniotic fluid.

There is a small risk that this procedure may cause uterine contractions or rupture the membranes, which could lead to labor and premature delivery. Additionally, it can be difficult to place the catheter in the right place and it can become dislodged later—often because the fetus pulls it out. Furthermore, not all fetuses with urinary tract obstruction and oligohydramnios benefit from this procedure. If the kidneys have suffered too much damage, they cannot produce any urine. For these fetuses, there is little that can be done. Often they die at birth of respiratory problems caused by severely underdeveloped lungs.

Nevertheless, this procedure is the most effective in restoring amniotic fluid and bypassing a blockage, thereby helping lung development and often preventing further damage to the kidneys.

What are my delivery options?

Unless there are signs that the fetus is in trouble, preterm delivery or Cesarean section is not necessary. Cesarean section may be necessary for obstetrical reasons, however. It is recommended that mothers deliver in a hospital that has immediate access to a specialized neonatal intensive care unit (NICU), with a pediatric surgical specialist present.

What will happen at birth?

Although some babies will need an operation after birth, it's usually not urgent. Some may only require antibiotics to prevent urinary infections. Most babies do not require intensive care, and can be evaluated in the nursery or even after they have left the hospital.

What is the long-term outcome?

After birth, urologists and nephrologists (kidney specialists) evaluate kidney and bladder function to determine what may occur as the baby grows. Postnatal treatment options depend on the type of obstruction. For posterior urethral valves, endoscopic resection is a minimally invasive technique performed within the first weeks of life, along with the removal of the shunt. Urologic surgeons attach specialized surgical instruments to a tool with a light and camera (endoscope) and insert it into the urethra to remove the tissue (valves) causing the obstruction.

In more complicated cases, a vesicostomy—an opening below the belly button that allows the bladder to drain directly into a diaper—diverts urine until the baby is healthy enough to undergo valve resection or urethral reconstruction.

Section 36.8

Vesicoureteral Reflux

Excerpted from "Vesicoureteral Reflux,"
National Institute of Diabetes and Digestive and Kidney Diseases,
National Institutes of Health, June 29, 2012.

What Is Vesicoureteral Reflux (VUR)?

Vesicoureteral reflux is the abnormal flow of urine from the bladder to the upper urinary tract. The urinary tract is the body's drainage system for removing wastes and extra water. The urinary tract includes two kidneys, two ureters, a bladder, and a urethra. Blood flows through the kidneys, and the kidneys filter out wastes and extra water, making urine. The urine travels down two narrow tubes called the ureters. The urine is then stored in a balloon-like organ called the bladder. When the bladder empties, urine flows out of the body through a tube called the urethra at the bottom of the bladder.

In VUR, urine may flow back—reflux—into one or both ureters and, in some cases, to one or both kidneys. VUR that affects only one ureter and kidney is called unilateral reflux, and VUR that affects both ureters and kidneys is called bilateral reflux.

Who Gets VUR?

Vesicoureteral reflux is more common in infants and young children, but older children and even adults can be affected. About 10 percent of children have VUR.[1] Studies estimate that VUR occurs in about 32 percent of siblings of an affected child. This rate may be as low as 7 percent in older siblings and as high as 100 percent in identical twins. These findings indicate that VUR is an inherited condition.[2]

What Are the Types of VUR?

The two types of VUR are primary and secondary. Most cases of VUR are primary and typically affect only one ureter and kidney. With primary VUR, a child is born with a ureter that did not grow long enough during the child's development in the womb. The valve formed by the ureter pressing against the bladder wall does not close properly, so urine refluxes from the bladder to the ureter and eventually to the kidney. This type of VUR can get better or disappear as a child gets older. As a child grows, the ureter gets longer and function of the valve improves.

Secondary VUR occurs when a blockage in the urinary tract causes an increase in pressure and pushes urine back up into the ureters. Children with secondary VUR often have bilateral reflux. VUR caused by a physical defect typically results from an abnormal fold of tissue in the urethra that keeps urine from flowing freely out of the bladder.

VUR is usually classified as grade I through V, with grade I being the least severe and grade V being the most severe.

What Are the Symptoms of VUR?

In many cases, a child with VUR has no symptoms. When symptoms are present, the most common is a urinary tract infection (UTI). VUR can lead to infection because urine that remains in the child's urinary tract provides a place for bacteria to grow. Studies estimate that 30 percent of children and up to 70 percent of infants with a UTI have VUR.[2]

What Are the Complications of VUR?

When a child with VUR gets a UTI, bacteria can move into the kidney and lead to scarring. Scarring of the kidney can be associated with high blood pressure and kidney failure. However, most children with VUR who get a UTI recover without long-term complications.

How Is VUR Diagnosed?

The most common tests used to diagnose VUR include:

- voiding cystourethrogram (VCUG);
- radionuclide cystogram (RNC);
- abdominal ultrasound.

Testing is usually done on:

- infants diagnosed during pregnancy with urine blockage affecting the kidneys;
- children younger than five years of age with a UTI;

- children with a UTI and fever, called febrile UTI, regardless of age;

- males with a UTI who are not sexually active, regardless of age or fever;

- children with a family history of VUR, including an affected sibling.

VUR is an unlikely cause of UTI in some children, so these tests are not done until other causes of UTI are ruled out for:

- children five years of age and older with a UTI;

- children with a UTI but no fever;

- sexually active males with a UTI.

What Other Tests Do Children with VUR Need?

Following diagnosis, children with VUR should have a general medical evaluation that includes blood pressure measurement, as high blood pressure is an indicator of kidney damage. If both kidneys are affected, a child's blood should be tested for creatinine—a waste product of normal muscle breakdown. Healthy kidneys remove creatinine from the blood; when the kidneys are damaged, creatinine builds up in the blood. The urine may be tested for the presence of protein and bacteria. Protein in the urine is another indication of damaged kidneys.

Children with VUR should also be assessed for bladder/bowel dysfunction (BBD).

Children who have VUR along with any BBD symptoms are at greater risk of kidney damage due to infection.

How Is Primary VUR Treated?

The standard treatment for primary VUR has included prompt treatment of UTIs and long-term use of antibiotics to prevent UTIs, also called antimicrobial prophylaxis, until VUR goes away on its own. Antibiotics are bacteria-fighting medications. Surgery has also been used in certain cases.

Several studies have raised questions about long-term use of antibiotics for prevention of UTIs. The studies found little or no effect on prevention of kidney damage. Long-term use may also make the child resistant to the antibiotic, meaning the medication does not work as well, and the child may be sicker longer and may need to take medications that are even stronger.

Current recommendations from the American Urological Association include the following:

- **Children younger than one year of age:** Continuous antibiotics should be used if a child has a history of febrile UTI or VUR grade III through V that was identified through screening.

- **Children older than one year of age with BBD:** Continuous antibiotics should be used while BBD is being treated.

- **Children older than one year of age without BBD:** Continuous antibiotics can be used at the discretion of the health care provider but is not automatically recommended; however, UTIs should be promptly treated

Surgery has traditionally been considered for a child with kidney infection, fever, and severe reflux that has not improved within a year. However, some health care providers recommend surgery when a scan of the kidneys shows evidence of inflammation. Several surgical approaches can be used to alter the ureter and prevent urine from refluxing.

Deflux, a gel-like liquid containing complex sugars, is an alternative to surgery for treatment of VUR. A small amount of Deflux is injected into the bladder wall near the opening of the ureter. This injection creates a bulge in the tissue that makes it harder for urine to flow back up the ureter. The health care provider uses a special tube to see inside the bladder during the procedure. Deflux injection is an outpatient procedure done under general anesthesia, so the child can go home the same day.

How Is Secondary VUR Treated?

Secondary VUR is treated by removing the blockage causing the reflux. Treatment may involve:

- surgery;

- antibiotics;

- intermittent catheterization—draining the bladder by inserting a thin tube, called a catheter, through the urethra to the bladder.

Eating, Diet, and Nutrition

Eating, diet, and nutrition have not been shown to play a role in causing or preventing VUR.

References

1. Pohl HG, Joyce GM, Wise M, Cilento BG. Pediatric urologic disorders. In: Litwin MS, Saigal CS, eds. *Urologic Diseases in America*. Washington, D.C.: U.S. Government Printing Office; 2007: 379–420. NIH Publication 07–5512.

2. Khoury A, Bagli DJ. Reflux and megaureter. In: Wein A, ed. *Campbell-Walsh Urology. 9th ed*. Philadelphia: Saunders Elsevier; 2007: 3423–81.

Part Four

Additional Help
and Information

Chapter 37

Glossary of Terms Related to Congenital Disorders

abdominal wall defects: Incomplete development of the skin and muscles of the belly, allowing internal organs to protrude into the umbilical cord (omphalocele) or outside the body (gastroschisis). Also called ventral wall defects.

agenesis: Failure to develop; absence.

alcohol-related birth defects: Children who had prenatal alcohol exposure, but do not manifest the full symptoms of fetal alcohol syndrome (FAS) may exhibit alcohol-related birth defects. Caused by prenatal alcohol exposure and refers to alcohol induced physical anomalies.

alcohol-related neurodevelopmental disorder: Children who had prenatal alcohol exposure but do not manifest the full symptoms of fetal alcohol syndrome (FAS) may exhibit alcohol-related neurodevelopmental disorder. Caused by prenatal alcohol exposure and refers to alcohol-induced cognitive and behavioral problems without the characteristic facial or growth abnormalities seen among children with FAS.

alpha fetoprotein: A plasma protein normally produced by the fetus that can be found in the mother's blood (the maternal serum AFP). It provides a screening test for neural tube defects. Prenatal maternal lab tests are done at fifteen to twenty weeks' gestation.

The terms in this glossary were excerpted from "Glossary," reprinted with permission from the California Birth Defects Monitoring Program, Maternal, Child and Adolescent Health Program, California Department of Public Health, http://www.cdph.ca.gov/programs/CBDMP. Copyright © 2013 State of California.

amniocentesis: A prenatal test where amniotic fluid is withdrawn using a needle inserted into the uterus. The fluid and the cells it contains can be used to perform tests on the fetus, including chromosome testing. Usually performed in the second trimester.

amniotic bands: Strands of tissue that float in the amniotic fluid as a consequence of tears or ruptures in the amniotic membrane which surrounds the fetus during development.

anal atresia: Incomplete development of the lowest part of the large intestine, preventing passage of stool (feces).

anencephaly: Neural tube defect where the brain and skull do not form completely. Affected babies die, either before birth (stillbirth) or shortly thereafter. Because the brain is only partly formed, affected newborns cannot control basic life functions like breathing.

aniridia: Congenital absence or defect of the iris.

anopthalmia: A developmental defect characterized by complete absence of the eyes or apparent absence of the globe in an otherwise normal orbit.

anotia: Congenital absence of the external ear.

aortic artery/valve (stenosis) defect: Heart defect involving the aorta (the main blood vessel leading from the heart). Defects include narrowing or complete closure of the vessel (artery) or valve (connection between the heart and the aorta).

atresia: Absence or blockage of an opening such as the intestinal tract.

atrial septal defect: An atrial septal defect is a hole (defect) in the wall (septum) that separates the two upper chambers of the heart, called atria. This hole between the heart chambers disrupts the flow of blood and oxygen to the body.

bilateral: Occurring on both sides. For example, bilateral limb defects affect both arms or both legs.

biliary atresia: Congenital absence or closure of the major bile ducts, the ducts that drain bile from the liver.

bladder exstrophy: A defect in the lower abdominal wall and anterior (front) wall of the bladder through which the lining of the bladder is exposed to the outside.

cardiac defects: See heart defects.

cerebral palsy: Condition where the brain does not properly control muscles and movement. Some people with cerebral palsy have additional disabilities, such as mental retardation or seizures. Although not a structural birth defect, cerebral palsy may have its origins in prenatal development and is sometimes accompanied by structural birth defects.

choanal atresia or stenosis: A congenital anomaly in which a bony or membranous formation blocks the passageway between the nose and the pharynx. This defect is usually repaired surgically after birth.

chorionic villus sampling: A prenatal test usually done in the first trimester to detect fetal abnormalities. A small piece of the developing placenta is withdrawn; because this has the same genetic make-up as the developing fetus, it can be used for genetic or chromosome tests.

cleft lip: Incomplete development of the lip, usually occurring on the upper lip. The split in the lip can occur on either or both sides (unilateral or bilateral cleft) and may be accompanied by a cleft palate. (Bilateral cleft lip was formerly called "harelip.")

cleft palate: Incomplete development of the roof of the mouth. It can occur alone or accompanied by a cleft lip.

coarctation of the aorta: Occurs when the aorta is pinched or constricted. This obstructs blood flow to the lower body and increases blood pressure above the constriction.

colorectal atresia: Abnormally formed segments in the colon or rectum (large intestine) block food movement during digestion; besides obstructions, there are often abnormal connections between the intestines and genitourinary tract. Surgery must be done at birth to remove the underdeveloped areas and reconnect the bowel.

congenital abnormality: A problem present at birth (see birth defects).

conotruncal heart defects: Heart defect occurring early in development, involving faulty septation / connection of the heart's chambers and/or the major blood vessels leaving the heart.

congenital cataract: An opacity (not transparent or translucent) of the lens of the eye that has its origin prenatally.

congenital hip dislocation: Location of the head of the femur (bone of the upper leg) outside its normal location in the cup-shaped cavity formed by the hip bones.

conjoined twins: Monozygotic (identical) twins who are physically united at birth. The defect can range from superficial (skin only) connection to one in which only a single body part is duplicated.

craniofacial: Involving the face and skull.

craniosynostosis: Too early closure of the skull bones, causing unusual head shape.

diaphragmatic hernia: Incompletely formed diaphragm (muscular sheet diving the chest and abdomen) allows the stomach, liver and other abdominal organs to move into the chest. This crowds the developing lungs, which may be too small to support breathing after birth, even if the diaphragm is surgically repaired.

duodenal atresia: Lacking a functional connection in the upper part of the intestine where it meets the stomach.

dysgenesis: Abnormal formation of an organ or body structure.

Ebstein anomaly: A very rare heart defect in which parts of the tricuspid valve are abnormal, giving the tricuspid valve a downward displacement. The tricuspid valve separates the lower heart chamber (right ventricle) from the upper heart chamber (right atrium).

encephalocele: A neural tube defect (NTD) present at birth that affects the brain. Involves a sac-like protrusion or projection of the brain, and the membranes that cover it, through an opening in the skull. Occurs when the neural tube does not close completely during pregnancy. See also neural tube defect (NTD).

epispadias: A congenital defect in which the urinary outlet opens above the normal position. The urinary sphincters are defective, so incontinence does occur.

esophageal atresia: Condition where the upper and lower ends of the esophagus (the swallowing tube leading from the mouth to the stomach) are not connected. Often associated with tracheal defects (involving the breathing tube connecting the mouth and lungs).

fetal alcohol syndrome: The sum total of the damage done to the child before birth as a result of the mother drinking alcohol during pregnancy. Fetal alcohol syndrome (FAS) always involved brain damage, impaired growth, and head and face abnormalities. One of the leading causes of mental retardation in the United States. FAS is an irreversible, lifelong condition.

fetal alcohol spectrum disorder: Physical findings and development disabilities caused by drinking alcohol during pregnancy. Characteristics include: low birth weight, poor growth after birth, small head, small eyelid openings, smooth philtrum (the area between the nose and lip) and thin upper lip. Alcohol-exposed children with developmental delays and behavior problems, but few of the physical features of FAS, may be designated as having "fetal alcohol effects."

fetal death (stillbirth): Spontaneous delivery of an infant or fetus at twenty weeks or greater gestation that does not exhibit signs of life. Transient cardiac contractions and fleeting respiratory efforts or gasps are not necessarily considered signs of life by all programs. A late fetal death is a fetal death that occurs at twenty-eight weeks or greater gestation.

folic acid: B vitamin found in green leafy vegetables and dried beans as well as in fortified cereal and flour. When taken around the time of conception and in early pregnancy, folic acid is associated with lower risk for neural tube defects, oral clefts, limb and heart defects.

gastroschisis: Condition where the intestines protrude through a hole in the abdomen to the side of the umbilical cord; part of the category abdominal wall defects.

gastrointestinal defects: Defects along the gastrointestinal tract (the mouth to the anus), including defects of the stomach and intestines.

gestation/gestational age: Pregnancy time span. For example, "twenty weeks' gestation" refers to the twentieth week of pregnancy. The normal human gestation is thirty-seven to forty-two weeks.

heart defects: Abnormal structures of the heart and/or large vessels leading from the heart; impairing distribution of oxygen and nutrients throughout the body. Also called cardiac defects.

Hirschsprung disease: A condition where sections of the intestine lack nerve stimulation; food is not moved through the gut, which becomes distended. Requires surgery to remove the faulty sections.

Holoprosencephaly: Serious brain abnormality where the developing forebrain fails to undergo normal division into two lobes. Facial development is often altered—there may be a single eye, closely spaced eyes with a single nostril, a midline cleft lip or a single central front incisor tooth. Holoprosencephaly often causes severe mental retardation and/or death.

591

hydrocephalus: Fluid accumulation in the brain, often due to a blockage in the canals that distribute fluid within the brain and spinal cord.

hyperplasia: Overgrowth characterized by an increase in the number of cells of a tissue. **hypoplasia:** A condition of arrested development in which an organ or part remains below the normal size or in an immature state.

hypoplastic left heart syndrome: The structures of the left side of the heart (the left ventricle, the mitral valve, and the aortic valve) are underdeveloped and unable to pump blood adequately to the entire body.

hypoplastic right heart syndrome: The structures of the right side of the heart (pulmonary valve, right ventricle, tricuspid valve, pulmonary artery) are underdeveloped and cause inadequate blood flow to the lungs.

hypospadias: Birth defect of the penis where the urinary opening is misplaced (on the shaft or in the scrotum in the more serious forms).

imperforate anus: Absence of an external opening from the rectum/ intestinal tract. Surgery is needed to allow the infant to pass feces.

intestinal atresia: Condition where abnormally formed segments in the intestine obstruct food movement during digestion. Often classified according to the part of the gut affected: from the stomach to the colon (small intestine), the colon and rectum (large intestine) or anus. See colorectal atresia and anal atresia.

intrauterine growth restriction: Refers to the poor growth of a baby while in the womb. Specifically, it refers to a fetus whose weight is below the tenth percentile for its gestational age.

kidney defects: Absence, underdevelopment or other structural abnormality of the kidneys. Also called renal defects.

limb reduction defects: Missing or malformed arms, legs, hands, fingers, feet, or toes.

malformation: A major anomaly that arises during the initial formation of a structure, i.e., during organogenesis. For most organs, this occurs during the first eight weeks after fertilization. The resulting structure may be abnormally formed, incompletely formed, or may fail to form altogether. Examples of malformations include spina bifida and hypoplastic left heart.

malrotation of the intestines: Unusual configuration of intestinal (bowel) loops.

maternal serum alpha-fetoprotein: The level of AFP, a plasma protein normally produced by the fetus, in the mother's blood (the maternal serum AFP) provides a screening test for neural tube defects. Prenatal maternal lab tests are done at fifteen to twenty weeks' gestation.

metabolic disease: Genetic disease caused by absent or defective substance. This disrupts metabolism at a cellular level—often the cell cannot create, use, or dispose of nutrients properly—leading to a variety of physical problems. Phenylketonuria (PKU) is an example where the inability to transform dietary protein leads to buildup of toxic waste and causes brain damage.

microcephaly: A cranial vault that is smaller than normal for age. The size of the cranial vault is an indicator of the size of the underlying brain.

microphthalmia: The congenital abnormal smallness of one or both eyes. Can occur in the presence of other ocular defects.

microtia: A congenital deformity of the outer ear in which the outer ear is incompletely formed. It can be unilateral (one side only) or bilateral (affecting both sides). Complete absence of the outer ear is anotia. (see anotia).

miscarriage: Pregnancy loss occurring before twenty weeks gestation (the first half of pregnancy). Also called spontaneous abortion.

mosaic: In genetics, this refers to an individual organism that has two or more kinds of genetically different cell types. The degree of abnormality depends on the type of tissue containing affected cells. Individuals may vary from near normal to full manifestation of the genetic syndrome. Can occur in any chromosome abnormality syndrome.

neonatal death: Death of a live-born infant within the first twenty-eight days after birth. Early neonatal death refers to death during the first seven days. Late neonatal death refers to death after seven days but before twenty-nine days.

neural tube defects: Abnormalities arising during early fetal development when the neural tube—the precursor of the spinal cord and brain—does not form correctly. Can cause absence of the brain (anencephaly) or spina bifida (open spine defect).

newborn screening: The examination of blood samples from a newborn infant to detect disease-related abnormalities or deficiencies in gene products. Newborn screening (NBS) programs collect dried blood spots (DBS) in every state.

obstructive genitourinary defect: Partial or complete obstruction of the flow of urine at any level. Severity of the defect depends largely upon the level of the obstruction. Urine accumulates behind the obstruction and damages the organs.

oligohydramnios: A condition in pregnancy where there is a lack of, or decrease in, amniotic fluid surrounding the fetus.

omphalocele: Condition where the abdominal wall is incompletely formed, allowing internal organs to protrude into the umbilical cord. Surgery to replace the organs can crowd the lungs, causing breathing problems. Omphalocele is part of the category abdominal wall defects.

open spine defect: See spina bifida.

oral cleft: Opening in the lip and/or palate occurring in early fetal development. Affected children need surgery to repair the cleft lip or cleft palate. They often need long-term help such as speech therapy and specialized dental care.

patent ductus arteriosus: This defect allows blood to mix between the pulmonary artery and the aorta. Before birth an open passageway (the ductus arteriosus) exists between these two blood vessels. Normally this closes within a few hours of birth. When this doesn't happen, some blood that should flow through the aorta and on to nourish the body returns to the lungs.

phenylketonuria (PKU): An inherited disorder of metabolism that can cause mental retardation if not treated. In PKU, the body cannot process a portion of the protein called phenylalanine (Phe), which is in almost all foods. If the Phe level gets too high, the brain can become damaged. All babies born in U.S. hospitals are now routinely tested for PKU soon after birth.

polydactyly: Extra digits (fingers or toes).

polyhydramnios: The presence of excessive amniotic fluid surrounding the unborn infant.

postnatal: After delivery

preconception care: Involves an assessment prior to becoming pregnant, of lifestyle, health, and fitness, by a health professional, in order to identify areas for improvement.

pregnancy termination: Abortion; often done when birth defects are detected with prenatal diagnosis.

premature birth: Birth of a baby before the standard period of pregnancy is completed. Prematurity is considered to occur when the baby is born sooner than thirty-seven weeks after the beginning of the last menstrual period (LMP). Also known as preterm birth.

prenatal: Before delivery.

prenatal diagnosis: Tests done during pregnancy to detect abnormalities. Some tests are for screening, determining whether a pregnancy is at higher or lower risk, such as the expanded AFP blood test. Other tests—like amniocentesis—are diagnostic, telling for certain whether the fetus is affected.

preterm infant: An infant born before thirty-seven completed weeks of gestation.

pulmonary artery/valve defect: Type of heart defect involving the outflow tract leading from the heart to the lungs, with narrowing/ closure of the blood vessel (pulmonary artery) or its connection to the heart (pulmonic valve).

pulmonary hypoplasia: Incomplete or defective development of the lungs.

pyloric stenosis: Overgrowth of the muscular connection between the stomach and intestines, blocking food passage and causing projectile vomiting a few weeks after birth. More common in boys.

radial defect: Underdeveloped or malformed radius, the larger of the two bones in the lower arm. This is often accompanied by defects in the surrounding tissue, especially the thumb, index, and middle fingers.

renal agenesis/dysgenesis: Condition where kidneys are absent (agenesis) or severely underdeveloped or malformed (dysgenesis). If both kidneys are affected, a fetus does not urinate prenatally and there is little or no amniotic fluid (which comes from fetal urine). This, in turn, prevents the fetal lungs from growing and expanding, leading to breathing problems and possibly death soon after birth.

renal defects: See kidney defects.

single ventricle: Major heart defect where the lower pumping chamber does not develop into two chambers (ventricles). Blood coming from the lungs carrying oxygen for the body is mixed with oxygen-depleted blood returning from the body.

spina bifida: Structural birth defect where the spine and spinal cord don't develop correctly. Depending on the size and location of the defect, it may cause paralysis or inability to control muscles in the legs or arms—affected children often use wheelchairs, walkers, or braces.

spontaneous abortion (miscarriage): Spontaneous delivery of a fetus at less than twenty weeks' gestation.

stillbirth (fetal death): Infant or fetus at twenty weeks or greater gestation that does not exhibit signs of life. Transient cardiac contractions and fleeting respiratory efforts or gasps are not necessarily considered signs of life by all programs.

structural birth defects: Problems in prenatal development affecting the body structure, whether external (for example, cleft lip or missing limbs) or internal (such as heart defects, kidney defects). Also called malformations.

term infant: An infant born after thirty-seven completed weeks and before forty-two completed weeks of gestation.

teratogen: An exposure that interferes with normal fetal development, causing a birth defect. Known teratogens include certain illnesses in the mother (German measles, diabetes), medications (thalidomide, Dilantin) and other exposures (excessive alcohol).

tetralogy of Fallot: Major defect of the heart's chambers and blood vessels leading to and from the heart. The four components are: underdeveloped right heart, hole between the lower heart chambers, overriding aorta and underdeveloped pulmonary artery.

tracheoesophageal fistula: Connection between the breathing tube (trachea) and swallowing tube (esophagus) causing life-threatening symptoms soon after birth. Surgery is needed to properly attach the trachea to the lungs and the esophagus to the stomach.

transposition of the great vessels/arteries: Major heart defect where the main blood vessels leading from heart are reversed, resulting in improper circulation of oxygenated and oxygen depleted blood.

tricuspid atresia: Major heart defect with absence of the tricuspid valve. This means that no blood can flow from the right atrium to the right ventricle. As a result, the right ventricle is small and not fully developed.

triphalangeal thumb: A thumb with three bones/two joints, resembling a finger.

truncus arteriosus: A conotruncal heart defect where a single blood vessel replaces the pulmonary artery (leading to the lungs) and the aorta (leading to the rest of the body); this results in mixing of oxygenated and oxygen-depleted blood.

ultrasound: Prenatal test using sound waves to create a picture of the developing fetus. Ultrasound can measure growth and examine body structures such as the heart and spine.

urethra: The tube leading from the bladder to outside the body.

urinary defects: Defects of the structures for collecting and excreting urine. This includes the bladder, the tubes connecting the kidneys to the bladder (ureters), and the tube leading from the bladder to outside the body (the urethra).

urinary tract obstruction: Defect in the tubes leading to and from the bladder, preventing normal urination. Backed-up urine damages the kidneys—children often need corrective surgery and possible dialysis (mechanized help with filtering waste from the blood). In severe cases, the absence of amniotic fluid (which comes from fetal urine) prevents the fetal lungs from growing and expanding; once born, these babies cannot breathe and soon die.

ventral wall defects: See abdominal wall defects.

ventricle: One of the two lower chambers of the heart (plural ventricles). The right ventricle sends blood to the lungs, and the left ventricle passes oxygen-rich blood to the rest of the body.

ventricular septal defect: Heart defect where a hole between the two bottom pumping heart chambers (ventricles) allows oxygenated and oxygen-depleted blood to mix.

vertebral defects: Abnormalities of the spinal bones.

very low birth weight: Birth weight less than 1,500 grams, regardless of gestational age.

Chapter 38

Congenital Disorders: Resources for Information and Support

General

AboutKidsHealth
The Hospital for Sick Children
555 University Avenue
Toronto, Ontario
Canada M5G 1X8
Website:
http://www.aboutkidshealth.ca

American Pregnancy Association
1425 Greenway Drive
Suite 440
Irving, TX 75038
Phone: 972-550-0140
Fax: 972-550-0800
Website:
http://www.americanpregnancy.org
E-mail: questions
@americanpregnancy.org

Boston Children's Hospital
300 Longwood Avenue
Boston, MA 02115
Phone: 617-355-6000
TTY: 617-730-0152
Website:
http://childrenshospital.org

Centers for Disease Control and Prevention
1600 Clifton Road
Atlanta, GA 30333
Toll-Free: 800-CDC-INFO
(800-232-4636)
Toll-Free TTY: 888-232-6348
Website: http://www.cdc.gov

Resources in this chapter were compiled from several sources deemed reliable. All contact information was verified and updated in January 2013.

Children's Hospital Colorado
Anschutz Medical Campus
13123 East 16th Avenue
Aurora, CO 80045
Toll Free: 800-624-6553
Phone: 720-777-1234
TTY: 720-777-6050
Website:
http://www.childrenscolorado.org

Children's Hospital of Philadelphia
34th St. and Civic Center Blvd.
Philadelphia, PA 19104
Phone: 215-590-1000
Website:
http://www.chop.edu

Children's Memorial Hermann Hospital
Texas Medical Center
6411 Fannin Street
Houston, TX 77030
Phone: 713-704-KIDS
(713-704-5437)
Website:
http://childrens.memorial
hermann.org

Cincinnati Children's Hospital Medical Center
3333 Burnet Avenue
Cincinnati, OH 45229-3026
Toll-Free: 800-344-2462
Toll-Free: 877-881-8479
(outside of tri-state area)
Phone: 513-636-4200
TTY: 513-636-4900
Website: https://www.cincinnati
childrens.org

Fetal Hope Foundation
9786 South Holland Street
Littleton, CO 80127
Toll-Free: 877-789-HOPE
(877-789-4673)
Phone: 303-932-0553
Website:
http://www.fetalhope.org
E-mail:
info@fetalhope.org

Fetal Treatment Program of New England
Bay Tower Medical Office
101 Plain Street
Providence, RI 02903
Phone: 401-228-0559
Website:
http://www.fetal-treatment.org
E-mail: coordinator@
fetal-treatment.org

Johns Hopkins Children's Center
1800 Orleans Street
Baltimore, MD 21287
Phone: 410-955-5000
Website:
http://www.hopkinschildrens.org

Madison's Foundation
P.O. Box 241956
Los Angeles, CA 90024
Phone: 310-264-0826
Fax: 310-264-4766
Website: http://www.madisons
foundation.org
E-mail: getinfo@
madisonsfoundation.org

March of Dimes
1275 Mamaroneck Avenue
White Plains, NY 10605
Phone: 914-997-4488
Website: http://
www.marchofdimes.com

**Organization
of Teratology
Information
Specialists (OTIS)**
5034A Thoroughbred Lane
Brentwood, TN 37027
Toll-Free: 866-626-OTIS
(866-626-6847)
Phone: (615) 649-3082
Fax: (615) 523-1715
Website:
http://www.otispregnancy.org
E-mail: contactus@
otispregnancy.org

**St. Louis Fetal
Care Institute**
SSM Cardinal Glennon
Children's Medical Center
1465 South Grand Boulevard
St. Louis, MO 63104-1095
Toll-Free: 877-SSM-FETL
(877-776-3385)
Phone: 314-268-4037
Website:
http://www.cardinalglennon.com/
fetalcareinstitute
E-mail: fetalcare@ssmhc.com

**University of California
San Francisco Benioff
Children's Hospital**
505 Parnassus Avenue
San Francisco, CA 94143
Phone: 415-476-1000
Website: https://www.ucsfbenioff
childrens.org

**University of
California San Francisco
Fetal Treatment Center**
400 Parnassus Avenue, A123
San Francisco, CA 94143-0570
Toll-Free: 800-RX-FETUS
(800-793-3887)
Fax: 415-502-0660
Website: http://fetus.ucsfmedical
center.org
E-mail: fetus@surgery.ucsf.edu

**University of Michigan
Fetal Diagnosis and
Treatment Center**
University of Michigan
Health System
1500 East Medical Center Drive
Ann Arbor, MI 48109
Phone: 734-936-6641
Website: http://www.med.umich
.edu/fdtc

**University of Texas
Medical School at
Houston-Department
of Pediatric Surgery**
6410 Fannin Street
Suite 950
Houston, TX 77030
Phone: 832-325-7234
Website: http://utsurg.uth.tmc
.edu/pedisurgery

Birthmarks

Vascular Birthmarks Foundation
P.O. Box 106
Latham, NY 12110
Toll-Free: 877-VBF-4646
(877-823-4646)
Website: http://birthmark.org
E-mail: hvbf@aol.com

Brain and Spinal Cord Defects

Dandy-Walker Alliance, Inc.
10325 Kensington Parkway
Suite 384
Kensington, MD 20895
Toll-Free: 877-Dandy-Walker
(877-326-3992)
Website: http://www.dandy
-walker.org
E-mail: comments@
dandy-walker.org

Hydrocephalus Association
4340 East West Highway
Suite 905
Bethesda, MD 20814
Toll-Free: 888-598-3789
Phone: 301-202-3811
Fax: 301-202-3813
Website:
http://www.hydroassoc.org
E-mail: info@hydroassoc.org

National Hydrocephalus Foundation
12413 Centralia Road
Lakewood, CA 90715-1653
Toll-Free: 888-857-3434
Phone: 562-924-6666
Website:
http://www.nhfonline.org

National Institute of Neurological Disorders and Stroke
NIH Neurological Institute
P.O. Box 5801
Bethesda, MD 20824
Toll-Free: 800-352-9424
Phone: 301-496-5751
TTY: 301-468-5981
Website:
http://www.ninds.nih.gov
E-mail: me20t@nih.gov

National Organization for Disorders of the Corpus Callosum
PMB 363
18032-C Lemon Drive
Yorba Linda, CA 92886
Phone: 714-747-0063
Fax: 714-693-0808
Website: http://www.nodcc.org
E-mail: info@nodcc.org

Pediatric Hydrocephalus Foundation
2004 Green Hollow Drive
Iselin, NJ 08830
Phone: 732-634-1283
Fax: 847-589-1250
Website:
http://www.HydrocephalusKids
.org/wordpress
E-mail:
info@hydrocephaluskids.org

Spina Bifida Association
4590 MacArthur Boulevard NW
Suite 250
Washington, DC 20007-4226
Toll Free: 800-621-3141
Phone: 202-944-3285
Fax: 202-944-3295
Website: http://www.spina
bifidaassociation.org
E-mail: sbaa@sbaa.org

United Cerebral Palsy
1825 K Street NW, Suite 600
Washington, DC 20006
Toll-Free: 800-872-5827
Phone: 202-776-0406
Fax: 202-776-0414
Website: http://www.ucp.org
E-mail: info@ucp.org

Cardiovascular Defects

Adult Congenital Heart Association (ACHA)
6757 Greene Street, Suite 335
Philadelphia, PA 19119-3508
Toll Free: 888-921-ACHA
(888-921-2242)
Phone: 215-849-1260
Fax: 215-849-1261
Website:
http://www.achaheart.org
E-mail: info@achaheart.org

American Heart Association
7272 Greenville Avenue
Dallas, TX 75231
Toll-Free: 800-AHA-USA-1
(800-242-8721)
Phone: 214-570-5978
Website: http://www.heart.org

Congenital Heart Information Network (C. H. I. N.)
P.O. Box 3397
Margate City, NJ 08402-0397
Phone: 609-822-1572
Fax: 609-822-1574
Website: http://www.tchin.org
E-mail: mb@tchin.org

National Heart Lung and Blood Institute (NHLBI)
NHLBI Health Information
Center
P.O. Box 30105
Bethesda, MD 20824-0105
Phone: 301-592-8573
TTY: 240-629-3255
Fax: 240-629-3246
Website:
http://www.nhlbi.nih.gov
E-mail:
nhlbiinfo@nhlbi.nih.gov

Craniofacial Defects

American Cleft Palate-Craniofacial Association
1504 East Franklin Street
Suite 102
Chapel Hill, NC 27514-2820
Phone: 919-933-9044
Fax: 919-933-9604
Website:
http://www.acpa-cpf.org
E-mail: info@acpa-cpf.org

Ameriface
P.O. Box 751112
Las Vegas, NV 89136-1112
Toll-Free: 888-486-1209
Phone: 702-769-9264
Fax: 702-341-5351
Website:
http://www.ameriface.org
E-mail: info@ameriface.org

Children's Craniofacial Association (CCA)
13140 Coit Road
Suite 517
Dallas, TX 75240
Toll-Free: 800-535-3643
Phone: 214-570-9099
Fax: 214-570-8811
Website:
http://www.ccakids.com
E-mail: contactCCA@
ccakids.com

Cleft Palate Foundation
1504 East Franklin Street
Suite 102
Chapel Hill, NC 27514-2820
Toll-Free: 800-242-5338
Phone: 919-933-9044
Fax: 919-933-9604
Website:
http://www.cleftline.org

FACES: The National Craniofacial Association
P.O. Box 11082
Chattanooga, TN 37401
Toll-Free: 800-332-2373
Website: http://
www.faces-cranio.org
E-mail: faces@faces-cranio.org

National Foundation for Facial Reconstruction
333 East 30th Street
Lobby Unit
New York, NY 10016
Phone: 212-263-6656
Fax: 212-263-7534
Website: http://www.nffr.org
E-mail: info@nffr.org

National Institute of Dental and Craniofacial Research
National Oral Health
Information Clearinghouse
Toll-Free: 866-232-4528
Phone: 301-496-4261
Fax: 301-480-4098
Website:
http://www.nidcr.nih.gov
E-mail: nidcrinfo@mail.nih.gov

World Craniofacial Foundation
7777 Forest Lane, Suite C-616
Dallas, TX 75230
Toll-Free: 800-533-3315
Phone: 972-566-6669
Fax: 972-566-3850
Website: http://www.worldcf.org

Digestive Tract Defects

American Liver Foundation
39 Broadway, Suite 2700
New York, NY 10006
Toll-Free: 800-GO-LIVER
(800-465-4837)
Phone: 212-668-1000
Fax: 212-483-8179
Website:
http://www.liverfoundation.org
E-mail:
info@liverfoundation.org

Association of Congenital Diaphragmatic Hernia Research Awareness and Support (CHERUBS)
3650 Rogers Road #290
Wake Forest, NC 27587
Phone: 919-610-0129
Fax: 815-425-9155
Website:
http://www.cherubs-cdh.org
E-mail: cpab@cherubs-cdh.org

Bowel Group for Kids Inc.
P.O. Box 40
Oakdale, NSW 2570
Australia
Website: http://www.bgk.org.au
E-mail: enquiries@bgk.org.au

Canadian Liver Foundation
3100 Steeles Avenue East
Suite 801
Markham, ON L3R 8T3
Canada
Toll-Free: 800-563-5483
Phone: 416-491-3353
Fax: 905-752-1540
Website: http://www.liver.ca
E-mail: clf@liver.ca

Children's Liver Association for Support Services
25379 Wayne Mills Place
Suite 143
Valencia, CA 91355
Toll-Free: 877-679-8256
Phone/Fax: 661-263-9099
Website:
http://www.classkids.org
E-mail: info@classkids.org

Children's Organ Transplant Association
2501 West COTA Drive
Bloomington, IN 47403
Toll-Free: 800-366-2682
Fax: 812-336-8885
Website: http://www.cota.org
E-mail: cota@cota.org

North American Society for Pediatric Gastroenterology, Hepatology and Nutrition (NASPGHAN)
P.O. Box 6
Flourtown, PA 19031
Phone: 215-233-0808
Fax: 215-233-3918
Website:
http://www.naspghan.org
E-mail: naspghan@naspghan.org

National Institute of Diabetes, Digestive & Kidney Diseases
Office of Communications &
Public Liaison
Building 31, Room 9A06
31 Center Drive, MSC 2560
Bethesda, MD 20892-2560
Phone: 301-496-3583
Website:
http://www2.niddk.nih.gov
E-mail:
NDDIC@info.niddk.nih.gov

Pull-Thru Network
1705 Wintergreen Parkway
Normal, IL 61761
Phone: 309-262-0786
Website:
http://www.PullthruNetwork.org
E-mail:
PullthruNetwork@gmail.com

Kidney and Urinary Tract Defects

American Association of Kidney Patients
2701 North Rocky Point Drive
Suite 150
Tampa, FL 33607
Toll-Free: 800-749-AAKP
(800-749-2257)
Phone: 813-636-8100
Fax: 813-636-8122
Website: http://www.aakp.org
E-mail: info@aakp.org

American Kidney Fund
11921 Rockville Pike
Suite 300
Rockville, MD 20852
Toll-Free: 800-638-8299
Phone: 301-881-3052
Website:
http://www.kidneyfund.org
E-mail:
helpline@kidneyfund.org

American Society of Pediatric Nephrology
3400 Research Forest Drive
Suite B-7
The Woodlands, TX 77381
Phone: 281-419-0052
Fax: 281-419-0082
Website:
http://www.aspneph.com
E-mail: info@aspneph.com

American Urological Association Foundation
1000 Corporate Boulevard
Linthicum, MD 21090
Toll-Free: 800-828-7866
Phone: 410-689-3700
Fax: 410-689-3998
Website:
http://www.urologyhealth.org
E-mail:
info@urologycarefoundation.org

Association for the Bladder Exstrophy Community
6737 West Washington Street
Suite 6737
West Allis, WI 53214
Phone: 414-918-9002 (U.S.)
or 519-679-8774 (Canada)
Fax: 414-918-9001
Website: http://www.
bladderexstrophy.com
E-mail: admin@
bladderexstrophy.com

Bladder Exstrophy Family Association
Website:
http://www.bladderexstrophy.co.uk

Bladder Exstrophy Research Foundation
P.O. Box 13083
Newport Beach, CA 92658
Phone: 949-922-9865
Website:
http://www.exstrophyresearch.org
E-mail: info@
exstrophyresearch.org

Georgia Urology
Toll-Free: 888-788-0770
Website:
http://www.gaurology.com

Hypospadias and Epispadias Association, Inc.
235 West 102nd Street, #5E
New York, NY 10025
Phone: 917-861-8339
Website: http://www.heainfo.org

Kidney and Urology Foundation of America, Inc.
2 West 47th Street, Suite 401
New York, NY 10036
Toll-Free: 800-633-6628
Phone: 212-629-9770
Fax: 212-629-5652
Website:
http://www.kidneyurology.org

National Kidney Foundation
30 East 33rd Street
New York, NY 10016
Toll-Free: 800-622-9010
Phone: 212-889-2210
Fax: 212-689-9261
Website: http://www.kidney.org

Limb and Joint Defects

American Academy of Orthopaedic Surgeons
6300 North River Road
Rosemont, IL 60018-4262
Phone: 847-823-7186
Fax: 847-823-8125
Website: http://www.aaos.org

American Society for Surgery of the Hand
822 West Washington Boulevard
Chicago, IL, 60607
Phone: 312-880-1900
Fax: 847-384-1435
Website: http://www.assh.org
E-mail: info@assh.org

Fibrous Dysplasia Foundation
Website:
https://www.fibrousdysplasia.org
E-mail: info@
fibrousdysplasia.org

Helping Hands Foundation
P.O. Box 332
Medfield, MA 02052
Website:
http://www.helpinghandsgroup.org
E-mail: info@
helpinghandsgroup.org

Maternal Alcohol Abuse

National Institute on Alcohol Abuse and Alcoholism
5635 Fishers Lane
Bethesda, MD 20892-9304
Phone: 301-443-3860
Fax: 301-480-1726
Website:
http://www.niaaa.nih.gov
E-mail: niaaaweb-r@
exchange.nih.gov

National Organization on Fetal Alcohol Syndrome
1200 Eton Court NW
Third Floor
Washington, DC 20007
Toll-Free: 800-66-NOFAS
(800-666-6327)
Phone: 202-785-4585
Fax: 202-466-6456
Website: http://www.nofas.org
E-mail: information@nofas.org

Index

Index

Page numbers followed by 'n' indicate a footnote. Page numbers in *italics* indicate a table or illustration.

Health Reference Series